YEOVIL COLLEGE
LIBRARY

KU-709-864

wjec
cbac

Psychology AS

The Complete Companion
Student Book for WJEC

SECOND EDITION

PSYCHOPATHY • MEMORY • THE FIRST FIVE YEARS OF LIFE • SIGMUND FREUD • CHILD PSYCHOLOGY • LEARNING and MEMORY • STRESS • EXPERIMENTAL PSYCHOLOGY • THE MIND • Social Psychology • THERAPY • EXPERIMENTAL PSYCHOLOGY • CHARLES DARWIN • EARLY CHILDHOOD • STATE OF MIND • ATTACHMENT • RESEARCH METHODS • Cognitive Psychology • PSYCHOLOGY • PSYCHOLOGY IN ACTION

Cara Flanagan • Lucy ... on Murray

OXFORD
UNIVERSITY PRESS

Yeovil College
Y0075817

OXFORD
UNIVERSITY PRESS

Great Clarendon Street, Oxford, OX2 6DP, United Kingdom

Oxford University Press is a department of the University of Oxford. It furthers the University's objective of excellence in research, scholarship, and education by publishing worldwide. Oxford is a registered trade mark of Oxford University Press in the UK and in certain other countries

© Oxford University Press 2015

The moral rights of the authors have been asserted

First published in 2015

All rights reserved. No part of this publication may be reproduced, stored in a retrieval system, or transmitted, in any form or by any means, without the prior permission in writing of Oxford University Press, or as expressly permitted by law, by licence or under terms agreed with the appropriate reprographics rights organization. Enquiries concerning reproduction outside the scope of the above should be sent to the Rights Department, Oxford University Press, at the address above.

You must not circulate this work in any other form and you must impose this same condition on any acquirer

British Library Cataloguing in Publication Data
Data available

ISBN 978-0-19-835917-3

1 3 5 7 9 10 8 6 4 2

Paper used in the production of this book is a natural, recyclable product made from wood grown in sustainable forests. The manufacturing process conforms to the environmental regulations of the country of origin.

Printed in Great Britain by Bell and Bain Ltd., Glasgow

Acknowledgements
Typesetting & project management: GreenGate Publishing Services

This material has been endorsed by WJEC and offers high quality support for the delivery of WJEC qualifications. While this material has been through a WJEC quality assurance process, all responsibility for the content remains with the publisher.

Credits
The publishers would like to thank the following for permissions to use copyright material:

Adbusters: p.13; **Adrian Raine:** p.19; **Alamy:** p.55 Interfoto, p.117 Pictorial Press Ltd; **Alexandra Milgram:** p.162; **Beck Institute for Cognitive Behavior Therapy:** p.72, www.beckinstitute. org; **Cartoonstock.com:** pp.42, 52, 79, 136; **Corbis:** pp.15, 75 Bettmann, p.38 Bernard Bisson/Sygma, p.53 Sunset Boulevard, p.79 Jodi Hilton/Pool/Reuters, p.162 Hulton-Deutsch Collection; **Dr Bill Swann:** p.115; **Getty Images:** p.51 Yvonne Hemsey, p.59 Hulton Archive/Stringer, p.164 Lee Lockwood; **John Palmer:** p.79; **Jon Kabat-Zinn:** p.93; **L. Brian Stauffer:** p.99, University of Illinois New Bureau; **Mark Stivers:** p.7; **Martin Seligman:** p.91; **Mary Evans Picture Library:** p.16, p.148 Mary Evans/Interfoto Agentur; **Michael B. Frisch:** p.95; **Randy Glasbergen:** p.99, glasbergen. com; **Rex Features:** p.156 Bruce Adams/Solo Syndication; **Science Photo Library:** p.18 Volker Steger, p.18 Frederic Comte, ISM, p.82 Dr Robert Friedland; **Shutterstock:** p.133, aastock, p.120, Aleksey Stemmer, p.54, Alex Mit, p.24, Alien Zagrebelnaya, p.111, Alila Medical Media, p.10, Anastasia Shilova, p.11, Andresr, pp.82, 158, Andrey_Kuzmin, p.48, Andy Dean Photography, p.41, antonsav, p.131, Ariwasabi, p.96, Artistan, p.34, Benoit Daoust, p.81, Bevan Goldswain, p.158, CristinaMuraca, p.119, Daniel Fung, p.127, Denis Cristo, p.108, Dirima, p.65, Dooder, p.101, Everett Collection, p.68, Feng Yu, p.130, Filipe Frazao, p.101, Flashon Studio, p.114, George Dolgikh, p.134, Hirurg, p.135, igor.stevanovic, p.104, Jaimie Duplass, p.39, Jasun, p.28, Jerax, p.122, Johnny Cash, p.5, Kachalkina Veronika, p.62, Ken Wolter, p.19, Kichigin, p.102, Kittichai, p.33, koya979, p.92, Kutlayev Dmitry, p.118, lathspell, p.144, lculig, p.36, Levent Konuk, p.141, LeventeGyori, p.144, Lightspring, p.4, Lissandra Melo, p.160, LTDean, p.120, luxorphoto, p.155, Mega Pixel, p.129, melis, p.88, Monkey Business Images, pp. 6, 138, 140, 150, Odua

DEDICATIONS

A Welsh book for my Welsh man – Robert George Jones.
  Cara Flanagan

For Niki, for always putting a smile on my face, love in my heart, and food in my tummy!
  Lucy Hartnoll

To my family, who still love me even when I go into 'hibernation' to write books like this.
  Rhiannon Murray

For Gethin, thanks for your continuous support and laughter. xx
  Jenny Hill

Acknowledgements

We would like to thank all those backroom 'boys' (and girls) who have helped in the production of the book – Rob Bircher and Sarah Flynn at OUP, Carrie Baker and the team at GreenGate, Katherine Cox and Natalie O'Brien for the reviewing work. All have been phenomenally helpful. We couldn't have done it without you.
  Cara Flanagan, Lucy Hartnoll, Rhiannon Murray and Jenny Hill

Images, p.91, Oleg Senkov, p.21, Pakhnyushchy, p.58, PathDoc, pp.54, 60, Pixsooz, p.149, Pushkin, p.78, Rido, p.158, Robert Crum, p.76, Ruth Black, p.125, Sascha Burkard, p.105, sdecoret, p.6, sibgat, p.104, Steven Frame, p.45, Stokkete, p.63, Subbotina Anna, p.105, Terry Eagling Joyce, p.46, Thitisan, p.43, Tomacco, p.84, tommaso79, p.128, totallyPic.com, pp.84, 142, Vepar5, p.113, Vlad Teodor, p.5, VLADGRIN, p.22, Vlue, p.164, Wollertz, p.105, XiXinXing, p.71, Yang Nan, p.8, z0w, p.94; **Statistical Science:** p.159, from R. Sampson and B. Spencer 1999 'A conversation with I. Richard Savage', Statistical Science, 14, p136; **The British Psychological Society:** p.5; **The Happy Movie:** p.98, www.TheHappyMovie.com; **The Open University:** p.118 Photo by John Oates, © The Open University 2015; **Topfoto:** p.123 © 2004 TopFoto; **UCL department of Psychology:** p.153; **University of Akron/Psychology Archives:** p.57; **Warren Anatomical Museum in the Francis A. Countway Library of Medicine:** p.139.

Although we have made every effort to trace and contact all copyright holders before publication this has not been possible in all cases. If notified, the publisher will rectify any errors or omissions at the earliest opportunity.

Links to third party websites are provided by Oxford in good faith and for information only. Oxford disclaims any responsibility for the materials contained in any third party website referenced in this work.

WJEC Psychology AS

YEOVIL COLLEGE
LIBRARY

CONTENTS

Each approaches chapter is divided into:

- Assumptions
- Therapy 1
- Therapy 2
- Classic evidence
- Contemporary debate
- Evaluation of the approach
- Activities
- Answering exam questions

WJEC AS EXAM

Unit 1 **Psychology: Past to Present**	1 hour 30 mins 80 marks 20% of A Level qualification
Five approaches. For each approach: • Assumptions • Explaining the formation of a relationship • One therapy • Evaluation of the therapy • Classic evidence • Evaluation of the approach	
Unit 2 **Psychology: Using Psychological Concepts**	1 hour 30 mins 80 marks 20% of A Level qualification
Section A Contemporary debates Section B Principles of research Section C Application of research methods to a novel scenario	

WJEC A2 EXAM

Unit 3 **Psychology: Implications in the Real World**	2 hours 30 mins 100 marks 40% of A Level qualification
Section A Study of behaviours Section B Controversies in psychology	
Unit 4 **Applied Research Methods**	1 hour 30 mins 60 marks 20% of A Level qualification
Section A Personal investigations Section B Application of research methods to a novel scenario	

Introduction

PSYCHE

The word psychology is derived from two Greek words – 'psyche' meaning mind, soul, spirit, and 'logos' meaning study. So literally, psychology means the study of the mind. However, definitions have changed as the discipline has evolved in terms of its focus; an accepted modern definition is:

The scientific study of the human mind and its functions, especially those affecting behaviour in a given context – Oxford English Dictionary.

WHAT DO PSYCHOLOGISTS DO?

You have probably chosen to study psychology because it will lead you to an interesting profession. This may be true; however, it is also true that studying the reasons why humans behave the way they do will help you in any situation you are in, not just in a job!

However, if you complete a degree in psychology, you may go on to work in one of the following professions:

- Educational psychologist
- Forensic (criminal) psychologist
- Clinical psychologist
- Sports psychologist
- Occupational (work or organisational) psychologist

TRY THIS

Divide your class into pairs or small groups.

Each pair/group should be given one of the professions on the left and they should research what is involved.

They should then give a brief presentation to the class.

A BRIEF HISTORY OF PSYCHOLOGY

The beginning of the history of psychology is very difficult to pinpoint. However, we know that interest in the mind is rooted in ancient history and philosophy. Way back, about 400 years BC, the leading philosopher Plato used the idea of the 'psyche' to describe the mind and soul. Through your course of studying Psychology at A Level, you will become familiar with some leading researchers in the field of more 'modern' psychology. Below are some of these important researchers, significant dates and their key interests:

1879 – **Wilhelm Wundt** founds the first experimental psychology laboratory in Leipzig, Germany. He is considered to be the '**father of psychology**' (see page 70).

1886 – **Sigmund Freud** sets up a private practice in Vienna, Austria and begins providing therapy to patients. He is considered the **founder of psychoanalysis** (see page 30).

1906 – **Ivan Pavlov** publishes his findings on **classical conditioning** following his famous experiment with dogs (see page 50).

1919 – **John B. Watson**, often referred to as the **founder of behaviourism**, publishes *Psychology from the Standpoint of a Behaviourist* (see page 50).

1954 – **Abraham Maslow** creates a third force in psychology – **humanistic psychology** (see page 103) joins psychoanalysis and behaviourism.

1963 – **Albert Bandura** first describes the concept of **observational learning** following his Bobo doll experiments.

1967 – **Ulric Neisser** publishes *Cognitive Psychology* – he describes his research as an assault on behaviourism. 1950s–1970 is often referred to as the cognitive revolution (see page 70).

1974 – **Stanley Milgram** presents his findings from his infamous **obedience to authority** experiments (see page 162).

1998 – **Martin Seligman** delivers President's address to the American Psychological Association, calling for a **positive psychology** (see page 91).

TRY THIS

History of psychology
Create a classroom poster entitled 'psychology timeline' where you represent the information on the left using pictures. You can research other events.

Or

Identify one significant figure in psychology. Write a brief biography of this person and present to the rest of the class.

TRY THIS

10 things you didn't know about psychology
The BPS website has a page devoted to this topic (go to www.bps.org.uk and search for 'Ten things you might not know' and select the first item offered).

Work in a small group and choose an interesting fact. Design and conduct a brief PowerPoint presentation informing the rest of the group about your research.

TRY THIS

Gender bias and psychology
Try to find significant female psychologists as you look at the history of psychology. What strikes you?

PSYCHOLOGY AND ETHICS

Ethics are standards that concern any group of professional people – solicitors, doctors, teachers all have documents advising what is expected of them in terms of right and wrong in their jobs. These are sometimes referred to as a **code of ethics**.

The British Psychological Society

Psychologists in the UK are advised by the **British Psychological Society (BPS)**. In the US there is the American Psychological Association (APA); in Canada the Canadian Psychological Association (CPA); and so on.

The most recent *Code of Ethics and Conduct* (BPS, 2009) identifies four principles:

1. *Respect* – Psychologists should show respect for the dignity and worth of all persons. This includes standards of **privacy** and **confidentiality** and **valid consent**.
   Intentional **deception** (lack of valid consent) is only acceptable when it is necessary to protect the integrity of research and when the deception is disclosed to participants at the earliest opportunity. One way to judge acceptability is to consider whether participants are likely to object or show unease when **debriefed**. Participants should be aware of the **right to withdraw** from the research at any time.
2. *Competence* – Psychologists should maintain high standards in their professional work.
3. *Responsibility* – Psychologists have a responsibility to their clients, to the general public and to the science of Psychology. This includes protecting participants from any **risk of physical or psychological harm** as well as debriefing them at the conclusion of their participation.
4. *Integrity* – Psychologists should be honest and accurate. This includes reporting the findings of any research accurately and acknowledging any potential limitations. It also includes bringing instances of misconduct by other psychologists to the attention of the BPS.

HOW DOES PSYCHOLOGY APPLY TO YOU?

Throughout your study of A Level Psychology, you will be looking at classic approaches and studies in psychology and considering key debates. However, you may wonder how psychology affects you and your everyday life, and what psychological research can tell you about your own behaviours (and that of those around you).

Consider the following questions:
- Are tattoos and piercings a sign of self-mutilation or self-expression?
- Is over-texting healthy for relationships?
- Is social networking good for friendships?

You will, no doubt, have some different views to your classmates, so why not have a discussion? There is a wealth of psychological research into these areas and you may, out of interest, wish to look into the research in these areas to use psychology to understand more about your own behaviour.

TRY THIS

Ethics

When psychologists conduct research they have to adhere to ethical guidelines; following these guidelines should ensure that participants are being treated in a moral way. Common ethical issues raised in research include: deception, valid consent, risk from harm, and confidentiality (see page 126).

Read the following scenarios and identify the types of ethical issues that could be raised:
- A researcher wanted to investigate the influence of friendship groups on stress in teenagers. He went into several local schools and gave out questionnaires to ask about these issues. He wrote back to the teenagers, giving them feedback about the study.
- A psychologist would like to find out if people are obedient. He sets up a situation at his university where participants are asked to give another person a (pretend) electric shock, which they believe to be real, when the experimenter instructs them to. The participants believe it is an experiment into teaching and learning.

- Psychology university students are acting as participants for their lecturers' research into the different qualities males and females look for in a partner. The students regularly meet with their lecturer to be interviewed to explore various issues. They feel that they cannot opt out because they want to successfully complete their course.

TRY THIS

Is texting good for you? And other ideas

Choose one of the questions on the left and discuss in class. The following links might help:

www.everydayhealth.com/columns/elizabeth-thompson-womens-wellness/tattoos-body-piercing-self-expression-self-mutilation

www.psychologytoday.com/blog/meet-catch-and-keep/201403/is-constant-texting-good-or-bad-your-relationship

htttp://friendship.about.com/od/Social_Networking/tp/Ways-Social-Networking-Ruins-Friendship.htm

Approaches in psychology

The backbone of your studies in psychology is the five main approaches. Each of the first five chapters in this textbook is focused on one of the approaches.

An approach is a perspective or view about human behaviour which involves beliefs about what causes behaviour, how behaviour can be changed, and how it can be studied.

MAIN APPROACHES IN PSYCHOLOGY

This is a very brief outline of the five main approaches:

The **biological approach** believes that behaviour can be explained in terms of inherited characteristics (genes), as well as other physiological factors (e.g. hormones, chemicals in the brain).

The **behaviourist approach** believes that the way a person is and behaves is due to life experiences. A person may be rewarded or punished for certain behaviour, and this determines how they behave in future. People might also imitate what they see others doing.

The **psychodynamic approach** believes that our behaviour is influenced by emotions that are beyond our conscious awareness. Such emotions are buried in the **unconscious** mind as a result of events in early childhood, which may have been traumatic.

The **cognitive approach** believes that behaviour is best explained in terms of how a person thinks about their actions (internal mental processes). For example, the expectation that a concert will be brilliant will increase the likelihood that it will be.

The **positive approach** believes that we should study what is best about human beings and how we can develop our positive qualities in order to lead fulfilled lives. This approach is grounded in the belief that people want to lead the best lives that they can, and want to enhance their experiences of love, work and play.

LOUISA

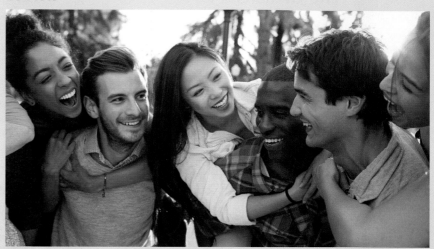

Louisa is seen by her friends as a rather 'needy' person. She is always seeking company, unable to feel at ease on her own. Every night and on weekends, when not around her college friends, she is either spending time with her mum, elder sister or visiting friends. She is also the same in romantic relationships – when she splits up with one boyfriend, she simply has to find another!

How would each of the approaches explain Louisa's behaviour?

The biological approach may consider the *physical* feelings that Louisa gets when she is around others. These feelings make her feel good and are physically addictive. For example, a **hormone** known as oxytocin (sometimes referred to as the love drug) is released when we are intimate with others, and this strengthens bonds between people.

The behaviourist approach would look at the *rewards* that people get from relationships, whether these are physical or psychological. Being around others induces feelings of happiness, comfort, safety, etc., and the behaviourist approach would say that this **positive reinforcement** would result in Louisa continuing to seek company.

The psychodynamic approach would look back at Louisa's childhood and the *early relationships* formed. It may consider that if Louisa was given too much attention at a very early age, this would result in her depending on others later in life. This approach would look closely at the attachment bond formed early on between Louisa and her mum, and would believe this to have an influence on her later relationships.

The cognitive approach would look at how Louisa perceives and interprets the relationships around her. For this approach, we may weigh up what she thinks she gets from relationships (e.g. lots of attention, social support) against what they 'cost' her (e.g. time invested in friends, boyfriends). If she perceives the benefits to be greater than the costs, she will continue these relationships.

The positive approach would say that the company of others allows Louisa to express her natural, positive qualities, for example kindness, altruism, humour. This approach proposes that we get greater life satisfaction from expressing and developing these qualities, compared with negative ones, and so Louisa is simply wanting to reach a greater sense of life satisfaction.

TRY THIS

John

John started stealing when he was just 10 years old. In the beginning, John just stole sweets from his local shop. However, by the time John was 17, he had joined a local gang. Along with the other members of the gang, he started stealing cars and breaking into houses to steal. An important part of being a gang member was acting tough and aggressive, regularly getting into fights with other gang members.

Try to explain his behaviour using the five approaches.

Issues and debates

There are four main issues and debates in psychology. They are issues because they are so important that we can't really ignore them. They are debates because there is no simple answer about which is right or wrong, better or worse.

These issues and debates will be very important in helping you to evaluate each of the approaches, something you may be required to do in the exam.

They are also crucial for comparing and contrasting the approaches, another requirement of the exam.

DETERMINISM OR FREE WILL

Determinism is the view that an individual's behaviour is shaped or controlled by internal or external forces rather than the individual's will to do something. This means that behaviour is predictable and lawful.

Free will is used to refer to the alternative end position in which an individual is seen as being capable of self-determination. According to this view, individuals have an active role in controlling their behaviour, i.e. they are free to choose and are not acting in response to any external or internal (biological) pressures.

Any approach, such as behaviourism or the biological approach, that takes the view that our behaviour is determined by factors other than our free will implies that people are not personally responsible for their behaviour. For example, according to the biological approach, low levels of **serotonin** in the brain may lead some individuals to behave aggressively. This poses a moral question about whether a person can be held personally responsible for his or her behaviour. We might argue that this is not acceptable, that people are responsible for their behaviour, and this kind of argument is therefore a limitation of such determinist explanations.

REDUCTIONISM OR HOLISM

Reductionism involves breaking down a complex phenomenon into more simple components. It also implies that this process is desirable because complex phenomena are best understood in terms of a simpler level of explanation. Psychologists (and all scientists) are drawn to reductionist explanations and methods of research because reductionism is a powerful tool that underlies experimental research (reducing complex behaviour to a set of variables).

The 'opposite' of reductionism is **holism**, or the holistic approach. Holism is the view that systems should be studied as a whole rather than focusing on their constituent parts, and suggests that we cannot predict how the whole system will behave from a knowledge of the individual components. Cognitive systems such as memory and intelligence are examples of the value of a holistic approach. They are complex systems, the behaviour of which is related to the activity of neurons, genes and so on, yet the whole system cannot be simply predicted from these lower level units.

NATURE OR NURTURE

The **nature or nurture debate** suggests that people are either (mainly) the product of their genes and biology (nature) or of their environment (nurture). The term nature does not simply refer to abilities present at birth, but to any ability determined by the genes, including those that appear through maturation. 'Nurture' is everything learned through interactions with the environment, both the physical and social environment, and may be more widely referred to as 'experience'.

At one time, nature and nurture were seen as largely independent and additive factors. However, a more contemporary view is that the two processes do not just interact, but are inextricably entwined. It is no longer really a debate at all but a new understanding of how genetics works.

IDIOGRAPHIC OR NOMOTHETIC

The **idiographic** approach involves the study of individuals and the unique insights each individual gives us about human behaviour. Psychologists who use idiographic methods study individuals or small groups over a long period of time, and in great detail. They do not try to make generalisations about the behaviour of whole populations.

The **nomothetic** approach involves the study of a large number of people and then seeks to make generalisations or develop laws/theories about their behaviour. This is the goal of the scientific approach – to produce general laws of behaviour.

TRY THIS

What makes a person intelligent? Can we influence our level of intelligence or is it fixed? How do psychologists measure intelligence? (You might want to do some research on the internet, for example http://general-psychology.weebly.com/how-do-we-measure-intelligence.html)

In small groups consider the questions above as fully as you can and then try answering the further questions below:
- Does your explanation support the nature or nurture debate?
- Is your explanation determinist?
- Is your explanation reductionist?
- Is the approach to measuring intelligence nomothetic or idiographic?

Chapter 1
The biological approach

SPECIFICATION

Approach	Assumptions and behaviour to be explained (including)	Therapy (one per approach)	Classic research	Contemporary debate
Biological	• evolutionary influences • localisation of brain function • neurotransmitters Learners will be expected to apply one of the given assumptions to the formation of a relationship	drug therapy OR psychosurgery	Raine, A., Buchsbaum, M. and LaCasse, L. (1997) Brain abnormalities in murderers indicated by positron emission tomography. *Biological Psychiatry*, *42(6)*, 495–508.	the ethics of neuroscience

CHAPTER CONTENT

What do you know about genes?

How do you think genes affect behaviour?

Can your behaviour be explained in terms of your genes?

What else influences your behaviour?

Biological approach assumptions

SPECIFICATION REQUIREMENT

For each approach it will be necessary to:
- Know and understand the assumptions.
- Apply the assumptions to explain the formation of a relationship.

The key assumption of the biological approach is that all behaviours can be explained at the level of functioning of our biological systems. There are several general 'strands' to this approach, including:

- The **physiological approach** – this approach believes that all behaviour is due to the functioning of internal body parts, for example the brain, nervous systems, hormones and chemicals.
- The **nativist approach** – this is based on the assumption that all behaviour is inherited; behaviour is passed down through our **genes** from one generation to the next.
- The **medical model** – this refers to the treatment of psychological disorders based on the same principles used to treat physical diseases. The argument is that psychological problems ultimately have a physical cause and thus can be treated using physical (medical) methods.

ASSUMPTION 1: EVOLUTIONARY INFLUENCES

To evolve means to change with time. In psychology the theory of **evolution** has been used to explain how the human mind and behaviour have changed over millions of years so that they are **adapted** to the demands of our individual environments.

Theory of natural selection

The notion of adaptiveness is based on Darwin's theory of **natural selection** – this is the idea that any genetically determined behaviour that enhances an individual's chance of survival and reproduction will be naturally selected, i.e. the genes will be passed on to the next generation. Natural selection takes place at the level of the genes. An example of this is altruistic behaviour, where parents risk their lives to save their offspring. The theory of natural selection would say that altruism is an inherited, adaptive trait because saving an offspring (or other relative) enhances the survival of that individual's gene pool.

EEA

One of the key concepts of the evolutionary approach is the environment of evolutionary adaptiveness (**EEA**). This is the environment to which any species is adapted and the selective pressures that existed at that time. Evolutionary psychologists don't assume that all forms of behaviour are adaptive – only the ones that will ensure the survival in that individual's particular environment. For humans, the most recent period of evolutionary change was about two million years ago when humans moved from forest life to the developing savannahs in Africa. EEA can explain why humans have such large brains relative to their body size. This theory would propose that the human brain has evolved in response to the complex social organisation of our species. Those humans with particular abilities would be more likely to survive: for example, those who are better at forming alliances and forming good relationships are more likely to survive in a complex social world. Therefore the genes for such behaviours are the ones that are passed on.

ASSUMPTION 2: LOCALISATION OF BRAIN FUNCTION

Localisation of brain function refers to the principle that certain areas of the brain are responsible for different functions – they have certain jobs or tasks to carry out. The cerebral cortex covers the brain much like a tea cosy covers a teapot, and is the area of the brain responsible for higher order cognitive functions.

Four lobes

The cerebral cortex is divided into four regions: frontal, parietal, temporal and occipital. Each of the four regions or 'lobes' has specific functions. The **frontal lobes** are involved in thinking and creativity, and have been linked to our personalities. The **parietal lobes** receive sensory information such as temperature, touch and pain. The **temporal lobes** are responsible for much of our memory processing as well as the processing of auditory information (hence speech). Lastly, the **occipital lobes** are concerned with visual processing and receive information directly from the eyes.

Lobes of the Brain

Lateral view *Superior view*

Anterior Posterior Anterior

- Frontal lobe
- Parietal lobe
- Occipital lobe
- Temporal lobe

Posterior

Left Right

Localisation of language

There are specific areas of the brain linked to the processing of language. Our understanding of this dates back to the middle of the 19th century, when the French neurosurgeon Paul Broca studied eight patients with language problems. He examined their brains after death and found that they had damage to a specific area of their left hemispheres. This area has been named 'Broca's area' and is associated with speech production. It is located in the posterior portion of the frontal lobe.

Carl Wernicke, a German neurologist, discovered another area of the brain that was involved in understanding language. This area, named 'Wernicke's area', is in the posterior portion of the left temporal lobe. His patients could speak but were unable to *understand* language.

◄ Kin selection can explain why siblings form close relationships.

Exam advice…
For each assumption it may be useful to be able to write approximately 150–200 words (about 4 marks' worth) and it's useful to follow the SEE format:
State the assumption,
Explain and elaborate, and give an
Example in psychology.
Try this for each of the assumptions throughout this book.

ASSUMPTION 3: NEUROTRANSMITTERS

Neurons are electrically excitable cells that form the basis of the nervous system. The flexibility of the nervous system is enhanced by having many branches at the end of each neuron (called *dendrites*) so that each neuron connects with many others.

One neuron communicates with another neuron at a **synapse**, where the message is relayed by chemical messengers (**neurotransmitters**). There is a diagram of a synapse on the following spread. These neurotransmitters are released from **presynaptic vesicles** in one neuron, and will either stimulate or inhibit receptors in the other neuron. The **synaptic cleft** or gap is about 20 nm (nanometres) wide.

Neurotransmitters and mental health

Neurotransmitters have been found to play a significant role in our mental health. For example, **serotonin** plays a role in our mood, sleep and appetite. Too little serotonin has been found in people suffering from depression. Some antidepressant medications therefore work by increasing the availability of serotonin at the **postsynaptic receptor** sites.

High levels of the neurotransmitter **dopamine** have been associated with symptoms of **schizophrenia**. This is supported by the fact that drugs that block dopamine activity reduce schizophrenic symptoms.

BIOLOGICAL EXPLANATION FOR RELATIONSHIP FORMATION

Evolutionary theory

Evolutionary theory proposes that relationships form with individuals who possess certain traits. Traits that enhance successful reproduction are naturally selected. However, males and females experience different selective pressures. Males do well to mate as frequently as they can and select women who are more fertile (young) and healthy – smooth skin, glossy hair, red lips and thin waist are all indicators of youthfulness and healthiness, and add up to what we see as 'physical attractiveness'. Females also seek signs of fertility and healthiness in their partner, but are more concerned to find a partner who can provide the resources needed for offspring to survive (e.g. food, shelter).

Further evolutionary processes can be seen in parental investment theory (Trivers, 1972), which offers an explanation about why certain relationships are formed, for example between younger women and older men. According to parental investment theory, as female mammals invest more in their offspring (e.g. they carry the baby), they must be 'choosier' in finding a partner, hence will seek out the male that can provide the most resources.

Neurotransmitters

The chemicals in our brain have a powerful effect on our emotions, and in turn will influence our perceptions of others, including those who we may enter into relationships with. Dopamine, for example, has been associated with pleasure seeking and reward-driven behaviour, so setting the goal of finding a partner, and being driven to achieve this, will give us a 'hit' of dopamine. This can explain why, as humans, we are driven to form relationships – they give us a natural 'high'.

Oxytocin is a hormone linked to human bonding and increasing trust and loyalty, and high levels of oxytocin have been linked to romantic attachment; it is thought that a lack of physical contact with one's partner will reduce levels of oxytocin, leading to feelings of longing to bond with one's partner again. This could also offer another explanation for forming relationships, specifically romantic ones – we have a natural chemical drive to bond with others.

Example: Explaining the formation of sibling relationships

Evolutionary theory can also explain the close relationships often found between brothers and sisters. In addition to natural selection there is also **kin selection** – traits that enhance the survival of those who have similar genes are also selected to promote the survival of our group's genes. Therefore, we have a natural incentive to look after our siblings, and to invest time, energy and other resources into ensuring they are protected and healthy.

TRY THIS

We have applied biological explanations for relationships to sibling relationships, just one of the examples given in the specification.

Try to do the same for some of the other examples in the specification: mother and child, pet and owner, romantic partners and friends. Try to make each one different.

EXAM CORNER

For each assumption named in the specification, you need to be able to:

- Outline the assumption.
- Fully elaborate this assumption, drawing on examples in psychology.

In addition, you need to be able to:

- Use at least **one** assumption to explain the formation of **one** relationship.

Possible exam questions:

1. Describe **two** assumptions of the biological approach. [8]
2. Explain the biological assumption 'localisation of brain function'. [4]
3. Describe the formation of **one** relationship using **one** assumption of the biological approach. [3]

Therapy 1: Drug therapy

Exam advice…
An exam question may ask you to focus only on how the assumptions apply in the therapy, so you need to be able to relate at least two assumptions to the aims/ components (principles) of each therapy. This could include the overall assumption or more specific assumptions.

Biological psychologists believe that we can explain all behaviour in terms of our biological make-up. This approach to explaining behaviour has a number of sub-assumptions, including the **physiological approach**, which looks at the influence of neurochemicals, hormones, the brain and nervous systems, and the **nativist approach**, which looks at **evolutionary** and **genetic** influences on our behaviour.

SPECIFICATION REQUIREMENT

For each approach it will be necessary to:
- Know and understand how the approach can be used in therapy (one therapy per approach).
- Know and understand the main components (principles) of the therapy.
- Evaluate the therapy (including its effectiveness and ethical considerations).

HOW BIOLOGICAL ASSUMPTIONS APPLY TO DRUG THERAPY

The **biological approach** assumes that psychological disorders such as depression, anxiety and **schizophrenia** have a physiological cause. This approach to therapy is known as the **medical model** and is based on the view that mental illnesses are like physical illnesses – they have a physical cause characterised by clusters of symptoms (a 'syndrome'), and therefore can be treated in a physical way. The medical model recommends that a patient should be treated for their mental illness through direct manipulation of their physical bodily processes, for example through drug therapy.

A second assumption of the biological approach is that changes in the brain's neurotransmitter systems will affect our mood, feelings, perceptions and behaviour. Therefore, advocates of the biological approach would suggest that psychotherapeutic drugs can be used to alter the action of neurotransmitters and treat mental disorder. In general, drug therapy operates by increasing or blocking the action of neurotransmitters in the brain, which will, in turn, influence our emotions, thoughts and actions.

A third assumption of the biological approach is that of **localisation of brain function**; drugs target specific regions of the brain which are involved in psychological disorder. For example, the **limbic system** regulates emotions, and disturbances in this part of the brain may affect mood.

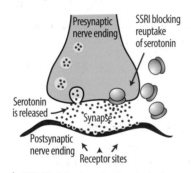

▲ SSRIs block the reuptake of serotonin at the presynaptic membrane, increasing serotonin concentration at receptor sites on the postsynaptic membrane.

SYMPATHETIC NERVOUS SYSTEM

When a person is scared their sympathetic nervous system is aroused so that the person is ready to deal with a potentially dangerous situation. This is called the 'fight or flight' response – because people (and animals) respond to such situations by fighting or fleeing.

When you (or an animal) are scared the body produces adrenaline and noradrenaline which create all the physiological symptoms you have experienced when scared or anxious. Imagine that you have to speak to a group of 100 people – your heart starts to beat rapidly, your mouth goes dry, you feel sweaty – these are all part of sympathetic arousal.

MAIN COMPONENTS (PRINCIPLES) OF DRUG THERAPY

The three main types of psychoactive drugs are antipsychotics, antidepressants and antianxiety drugs.

Antipsychotic drugs

Antipsychotic drugs treat **psychotic** mental disorders such as schizophrenia. A patient with a psychotic mental disorder has lost touch with reality and has little insight into his or her condition. **Conventional antipsychotics** are used primarily to combat the positive symptoms of schizophrenia (e.g. delusions and hallucinations). These drugs block the action of the neurotransmitter **dopamine** in the brain by binding to, but not stimulating, dopamine receptors (see diagram on left).

The **atypical antipsychotic drugs** (such as *Clozaril*) act by only temporarily occupying dopamine receptors, and then rapidly dissociating to allow normal dopamine transmission. This may explain why such atypical antipsychotics have lower levels of side effects (such as *tardive dyskinesia* – involuntary movements of the mouth and tongue) compared with conventional antipsychotics.

Antidepressant drugs

Depression is thought to be due to insufficient amounts of neurotransmitters such as **serotonin** being produced in the nerve endings (**synapse**). In normal brains, neurotransmitters are constantly being released from the nerve endings, stimulating the neighbouring neurons. To terminate their action, neurotransmitters are reabsorbed into the nerve endings and are broken down by an enzyme. Antidepressants work either by reducing the rate of reabsorption, or by blocking the enzyme that breaks down the neurotransmitters. Both of these mechanisms increase the amount of neurotransmitter available to excite neighbouring cells.

The most commonly prescribed antidepressant drugs are **selective serotonin reuptake inhibitors** (**SSRIs**) such as *Prozac*. These work by blocking the transporter mechanism that reabsorbs serotonin into the presynaptic cell after it has fired. As a result, more of the serotonin is left in the synapse, prolonging its activity and making transmission of the next impulse easier.

Antianxiety drugs

The group of drugs most commonly used to treat anxiety and **stress** are **benzodiazepines** (**BZs**). They are sold under various trade names such as *Librium* and *Valium*. BZs slow down the activity of the **central nervous system**. They do this by enhancing the activity of **GABA**, a biochemical substance (or neurotransmitter) that is the body's natural form of anxiety relief.

Beta-blockers (**BBs**) are also used to reduce anxiety. They reduce the activity of **adrenaline** and **noradrenaline**, which are part of the response to stress. BBs bind to receptors on the cells of the heart and other parts of the body that are usually stimulated during sympathetic arousal. By blocking these receptors, it is harder to stimulate cells in this part of the body, so the heart beats slower and with less force, and blood vessels do not contract so easily. This results in a fall in blood pressure, and therefore less stress on the heart. The person feels calmer and less anxious.

You only study one biological therapy as part of your course – drug therapy OR psychosurgery.

EXAM CORNER

For each therapy, you will need to be able to:
- Describe how the assumptions of the approach are applied in the therapy.
- Describe the main components (principles) of the therapy.
- Evaluate the therapy in terms of its effectiveness.
- Evaluate the therapy in terms of ethical considerations.

Possible exam questions:
1. Describe how the assumptions of the biological approach are applied in **one** therapy. [6]
2. Describe **two** components (principles) of drug therapy. [8]
3. Evaluate the ethical issues raised in drug therapy. [8]
4. Evaluate the effectiveness of drug therapy. [8]

EVALUATION: EFFECTIVENESS

Drugs versus placebo

There is considerable evidence for the effectiveness of drug treatments. Typically a **randomised control trial** is used to compare the effectiveness of the drug versus a **placebo** (a substance that has no pharmacological value but controls for the belief that the pill you are taking will affect you). Soomro *et al.* (2008) reviewed 17 studies of the use of SSRIs with **OCD** (which has a component of depression) patients and found them to be more effective than placebos in reducing the symptoms of OCD up to three months after treatment, i.e. in the short term.

In a further study highlighting the superiority of drugs compared with placebos, Kahn *et al.* (1986) followed 250 patients over 8 weeks and found BZs to be significantly superior to placebos.

However, one of the issues regarding the evaluation of treatment is that most studies are only of three to four months' duration, and therefore little long-term data exists (Koran *et al.*, 2007).

Side effects

While drugs are generally extremely effective in treating psychological disorders, many have serious side effects. For example, nausea, headache and insomnia are common side effects of SSRIs (Soomro *et al.*, 2008). These may not seem that terrible but often are enough to make a person prefer not to take the drug. **Tricyclic antidepressants** tend to have more side effects (such as hallucinations and irregular heartbeat) than SSRIs so they are more likely to be used in cases where SSRIs were not effective.

Symptoms not cause

One of the common criticisms of drug therapy is that, while drugs may be effective in treating the symptoms of psychological disorders, this type of therapy does not address the underlying cause(s). For example, if a person is suffering depression in adulthood because of serious childhood trauma, then antidepressants may provide an effective short-term solution for the individual, but in the long term the disorder will not be dealt with. This will lead to what is known as the 'revolving door syndrome' where a patient is back and forth to their doctor as their disorder is never really cured.

Comparison with other treatments

Relative to other treatments (e.g. **psychotherapy**), drug therapy is cheap for the patient – in the UK they would be prescribed their drugs on the NHS. The practitioner has to invest less time in the patient, because they only need to meet with the patient every couple of months after initial consultation to discuss whether the drugs are having a positive effect and whether the patient is making progress. Therefore this type of therapy is efficient and easy to administer compared to other forms of therapy.

EVALUATION: ETHICAL ISSUES

Use of placebos

Biological treatments raise important **ethical issues**. First, there is an issue related to studying the effectiveness of drugs. A fundamental research ethic is that no patient should be given a treatment known to be inferior. If effective treatments exist, they should be used as the **control condition** when new treatments are tested. Substituting a placebo for an effective treatment does not satisfy this duty as it exposes individuals to a treatment known to be inferior.

Patient information

Another ethical problem is the issue of **valid consent**, or lack of it. Many patients will find it difficult to remember all the facts relating to the potential side effects of the drug prescribed or they simply may not be in a frame of mind to digest this information. Therefore truly valid consent is an illusion.

Furthermore, medical professionals may withhold some information about the drugs, for example they may not fully explain that the pharmacological benefits of the drugs are slim. Some medical professionals may also exaggerate the benefits of taking medication and may fail to inform the patient of other therapeutic options due to the 'quick fix' nature of drug therapy.

Dopamine and *serotonin* are both neurotransmitters that have been associated with a number of behaviours. Dopamine is linked to schizophrenia. Low levels of serotonin are related to depression, and high levels have been linked to anxiety.

TRY THIS

In small groups produce a leaflet, to be placed in hospitals/GP surgeries, on one type of drug therapy (antipsychotics, antidepressants or antianxiety drugs). Your leaflet should be concise, interesting and inform the reader of the following:
- The mental health disorders that are treated with the drug therapy.
- The different types of drugs.
- The effectiveness of the drugs.
- Some of the issues with using drug therapy.

Therapy 2: Psychosurgery

SPECIFICATION REQUIREMENT

For each approach it will be necessary to:
- Know and understand how the approach can be used in therapy (one therapy per approach).
- Know and understand the main components (principles) of the therapy.
- Evaluate the therapy (including its effectiveness and ethical considerations).

You only study one biological therapy as part of your course – drug therapy OR psychosurgery.

▲ In the 1940s and 1950s, it was common to perform a lobotomy on patients with mental illness to control aggressive symptoms. One form of lobotomy – a transorbital lobotomy – was performed by inserting a sharp instrument into the brain through the eye socket. The prefrontal cortex, lying at the front, is thus damaged and this was thought to reduce aggressive behaviour.

Deep brain stimulation

A possible alternative to psychosurgery is **deep brain stimulation** (**DBS**), where surgeons thread wires through the skull. This more modern type of psychosurgery involves no tissue destruction and is thus only temporary. The wires, which remain embedded in the brain, are connected to a battery pack implanted in the patient's chest. The batteries produce an adjustable high-frequency current that interrupts the brain circuitry involved in, for example, OCD. If it doesn't work, it can always be turned off.

Biological psychologists believe that we can explain all behaviour in terms of our biological make-up. This approach to explaining behaviour has a number of sub-assumptions, including the **physiological approach**, which looks at the influence of neurochemicals, hormones, the brain and nervous systems, and the *nativist approach*, which looks at **evolutionary** and **genetic** influences on our behaviour.

Exam advice...
An exam question may ask you to focus only on how the assumptions apply in the therapy, so you need to be able to relate at least two assumptions to the aims/ components (principles) of each therapy. This could include the overall assumption or more specific assumptions.

HOW BIOLOGICAL ASSUMPTIONS APPLY TO PSYCHOSURGERY

The **biological approach** would assume that psychological disorders such as depression, anxiety and **schizophrenia** have a physiological cause. This approach to therapy is known as the **medical model** and is based on the view that mental illnesses are like physical illnesses – they have a physical cause characterised by clusters of symptoms (a 'syndrome'), and therefore can be treated in a physical way. The medical model recommends that a patient should be treated for their mental illness through direct manipulation of their physical bodily processes, for example through altering parts of the brain (psychosurgery).

A second assumption is **localisation of brain function** – the idea that certain areas of the brain have different 'jobs' or functions that they carry out. Treating psychological disorders in a physical way involves destroying or removing certain areas of the brain that are thought to contribute to psychological problems, such as depression or anxiety.

A third assumption is the role of **neurotransmitters**. Modern methods of psychosurgery involve stimulating areas of the brain, which has an effect on neurotransmitters in the brain. Low levels of certain neurotransmitters in the brain are associated with mental disorder, for example low levels of **serotonin** are linked with depression. If the brain is stimulated and serotonin levels increased, the patient will experience improved mental health.

MAIN COMPONENTS (PRINCIPLES) OF PSYCHOSURGERY

Prefrontal lobotomy

The **prefrontal lobotomy** is a surgical procedure involving selective destruction of nerve fibres. It is performed on the **frontal lobe** of the brain, an area that is involved in impulse control and mood regulation. Its purpose is to alleviate some of the severe symptoms of mental illness. Initially, operations were performed on patients with *affective disorders* (i.e. various types of **depression**); other groups of patients included those with severe **obsessive-compulsive disorder** (**OCD**), and, less successfully, with schizophrenia. As a rule, the *severity* of the illness was a more important factor than the *type* of illness, along with consideration of how dangerous the patient was.

The Portuguese neurologist Egas Moniz developed a surgical procedure called a **prefrontal leucotomy** in the 1930s. This involved drilling a hole on each side of the skull and inserting an instrument that resembled an ice-pick to destroy the nerve fibres underneath. Moniz later refined his technique by designing a 'leucotome', an instrument with a retractable wire loop that could cut into the white matter of the brain and sever nerve fibres. It was hoped that cutting into nerve pathways that carried thoughts from one part of the brain to the other would relieve patients of their distressing thoughts and behaviours.

Stereotactic psychosurgery

More recently, neurosurgeons have developed far more precise ways of surgically treating mental disorders such as OCD, bipolar disorder, depression and eating disorders that fail to respond to psychotherapy or other forms of treatment.

Instead of removing large sections of frontal lobe tissue, neurosurgeons nowadays use brain scanning, such as **MRI scans**, to locate exact points within the brain and sever connections very precisely. The procedure is done using an anaesthetic.

In OCD, for example, a circuit linking the orbital frontal lobe to deeper structures in the brain, such as the **thalamus**, appears to be more active than normal. The bilateral **cingulotomy** is designed surgically to interrupt this circuit. Surgeons can either burn away tissue by heating the tip of the electrode, or use a non-invasive tool known as a *gamma knife* to focus beams of radiation at the target site.

In a **capsulotomy**, surgeons insert probes through the top of the skull and down into the capsule, a region of the brain near the **hypothalamus** that is part of the circuit. They then heat the tips of the probes, burning away tiny portions of tissue.

EXAM CORNER

For each therapy, you will need to be able to:

- Describe how the assumptions of the approach are applied in the therapy.
- Describe the main components (principles) of the therapy.
- Evaluate the therapy in terms of its effectiveness.
- Evaluate the therapy in terms of ethical considerations.

Possible exam questions:

1. Describe how the assumptions of the biological approach are applied in **one** therapy. [6]
2. Describe the main components (principles) of psychosurgery. [12]
3. Outline **two** components (principles) of psychosurgery. [4 + 4]
4. Evaluate psychosurgery in terms of its effectiveness and ethical issues. [8]

▶ The film *Frances* is about the Hollywood actress Frances Farmer. In the film, she is subject to a transorbital lobotomy. In real life, she did spend a number of years in a mental hospital but in fact never had a lobotomy. The film shows graphic detail of some of the horrors of early lobotomies.

Recently Howard Dully (2007) produced a book called *My Lobotomy*, vividly describing his experiences as a lobotomy patient, which gives disturbing insights into the whole process.

However, it is important to recognise that modern-day lobotomies are much less primitive, although the end result may be the same. For example, Mary Lou Zimmerman received psychosurgery (a cingulotomy and a capsulotomy) for untreatable OCD. Unfortunately, the operation resulted in crippling brain damage rather than a cure. Her family sued the US clinic that treated her, claiming they had not been informed of the dangerous and experimental nature of the surgery. A jury, after hearing expert witnesses, awarded her $7.5 million in damages.

EVALUATION: EFFECTIVENESS

Early psychosurgery

There is no doubt that the early practice of psychosurgery was both inappropriate and ineffective. Lobotomies had a fatality rate of up to 6%, and a range of severe physical side effects such as brain seizures and lack of emotional responsiveness (Comer, 2002). Modern psychosurgery is a different matter, although fundamentally the same objections could apply.

Modern psychosurgery

In a general review of research, Cosgrove and Rauch (2001) reported that cingulotomy was effective in 56% of OCD patients, and **capsulotomy** in 67%. In patients with major affective disorder, cingulotomy was effective in 65%, and capsulotomy in 55%. However, given that the authors claimed that only about 25 patients per year are currently treated in this way in the USA, the number of patients studied is very small. Also, Bridges *et al.* (1994) have pointed out that, as a treatment of last resort, no controlled trial against a comparable treatment is possible.

DBS has been found to be effective in patients suffering with severe depression. For example, Mayberg *et al.* (2005) found that in four out of six patients with this disorder, striking improvements were noted following treatment involving stimulation of a small area of the frontal cortex.

Appropriateness of psychosurgery

Psychosurgery is limited in its use, for example it is rarely used for treatment of phobias, and then only for extreme cases that have proven otherwise untreatable. It is not used to treat schizophrenia, although some researchers have called for controlled trials into its effectiveness in treating it. Szasz (1978) criticised psychosurgery generally because a person's psychological self is not something physical and therefore it is illogical to suggest it can be operated on.

Future directions

DBS is evolving as a research tool as well as a form of treatment. This is due to the fact that this procedure can provide the researcher with information that other scanning methods cannot. For example, the electroencephalograph (**EEG**) is able to tell us *when* activity in the brain is happening, but not *where*. By contrast, functional magnetic resonance imaging (**fMRI**) does the opposite – it tells us where the activity us, but is too slow to pinpoint when. DBS can give us precise information about both these things.

EVALUATION: ETHICAL ISSUES

Valid consent

Early psychosurgical techniques were used in mental asylums and prisons on patients who had not necessarily given their **valid consent** to the operation.

The ethical debate in relation to consent continues to this day. Patients with severe depression, for example, arguably are not in the right frame of mind to be able to give fully informed consent. In 1983 in Britain the Mental Health Act (MHA) incorporated more stringent provisions regarding consent to psychosurgical treatment. For example, those who are detained under the MHA, but have not committed a crime, have the same rights to consent as people who are not detained.

Irreversible damage

A major concern is that the effects of psychosurgery cannot be reversed. Early procedures resulted in significant changes to a patient's cognitive capabilities such as memory loss, as well as, in some cases, the severe blunting of emotions. Following early methods such as prefrontal lobotomy, many patients returned to the community zombie like, devoid of emotions.

Modern methods have reduced the risk of severe damage to the brain because of techniques that can target precise locations in the brain. However, procedures such as DBS still carry risks of long-term side effects such as seizures and altered states of mood.

TRY THIS

Divide your class into groups. Each group should take one form of psychosurgery and prepare:

- An engaging and informative talk about that technique.
- A poster display.
- A handout of notes.
- A quick quiz about the topic, including the answers.

Classic evidence: Raine, Buchsbaum and LaCasse (1997)

SPECIFICATION REQUIREMENT

For each approach it will be necessary to:
- Know and understand a classic piece of evidence (including methodology, procedures, findings and conclusions).

BRAIN ABNORMALITIES IN MURDERERS INDICATED BY POSITRON EMISSION TOMOGRAPHY

Early theories about criminal behaviour suggested that there might be a physical difference between criminals and non-criminals that would enable us to identify individuals before they committed a crime. For example, Cesare Lombroso (1876) suggested that criminals typically had a narrow, sloping forehead, prominent eye ridges, large ears and a protruding chin.

The advent of **brain scanning** techniques opened a new way to research the differences between criminals and non-criminals. It might be that specific areas of the brain are different in criminals and such differences may predispose those individuals to violent behaviour. There are clues as to which areas might be involved from animal research and also from studies of people with brain damage.

Adrian Raine, Monte Buchsbaum and Lori LaCasse focused on one particular group of criminals – individuals who had committed a murder and entered a plea of not guilty by reason of insanity (NGRI). The researchers proposed, on the basis of previous research, that seriously violent individuals:
- Would have brain dysfunction in the prefrontal cortex, angular gyrus, amygdala, hippocampus, thalamus and corpus callosum.
- Would not have brain dysfunction in the areas of the brain that have been implicated in mental illnesses but not previously related to violence (caudate, putamen, globus pallidus, midbrain, cerebellum).

▲ One of Lombroso's drawings of a criminal type (Lombroso, 1876). Although his theory seems quite cruel, Lombroso was an advocate for the humane treatment of criminals by arguing for rehabilitation and against capital punishment.

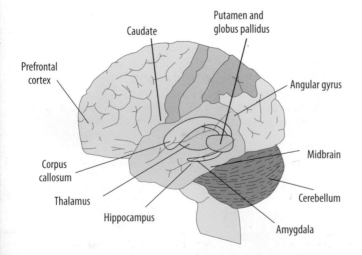

▲ The diagram shows the areas of the brain that were the focus of this study.

The limbic system is associated with emotion and includes the prefrontal cortex, amygdala, hippocampus and thalamus. These structures plus the angular gyrus and corpus callosum have been linked to violent behaviour in previous research.

The other structures labelled have all been implicated in other psychiatric conditions but have not been found to be related to violence.

METHODOLOGY

This was a **quasi-experiment** with a **matched pairs design**. The **IV** is NGRI or not, the **DV** is brain differences.

Participants

Murderers (experimental group)

There were 41 murderers (39 men and 2 women) who had a **mean** age of 34.3 years. They had all been charged with murder or manslaughter *and* all pleaded not guilty by reason of insanity (NGRI) or incompetence to stand trial. The participants were referred to the University of California for examination to obtain proof of their diminished capacity. The reasons for referral were that the murderers had some form of mental impairment as shown in the table below.

Mental disorder	Number
Schizophrenia	6
History of head injury or organic brain damage	23
History of psychoactive drug abuse	3
Affective disorder	2
Epilepsy	2
History of hyperactivity and learning disability	3
Personality disorder	2

The participants were instructed to be medication free, which was checked with a urine scan, for two weeks prior to brain scanning.

Control group

The **control group** was formed by matching each murderer with a normal individual of the same sex and age. The six **schizophrenics** were matched with six schizophrenics from a mental hospital. The other controls had no history of psychiatric illness, nor was there a history of psychiatric illness in any close relatives, and no significant physical illness. None were taking medication.

PROCEDURES

The sample was obtained using **opportunity sampling**. A **PET scan** was used to study the active brain.

All participants were given an injection of a 'tracer' (fluorodeoxyglucose or FDG). This tracer is taken up by active areas of the brain and thus it was possible to compare the brains of the NGRI and control groups.

All participants were asked to do a continuous performance task (CPT). This task specifically aimed to activate the target areas of the brain so the investigators could see how the different areas functioned.

1. Participants were given a chance to practise the CPT before receiving the FDG injection.
2. Thirty seconds before the FDG injection participants started the CPT so that the initial task novelty wouldn't be FDG labelled.
3. Thirty-two minutes after the FDG injection a PET scan was done of each participant. Ten horizontal slices (pictures) of their brain were recorded using the cortical peel and box techniques. The article provides precise details of the scanning techniques so that the study could be **replicated**.

FINDINGS

Brain differences

The study found *reduced* activity in the brain of NGRI participants in areas previously linked to violence:

- prefrontal cortex
- left angular gyrus
- corpus callosum
- in the left hemisphere only there was reduced activity in the amygdala, thalamus and hippocampus

The study found *increased* activity in the brain of NGRI participants in areas *not* previously linked to violence:

- cerebellum
- in the right hemisphere there was increased activity in the amygdala, thalamus and hippocampus

The study found *no difference* between NGRI group and controls in areas not previously linked to violence:

- caudate
- putamen
- globus pallidus
- midbrain

In summary, murderers had:

- **Reduced activity** (i.e. reduced glucose metabolism) in some areas, notably the areas previously linked to violence.
- **Abnormal asymmetries** – reduced activity on left side of the brain, greater activity on the right. This applied to some of the areas identified in the hypothesis as being linked to violence (the amygdala, thalamus and hippocampus).
- **No differences** in many brain structures, notably structures associated with mental illness but not violence.

Performance on CPT

Both groups performed similarly on the continuous performance task. Therefore any observed brain differences were not related to task performance.

Other differences not controlled for

Some differences between the NGRI group and control group were noted:

- *Handedness:* Six of the murderers were left handed but in fact they had less amygdala asymmetry and higher medial prefrontal activity than right-handed murderers.
- *Ethnicity:* 14 of the murderers were non-white but a comparison between them and white murderers showed no significant difference in brain activity.
- *Head injury:* 23 of the murderers had a history of head injury, but they didn't differ from murderers with no history of brain injury.

TRY THIS

Use a cauliflower to label the key areas of the brain just to get a 'feel' for it!

Later you can attach new labels showing what the study found for each of these key areas.

Finally, you can add a few onions and make a stir fry – education and nutrition!

CONCLUSIONS

Past research (animal and human studies) has identified links between areas of the brain and aggression as shown in the table below. These findings are supported by this study. Taken together these findings provide preliminary evidence that murderers pleading NGRI have different brain functioning to normal individuals.

However, neural processes underlying violence are complex and can't be reduced to a single brain mechanism. Violent behaviour can probably best be explained by the disruption of a *network* of interacting brain mechanisms rather than any single structure. Such disruption would not *cause* violent behaviour but would *predispose* an individual to violent behaviour.

Confounding variables

The study was carefully designed, involving a large sample and matched controls. However, Raine *et al.* acknowledge that head injury and IQ have not been ruled out as contributory factors.

Warning

Raine *et al.* emphasise that it is important to recognise what these results do *not* demonstrate:

1. The results do not show that violent behaviour is determined by biology alone; clearly social, psychological, cultural and situational factors play important roles in predisposition to violence.
2. The results do not show that murderers pleading NGRI are not responsible for their actions, nor that PET can be used as a means of diagnosing violent individuals.
3. The results do not show that brain dysfunction causes violence. It may even be that brain dysfunction is an effect of violence.
4. The results do not show that violence can be explained by the results; the results relate only to criminal behaviour.

Nevertheless the findings do suggest a link between brain dysfunction and a predisposition towards violence in this specific group (NGRI murderers), which should be further investigated.

Raine *et al.* presented this summary of past research findings.

Brain structure	Associated behaviours found in past research	Might explain
Limbic system (prefrontal cortex, amygdala, hippocampus and thalamus)	Emotion.	Abnormal emotional responses.
	Learning, memory and attention; abnormalities in their functioning may result in reduced sensitivity to conditioning.	Failure of violent offenders to learn from experience.
Prefrontal cortex	Deficit linked to impulsivity, loss of control, immaturity, and inability to modify behaviour. All of these are associated with increased aggressive behaviour.	Aggressive behaviour.
Amygdala	Aggressive behaviour in animals and humans. The destruction of the amygdala in animals results in lack of fear.	Fearlessness associated with violent activity.
Hippocampus	Modulates aggression in cats and, together with the *prefrontal cortex*, may be responsible for inhibiting aggressive behaviour.	Lack of inhibition of aggression.
Angular gyrus	Damage to the left: deficits in verbal and arithmetic abilities.	Low verbal IQs and poor school performance of violent offenders, which might predispose them to a life of crime.
Corpus callosum	Dysfunction related to a predisposition to violence, and poor transfer of information between hemispheres.	Reduced processing of linguistic information that has been found in violent groups.
Right hemisphere	Dominance of right hemisphere: less regulation by left hemisphere inhibitory processes, negative emotions, inappropriate emotional expression.	Lack of control over expressing violence.

Classic evidence: Raine, Buchsbaum and LaCasse (1997) (continued)

SPECIFICATION REQUIREMENT

For each approach it will be necessary to:
- Make judgements on a classic piece of evidence including ethical issues and social implications.

On this spread we are going to evaluate the classic study by looking at issues related to its methodology, and comparing the study to alternative evidence. When it comes to evaluation, you can make up your own mind. We have presented some evidence and statements, and invite you to use these to construct your own view of the classic study. You can use your knowledge of research methods as well.

TRY THIS

Do some further research (see 'Things to do') and have a debate in class.

Are criminals born or made? Nature or nurture?
Some people take the view that criminals are made not born, i.e. they become criminal because of social factors such as poverty and unemployment, or because of their upbringing.

One of the implications of this classic study is that criminals are 'born not made'. What do you think?

Divide your class into groups to prepare arguments for and against the view that criminals are born, not made.

▲ A patient is being moved into a PET scanner (left). An example of a PET scan is shown on the right. The damaged areas of the brain have reduced blood flow and no glucose metabolism. In this image damage has been caused by a blow to the head by a rock. The red areas are most active.

THINGS TO DO

WWW
There is a good BBC Horizon programme on the topic 'Are you Good or Evil?', broadcast in 2011; see www.bbc.co.uk/programmes/b014kj65

Original article
The full reference for this classic study is Raine, A., Buchsbaum, M. and LaCasse, L. (1997) Brain abnormalities in murderers indicated by positron emission tomography. *Biological Psychiatry, 42(6)*, 495–508.

You can read this article in full for a fee of $31.50 at: www.biologicalpsychiatryjournal.com/article/S0006-3223(96)00362-9/pdf

Other resources
Read Raine's arguments and Steven Rose's counter arguments at http://news.bbc.co.uk/1/hi/programmes/if/4102371.stm

Look up articles on criminal genes, for example: www.independent.co.uk/news/uk/do-your-genes-make-you-a-criminal-1572714.html

EVALUATION: METHODOLOGY AND PROCEDURES

A quasi-experiment
The study is an experiment because there is an **independent variable** (NGRI or not) and a **dependent variable** (activity of brain regions). However, the independent variable in this study (criminal status of the participant) was an existing condition of the individual, not something that was manipulated by the experimenter.

This means the study is a **quasi-experiment** and causal conclusions are not justified. As Raine *et al.* point out in their conclusions, the findings do not show that violent behaviour is *determined* by biology alone. Raine *et al.* suggest that psychological, cultural and situational factors play important roles in predisposition to violence.

Thus the limitation of this method is that no causal conclusions can be drawn. The danger is that readers misinterpret the findings and assume that criminal behaviour is predetermined and inescapable.

The research technique
Data was collected in this study using **PET scans**. Such techniques have permitted researchers to study the brain in a way not possible until recently. In the past, researchers relied on post-mortem examinations where brain physiology could not be linked to behaviour. PET scans permit researchers to study detailed regions of the brain. PET scans also enable the brain in action to be examined, which in this study meant that Raine *et al.* could see how the brains of different individuals differed in the way they processed information.

The sample
The murderers were not typical of all violent individuals. This is again something that Raine *et al.* acknowledge. The findings do not show that all violent offenders have such brain dysfunctions; the study can only draw conclusions about this kind of violent offender – namely an individual with some recognised form of mental impairment. Furthermore, the crime is one of murder and many violent crimes do not involve murder. This means that the conclusions are restricted to a very particular group of people.

EVALUATION: ALTERNATIVE EVIDENCE

Adrian Raine has continued to conduct research on the association between criminal behaviour and brain dysfunction. For example, a study by Yang and Raine (2009) was a **meta-analysis** of 43 imaging studies that considered both antisocial and violent behaviour. The conclusion of this meta-analysis was that there is significantly reduced prefrontal activity in antisocial and/or violent individuals.

Such findings are further supported by **genetic** studies that indicate a 'criminal gene'. One candidate for this is the MAOA gene (monoamine oxidase A) that causes abnormally high levels of the **neurotransmitter dopamine**. A recent study by Tiihonen *et al.* (2015) analysed the genes of 895 Finnish prisoners and found an association between this gene and an increased likelihood of committing a violent crime.

However, it also should be remembered that genes are only predisposing factors. One neuroscientist researching this topic, James Fallon, analysed his own genes and found that he had the genetic and brain characteristics of a violent criminal – but he wasn't one. He suggested that his positive experiences during childhood meant that his potentially criminal tendencies were not triggered. This is a **diathesis-stress** explanation – a diathesis is a genetic predisposition which is only manifested if certain stressors trigger it, such as a difficult childhood.

Exam advice…
Always make sure you carefully read any exam question about one of the classic studies. If a question is quite specific and just asks you to describe the 'findings' then describing content that relates to procedures, methodology or conclusions is going to waste your time as it won't receive credit.

ETHICAL ISSUES AND SOCIAL IMPLICATIONS

Valid consent

The main group of participants in this study were murderers who pleaded guilty by reason of insanity. This suggests that they may not have been mentally competent to provide **valid consent**.

The participants may not have fully understood what they would be required to do. For example, they may have found the performance task difficult and this would have the potential to lower their self-esteem, an example of **psychological harm**.

They may also not have realised what would be involved in a PET scan and may have found that a distressing experience.

Finally they may not have fully understood their **right to withdraw** at any time, especially as they were prisoners. They may have felt they couldn't simply say they no longer wished to take part.

Socially sensitive research

Another important **ethical issue** is the broader social implications of this research. 'Socially sensitive research' refers to any research that has consequences for the larger group of which the participants are members. An example of this would be research on drug addiction or homosexuality.

In the case of the research on murderers the question is whether our understanding of criminal behaviour is advanced by this research. If the research indicates that murderers are born rather than made this may have consequences that would be disadvantageous for people with similar brain abnormalities – they might be imprisoned without any trial or any reference to their social circumstances. Thus the research findings have implications for the prisoners.

This means that important decisions have to be made about the way such research is conducted and reported.

See the next spread for a discussion of further ethical and social implications of this topic.

EXAM CORNER

You will need to be able to do the following with respect to the study by Raine, Buchsbaum and LaCasse (1997):

Describe:
- The methodology of the study (describe and justify; includes characteristics of the sample but not the sampling technique).
- The procedures of the study (what the researcher did; includes the sampling technique).
- The findings of the study.
- The conclusions of the study.

Evaluate:
- The methodology of the study.
- The procedures of the study.
- The findings of the study (use methodology and/or alternative evidence).
- The conclusions of the study (use methodology and/or alternative evidence).
- The ethical issues and social implications.

Possible exam questions:
1. 'The value of research such as Raine, Buchsbaum and LaCasse is undermined by weaknesses in the methodology of the research'. Evaluate the methodology used by Raine, Buchsbaum and LaCasse's (1997) research *'Brain abnormalities in murderers indicated by positron emission tomography'*. [12]
2. Outline the findings and conclusions of Raine, Buchsbaum and LaCasse's (1997) research *'Brain abnormalities in murderers indicated by positron emission tomography'*. [8]
3. Discuss the ethical and social implications raised by Raine, Buchsbaum and LaCasse's (1997) research *'Brain abnormalities in murderers indicated by positron emission tomography'*. [12]

◄ On 1 August 1966, Charles Whitman murdered 16 and wounded 32 people whilst shooting from the 28th floor of the main building at the University of Texas in Austin (pictured). In an autopsy, it was found that Whitman had a 'pecan-sized' tumour situated near his amygdala; however, it is unclear if this or his strict and abusive upbringing is responsible for determining his murderous behaviour. Or there might be some other explanation.

MEET THE RESEARCHER

Adrian Raine (1954–) started out as an airline accountant with British Airways, but then did a degree in psychology. His first job was as a prison psychologist in top-security prisons in England. Then, in 1987, he emigrated to the USA where he now works at the University of Pennsylvania.

He has been involved for many years in research on criminal behaviour but also is involved in the Mauritius Child Health Project, a longitudinal study investigating the effects of various factors on mental health. In contrast to the findings of the classic study described here, the Mauritius Project has identified the importance of environmental factors. For example, Raine *et al.* (2003) found that children who received an enriched early education were less likely to become antisocial or develop schizotypal symptoms in late teens – in other words, the study showed there were important environmental rather than biological influences on development.

Contemporary debate: The ethics of neuroscience

SPECIFICATION REQUIREMENT

SPECIFICATION REQUIREMENT

For each approach it will be necessary to:
- Understand what is at the core of the debate.
- Refer to psychological studies and theories.
- Explore both sides of the contemporary debate from a psychological perspective (including the ethical, economic and social implications).

If you visit the Countway Library of Medicine in Boston, you will see a case which contains an iron bar 13 cm in circumference and just over a metre in length. It is displayed alongside a skull (see photo on page 139). It is claimed that these artefacts triggered the beginning of modern **neuroscience**. In September 1848, the *Boston Post* reported on a 'Horrible Accident' involving a railway foreman. An explosion had forced an iron bar through his left cheek and out of the top of his skull. The newspaper reported that '*he was alive at two o'clock this afternoon, and in full possession of his reason, and free from pain*'. This case of Phineas Gage became one of the first which allowed doctors to investigate neuroanatomy. Since then, improving technology has allowed neuroscientists to find out so much more about the brain. However, there is considerable debate as to whether the knowledge that neuroscience produces is always being used **ethically**.

ETHICAL, SOCIAL AND ECONOMIC IMPLICATIONS

Improving marketing techniques can aid the economy by stimulating sales and profits, as discussed on the right. However, these are by no means the only social and economic implications of neuroscience. Some are more beneficial to us all.

For example, the Nuffield Trust (2014) points out that since the financial crisis started in 2008, there has been an increase in the amount of **antidepressants** being prescribed. The Trust also noted a greater rise in antidepressant usage amongst areas of the population with higher rates of unemployment. Thomas and Morris (2003) estimated that the total cost of depression in adults in England alone was £9.1 billion in 2000. According to Alzheimer's Research UK, the cost to the UK economy of treating dementia is £23 billion per year.

Neuroscientists who help treat or even cure these disorders could save the UK economy billions of pounds.

Neuroscientists have a responsibility to ensure that the societies in which they work are informed and aware of the implications of their work.

Exam advice...

In preparation for this part of the exam it is really useful if you can actually hold debates about the issues being covered.

Don't limit your evidence to that included here. Collect evidence from other sources and ask people their opinions on the matter.

NEUROSCIENCE IS ETHICAL AS IT PROVIDES ANSWERS

The question of ethics is often resolved in terms of costs versus benefits – something is ethical if the benefits outweigh the costs. Therefore on this side of the spread we consider the benefits of neuroscience, which suggest that it is ethical.

Understand consciousness

For centuries, philosophers have tried to determine what 'consciousness' is. Neuroscientists Francis Crick and Christof Koch (1998) think they have a solution. They propose that the *claustrum*, a thin sheet of **neurons** found in the centre of the brain, is the seat of the consciousness. They believe the *claustrum* acts like the conductor of an orchestra, combining information from distinct brain regions.

The experiences of a 54-year-old woman support this. She suffered from severe epilepsy and, during some tests of her brain, an electrode placed near the *claustrum* was electrically stimulated. The woman stopped reading, stared blankly and didn't respond to visual or auditory commands. When the stimulation stopped, she regained consciousness immediately with no recollection of the event. When the stimulation was repeated, the same thing happened (Koubeissi *et al.*, 2014).

This knowledge could help us make decisions about patients who are in a persistent vegetative state. The decision to end their life could be based on the knowledge of whether they remain conscious or not.

Treat criminal behaviour

Part of the role of any Criminal Justice System is to rehabilitate offenders in order to prevent further criminal behaviour. One possible solution lies in neuroscience. Some people believe that criminal behaviour stems from abnormal levels of certain **neurotransmitters**. If this is true then drugs could be used to 'treat' criminals.

Cherek *et al.* (2002) investigated the levels of impulsivity and aggression in males with a history of conduct disorder and criminal behaviour. Half received a **placebo** for 21 days, whereas the other half were administered *paroxetine* (an SSRI antidepressant). Those who received *paroxetine* showed a significant decrease in impulsive responses, and aggression declined by the end of the study. Offering pharmacological treatments to criminals could therefore reduce recidivism and make society safer for all.

Enhance neurological function

Neuroscience could be used to improve the abilities of 'normal' individuals, such as improved performance on complex academic tasks. *Transcranial Direct Current Stimulation* (TDCS) involves passing a small electric current across specific regions in the brain. Cohen Kadosh *et al.* (2012) found that TDCS leads to improvements in problem-solving and mathematical, language, memory and attention capabilities. Students could use the TDCS apparatus in preparation for examinations.

It could be argued that neuroenhancement is not such a new thing. Many students already 'neuroenhance' themselves whenever they use caffeine-based drinks to block adenosine receptors in the brain and are hence more alert to revise.

Improve marketing techniques

A recent application of neuroscience has been in the world of advertising and marketing – 'neuromarketing'. When interviewed by market researchers we may not give our true opinions because we want to appear in a 'good light'. This **social desirability bias** can be avoided using eye tracking equipment which provides objective evidence of what really catches a person's eye when shopping or watching advertisements. **EEG** can also be used to analyse neurological responses.

One company, Sands Research, used this kind of neuromarketing research when devising the highly successful ad 'The Force' (Volkswagen). Doug Van Praet, part of the creative team behind this ad, notes that it 'upped traffic to the VW website by half, and contributed to a hugely successful sales year for the brand'.

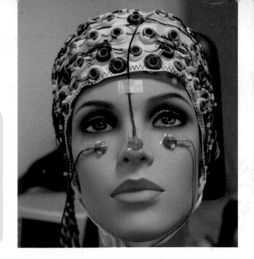

▶ A manikin wearing an **EEG** hat similar to those used by marketing consultants to 'read your mind' – or at least find out what you really think about their products.

TRY THIS

1. Look at some advertisements yourself and consider why they are effective.
   - The Volkswagen ad can be viewed here: *www.youtube.com/watch?v=R55e-uHQna0*
   - Or you can watch a Superbowl ad here: *www.superbowl-commercials.org*
   - Look at neuro-engagement scores here: *www.sandsresearch.com/2013SBMovies.aspx*
2. Conduct a group debate/discussion on the following topic: *'Universities should not accept applications from those who have undergone neuroenhancing treatments'.*

NEUROSCIENCE IS NOT ETHICAL

Neuroscience could be considered 'unethical' if the benefits are not real or actually go on to create more difficulties.

Understand consciousness

If neuroscientists are able to locate consciousness in the brain, what sort of implications might that have? One area of contention is whether those individuals in a persistent vegetative state should have life-support withdrawn. Just because a patient has currently lost consciousness, does that mean we have the moral right to withdraw care?

There is also doubt about the soundness of the evidence as it is derived from the **case study** of one 'abnormal' brain (a person suffering from severe epilepsy).

Treat criminal behaviour

Although neuroscientists may link criminal behaviours to neurological imbalances, many see crime as a response to the social context. Even if there is a neurological basis to criminal behaviour, there is the question about whether it is acceptable to include mandatory neurological interventions for prisoners. Martha Farah (2004) argues that, if courts use neurological interventions, it signals the denial of an individual's freedom, something that even prisoners have not been denied previously, i.e. the freedom to have your own personality and to think your own thoughts.

Furthermore, a court may offer a convicted criminal the choice of a prison term or a course of medication. This introduces the ethical issue of implicit coercion – the criminal is left with very little choice about medication.

Enhance neurological function

Cohen Kadosh *et al.* warn of ethical limitations to TDCS technology. First of all there are no training or licensing rules for practitioners. This could lead to poorly qualified clinicians at best administering ineffective treatments or at worst causing brain damage to patients.

Although comparatively cheap, TDCS apparatus is not available to everyone. It may not be fair to allow some individuals to benefit from a treatment not available to all.

Therefore should we consider banning the use of neuroenhancing technologies in the same way as performance-enhancing substances are banned in sport? This might be especially important when using the treatment with brains that are still developing.

Improve marketing techniques

Accessing information about consumer preferences and behaviours is not new. The use of loyalty cards and analysing the online browsing records of individuals have helped make product marketing much more effective.

However, there is a difference; neuromarketing has access to our inner thoughts. Wilson *et al.* (2008) believe commercial integration of neuromarketing research will allow advertisers to deliver individualised messages where our **free will** is potentially manipulated by big brands. Do we really want corporations to be able to produce marketing messages that remove our ability to make informed decisions about whether we purchase a product or not?

Currently neuromarketing firms are not obliged to abide by ethical codes of practice. In fact, Nelson (2008) found that 5% of the brain scans recorded by marketing firms produced 'incidental findings'. For example, researchers might see evidence of a brain tumour or some other problem with a person's brain function. As the researchers are not 'board-certified' they are not obliged to follow appropriate ethical protocols such as advising the person of their findings.

EXAM CORNER

You will need to be able to:
- Discuss the argument and evidence in favour of neuroscience being ethical.
- Discuss the argument and evidence against neuroscience being ethical.
- Present a conclusion about the debate.
- Include discussion of the ethical, economic and social implications of this debate.

Possible exam questions:

1. Ethical issues involved within neuroscience only really arise because neuroscientists are trying to apply their knowledge to address sensitive issues in society.
   Using your psychological knowledge, discuss the extent to which you agree with this statement. [20]
2. *'Neuroscience findings need to be treated with caution'.*
   Discuss evidence which supports the above view. [20]

CONCLUSION

It is clear that knowledge in the field of neuroscience has grown exponentially since the time of Phineas Gage. It has offered us great insight into understanding how our brain works and as a result has led to the development of many explanations of both normal and abnormal behaviour. It offers 'stigma-free' explanations of behaviour.

However, like every other area of science, the knowledge it produces when published becomes accessible to all, whether their intentions for its use are good or not good. Neuroscientists are not solely responsible for the way their research is used but it is also the responsibility of governments, regulatory bodies and other institutions in society to ensure that neuroscientific knowledge is applied in an appropriate ethical way.

Evaluating the biological approach

SPECIFICATION REQUIREMENT

For each approach it will be necessary to:
- Evaluate the approach (including strengths, weaknesses and comparison with the four other approaches).

You have studied several assumptions of the biological approach as well as gained an insight into how the approach might explain particular behaviours (e.g. relationship formation and therapies). Now you must consider some of the strengths and weaknesses of explaining human behaviour from a biological perspective.

STRENGTHS OF THE BIOLOGICAL APPROACH

1. Scientific approach

At the beginning of this chapter we looked at the assumptions of the biological approach, which were that behaviour can be explained in terms of the brain, **neurotransmitters** and **localisation of brain function** (i.e. biological systems). This means that biological explanations have clear variables that can be measured, tracked and examined. This enables psychologists to conduct scientific research studying these variables.

For example, research on **drug therapy** has investigated the links between psychoactive drugs and the production of certain neurotransmitters (such as **dopamine**), and linked this to behaviour.

Psychosurgery involves functionally removing parts of the brain. Such procedures are based on earlier research that has linked areas of the brain to certain behaviours such as aggression.

Raine *et al.* made use of **PET scans** to compare 14 areas of the brain in murderers (pleading NGRI) compared with non-murderers.

All of these examples of research are scientific insofar as they fulfil the aims of scientific research – to conduct objective, well-controlled studies and, ideally, to demonstrate causal relationships. Thus a strength of the biological approach is that it lends itself to scientific research that can then be used to support biological explanations.

2. Determinist approach

As well as being scientific, the biological approach is also **determinist**. One strength of being determinist is that if we know what 'predetermines' our behaviour, we are more likely to be able to treat people with abnormal behaviour. Psychologists seek, for example, to understand the functioning of neurotransmitters so they can predict the effects of neurotransmitters on normal and abnormal behaviour.

For instance, the neurotransmitter dopamine has been linked with the mental disorder of **schizophrenia**. The evidence comes from a number of sources. For example, the drug *amphetamine* is known to increase levels of dopamine and the large doses of the drug can cause some of the symptoms associated with schizophrenia (e.g. hallucinations). A second line of evidence comes from the drugs that are used to treat schizophrenia (**antipsychotics**), which reduce some of the symptoms and are known to reduce dopamine levels. This suggests that high levels of dopamine are causing the symptoms.

Similar research has been conducted in relation to psychosurgery. For example, **brain scans** have shown that certain areas of the brain are more active than others in patients with **OCD**. The **cingulotomy** (a form of psychosurgery) is therefore designed functionally to sever these areas in order to reduce the symptoms of OCD. The research suggests that OCD is caused by activity in these areas of the brain – a determinist explanation.

The strength of causal understandings is that they enable us to control our world. If we understand that prolonged stress causes physical illness, then we can reduce the negative effects by treating stress in the short term. If mental illness is caused by biological factors, then we can treat mental illness using biological methods. Thus one strength of the biological approach is that it is determinist and provides explanations about the causes of behaviour so that we can use such understanding to improve people's lives.

3. Successful applications

The biological approach has led to many successful applications. For example, research into the relationship between abnormal levels of neurotransmitters and criminal behaviour has implications for offering pharmacological treatments to criminals, leading to lowered recidivism rates, and ultimately safer societies. For example, Cherek *et al.* (2002) showed that males with conduct disorder and criminal behaviour had reduced levels of aggression and impulsivity after a 21-day course of an SSRI antidepressant compared to a control group taking **placebos**.

The biological approach has also led to many forms of treatment for mental disorder, such as drug therapy and psychosurgery. For example, the effectiveness of **capsulotomy** (a form of psychosurgery) in the treatment of OCD is discussed on page 15. Cosgrove and Rauch (2001) reported recovery rates of 67%, which is reasonably high.

Drug therapy produces rather mixed results because drugs affect people differently. However, it is a particularly popular form of treatment because it is easy and enables many people with mental disorders to live relatively normal lives outside mental hospitals. For example, **bipolar disorder** (manic depression) has been successfully treated with drugs – Viguera *et al.* (2000), for instance, report that more than 60% of bipolar patients improve when taking the drug *lithium*.

▲ The biological approach sees behaviour as the consequence of biological systems, such as activity in the brain, neurotransmitters and hormones.

Exam advice…

When writing an exam answer for each strength/weakness you need to follow the SEEW format:

State the strength/weakness,

Explain and elaborate, and give an

Example in psychology; finally explain

Why it is a strength/weakness

This will maximise your marks.

TRY THIS

Vince has a particular talent for rugby. Since the age of five his Dad, who is also a keen rugby player, has practised with him every weekend. Vince feels that he can release a lot of pent-up aggression on the rugby pitch.

Recently, Abi has felt a little down and is tired easily. She sometimes gets upset during the college day and has to go home to bed. Her parents have started to get a little worried.

For the two scenarios above:
- Outline how the biological approach might explain these behaviours.
- Think of **two** strengths and **two** weaknesses of explaining these behaviours in this way.

WEAKNESSES OF THE BIOLOGICAL APPROACH

1. Reductionist approach

Biological explanations reduce complex behaviours to a set of simple explanations, for example reducing the experience of stress to the action of the hormone **adrenaline**.

Reductionism is a part of understanding how systems work, but the problem is that, in the process, we may lose a real understanding of the thing we are investigating. For example, the biological approach suggests that an illness such as schizophrenia is basically a complex physical–chemical system that has gone wrong. The psychiatrist R.D. Laing (1965) claimed that such an approach ignores the *experience* of distress that goes along with any mental illness, and is therefore at best an incomplete explanation.

Furthermore, a simplified explanation may prevent us reaching a true understanding of the target behaviour.

2. Nature rather than nurture

Mental illness has multiple causes, yet the biological approach focuses on just biology (**nature**), tending to ignore life experiences (**nurture**) and psychological factors such as how people think and feel.

For example, the biological approach to explaining schizophrenia is concerned with abnormal levels of certain neurotransmitters rather than with how patients feel about their illness. The biological approach to treatment is therefore concerned with adjusting the abnormal biological systems rather than with talking to patients about how they feel.

3. Individual differences

The biological approach is a **nomothetic** approach, looking to make generalisations about people and find similarities. It tends to ignore differences between individuals. For example, when stressed, some people produce higher levels of adrenaline than others, which, in turn, affects the long-term effects of stress.

Biological research often focuses on just a few individuals and assumes that everyone's biological systems behave in the same way. In fact, research on biological systems has tended to use male rather than female participants (both animals and humans) because female hormone cycles may interfere with biological research. Such research bias could, however, produce an erroneous picture of behaviour: one with a male bias.

For example, Taylor *et al.* (2000) suggest that men usually react to stress with a 'fight or flight' response, but women show a 'tend and befriend' response. This gender difference is seen in many species, with females responding to stressful conditions by protecting and nurturing their young (the 'tend' response), and by seeking social contact and support from other females (the 'befriend' response). The difference has been attributed to the fact that women produce the hormone **oxytocin** when stressed, sometimes called the 'love hormone'.

COMPARING APPROACHES

You will need to be able to compare and contrast the biological approach with the other four approaches that you will learn about. To do this, you will need to understand how the key issues and debates (see page 7) relate to the biological approach.

In pairs, try to complete the table below, outlining how the key issues/debates (discussed in the introduction) relate to the approach.

Issue/debate	Biological approach
Nature–Nurture	
Scientific–Non-scientific	
Reductionism–Holism	
Determinism–Free will	

EXAM CORNER

To evaluate the approach you need to be able to:
- Fully discuss the strengths (at least **two**).
- Fully discuss the weaknesses (at least **two**).
- Compare and contrast the approach with the four other approaches in terms of key issues and debates.

Possible exam questions:
1. Discuss **two or more** weaknesses of the biological approach. [8]
2. Evaluate **one** strength and **one** weakness of the biological approach. [6]
3. 'At first you might think that the biological and behaviourist approaches are very different, but there are quite a few similarities.' Compare and contrast the biological and behaviourist approaches. [8]
4. 'The biological approach offers both strengths and weaknesses.' Evaluate the biological approach in psychology. [16]

Some activities for you

ASSUMPTIONS

ANSWERS ON PAGE 172

True or false?

Are the following true or false in relation to the assumptions of the biological approach? Copy the table and circle the correct answer.

1	Evolutionary theory is a modern idea in psychology.	T or F
2	Evolutionary theory looks at which characteristics and behaviours are essential for survival.	T or F
3	Adaptive traits are those which have helped us to survive.	T or F
4	Humans have the smallest brain relative to their size, compared with other species.	T or F
5	EEA stands for external evolutionary approach.	T or F
6	Neurons are electrically excitable cells that form the basis of the nervous system.	T or F
7	One neuron communicates with another neuron at the synapse.	T or F
8	Neurotransmitters will either stimulate or inhibit receptors in the other neurons.	T or F
9	Serotonin is an example of a neurotransmitter that influences our moods.	T or F

CLASSIC EVIDENCE

ANSWER ON PAG 172

True or false?

Read the statements below from Raine, Buchsbaum and LaCasse (1997) and decide if they are true or false. Copy the table and re-write any that are false.

1	The sample included 45 murderers (39 males and 6 females).	T or F
2	All murderers used in the study had some form of mental impairment.	T or F
3	A CAT scan was used to study the active brain.	T or F
4	CPT stands for central performance task.	T or F
5	Murderers had reduced activity in the amygdala in the left hemisphere.	T or F
6	Murderers had abnormal asymmetrical brains.	T or F
7	Murderers performed better than the control group on the CPT.	T or F

The brain

1. Label the four lobes on the diagram below, and write one sentence explaining the function of each of the lobes.
2. Joe has always been close to his younger brother. They are both now in their 30s and have separate family lives; however, Joe still sees his brother a lot and ensures that both families spend lots of time together.
   Using your knowledge of the biological approach, explain Joe's close relationship with his brother.

CLASSIC EVIDENCE

Evaluation

In pairs prepare a set of revision cards to help you learn the strengths and weaknesses of Raine, Buchsbaum and LaCasse (1997). One person in the pair needs to prepare the strengths, the other person the weaknesses. Include some brief notes explaining each strength/weakness.

Once you have prepared your revision cards you need to be able to explain to your partner the key strengths/weaknesses using the cards alone.

ANSWER ON PAG 172

What's active?

State and explain which areas of the brain would be most active during the following activities:

1. Driving a forklift truck.
2. Learning how to count to 10 in a new language.
3. Trying to solve an algebraic equation.
4. Operating CCTV cameras.
5. Learning a script for a film role.

THERAPIES

Mind maps

A mind map is a visual representation of a topic, showing the links between the various elements. The links usually form a branching pattern, with the main topic in the centre and component elements/ideas radiating outwards. Small sketches/doodles can be added, as well as colours (using highlighters, felt-tips). Each page of notes therefore has a unique, distinctive visual appearance (whereas pages of ordinary/linear notes all look very similar) (Buzan, 1993).

Your task

Choosing either psychotherapy or drug therapy, complete a mind map covering all specification requirements, namely:
- How the approach applies in the therapy.
- Main components.
- Evaluation – effectiveness and ethical issues.

You can use some of the review activities described at the ends of the other chapters. For example, you could produce a comic strip or design your own crossword (see page 45).

You should certainly list again the key words in this chapter and make sure you understand them.

Key words game

Go through the chapter and identify all the key terms in blue bold. Create a set of key cards for these words – write the key term on one card and write its definition on another card (you can find the definitions in the glossary/index).

One game you can play with these is called 'Concentration', which works best with two or three players. Place all the cards face down, with the key terms on the left and the definitions on the right. Turn over two cards – one from the left and one from the right. Do they match? If not, turn them face down again and let the next player have a go. If they do match, then you keep the cards and have another go.

Mind maps

On the left is a mind map. Psychological research shows that memory is improved by processing information – and that's what you do when you create a mind map. Furthermore, the visual image and strong colours help create enduring memories. So create one for every topic.

DEBATE

Hypothetical neuroscience activity

Newsflash: Neuroscientists have found that a certain part of the brain (the *madeupamus*) is responsible for people being bigots.

Those with a small madeupamus are more likely to hold racist or homophobic views, whereas those with a large madeupamus are more likely to be tolerant of those from different backgrounds to themselves.

Write a newspaper article in which you discuss what the potential impact of this finding might be.

Remember to consider the impact on:
- Social policies held by government.
- Treatment options for bigots.
- Society in general.

EVALUATION

Four corners

Section the classroom into four corners, each with one of four large titles:

IS THIS A STRENGTH OR WEAKNESS OF THE BIOLOGICAL APPROACH?

EXPLAIN WHAT THIS MEANS.

GIVE AN EXAMPLE OF THIS WITH RESPECT TO THE BIOLOGICAL APPROACH.

WHY IS THIS A STRENGTH/WEAKNESS?

Each pair of students is given one of the following evaluation points:
- reductionism
- determinism
- scientific
- nomothetic
- nature/nurture
- usefulness

The student pair then has to visit each section in the classroom in order, and on a piece of paper answer the four questions for their evaluation point.

They then share their point with the rest of the class.

At the end of the task the whole class should be able to evaluate the biological approach in some detail.

Exam questions and answers

QUESTION ON EXPLAINING BEHAVIOURS

Using your knowledge of the biological approach explain why a relationship is formed. [5]

Mark scheme for this question

Mark	Description
5	Explanation is **well detailed** and **clearly linked** to forming a relationship.
3–4	Explanation is **detailed** and **linked** to forming a relationship. There may be inaccuracies which do not detract from the overall meaning.
1–2	Explanation is **superficial/limited** and **links** to forming a relationship are **unclear**.
0	**Inappropriate** answer given / **no response** attempted.

Bob's answer

Evolutionary theory says that we should retain behaviours that are adaptive and promote the survival of the species. Forming romantic relationships is one way of doing this. When forming these relationships males and females have different evolutionary pressures as females have limited fertility while males do not. As a result males will favour females who are youthful and attractive as this indicates health and fertility. In contrast, females are more concerned with a male's ability to provide as this will allow the limited offspring she produces to survive and with age men accrue more resources. This assumption helps explain why females and males are attracted to reproduce and have relationships with certain mates and not others.

In addition to this we can apply a second biological assumption to help explain romantic relationships. Neurotransmitters can help explain the maintenance of romantic relationships after reproduction. Oxytocin is a hormone that is boosted by physical contact with one's partner. We clearly have a natural chemical drive to bond and have romantic relationships and this is a fundamental assumption of the biological approach. 179 words

Bob has not simply repeated the biological assumptions but has clearly linked them to forming a romantic relationship.

Bob's explanation is well-detailed and accurate.

Megan's answer

The biological approach can help us understand relationships in many ways. Evolutionary theory was first proposed by Darwin and is based on the notion of survival of the fittest. The theory says that we will keep behaviours that help us survive and lose behaviours and traits that do not help us to survive. Genes containing these survival behaviours will be passed on to the next generation and we have relationships to do this. Another way that the biological approach explains relationships is through neurotransmitters. These are chemical messengers that pass messages around the body and are released from vesicles in one neuron and stimulate or inhibit receptors in another neuron. Examples of neurotransmitters are serotonin and dopamine, and when we have high levels this can be associated with excitement and arousal. It might be that when we meet new people, especially romantically, we have high levels of neurotransmitters and this is why we want to have relationships. 164 words

Megan has focused on the assumptions of the biological approach. Links to relationships and how they are formed are unclear and lacking focus.

Examiner comments and marks on page 173

QUESTION ON ASSUMPTIONS AND THERAPIES

Describe how the assumptions of the biological approach are applied to either psychosurgery or drug therapy. [6]

Mark scheme for this question

Mark	Description
5–6	Explanation is **well detailed** and **clearly linked** to assumptions.
3–4	Explanation is **detailed** and **linked** to assumptions. There may be inaccuracies which do not detract from the overall meaning.
1–2	Explanation is **superficial/limited** and **links** to the assumptions are **unclear**.
0	**Inappropriate** answer given / **no response** attempted.

Bob's answer

The biological approach sees all behaviour, normal or abnormal, as having a biological origin. It advocates the medical model which suggests that mental illnesses are like physical illnesses, with a physical cause and are best treated in a physical way, e.g. through the use of drugs. Drug therapy is based on the assumption that neurotransmitters affect our behaviour. For example, the neurotransmitter serotonin plays a role in our mood and sleep patterns and too little of it can lead people to suffer from depression.

The biological approach would therefore want to adopt a therapy which aims to alter and restore neurotransmitter levels back to normal in the hope that it would cause behaviour to become more normal. Drugs work by affecting the action of neurotransmitters by increasing or blocking the action of the neurotransmitter at the synapse. For example, you would want to increase the amount of serotonin for people with depression, whereas you would want to block dopamine for people suffering with schizophrenia. Restoring neurotransmitter levels to normal should reduce any symptoms experienced. 175 words

Megan's answer

The biological approach believes that all behaviour has a physical cause, for example our genes, biochemistry and brain all influence our behaviour. The biological approach suggests something called localisation of function which basically means that each area of our brain controls specific behaviours, for example the frontal lobe is responsible for thinking and problem solving whilst the temporal lobes are responsible for memory. The brain also has two hemispheres and Broca found that our language skills can be found in the left hemisphere. It is clear to see that our brain does affect our behaviour and if something goes wrong with the brain this will affect your behaviour and may lead you to have a mental illness. If the cause of the illness is the brain, it makes sense that you should use a treatment that focuses on the brain. Psychosurgery is a type of treatment that does focus on the brain and is a type of brain surgery. 160 words

TRY THIS

Have a go at being the examiner

Choose Bob or Megan's answer, depending on which therapy you have covered. Assess the relevant answer using the mark scheme, and write an examiner's comment highlighting what has been done well and what could be improved, before giving it a final mark.

QUESTION ON CLASSIC EVIDENCE

Evaluate the research of Raine, Buchsbaum and LaCasse (1997) *'Brain abnormalities in murderers indicated by positron emission tomography.'* [16]

Mark scheme for this question

Mark	Description
13–16	A **sophisticated** and **well-developed** evaluation of the research and its methodology. **Range** and **depth** is displayed.
10–12	A **thorough** evaluation of the research and its methodology is demonstrated, and **well-balanced** arguments are made. **Range** or **depth** is displayed.
7–9	A **reasonable** evaluation of the research and its methodology. Arguments although reasonable may be **one-sided**. Evaluative comments tend to be **generic** and **not contextualised**.
4–6	**Basic** evaluation of the research and its methodology.
1–3	**Identification** of methodological issues with **no evaluative commentary**.
0	**Inappropriate** answer given / **no response**.

TRY THIS

Reflect on the examiner's comments in the table below and decide which ones relate to Bob and which to Megan – and some comments might relate to both.

Evaluation is quite generic	Arguments are well structured
Well-developed evaluation	Evaluation lacks contextualisation
Terminology is used well	Evaluation is contextualised well
Range and depth	Range only
Mark = 15/16	Mark = 10/16

Bob's answer

I think this is a good study and certainly better than most psychological research, mainly because it uses a quasi-experiment as its research method. This is simply the study of a naturally occurring event and requires no manipulation of the IV and as a result is a lot more realistic than most psychology studies that use laboratory experiments. However, this comes at a cost because quasi-experiments do not allow us to draw causal relationships, e.g. we cannot say that it is definitely the IV that caused the DV because the researcher does not have full control over the variables.

This study uses a group of murderers who pleaded insanity as its sample. This is quite limited because they may not be representative of all criminals.

This study uses PET scans to collect data about the brain. This is good because it is objective and a good way to see the brain in action but it might be quite uncomfortable for the people involved as they can take some time and many report the process to be quite unpleasant. This is an example of the ethical issue of risk of harm. In psychology you are not allowed to harm your participants physically or psychologically so making them have a PET scan might violate this. Another ethical issue in this study is valid consent. This is because Raine's sample were vulnerable and labelled insane, so may not be able to fully understand what the study entails and thus cannot give their valid consent.

This study has been proven to be fairly reliable because other studies that have been done have come up with similar findings, for example a later study done by Yang and Raine found that violent people have less activity in the prefrontal lobe. This is similar to what was found in this study and shows that the findings are true and trustworthy, rather than a 'one off' finding.

One big problem with this study is that it cannot make clear conclusions about the causes of behaviour. It cannot say that the murderers committed their crime because of biology or because of something else. This is due to cause and effect and the fact they did not use a lab experiment. *378 words*

Megan's answer

Methodologically this study can be both praised and criticised. Its use of a quasi-experiment means it required no experimental manipulation of the IV (criminal status). It was a naturally occurring event that was simply studied. This raises the ecological validity of the study and reduces the impact of demand characteristics but does raise questions regarding causality. The findings do not show that violence is determined by biology alone as Raine was unable to control or assess the impact of situational factors like e.g. upbringing may have had on their behaviour. This raises a concern as readers may misinterpret findings and assume that criminality is determined by biology alone.

The sample although appropriate raises a number of issues. Raine's sample were not typical of all violent people and Raine was keen to point out that, based on this, we cannot say that all violent offenders have such brain dysfunctions. Furthermore it is gender-biased and only focused on one crime type – murder. This means findings are restrictive and only apply to a small subsection.

Ethically this study is dubious for a number of reasons. First we can question to what extent a group of murderers claiming insanity can actually give valid consent as they may not understand what having a PET scan means nor how unpleasant it can be, furthermore exposing them to a performance task that may have been confusing and distressing. Also, we can question whether they understood that they did not have to participate or could withdraw at any time. The determinist nature of this type of research makes it quite socially sensitive – if biology plays a role in criminality this has implications for the identification and punishment of criminals.

A key strength of the study is that it uses PET scans that are objective and show the brain in action so Raine could clearly see the difference in brain activity between the murderers and the control group. Furthermore, subsequent research by Yang and Raine provides support for reduced prefrontal brain activity and demonstrates these findings to be reliable. *341 words*

Examiner comments and marks on page 173

Chapter 1 The biological approach

Chapter 2
The psychodynamic approach

SPECIFICATION

Approach	Assumptions and behaviour to be explained (including)	Therapy (one per approach)	Classic research	Contemporary debate
Psychodynamic	• influence of childhood experiences • the unconcious mind • tripartite personality Learners will be expected to apply one of the given assumptions to the formation of a relationship	dream analysis OR group analysis psychotherapy	Bowlby, J. (1944) Forty-four juvenile thieves: Their characters and home-life. *International Journal of Psychoanalysis, 25(19–52)*, 107–127.	the mother as the primary care-giver of an infant

CHAPTER CONTENT

DREAMS

What do they mean?

Psychodynamic approach assumptions

WHAT'S ON A MAN'S MIND

SIGMUND FREUD

SPECIFICATION REQUIREMENT

For each approach it will be necessary to:
- Know and understand the assumptions.
- Apply the assumptions to explain the formation of a relationship.

The essence of the psychodynamic approach is to explain behaviour in terms of its 'dynamics', i.e. the forces that drive an individual to behave the way they do. The best known example of this approach is Freud's psychoanalytic theory of personality.

Sigmund Freud (writing between the 1890s and the 1930s) put forward several theories and ideas which have formed the basis of the **psychodynamic approach** to psychology. Freud specialised in treating neurotic disorders, such as hysteria, for which there was no physical cause. His work led him to believe in **psychic determinism** – the idea that personality and behaviour are determined more by psychological factors than by biological conditions or current life events. Freud's theory and his method of therapy are both called **psychoanalysis** and this perspective seeks to explain human behaviour as an interaction between innate (inborn) drives and early experiences.

ASSUMPTION 1: INFLUENCE OF CHILDHOOD EXPERIENCES

For Freud, experiences during childhood shape our adult personality. He proposed that psychological development in childhood takes place in a series of key developmental stages. These are called **psychosexual stages** and each stage represents the fixation of **libido** (roughly translated as sexual drives or instincts) on a different area of the body.

There are five psychosexual stages (see table below). Each stage is associated with a particular part of the body. Problems at any stage of development can result in the child getting **fixated** (stuck) at the body part associated with that stage, which will have a long-lasting effect on personality. Fixation at any of these stages can occur through:

- Frustration – when the stage has not been resolved because needs have not been met, for example the child is undersatisfied.
- Overindulgence – this is when the needs of the child have been more than satisfied, and the result is that the child feels too comfortable and reluctant to move on to the next stage.

Stage	Origin of libido and source of pleasure	Key events	Outcome of fixation
Oral (0–18 months)	Mouth: Sucking, chewing, swallowing and biting.	Breast feeding. Weaning onto solid food.	Frustration = pessimism, envy, sarcasm. Overindulgence = optimism, gullibility, neediness.
Anal (18 months – 3 years)	Anus: Withholding, expelling, playing with faeces.	Potty training.	Frustration = stubborn, possessive, overly tidy. Overindulgence = messy, disorganised, reckless.
Phallic (3–5 years)	Genitals: Masturbation.	The Oedipus complex leads to superego and gender identity.	Self-assured, vain, may have problems with sexuality and difficulty building and maintaining relationships in adulthood.
Latency (5 years – puberty)	Little/no sexual motivation.	Acquiring knowledge and understanding of the world.	No fixations as no pleasure focus.
Genital (puberty onwards)	Genitals: Heterosexual intercourse.		Well-developed adult personality, well adjusted (if complexes during phallic stage are resolved).

ASSUMPTION 2: THE UNCONSCIOUS MIND

Freud proposed that the mind is like an iceberg – much of what goes on inside the mind lies under the surface. This is the **preconscious** and **unconscious** mind. The conscious mind is logical, whereas the unconscious mind is not and is ruled by pleasure seeking. The unconscious mind cannot be directly accessed, but expresses itself indirectly through, for example, dreams.

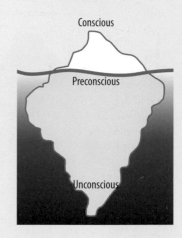

Freud believed that the unconscious mind determines much of our behaviour and that we are motivated by unconscious emotional drives. Freud believed that the unconscious contains unresolved conflicts that have a powerful effect on our behaviour and experience. He argued that many of these conflicts will show up in our fantasies and dreams, but the conflicts are so threatening that they appear in disguised forms, in the shape of symbols.

The unconscious is also related to **ego defence mechanisms**. Conflicts between the id, ego and superego create anxiety. The ego protects itself with various ego defences. These defences can be the cause of disturbed behaviour if they are overused. For example, a boy who cannot deal with what he perceives as maternal rejection when a new baby brother is born may **regress** to an earlier developmental stage, soiling his clothes and becoming more helpless. Other examples of defence mechanisms include:

- **Displacement** (transfer of impulses from one person or object to another).
- **Projection** (undesirable thoughts are attributed to someone else).
- **Repression** (pushing painful memories deep down into our unconscious mind, so they are effectively forgotten).

TRY THIS

Find out about Sigmund Freud – write your own biography. What factors in his background might have led him to develop his theory of personality? For example, what was his relationship with his own mother and father?

ASSUMPTION 3: TRIPARTITE PERSONALITY

Freud believed that the adult personality is structured into three parts that develop at different stages in our lives.

- **Id** – This is the impulsive (and unconscious) part of our personality, and is present at birth. It demands immediate satisfaction, which can be referred to as the **pleasure principle**. The main aim of the id is to gain pleasure and gratification at any cost.
- **Ego** – This is the conscious, rational part of the mind that develops around the age of two years. Its function is to work out realistic ways of balancing the demands of the id in a socially acceptable way. It is governed by the **reality principle**.
- **Superego** – This is the last part of our personality to develop. Forming at around the age of four years, it embodies the child's sense of right and wrong as well as his or her ideal self. The superego seeks to perfect and civilise our behaviour. It is learned through identification with one's parents and others.

The id and the superego are often in conflict (i.e. the battle between right and wrong). Thus the ego has to act as a referee and resolve the conflict, considering consequences of a person's actions.

Although this is described as a 'structural' model, it is important to remember that the three parts are symbolic processes.

PSYCHODYNAMIC EXPLANATION FOR RELATIONSHIP FORMATION

The psychodynamic approach would emphasise the importance of forming healthy, early relationships, in order to be able to achieve the same later on in life.

Childhood experiences (psychosexual development)

The psychodynamic approach would consider the different stages of psychosexual development and use the idea of fixation to explain the nature of relationships in adulthood. For example, over-indulgence during the oral stage could result in an unhealthy dependency on others later on in life. This could mean a person becomes too 'needy' in a relationship.

The phallic stage was also very important for Freud in influencing later relationships. During this stage, the superego, conscience and **ego-ideal** are developing, and it is possible that fixation at this stage will result in an adult who is not capable of loving another person and entering into a relationship.

Successful passing through this stage will affect the later genital stage of development. For example, in boys the **Oedipus complex** needs to be resolved. In the phallic stage a young boy comes to desire his mother and regard his father as a rival, wishing him dead. The boy's wish that the father was dead creates anxiety. It is eventually resolved when a boy comes to identify with his father. This resolution allows a boy, during the genital stage, to develop normal, healthy friendships and heterosexual relationships. However, if the Oedipus complex is not successfully resolved, then relationship problems can occur. According to Freud this may lead to the development of homosexuality.

Defence mechanisms

Forming a relationship in adulthood may, for some people, bring up unpleasant emotions from the past. In these instances, people may use ego defences to help them avoid anxiety. Freud spoke about many defence mechanisms, and how they affect all aspects of behaviour, and this can include our relationships. For example, a person who is in denial about their sexuality might try to form relationships which are not in line with their true feelings, resulting in these relationships being dysfunctional and eventually breaking down. Those who are being dishonest in a relationship (e.g. having an affair) may deal with their guilt through rationalisation ('they deserve it as they don't pay me any attention!'). Defence mechanisms affect our overall personality and will inevitably affect our relationships.

Example: Explaining the formation of parent–child relationships

Later in this chapter you will learn about John Bowlby's classic study about 44 juvenile thieves. Bowlby was a Freudian psychiatrist and he formed the view that early unhealthy experiences shaped the behaviour of some children. In particular, some of the young 'thieves' that he studied had formed an 'affectionless' character – an inability to show affection or concern for others. Bowlby also found that most of these affectionless thieves had experienced prolonged early separations from their mothers.

This led Bowlby to develop the **maternal deprivation hypothesis**, the view that the ability to form meaningful social relationships in adulthood was dependent on a close, warm and continuous relationship with the mother (or mother figure) in the first few years of one's life. The first two and a half years are especially important but there is continuing sensitivity up to the age of five years. Since this relationship acts as the prototype for all future relationships, its disruption would impair the person's ability to relate to others.

EXAM CORNER

For each assumption named in the specification, you need to be able to:
- Outline the assumption.
- Fully elaborate this assumption, drawing on examples in psychology.

In addition, you need to be able to:
- Use at least **one** assumption to explain the formation of **one** relationship.

Possible exam questions:
1. Describe **two** assumptions of the psychodynamic approach. [8]
2. 'A child's primary relationships are the most important in influencing later development.' With reference to this quote, explain how **one or more** assumptions of the psychodynamic approach might explain relationship formation. [4]

TRY THIS

We have applied psychodynamic explanations for relationships to mother and child relationships, just one of the examples given in the specification.

Try to do the same for some of the other examples in the specification: siblings, pet and owner, romantic partners and friends. Try to make each one different.

Therapy 1: Dream analysis

You only study one psychodynamic therapy as part of your course – dream analysis OR group analysis psychotherapy.

SPECIFICATION REQUIREMENT

For each approach it will be necessary to:

- Know and understand how the approach can be used in therapy (one therapy per approach).
- Know and understand the main components (principles) of the therapy.
- Evaluate the therapy (including its effectiveness and ethical considerations).

The **psychodynamic approach** believes that human behaviour is largely influenced by **unconscious** drives, and that what goes on 'under the surface' cannot be easily accessed yet has the greatest influence on behaviour. In addition, this approach sees childhood experiences as having a significant influence on adult emotions and behaviour.

HOW PSYCHODYNAMIC ASSUMPTIONS APPLY TO DREAM ANALYSIS

The main assumption of the psychodynamic approach is that we behave the way we do largely because of unconscious drives. **Psychoanalysis** (the therapy based on psychodynamic principles) is a form of therapy that aims to make the 'unconscious conscious', so that people gain 'insight' (i.e. become aware of them) and so can be cured. Psychoanalysis will involve establishing whether repression (a defence mechanism) is causing the person's psychological illness. Dream analysis is a technique used in psychoanalysis. Freud proposed that one way that the unconscious mind expresses itself is through dreams. The threatening nature of unconscious thoughts is disguised in dreams. The purpose of dream analysis is to decode what is in the unconscious mind as it expresses itself in the 'storyline'.

A second assumption of the psychodynamic approach relates to the influence of childhood experiences. Traumatic memories buried in the unconscious may be related to current experiences but may also be related to childhood events that are still troubling. These may surface during dreams as a means of working through traumatic past events.

Another assumption of the psychodynamic approach is that of the **tripartite personality**. It is thought that the demands of the id, the desires that are unacceptable during waking hours, are relegated to our dreams. Thus the purpose of dreaming is to act out our wishes and desires in an acceptable way, rather than allowing them to build up and threaten our sanity. For Freud, the **ego** would usually block out the unacceptable demands of the **id**, and **ego defences** such as **displacement** would be in operation. However, during dreaming, our ego defences are low, and therefore the id 'comes to life'.

Exam advice…

An exam question may ask you to describe one or two components (principles) of the therapy, so you need to make sure you know each component in sufficient detail. Make sure you can write 300–400 words on two of the components.

DREAMWORK PROCESSES

- **Condensation** – Dream thoughts are rich in detail and content but these are condensed to the brief images in a dream where one dream image stands for several associations and ideas.
- **Displacement** – The emotional significance of a dream object is separated from its real object or content and attached to an entirely different one so that the dream content is not 'censored'. (Freud used the concept of a 'censor' who prevents disturbing thoughts reaching the conscious mind except in a disguised form.)
- **Representation** – A thought is translated into visual images.
- **Symbolism** – A symbol replaces an action, person or idea.
- **Secondary elaboration** – The unconscious mind collects all the different images and ties them together to form a logical story, further disguising the latent content. The actual dream material may be supplied from recent events in a person's waking life.

MAIN COMPONENTS (PRINCIPLES) OF DREAM ANALYSIS

Freud famously described dreams as 'the royal road to a knowledge of the unconscious activities of the mind' (Freud, 1900, page 769). He proposed that the unconscious mind expresses itself through dreams, and that the content of a person's dreams can therefore reveal what is in their unconscious. Dream analysis is the process of assigning meaning to dreams.

Dreams as wish fulfilment

Freud believed that all dreams were the unconscious fulfilment of wishes that could not be satisfied in the conscious mind. Dreams therefore protect the sleeper (primary-process thought), but also allow some expression to these buried urges (wish fulfilment).

The symbolic nature of dreams

According to Freud, although dreams represent unfulfilled wishes, their contents are expressed *symbolically*. The real meaning of a dream (**latent content**) is transformed into a more innocuous form (**manifest content**, the content you actually experience) that may be meaningless to anybody but a psychoanalyst trained to interpret these symbols. For example, a penis may be represented by a snake or a gun, a vagina by a tunnel or a cave. In order to understand the meaning of dream symbols fully, however, Freud believed it was necessary to consider them in the context of a person's life. For example, a fish could represent a person's friend who is a fisherman or another friend who has a Piscean star sign. Freud did not support the idea of dream dictionaries. Freud also recognised that not everything in a dream is symbolic; as Freud himself said, *'sometimes a cigar is just a cigar'*.

Dreamwork

The latent content of a dream is transformed into manifest content through the process of **dreamwork**. Dreamwork consists of the various processes listed on the left. These processes are applied to repressed wishes to produce the content of the dream that is experienced.

Role of the therapist

The role of the therapist is to reverse the dreamwork process – to decode the manifest content back to the latent content. They should not offer one interpretation of a dream, but suggest various interpretations based on the patient's feedback and knowledge of their life experiences, allowing the patient to select those that make sense.

EXAM CORNER

For each therapy, you will need to be able to:
- Describe how the assumptions of the approach are applied in the therapy.
- Describe the main components (principles) of the therapy.
- Evaluate the therapy in terms of its effectiveness.
- Evaluate the therapy in terms of ethical considerations.

Possible exam questions:
1. Describe how the assumptions of the psychodynamic approach are applied in **one** therapy. [6]
2. Describe the main components (principles) of dream analysis. [10]
3. Evaluate dream analysis in terms of its effectiveness. [10]
4. Evaluate **two** ethical issues in dream analysis. [4 + 4]

▲ Are dreams always symbolic? Freud famously said 'sometimes a cigar is just a cigar'.

EVALUATION: EFFECTIVENESS

Research evidence

Recent research has provided support for Freud's link between dreaming and primary-process thinking. Solms (2000) used **PET scans** to highlight the regions of the brain that are active during dreaming. The results showed that the rational part of the brain is indeed *inactive* during **rapid eye movement (REM) sleep**, whereas the centres concerned with memory and motivation are very active. In Freud's language, the ego (rational and conscious thought) becomes suspended while the id (the more primitive, unconscious-'driven' parts of the mind) is given free rein.

Another source of support comes from earlier research by Hopfield *et al.* (1983) on **neural networks** – computer simulations that aim to mimic the action of the brain. Such computer simulations show that neural networks deal with an overloaded memory by conflating or condensing 'memories'. This supports Freud's notion of condensation – when unacceptable desires are censored and dealt with by recombining fragments until they emerge in a new form (the manifest content of the dream).

Methodological issues

Much of the research into dreaming (e.g. relationship between REM sleep and dreams) is conducted in sleep laboratories. It can therefore be questioned whether the sleep/dream state is as authentic as when under normal conditions, as the patient is wired up with various electrodes taking measurements. This set up makes it impossible to conclude that dreaming is the same as in everyday life, and so the **ecological validity** of dream research is questioned.

Many studies into dreaming are conducted on humans and animals that have been deprived of (significant amounts of) sleep, or particular stages of sleep, such as **REM sleep** (when a person's eyes dart about under their eyelids). Significant disruption will impair important biological functions such as the secretion of hormones and neurotransmitters. These may act as **confounding variables**, so any results may be due to these factors and should be interpreted with caution.

Subjective interpretation

Interpreting the manifest content and coming up with its underlying meaning (latent content) relies on the subjective interpretation of the therapist. Further, the dream that is being interpreted is a subjective report of the dreamer and may not be reliable information. This means that dream analysis is a highly subjective process, going against the objective scientific aims of psychology.

EVALUATION: ETHICAL ISSUES

Therapist–client relationship

Therapies based on the psychodynamic approach have come under fire from an **ethical** perspective because of the potential power imbalance between therapist and patient. Generally, the therapist takes the expert role, offering the patient insight into their unconscious, and for this reason, the patient is reliant on the therapist in making progress through the therapy. This may create a power imbalance and also can lead to over-dependence on the therapist. This may be especially true in people suffering from **depression**, as they may have a tendency to over-rely on important people in their lives.

False memory syndrome (FMS)

FMS is a condition in which a person's identity and relationships are affected by strongly believed but false memories of traumatic experiences. These false memories can come to light during psychoanalysis when the therapist claims to have uncovered past, traumatic events. Supporters of FMS suggest that a patient is likely to succumb to the belief of the therapist as they are an authority figure. Toon *et al.* (1996) even go as far as to suggest that therapists may induce false memories so that the therapy will take longer, and they will make more financial gain. The result of FMS is that the patients may experience much anxiety because of 'memories' of events that didn't even happen.

Emotional harm

During dream analysis, a therapist may guide a client towards an insight or interpretation that proves to be emotionally distressing. Although this insight may be necessary for recovery, the distress caused may be greater than the distress that the client is experiencing as a result of current problems. It is important that psychotherapists warn their clients of this danger before they engage in the therapy.

TRY THIS

Try to analyse one of your own dreams.
1. Record your dream, including as much detail as possible.
2. Break the report down into specific items and events.
3. For each item/event, write down any associations, such as recent events, old memories and personal interests. These should point to the latent content of your dream. (Remember the processes of dreamwork and try to ignore the 'logic' of the manifest content.)
4. Find the wish fulfilment in your dream.

If your dreams aren't very interesting (!), try searching for dream reports on the internet. For example: *www.ablongman.com/html/psychplace_acts/dreams/descr.html*

Therapy 2: Group analysis psychotherapy

You only study one psychodynamic therapy as part of your course – dream analysis OR group analysis psychotherapy.

The **psychodynamic approach** believes that human behaviour is largely influenced by **unconscious** drives, and that what goes on 'under the surface' cannot be easily accessed yet has the greatest influence on behaviour. In addition, this approach sees childhood experiences as having a significant influence on adult emotions and behaviour.

SPECIFICATION REQUIREMENT

For each approach it will be necessary to:
- Know and understand how the approach can be used in therapy (one therapy per approach).
- Know and understand the main components (principles) of the therapy.
- Evaluate the therapy (including its effectiveness and ethical considerations).

Exam advice…
An exam question may ask you to describe one or two components (principles) of the therapy, so you need to make sure you know each component in sufficient detail. Make sure you can write 300–400 words on two of the components.

HOW PSYCHODYNAMIC ASSUMPTIONS APPLY TO GROUP ANALYSIS PSYCHOTHERAPY

Therapies based on the psychodynamic approach are largely influenced by the work of Sigmund Freud, who in the late 19th century developed the method of **psychoanalysis**. Psychoanalysis is a form of therapy which works on the assumption that if we make unconscious thoughts conscious, people gain 'insight' (i.e. become aware of them) and so can be cured of the problems the unconscious thoughts create. **Group analysis** combines these psychoanalytic principles with an appreciation of the social nature of human beings. During group analysis, there is recognition of a group unconscious (underlying issues that may be pertinent to several members of the group), and through feedback, role play and problem-solving, people will gain insight into their own behaviour through that of others.

A second assumption of the psychodynamic approach is the importance of early childhood experiences, and our relationships with others. In group analysis, members often identify others as representing their own parents and siblings, and this will provoke feelings and behaviours towards the 'group' that is representative of their feelings towards significant others in their lives. The therapist will listen, watch and offer an interpretation for their emotions/behaviour which helps the whole group gain an understanding of the effect of their childhood experiences on their personality.

Another important aspect of group analysis relates to the assumption that **ego defences** affect our personality. During group analysis, members may often use defence mechanisms such as **projection** to transfer their real feelings towards family members onto the group and then deal with their feelings. Alternatively, a person may become aware of a **repressed** aspect of themselves in another person.

MAIN COMPONENTS (PRINCIPLES) OF GROUP ANALYSIS PSYCHOTHERAPY

Group analysis is a method of group psychotherapy and was developed by S.H. Foulkes in the 1940s. Group analysis emphasises the relationship between the individual and the group, drawing on the social nature of human beings as a way of aiding recovery from psychological problems.

Interaction between group members

At the core of group analysis is the carefully formed group, who are representing wider society. A typical group will consist of up to eight members and will meet at least once per week. Treatment is based upon stimulating interaction between these members, where conversation and frank discussion become a powerful way of learning about the self. Once mutual confidence is developed, and each individual completely 'opens up', past patterns of attitudes, feelings and behaviours will appear in the group, and the whole group can offer thoughts about these patterns as well as solutions. Problems are seen at the level of the group, with members often viewing their own behaviours/issues in others, and so the problems are not solely assigned to the individual sufferer. Thus, democracy and cooperation form the pillars of group-mediated solutions.

Role of the therapist

One of the key features of group analysis is that the therapist takes a much less intrusive role than in other forms of psychotherapy. The therapist is seen as a 'conductor' of the group, encouraging all members to be 'therapists' for the other group members as well as themselves. In the early sessions, the therapist is likely to have to facilitate discussion, but gradually this will be taken over by members of the group and the therapist will sit back and let interactions develop between group members and tensions build up. However, some individuals may remain persistently silent (while others will dominate), and here the role of the therapist is to step in to encourage all members to verbalise, through directive questioning and facilitation.

Mirroring

During the therapy sessions, it is highly likely that individuals will see themselves in others. This is known as *mirroring*. A group member may explain a thought/feeling/reaction to an event that another will identify with; they may also see how the reactions are dysfunctional and translated into neurotic behaviour. Foulkes described the group as a 'hall of mirrors', suggesting that individuals discovered themselves in others; this enhances self-awareness. Pines (1998) described several forms of mirroring reactions which are prevalent in groups, including:
- *Antagonistic mirroring* develops when two individuals evoke feelings of impatience, fury or despair in each other, leading to regular confrontation. These confrontations have the danger of destroying the group and need intense mediation from the therapist.
- *Dialogue mirror reaction* is when group members are able to respond to the experiences of others without being overly defensive. They see themselves in others and accept the reality. Such interactions are positive and strengthen both the individual and the group.

▲ Mirroring is an important aspect of group analysis. Look on the internet – can you find any other types of mirror reactions?

EXAM CORNER

For each therapy, you will need to be able to:

- Describe how the assumptions of the approach are applied in the therapy.
- Describe the main components (principles) of the therapy.
- Evaluate the therapy in terms of its effectiveness.
- Evaluate the therapy in terms of ethical considerations.

Possible exam questions:

1. Describe how the assumptions of the psychodynamic approach are applied in **one** therapy. [6]
2. Describe the main components (principles) of group analysis psychotherapy. [12]
3. Evaluate group analysis psychotherapy in terms of its effectiveness and ethical considerations. [20]
4. Evaluate **two** ethical issues in group analysis psychotherapy. [4 + 4]

MEET THE RESEARCHER

Siegmund Heinrich Foulkes (1898–1976) was born in Germany where he studied medicine. From 1928–30 he trained as a psychoanalyst in Vienna before emigrating to England in 1933 as a refugee. His early work with WWII soldiers in the UK, who were suffering war neuroses, contributed to his co-founding of the Group Analytic Society (GAS) in 1952. This was a new form of group psychotherapy which combined psychoanalytic insights with an understanding of social and interpersonal functioning. In 1971, leading members of the GAS set up the Institute of Group Analysis which became responsible for training in group analysis therapy.

Foulkes didn't meet with Freud while a student in Vienna but later, in 1936, had the opportunity to meet the man he called the single greatest influence on his life.

TRY THIS

There are many different types of mirroring techniques used in group analysis. There are two described on this spread but try and research at least one other.

Divide the class into small groups. Each group is to be given a mirroring technique to act out for the rest of the class in order to help each other understand the different types of mirroring.

EVALUATION: EFFECTIVENESS

Applications

The principles used in group analysis have many different applications. As well as for those suffering mental health problems, the underlying principles have been used in education, prisons, management consultancy and survivors of trauma. In prisons, for example, specialised therapy groups may be organised around shared life experiences (e.g. children of alcoholics, incest survivors), or common problems (e.g. anger management, parenting). These specialised groups offer the perfect opportunity for group analysis principles (e.g. mirroring, reflection, trust) to reign in order to help in the rehabilitation process.

Group therapy and depression

McDermut *et al.* (2001) conducted a **meta-analysis** of 49 studies into group psychotherapy for depression in adults. The researchers reported that, in 45 out of the 48 studies, group psychotherapy was effective in reducing depressive symptoms and 43 studies showed significant decreases in these symptoms. Although in nine of the studies, group psychotherapy and individual psychotherapy did not differ in terms of effectiveness.

Lack of support

Blackmore *et al.* (2009) carried out a systematic review of the **clinical** effectiveness of group analysis (commissioned by the Institute of Group Analysis in London). From 34 studies and 19 relevant reviews, they concluded that, while group psychotherapy is an effective approach to treatment, there is a lack of evidence in relation to:

- The types of patients for whom group analysis therapies are effective.
- The comparative cost effectiveness of group versus individual therapy.
- The number of high quality **randomised control trials**, i.e. trials that have excluded **confounding variables**.

Moderating factors

In a meta-analysis conducted by Burlingame *et al.* (2003), 111 studies which had been published in the 20 years previous were reviewed. Burlingame *et al.* concluded that those receiving group therapy were better off than in 72% of untreated controls; however, improvement is moderated by:

- Composition of the group (mixed genders responded better to treatment).
- Nature of client problems (homogeneous groups responded better than heterogeneous ones).
- Nature of patient treatment programme (outpatients responded better than inpatients).

The researchers suggest that further research is needed into the nature of client variables in group analysis.

EVALUATION: ETHICAL ISSUES

Confidentiality

One of the most important **ethical** considerations of the group is that of **confidentiality**. All group members have a responsibility to hold information about others in confidence, and it is the therapist's responsibility to create this sense of safety and trust within the group. Protecting confidentiality is vital in encouraging self-disclosure and trust between all group members. As part of this, individuals are discouraged from meeting outside of the group, or from discussing issues outside of the sessions, to preserve confidentiality and the therapeutic setting. It is likely that all group members will have to sign a confidentiality agreement prior to therapy commencing. Therapists have a legal obligation to disclose confidential material without consent if there is an immediate **risk of harm** to the client or someone else (e.g. to the police, their GP or social services).

The Institute of Group Analysis

The Institute of Group Analysis (IGA) was founded in 1971 by Dr Foulkes and colleagues to provide clinical training in Group Analytic Psychotherapy. The IGA has developed a *Code of Ethics and Professional Conduct* which all therapists carrying out group analysis must adhere to. In addition, the IGA has an ethics committee whose role is to ensure consistent ethical practice in group analysis by:

- Advising members on the IGA Code of Practice and Professional Conduct.
- Overseeing the IGA's complaints process.
- Regularly reviewing the IGA Code of Practice and Professional Conduct.
- Responding to ethical queries raised by IGA members or others.

Classic evidence: Bowlby (1944)

FORTY-FOUR JUVENILE THIEVES: THEIR CHARACTERS AND HOME-LIFE

SPECIFICATION REQUIREMENT

For each approach it will be necessary to:
- Know and understand a classic piece of evidence (including methodology, procedures, findings and conclusions).

▲ A delinquent is someone who breaks the law, usually committing minor crimes. Bowlby proposed that one cause of such behaviour might be a disrupted relationship between a mother and her child.

PSYCHOANALYST, PSYCHIATRIST AND PSYCHOLOGIST

A psychoanalyst is a psychiatrist who has been trained in the tradition of Freudian psychoanalysis, i.e. Freud's ways of understanding and treating mental disorder. John Bowlby trained as a Freudian psychoanalyst, which means that his views about the causes of abnormal behaviour and its treatment were shaped by the assumptions of the psychodynamic approach.

A psychiatrist is a person who has initially trained as a medical doctor and subsequently spent a number of years training to be a psychiatrist.

A psychologist working in a child guidance clinic has often taken a first degree in psychology and a further masters degree in clinical psychology. 'Clinical' simply means related to health care practices.

Research in the 1930s and 40s suggested that separation between a child and his/her mother might have long-lasting effects. For example, Spitz and Wolf (1946) studied about 90 infants who had been separated from their mothers, and found that the infants became severely **depressed**. In fact a third of the children studied died before they reached their first birthday.

Skeels and Dye (1939) also observed the negative effects of separation, finding that children in orphanages suffered impaired intellectual development. However, a later study (Skodak and Skeels 1949) showed that the children improved when they were moved from the orphanage to a home for mentally retarded adults. The adults gave the children special attention, suggesting that the damage was caused by a lack of emotional care.

During this time John Bowlby was working in London as a psychoanalyst in a child guidance clinic, where he treated many emotionally disturbed children. This provided him with the opportunity to observe at first hand the effects of separation on the children he treated. He formed the view that 'habitual delinquency' might be explained in terms of early prolonged separations between a child and his/her mother.

METHODOLOGY

Participants

This study was a series of **case studies**. There was a **control group** but the study was not an experiment. The final analysis looked at an *association* between the two groups of participants (thieves and control group) and experiences of separation.

Focus of the study: The thieves

The focus of this study was on 44 children who attended a child guidance clinic in London. These children were described as 'thieves' because stealing was one of their 'symptoms'. Only a few had actually been charged in Court partly because many of them were too young to be charged.

The sample consisted of 31 boys and 13 girls, aged between 5 and 17 years old. They were graded in terms of the seriousness of their stealing. Grade IV thieves (22 of the children) had been stealing for a long time, some for more than three years. Grade I thieves had committed only one theft – four children fell into this category.

The 'thieves' were mainly of average intelligence – about 50% had an IQ score in the range of 85–114 (100 is the mean score for IQ). A further 15 of the 'thieves' had a higher IQ and just two were below 85.

Control group

A control group was also used in this study, consisting of a further 44 children who attended the clinic. This group was similar in age, sex and IQ to the 'thieves'. Like the 'thieves' this group were emotionally disturbed but they did not steal.

Thus, altogether, 88 children were involved in this study, all of whom had been referred to the child guidance clinic for emotional problems.

Mothers

In addition, the mothers of the thieves and of the control group participants were also involved in the study. The mothers were interviewed in order to assess the case histories of the children.

PROCEDURES

Initial examination

The sample was obtained through **opportunity sampling**. On arrival at the clinic each child was given mental tests by a psychologist to assess their intelligence (the Binet Scale was used). The psychologist who conducted the test also noted the emotional attitude of the child.

At the same time a social worker interviewed the child's mother and recorded preliminary details of the child's early psychiatric history.

Finally, both the psychologist and social worker reported to the psychiatrist (John Bowlby). The psychiatrist then interviewed the child and the mother.

After this two-hour examination the team considered school and other reports and discussed their conclusions.

Therapy

Many of the children continued to meet with the psychiatrist weekly over a period of six months or more. The mothers talked over their problems with the social worker.

These meetings and discussions enabled a detailed case history to be recorded, and also enabled the psychiatrist to diagnose the children's emotional problems.

TRY THIS

You may find it difficult to remember the details of the method and findings of this study. A useful way to remember the right amount of detail is to identify ten key points for the method and ten key points for the findings – we have selected 'ten' because that's about the right amount for likely exam questions.

Once you have identified the key points reduce each to just a 'trigger' phrase. Close your book and look at each trigger phrase and write down what you remember for each. Open your book and remind yourself what else you might have included. Psychological research shows that testing your memory in this way is one of the best ways to improve what you can recall.

FINDINGS

Diagnosis

In order to determine what previous experiences might have caused the 44 thieves to turn to stealing it was first necessary to distinguish between different possible personality types. Bowlby recognised that it was difficult to do this with children whose whole personalities are not yet formed, but his overall view was that there were six main personality types in his sample:

- *Normal* – children whose characters appear fairly normal and stable.
- *Depressed* – children who have been unstable and are now in a more or less depressed state of mind.
- *Circular* – unstable children who show alternating depression and over-activity.
- *Hyperthymic* – children who tend to be constantly over-active.
- *Affectionless* – children characterised by lack of normal affection, shame or sense of responsibility.
- *Schizoid* – children who show marked schizoid or schizophrenic symptoms.

The affectionless character

Having identified one group of children as affectionless, a very clear pattern emerged in relation to delinquency.

Looking at all 44 thieves, Bowlby found that 14 were classified as 'affectionless'. Of these 14 'affectionless' children 12 had experienced frequent separations from their mothers. For example:

- Betty I. – placed in a foster home at age seven months when her parents split up, she moved from one foster home to another and then spent a year in a convent school before she returned home at the age of five years.
- Derek B. – at age 18 months was hospitalised because he developed diphtheria. He stayed there for nine months and, during that time, was not visited by his parents.
- Kenneth W. – between the ages of three and nine years old he was primarily cared for by his grandfather who had no control over him.

Such separations were very rare amongst the other types of thieves. There were 30 non-affectionless thieves, only three of whom had experienced separations.

In the control group (44 of them) only two had experienced prolonged separations.

Other factors

Altogether 17 of the thieves experienced early separation. When considering the remaining 27 thieves Bowlby reported that 17 had mothers who were:

'either extremely anxious, irritable or fussy or else were rigid, domineering and oppressive . . . These are traits that mask unconscious hostility' (page 55).

Five of the 27 had fathers who hated them and expressed their hatred openly.

However, these experiences were also reported by the non-delinquent group. Therefore, such early experiences might explain emotional problems but not delinquency.

CONCLUSIONS

The conclusion to be drawn is that the children would not have become offenders if they had not had experiences that were harmful to healthy development.

Bowlby subscribed to the psychoanalytic (psychodynamic) view that early experiences are of vital importance in later development. The particular experience he focused on was the relationship between a mother and child, and the importance this has in emotional development. He proposed that the damage to this relationship would affect the development of the **superego**, leading to a reduced sense of right and wrong.

Juvenile delinquency is undoubtedly the consequence of many and complex factors, such as poverty, bad housing and lack of recreational facilities. However, this classic study has placed an emphasis on psychoanalytic factors, i.e. early experiences.

Implications for treatment

If the findings of this study are correct, the implication is that treatment should be offered to delinquents, though this process is extremely slow and difficult. The earlier that a diagnosis is made the better for treatment.

A preferable approach is prevention rather than treatment. The prolonged separation of a mother and her child may on occasion be unavoidable, for example in the case of a mother's death or ill health or simply because of social circumstances.

'However, if all of those people who advise on the upbringing of small children, not least among them doctors, were aware of the appalling damage which separations of this kind have on the development of a child's character, many could be avoided and many of the most distressing cases of chronic delinquency prevented' (page 54).

A table summarising Bowlby's findings about the relationships between affectionless character and early separations between mother and child. The same data is illustrated in the graph below.

	Separations from mother before the age of two		Total
	Frequent	**None**	
Affectionless thieves	12 (86%)	2 (14%)	14
Other thieves	5 (17%)	25 (83%)	30
All thieves	17 (39%)	27 (61%)	44
Control participants	2 (4%)	42 (96%)	44

▼ Graph illustrating the data in the table above.

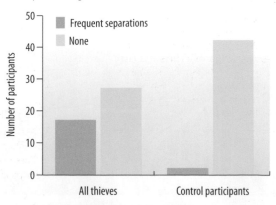

Classic evidence: Bowlby (1944) (continued)

SPECIFICATION REQUIREMENT

For each approach it will be necessary to:
- Make judgements on a classic piece of evidence including ethical issues and social implications.

On this spread we are going to evaluate the classic study by looking at issues related to its methodology, and comparing the study to alternative evidence. When it comes to evaluation, you can make up your own mind. We have presented some evidence and statements, and invite you to use these to construct your own view of the classic study. You can use your knowledge of research methods as well.

THINGS TO DO

WWW
There's a clearly narrated seven-minute video on this study, along with other research, at: www.youtube.com/watch?v=Polyrv5GPUc

Original article
The full reference for this classic study is Bowlby, J. (1944) Forty-four juvenile thieves: Their characters and their home-life. *International Journal of Psychoanalysis*, 25(19–52), 107–207.

You can download the article from scribd, free on a one-month trial: www.scribd.com/doc/125866662/John-Bowlby-Fourty-Four-Juvenile-Thieves-Their-Caracter-and-Home-life#scribd

Other resources
Bowlby went on to propose the maternal deprivation hypothesis – the view that children's emotional development depends on a warm, intimate and continuous relationship with a mother (or permanent mother-substitute). Listen to Michael Rutter talking about this here: www.youtube.com/watch?v=igC9R45TS5E&index=7&list=PLCEB6B1E1057EE9FB

EVALUATION: METHODOLOGY AND PROCEDURES

No causal findings

It is tempting to draw the conclusion from this study that prolonged separation caused the emotional problems experienced by many of the thieves. However, this variable was not manipulated. All that is demonstrated is a relationship between these variables. There may be other variables that caused the emotional problems. For example, it might be that discord in the home 'caused' prolonged separations between mother and child and also caused the affectionless nature of some of the children. It could even be that the affectionless character caused the separations in some cases (for example, a difficult child might be more likely to be placed in care).

This means that no causal conclusions should be drawn.

Biased data

Bowlby produced a rich record of **qualitative data** on each of his participants, based on extensive interviews with the children and their families. In total there are over 25 pages in the report simply detailing the case histories of the 44 thieves. Such data has the advantage of providing many insights into the events that preceded the children's problems.

However, the data is limited because it is based on the view of one person – albeit a very experienced psychiatrist. His perceptions may have been biased by his own beliefs – for example his belief in the importance of early experience.

There is a further source of bias in the data collected. The case histories were largely based on the recollections of the parents about events that happened many years previously. Such recollections are likely to be inaccurate, though we would expect such inaccuracy to lean towards portraying the events more positively, which would lead to a 'rosier' picture of the early childhoods.

The sample

All 88 children in this study were emotionally disturbed. Therefore it may not be appropriate to generalise from this sample to all children. For example, there may well be delinquents who have no emotional disturbance and the cause of their delinquency may be more social than emotional. Bowlby suggests that it would be useful to examine a sample of children appearing in court for stealing in order to determine whether all cases of delinquency have a similar explanation.

▼ In 1966 the Romanian government, under the dictator Nicolae Ceaușescu, tried to boost the population of Romania by encouraging parents to have large families and also by banning abortion. The consequence was that many babies were born who could not be cared for by their families.

When the regime collapsed in 1989 there were more than 100,000 orphans in 600 state-run orphanages. Many were adopted by Western families. Researchers have studied these children to see how early separation has affected their emotional development (see text on right).

EVALUATION: ALTERNATIVE EVIDENCE

One criticism that has been made of Bowlby's research is that he muddled together several different experiences. Separation alone may not cause long-lasting damage, especially if a child is given good substitute emotional care. Furthermore, research has shown that there is a sensitive period in development – a lack of emotional care before the age of six months appears to be something that children can recover from (as in the case of Romanian orphans) (Rutter and Sonuga-Barke, 2010).

However, Bowlby's basic conclusion has been supported in subsequent research. The lack of emotional care during key periods of development appears to have lasting and serious consequences. These consequences include physical underdevelopment, intellectual retardation, and difficulties in later relationships with friends, romantic partners and one's own children.

In the study mentioned above Michael Rutter *et al.* (2010) compared Romanian orphans who were adopted before or after the age of six months. Those who were adopted later (i.e. continued to lack emotional care at a very important time in their development) lagged behind a control group of UK children on all measures of physical, cognitive and social development.

ETHICAL ISSUES AND SOCIAL IMPLICATIONS

Confidentiality and privacy

The participants in this study were not afforded **confidentiality**. The report gives their first names and initial letter of their last name. Their case histories provide considerable detail of their lives. Both make it easy for anyone to identify the individual and their families.

It is not clear from the report to what extent the children and their families were aware that this information would be published. Remember that the details were collected during interviews with the psychiatrist (John Bowlby) as part of treatment. In retrospect some of the participants may have preferred that their details were not published.

Valid consent

Where children are involved in research it is usually accepted that parents are asked to provide **valid consent**. However, it is more usual today for children to also be informed about the nature and purpose of any research.

It appears from the article that data were collected as a routine part of treating patients at the clinic and that the decision to use the data was retrospective. The children and their families were seen at the clinic in the years 1936–1939 whereas the report was published in 1946. This suggests that the clinic team would not have decided to use the data for this study at the time the children were treated. It would have been difficult to obtain consent five or more years later.

It is worth noting that attitudes about the ethics of research changed in the period after the war when the first ethical guidelines were published. We are much more sensitive about these issues today.

See the next spread for a discussion of further ethical and social implications of this topic.

TRY THIS

When researchers wish to conduct a new study they usually have to present their plans to an **ethical committee** who will decide whether the study is acceptable.

Elect members of your class to serve as an ethical committee. Other class members should consider what details would need to be provided to gain ethical approval for this study, e.g. what you would do about informed consent and the right to withdraw.

The ethical committee should then consider the costs and benefits of the study, and make recommendations about whether the study is acceptable and, if not, what could be done to make it acceptable.

MEET THE RESEARCHER

John Bowlby (1907–1990) was born into an upper middle class family and raised mainly by a nanny. His son, Sir Richard Bowlby, explains how this led to his father's interest in the relationship – or lack of relationship – between a mother and child:

The origin of my father's motivation for working on the conundrum of the parent child attachment bond, probably stems from a traumatic childhood. His father, my grandfather, was a successful surgeon who lived in a large London townhouse with his wife and six children. The children, as was normal for the time, were raised by nannies. The children only saw their mother for one hour each day, and even then the children went to see her all together, so there wasn't exactly individual quality time. My father grew to love his nanny called Minnie, and I have little doubt that she was his surrogate [mother] figure, but when he was 4 years old Minnie left the family. He lost his 'mother figure', and his primary attachment bond was broken. He was then sent away to boarding school when he was 8 years old causing further trauma. I think one thing that saved him was that he did have those 4 years of secure attachment with Minnie. (personal communication)

These early experiences of separation shaped Bowlby as a person and also shaped his work; like many psychologists he was drawn to investigate an area of behaviour that was personally difficult.

EXAM CORNER

You will need to be able to do the following with respect to the study by Bowlby (1944):

Describe:
- The methodology of the study (describe and justify; includes characteristics of the sample but not the sampling technique).
- The procedures of the study (what the researcher did; includes the sampling technique).
- The findings of the study.
- The conclusions of the study.

Evaluate:
- The methodology of the study.
- The procedures of the study.
- The findings of the study (use methodology and/or alternative evidence).
- The conclusions of the study (use methodology and/or alternative evidence).
- The ethical issues and social implications.

Possible exam questions:
1. Critically assess the findings and conclusions of Bowlby's (1944) research *'Forty-four juvenile thieves: Their characters and home-life'.* [10]
2. Outline the procedures used in Bowlby's (1944) research *'Forty-four juvenile thieves: Their characters and home-life'.* [10]
3. Discuss the ethical issues and social implications that arise from Bowlby's (1944) research *'Forty-four juvenile thieves: Their characters and home-life'.* [12]

◀ Bowlby's research emphasised the importance of a mother's care – which was very important. At the time of Bowlby's research a mother's role was undervalued and divorce courts often gave custody to fathers.

Subsequently our society has recognised the importance of a mother's care and many believe a father is not an adequate substitute. It is important to recognise that mothering can be done by fathers too. The role that Bowlby was talking about is the provision of continuous emotional care.

Contemporary debate: The mother as primary care-giver of an infant

SPECIFICATION REQUIREMENT

For each approach it will be necessary to:
- Understand what is at the core of the debate.
- Refer to psychological studies and theories.
- Explore both sides of the contemporary debate from a psychological perspective (including the ethical, economic and social implications).

A primary care-giver of an infant is the person who is most responsible for an infant's health, development and well-being. This debate presupposes that there is such a thing as a 'primary care-giver' but, even more, this debate concerns a sensitive issue. We now live in a society that promotes equality and opportunity for all, irrespective of gender. However, if the evidence suggests that the mother is the 'best' primary care-giver of an infant, what impact might that have on the career prospects of women? In addition, fathers, who may desperately want to care for their infants, would be sidelined.

ETHICAL, SOCIAL AND ECONOMIC IMPLICATIONS

Childcare arrangements have significant economic implications. Increasing industrialisation in the 19th and 20th centuries led to the need for an expanding workforce which included women. It also meant that childcare needed to be provided – so the debate about stay-at-home mums versus go-to-work mums began.

One of the forms of support offered to parents is time off work following the birth of their infant. Traditionally, this has only been offered to women in the form of maternity leave; however, from April 2015, parents are entitled to 'shared parental leave'. This means fathers and mothers can divide the 52-week entitlement as they see fit. This change in social policy reflects how parents in the UK are moving away from the traditional view that the mother should be the primary care-giver of an infant.

The economic costs of childcare at both the family and societal level are significant. In March 2014, the Family and Childcare Trust reported that the average annual cost to parents of sending an infant to nursery school full-time is £9,850. In March 2014, the UK government introduced a scheme that allows parents to claim tax relief on childcare costs, thereby incentivising parents to work. The costs to the Treasury of schemes such as these are significant, but there may be a greater cost to our economy if we are unable to sustain an effective workforce.

Exam advice…

In preparation for this part of the exam it is really useful if you can actually hold debates about the issues being covered.

Don't limit your evidence to that included here. Collect evidence from other sources and ask people their opinions on the matter.

THE MOTHER SHOULD BE THE PRIMARY CARE-GIVER OF AN INFANT

Feeding

The NHS recommends that, if possible, infants are breastfed for at least the first six months of their lives. Breastfeeding, they report, offers the healthiest start for infants because it protects the infant from numerous infections and diseases. The NHS also claims that 'it can build a strong physical and emotional bond between mother and baby', important in subsequent emotional development.

This feeding argument obviously means that the infant's mother is the individual who is going to need to be available to feed the infant, possibly every two hours. This argument alone means that it is practical, and essential to the infant's survival, that the mother be the primary care-giver.

This means that anyone else, including the father, is obviously limited to a supporting care-giving role; perhaps similar to the relationship between a pit crew and a Formula One driver.

Freud's views on the importance of the mother

Sigmund Freud believed that the mother–infant dyad was of the greatest importance in the initial **oral stage** of **psychosexual development**. Infants depend upon their mother to satisfy the needs of their libido. Overindulgence or frustration leads to emotional problems later in life, such as neediness or pessimism respectively.

Freud also claimed that separation anxiety is caused by the infant realising that their bodily needs will go unsatisfied if separation is allowed to occur. In 1938, Freud wrote that the infant's relationship with the mother was *'unique, without parallel, laid down unilaterally for a whole lifetime as the first and strongest love object'*. In this Freud is claiming that a mother's love acts as a prototype for every relationship the infant will go on to have in their lifetime.

Deprivation damage

John Bowlby's classic research is described on the previous two spreads. He demonstrated that early and prolonged separation between a child and its mother can have lasting emotional effects. Most especially, that such separation is likely to lead to an affectionless character, someone who lacks the ability to feel normal affection, shame or sense of responsibility. Such a character is more likely to become a thief and also is likely to have difficulty forming relationships. Bowlby developed these views into the **maternal deprivation hypothesis**. He famously noted *'Mother love in infancy is just as important for a child's mental health, as vitamins and minerals are for physical health'*.

Bowlby thus identified a central role for the mother in healthy emotional development. Initially his ideas were based on his training as a Freudian psychiatrist. Subsequently Bowlby (1969) was influenced by evolutionary theory and proposed that attachment to one caregiver has special importance for survival. He called this one special emotional bond **monotropy** (leaning towards one person).

Mothers not fathers

It is possible that women are best as primary care-givers because most men are just not psychologically equipped to form this kind of intense emotional relationship. This may be due to biological or social factors. In terms of biology the female **hormone oestrogen** underlies caring behaviour so that women, generally, are more oriented towards emotional relationships than men.

In terms of social factors, there continue to be sex-**stereotypes** that affect male behaviour, such as it is being rather feminine to be sensitive to the needs of others. There is evidence that men are indeed less sensitive to infant cues than mothers (e.g. Heermann *et al.* 1994). However, Frodi *et al.* (1978) showed videotapes of infants crying and found no differences in the *biological* responses of men and women.

TRY THIS

Interview people of various ages who have been parents, asking them what they think about the proposal that 'mothers should be the primary care-givers of infants'.

Compare the results you get from younger parents and older parents.

▲   Who says fathers can't be the primary care-giver?

THE MOTHER DOESN'T NEED TO BE THE PRIMARY CARE-GIVER OF AN INFANT

Feeding

In the 1950s **behaviourists** promoted the view that infants were **classically conditioned** to associate their mother with a sense of pleasure: food (**unconditioned stimulus**) creates pleasure (**unconditioned response**); mother is associated with feeding and hence becomes a **conditioned stimulus** producing a **conditioned response** of pleasure (see page 50 for an explanation of classical conditioning).

However, a number of studies demonstrated that food does not equal love. Harry Harlow (1959) placed infant monkeys with two wire 'mothers'. One had a feeding bottle attached and the other was covered in soft cloth. The monkeys spent most of their time on the cloth-covered 'mother', most especially clinging to this 'mother' when frightened. This demonstrated that food does not create an emotional bond – contact comfort does.

Schaffer and Emerson (1964) supported this finding in a study of human behaviour. They found that primary attachments were not formed with the person who fed or spent more time with the infant. Strongly attached infants had carers who responded quickly and sensitively to their 'signals' and who offered their child the most interaction.

Freud's views on the importance of the mother

It is important to consider the historical context of Freud's ideas. At the time he was writing, women did not even have the right to vote. His ideas about the different roles played by the mother and father really may simply reflect the norms and values that were held by society in the early half of the 20th century. If Freud were writing today, he might portray quite a different picture of the father's role.

Freud did recognise the importance of the role of the father. For example, in 1930, Freud claimed *I cannot think of any need in childhood as strong as the need for a father's protection*. In addition, Freud recognised the special importance of a father in a boy's development (see the **Oedipus complex**, page 31).

Deprivation damage

Although Bowlby used the term 'maternal' in the maternal deprivation hypothesis, he did not mean this was exclusively the child's mother. He wrote *'a child should experience a warm, intimate and continuous relationship with his mother (or permanent mother substitute – one person who steadily "mothers" him)'* (1953). In other words 'mothering' is not exclusive to a child's mother.

Further issue can be taken with the claim that such a relationship is indeed of crucial importance. Bowlby himself presented research that some children show no ill effects from early separation (Bowlby *et al.,* 1956). The children in this study were very ill with tuberculosis and spent years in hospital with little contact with their families. Nevertheless most of them showed few problems later in life. Bowlby *et al.* suggest that those children who coped better may have been better attached to their mothers (or mother substitute) in the first place and thus more resilient.

Mothers not fathers

There is plenty of evidence that men are quite capable of forming close attachments with their children, as is the case in single (male) parent families. The view that men are not emotional is outdated. Our changing stereotypes have meant that both men and women feel freer to take on roles traditionally reserved for the opposite sex. Women are not the only parent who becomes hormonally adapted to parenthood. Gettler *et al.* (2011) suggest that a father's testosterone level drops in order to help *'a man respond more sensitively to his children's needs.'*

EXAM CORNER

You will need to be able to:

- Discuss the argument and evidence in favour of the mother as primary care-giver of an infant.
- Discuss the argument and evidence against the mother as sole primary care-giver of an infant.
- Present a conclusion to the debate.
- Include discussion of the ethical, economic and social implications of this debate.

Possible exam questions:

1. *'Without mothers as the primary care-giver, infants would fail to develop in a healthy way'.*
   With reference to this quote, discuss evidence which supports this point of view. [20]
2. Discuss the view in today's society that the primary care-giver does not always need to be the mother of the infant. [20]

Exam advice…

In the second exam-style question above the view is proposing that the mother does not need to be the primary care-giver of an infant. However, it also makes reference to 'today's society'. This means that in your answer, possibly in your conclusion, you could incorporate some discussion of the current social implications of this issue, such as recent legal changes in parental leave.

CONCLUSION

The view of mother as primary care-giver is out of date for two main reasons. First of all there is no conclusive evidence to suggest that the primary care-giver has to be female.

Second, it mistakenly emphasises the fact that children have one primary carer. The reality is that healthy development relies on multiple important relationships. Bowlby proposed that there is one primary attachment figure – but he also proposed that secondary attachments provided a vital emotional safety net for situations where the primary carer is absent. Research has also shown that, while women more often are the main emotional figure in a child's life, men typically provide an equally important ingredient in development. For example, fathers are more playful, physically active and generally better at providing challenging situations for their children (Geiger, 1996).

Perhaps the biggest mistake is thinking that any care-giver has to be 'primary'.

Evaluating the psychodynamic approach

SPECIFICATION REQUIREMENT

For each approach it will be necessary to:
- Evaluate the approach (including strengths, weaknesses and comparison with the four other approaches).

You have studied many aspects of the psychodynamic approach, including the assumptions of the approach, so now you need to consider the strengths and weaknesses of this approach.

As well as the strengths and weaknesses outlined below, you should also try and think about some of the problems relating to psychodynamic therapies, as these could link with weaknesses of the approach in general.

STRENGTHS OF THE PSYCHODYNAMIC APPROACH

1. Nature and nurture

One strength of the psychodynamic approach is that it takes into account both sides of the **nature–nurture debate**. Freud claimed that adult personality is the product of **innate** drives (**nature**) and childhood experiences (**nurture**). For Freud, the **id** is instinctual, and is the biological aspect of our personality. The id is driven by *Eros* (the life drive, the drive to preserve and create life) and *Thanatos* (the death drive which motivates antisocial acts such as aggression).

The influence of nurture (experience) comes in the form of the **psychosexual stages** that every child passes through. In each of these stages, frustration or overindulgence may lead to a fixation on that stage and predictable adult personality characteristics. Freud's theory therefore considers the influence of nature (things we are born with) and nurture (things that develop through experience). The *interactionist* nature of this approach is a key strength.

2. Usefulness

The psychodynamic approach has proved to be useful in several ways.
- It highlights the fact that childhood is a critical period in development; who we are and become is greatly influenced by our childhood experiences.
- Ideas put forward by Freud have greatly influenced the therapies used to treat mental disorders. Freud was the first person to recognise that psychological factors could be used to explain physical symptoms such as paralysis. **Psychoanalysis** (the general term for therapy developed from this approach) has been widely used to help people overcome psychological problems. There is research evidence to support this.
- Generally, this is a useful approach for helping to understand mental health problems, i.e. that mental health can be caused by childhood trauma and/or unconscious conflicts.

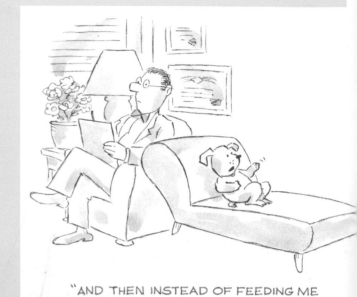

"AND THEN INSTEAD OF FEEDING ME HE WOULD RING A LITTLE BELL."

3. Reflects the complexity of human behaviour

One of the common criticisms of the other approaches in this book is that the explanations of behaviour are **reductionist**. In contrast, Freud's explanations reflect the complexity of human behaviour and experience. Therefore the psychodynamic approach can be seen as an approach that is **holistic** – it recognises that human behaviour is influenced by multiple factors which cannot be separated.

The psychodynamic approach improves on those other approaches that reduce explanations for human behaviour to one factor. For example, the **behaviourist approach** proposes that recovery from mental disorder can be achieved through re-learning, and does not require any consideration of what may have caused the disorder in the first place. The problem with this approach is that the original symptoms may simply reappear again because the actual cause has been ignored (called '**symptom substitution**'). Freud's method of psychoanalysis (see left) seeks to uncover deep meanings and acknowledges that understanding behaviour is a lengthy process.

PSYCHOANALYSIS

Freud used the term psychoanalysis to describe both his theory of personality and his therapy. The aim of the therapy is to bring unconscious feelings and thoughts into conscious awareness where they can be dealt with.

A key technique used to do this is free association. In free association, patients express their thoughts exactly as they occur, even though the thoughts may seem unimportant or irrelevant. Patients should not censor their thoughts in any way. Freud believed that the value of free association lies in the fact that the patients are making links (or associations) as they express their thoughts, and these associations are determined by the unconscious factors that the analysis is aiming to uncover. This procedure is designed to reveal areas of conflict, and to bring into consciousness those memories that have been repressed. The therapist helps interpret these for patients, who correct, reject, and add further thoughts and feelings.

Psychoanalysis (and free association) is not a brief form of therapy. Together, patients and therapist examine the same issues over and over again, sometimes over a period of years, in an attempt to gain greater clarity concerning the causes of their neurotic behaviour.

WEAKNESSES OF THE PSYCHODYNAMIC APPROACH

1. Reductionist and oversimplified approach

On the facing page, we identified one of the strengths of the psychodynamic approach being that it reflects the complexity of human behaviour and experience. However, in some ways the psychodynamic approach can also be seen as being reductionist. It can be accused of 'mechanistic reductionism' because it simplifies complex human behaviour to the mechanics of the mind (i.e. the battle between the **id**, **ego** and **superego**) and early childhood experience (psychosexual stages).

This approach thus ignores other important influences on behaviour, such as biochemistry and **genetics**. For example, during the 1950s and 60s, one of the main explanations for **autism** was that some mothers were very distant from their children ('refrigerator mother') and autism was a withdrawal from the lack of involvement. Such a psychodynamic explanation was an oversimplification of the underlying processes of autism. Therefore, in some ways, this approach does have the weakness of being an oversimplification and ignoring other important factors.

2. Determinist approach

Freud saw infant behaviour as determined by innate forces (**libido**), and adult behaviour as determined by childhood experiences. It therefore follows that we have no **free will** (choice) in who we become or how we behave. We call this a **determinist** viewpoint, as it sees our personality as shaped (pre-determined) by forces that we cannot change or do not have a choice about – as humans we have no free will when it comes to our personality and behaviour.

This is a weakness, as we *are* able to change the way we behave if we want to. This determinist viewpoint may give some people a plausible excuse for behaving unreasonably (*'I can't help the way I am'*) or an excuse for criminal behaviour (*'It's not my fault'*). It also implies that people cannot be held responsible for their behaviour.

3. Cannot be proven wrong

The major objection to Freud's theory is that it is difficult to **falsify**. A good theory is one that can be tested to see if it is wrong. Karl Popper (1934) argued that falsification is the only way to be certain: *'no amount of observations of white swans can allow the inference that all swans are white, but the observation of a single black swan is sufficient to refute that conclusion.'* In other words, you can't prove that a theory is right – you can only falsify a theory.

Many of Freud's predictions are notoriously 'slippery'. For example, his view that all men have repressed homosexual tendencies cannot be disproved. If you do find men who have no repressed homosexual tendencies then it could be argued that they have them – it's just that they are so repressed they are not apparent. In other words, the prediction cannot be falsified.

However, while it is difficult to generate testable hypotheses from Freud's theory of personality, it is not impossible. For example, research has looked at the relationship between guilt and wrongdoing – Freud predicted an inverse relationship, and MacKinnon (1938) did find that individuals who cheated at a task tended to express less guilt when questioned about life in general than those who did not cheat.

▲ A person might believe all swans are white, and this picture appears to support this hypothesis – but it does not prove it to be right. In fact, you cannot prove that this hypothesis is right – you can only prove it is wrong (falsify it) by seeing a black swan.

COMPARING APPROACHES

You need to be able to compare and contrast the psychodynamic approach with the other approaches that you have studied. In groups of three or four students, discuss how the psychodynamic approach compares with the other approaches you have studied in terms of the following:

- Recognition of the role of nature and nurture.
- Its usefulness.
- Determinist nature.
- Reductionist nature.
- Whether its concepts/ideas can be measured scientifically and objectively (i.e. are they falsifiable)?
- Therapeutic intervention.

Use this information to prepare for the following exam question:

Compare and contrast the biological and psychodynamic approaches. [12]

EXAM CORNER

To evaluate the approach you need to be able to:
- Fully discuss the strengths (at least **two**).
- Fully discuss the weaknesses (at least **two**).
- Compare and contrast the approach with the four other approaches in terms of key issues and debates.

Possible exam questions:
1. 'The weaknesses of the psychodynamic approach are that it cannot be scientifically observed or tested'. Critically assess this statement with reference to your knowledge of the strengths and weaknesses of the psychodynamic approach. [8]
2. Evaluate **two** strengths of the psychodynamic approach. [8]
3. Discuss the similarities and differences of the psychodynamic and behaviourist approaches in psychology. [10]
4. Discuss the psychodynamic approach in terms of its strengths and weaknesses. [16]

Some activities for you

ASSUMPTIONS

What would you do?

In pairs, decide what your id, ego and superego would be telling you to do in the following scenarios (or this can be done as a role play).

a) You haven't got any money but you go into your favourite clothes shop anyway, and try on a lovely item. You discover the item is not tagged, and no one saw you take it into the changing room.

b) Your best friend has just split up from their boyfriend/girlfriend and is devastated. The problem is the ex-boyfriend/girlfriend has asked you out on a date, and you have secretly liked them for ages.

c) In your psychology test, you realise that you have left some revision notes in your pencil case, which is on the desk in front of you. Your teacher is busy marking some work at the front of the classroom.

The id, ego and superego

ANSWERS ON PAGE 172

Create a chart with the headings 'id', 'ego' and 'superego' and, working in pairs, place the following phrases under the appropriate headings. Try to think of some more of your own as well.

- Demands immediate pleasure.
- Function is to control the impulses of the id, especially those that society forbids.
- Concerned with devising a realistic strategy to obtain pleasure.
- Not concerned with the consequences of an action.
- Can punish the ego through causing feelings of guilt.
- Works out realistic ways of satisfying the id's demands.
- Develops in order to mediate between the unrealistic demands of the id and the superego.

Ego defences

ANSWERS ON PAGE 172

Decide which defence mechanisms (repression, displacement, regression, projection) are being
used in the examples below:

a) Sarah really wants to punch her cheeky little brother in the face. Instead she punches her pillow.

b) Every time Kathy feels anxious she bites her nails as this provides her with the comfort she associates with being a toddler.

c) Tommy constantly accuses his girlfriend of cheating on him.

d) Julie suddenly remembered as an adult, while talking about her feelings in therapy, that her father had committed suicide when she was a girl.

Fill in the blanks

ANSWERS ON PAGE 172

Copy the text below and try to fill in the blanks without looking back through the book to see how much you remember. The words to choose from are listed at the end if you need them.

One assumption of the psychodynamic approach is that each child moves through five _____ _____ of development. He or she moves through these in the same _____. The stages are known as _____, _____, _____, _____ and _____. At each stage, a child's energy or _____ is attached to a body region. If conflicts occur at any stage and are not overcome or dealt with, _____ can occur, which may be due to _____ or _____ at a stage of development. This will affect our _____ later on in life. One example is the _____ _____ character. Such people typically have some of the following characteristics: _____, _____ and _____. Another personality type is the _____ _____ _____ character. Such people typically have some of the following characteristics: _____, _____ and _____.

orally fixated   phallic   personality   order   tidy   oral
latency   fixations   possessive   libido   over-indulgence
under-indulgence   psychosexual   stages
pessimistic   anally fixated   anal   sarcastic   envious   stubborn   genital

CLASSIC EVIDENCE

ANSWERS ON PAGE 172

Bowlby (1944) Forty-four juvenile thieves.

Copy and complete the crossword below to test your understanding of this classic study.

Across

4. The group used to compare the thieves against (C_ _ _ _ _ _)
8. The affectionless thieves experienced more P_ _ _ _ _ _ _ _   S_ _ _ _ _ _ _ _ _ _
9. The number of main personality types identified by Bowlby (_ _ _)
10. The name of the researcher who conducted research on Romanian orphans (R_ _ _ _ _)

Down

1. One key ethical issue in this study (C _ _ _ _ _ _ _ _ _ _ _ _ _ _)
2. The personality type identified by Bowlby for children who lack normal affection, shame or sense of responsibility (A_ _ _ _ _ _ _ _ _ _ _ _)
3. The test used by the psychologist to measure the children's intelligence (B_ _ _ _ S_ _ _ _)
5. The number of thieves characterised as affectionless by Bowlby (F_ _ _ _ _ _ _)
6. The type of data collected in this study (Q _ _ _ _ _ _ _ _ _ _)
7. The number of thieves used in the study (F_ _ _ _ F_ _ _)

THERAPIES

Exam answers

In order to understand therapies, you must understand how the assumptions apply to the general and specific aims of that therapy. Choosing either dream analysis or psychodrama, fill in a copy of the chart below as a guide to constructing an exam answer:

Example question – *Describe how the assumptions of the psychodynamic approach are applied to either dream analysis or psychodrama.*	
Therapies that arise from the psychodynamic approach are based on the underlying assumption(s) that…	
One specific assumption that applies in this therapy is…	
Another specific assumption that applies in this therapy is…	

EVALUATION

Some questions

Using the information on 'Evaluating the psychodynamic approach' (see previous spread), answer the following questions:

- Explain how the psychodynamic approach fits in with the nature–nurture debate.
- Explain **two** examples of the 'usefulness' of the psychodynamic approach.
- Why is the psychodynamic approach less reductionist than other approaches covered in this book?
- Why do some researchers argue that the psychodynamic approach does display reductionism?
- Explain why the psychodynamic approach is determinist.
- What elements of the psychodynamic approach cannot be falsified?

Make a crossword

Create a crossword (see above right for website).

In pairs, design a crossword with all the key concepts that you need to learn for the evaluation of the psychodynamic approach.

You will need to write appropriate clues for the crossword words. When you have finished, swap your crossword with another pair to help them learn and understand the evaluation better.

Here are some examples:

1. This term refers to a theory that cannot be proven wrong; in other words it lacks … (answer: falsification)
2. Freud's theory is criticised for this; it is the opposite of free will. (answer: determinist)

You can use some of the review activities described at the ends of the other chapters. For example, you could produce some multiple choice questions or make a mobile (see page 65).

You should certainly list again the key words in this chapter and make sure you understand them.

Produce a comic strip

Illustrate a topic you have studied in pictures. There are websites to help you, such as *www.toondoo.com*

Design your own crossword

There are many websites that will assist you in making your own crosswords, e.g. *www. crosswordpuzzlegames.com*

There are also sites to help make your own word search or other puzzles.

▲ Be a N.U.R.D.

Stands for nature/nurture, usefulness, reductionist, determinist.

All ways to evaluate the psychodynamic approach.

DEBATE

Collect examples of comments from various sources, such as news websites, and write your own blog post as to whether you think mothers are the best option for being the primary care-giver. You don't have to offer a balanced opinion – just be prepared to back up your point of view with evidence.

Exam questions and answers

QUESTION ON CLASSIC EVIDENCE

Describe the procedures of Bowlby (1944) *Forty-four juvenile thieves: Their characters and home-life*. [6]

Mark scheme for this question

Mark	Description
6	Description is **well detailed** with no major inaccuracies.
4–5	Description is **reasonably detailed**. There may be inaccuracies which do not detract from overall meaning.
2–3	Description is **basic** and **limited**. There may be a number of major/minor inaccuracies.
1	Description is **superficial/muddled**.
0	**Inappropriate** answer given / **no response** attempted.

TRY THIS

After assessing Bob and Megan's answers and reading the examiner's comments, explain three tips you would give a fellow student when answering this question and/or similar 6-mark 'Describe' questions.
  Issues to consider:
- Length
- Structure
- Making sure description is 'well detailed'
Have a go at writing the perfect answer.

Bob's answer

This is an experiment and Bowlby did not intervene in any way. Bowlby used 44 thieves from a child guidance clinic where he worked in London as his sample. It contained mainly boys but there were some girls and everyone was aged between 5 and 18. He tested their level of intelligence and found most were normal. Bowlby compared this group to a control group of 44 other children who were not thieves but did attend his clinic because they had other problems. Bowlby gave each child a few tests such as IQ and emotional state and a psychologist also tested them. Over time lots of experiments and interviews were done on the children and Bowlby built up a picture of the type of person they were. Bowlby collected lots of quantitative data. Bowlby did groundbreaking research and he was one of the first people to make links between children being separated from their mums and then having future emotional problems. This led to changes in thinking about how children should be cared for if they are unable to live with their parents.

184 words

Pay attention when reading Bob's answer – are there any inaccuracies?

Has Bob described procedures only or does he include methodological detail (not creditworthy)?

Pay attention to how Bob discusses the implications of the study. Remember this is an AO1 question.

Megan's answer

Bowlby worked as a psychoanalyst in a child guidance clinic treating emotionally disturbed children. He took advantage of this position to research the effects separation can have.

The sample he used were 88 service users – Group 1 contained 44 juvenile thieves, 31 boys and 13 girls aged between 6 and 14 years old. Bowlby rated these 44 thieves using a 4 point scale with over half the children being grade four thieves (the most severe) and only four were given a grade 1 (least severe). These were compared to a control group of 44 children who attended the clinic but had not been labelled a thief. This group was 'matched' in terms of age and IQ and was of average intelligence. The mothers of the children were also used and could be considered participants as well.

Bowlby assessed each child when they arrived at the clinic using mental tests and recruited a psychologist to help him. Mothers were also interviewed and were asked about their relationship and the child's history. Once completed, all those involved in the assessments met to discuss what personality type the child fell into and used reports from other sources such as school to help them do this.

201 words

Megan has given information about the sample – is she describing what the sample was or how it was obtained?

The term 'procedures' refers to what the researcher(s) actually did, which could include how the sample was obtained but not what the sample was.

Megan has provided basic details of the psychological assessments used.

This answer is a reasonable length for a 6-mark question.

▲ It's all in the detail.

Det**ail.**

Examiner comments and marks on page 173

QUESTION ON EVALUATING APPROACHES

A psychologist needs to explain to his client why they may be better using a therapy from a psychodynamic approach rather than a therapy from the behaviourist approach.

Using your knowledge of both approaches compare and contrast the psychodynamic and behaviourist approaches and their therapies. [16]

Mark scheme for this question

Mark	Description
13–16	A **thorough analysis** is made of the similarities and differences in the context of therapy. An **appropriate conclusion** is reached based on the evidence presented.
10–12	A **good analysis** is made of the similarities and differences in the context of therapy. A **reasonable conclusion** is reached based on the evidence presented.
7–9	A **basic analysis** is made of the similarities and differences in the context of therapy. A **basic conclusion** is reached.
4–6	A **basic analysis** is made of the similarities and/or differences but with little reference to therapy. **No conclusion** is reached.
1–3	A **superficial analysis** is made of the similarities and/or differences with little reference to therapy. **No conclusion** is reached.
0	**Inappropriate** answer given / **no response** attempted.

TRY THIS

Have a go at being the examiner
Read through both Bob and Megan's answers on this page and decide which one is best.
You might consider:
- How effectively both answers compare and contrast. You may find it useful to look at the number of comparative terms, e.g. in contrast, similarly, both, etc., that Bob and Megan use.
- How effectively both answers contextualise the points they make in therapy.
- How effectively both answers draw a meaningful conclusion based on the arguments presented.

You could highlight each of these three considerations in a different colour.
Once you have done this decide on a mark using the mark scheme on the left.
Finally, write three pieces of advice you would give a fellow student who was answering this question.

Bob's answer

One key difference between the approaches is effectiveness. Psychodynamic therapy (PT) such as dream analysis is extremely difficult to measure in terms of effectiveness and evidence tends to focus on dreams as a function rather than examining percentage success rates. In contrast, behaviourist therapy (BT) is able to quantitatively measure how successful it has been, e.g. Capafóns (1998) has found that clients with a phobia of flying showed less physiological signs and lower fear ratings after completing a 12–25 week treatment. The key difference is that BT is only concerned with objective, measurable concepts like fear ratings whilst PT focuses on concepts that are subjective and cannot be scientifically measured or confirmed, e.g. unconscious conflicts. Ultimately the behaviourist approach and its therapies are more scientific and rigorous than the psychodynamic approach and its therapies.

A key criticism with PT and BT is that they both have a limited use with BT only really examining phobias and addictions, although not all phobias can be cured, e.g. generalised phobias like agoraphobia and ancient fears as identified by Seligman, whilst PT is mainly used for anxiety and unconscious conflicts. Neither approach is recommended for the treatment of schizophrenia.

Ethically BT has a better approach to therapy than PT as they put the element of responsibility on the individual – it is their free will to attend, e.g. systematic desensitisation, and they are able to control their anxiety by not taking the next step on the anxiety hierarchy until they are ready. In contrast the PT removes the element of responsibility and is considered more unethical as there is a clear power balance distinction between client and therapist that can result in the client becoming over dependent on the therapist. This creates an important distinction between both approaches to therapy and it is clear to see that PT is more determinist, i.e. its success or not is down to the therapist not the individual. Whereas BT allows for a certain degree of free will as its success is more under the control of the individual rather than the therapist.

Another key difference is the extent to which BT and PT address the root of the problem. PT therapies come out on top as they do address the underlying cause of a disorder, in contrast BT often suffer from symptom substitution as they only address undesirable symptoms and not the underlying cause.

In conclusion, when weighing up BT in comparison to PT, we must consider what disorder the individual has as PT has less use and are only suitable for certain people, but they can be highly effective and offer long-term solutions. Whereas BT are ethically better and have lots of scientific evidence to prove their effectiveness but can sometimes result in symptom substitution. 461 words

Megan's answer

The behaviourist approach is highly scientific as it uses scientific methodology to collect data, e.g. lab experiments. It is only interested in behaviour that can be objectively observed and measured. The psychodynamic approach is completely unscientific because its ideas (e.g. the id) cannot be seen or measured or even falsified. This means that the psychodynamic approach has less proof than other approaches.

The behaviourist approach is determinist because it suggests the environment shapes our behaviour and an individual has no control over this. The psychodynamic approach is determinist as it says our behaviour is shaped by the unconscious mind which we are not aware of, let alone able to control.

The behaviourist approach uses therapies that are based on classical conditioning and sees the problem as stemming from external environmental causes. The psychodynamic approach uses therapies that try to access the unconscious mind as they believe the cause of mental problems lies there, e.g. internal causes. This is a big difference in their approach to therapy.

The behaviourist approach has therapies that are very effective for phobias. The psychodynamic approach has therapies that work for anxiety, depression and conflicts.

The behaviourist approach has therapies that suffer from symptom substitution and this means their effectiveness is reduced over time as symptoms can reappear, e.g. one year later. The psychodynamic approach does not really have symptom substitution but it does have ethical issues because it generally involves people having to rake up painful information that they have buried in their unconscious mind and this could be traumatic and make the person feel worse than if they had not had therapy.

Behaviourist therapies usually work fairly quickly, e.g. one researcher found that people were cured after 25 sessions for a phobia of flying. The psychodynamic therapies are very time consuming and in some cases it may take years for the individual to see any progress and at the end of it they may be no further forward in understanding why they behave as they do.

The behaviourist approach is traditionally based on animal research such as Pavlov's dogs. Pavlov did research on dogs and developed classical conditioning which was then applied to humans in a therapy like systematic desensitisation. The psychodynamic approach does not use animals and only does research on humans.

I think that the behaviourist approach is a better approach than the psychodynamic approach for many reasons. 395 words

Examiner comments and marks on page 173

Chapter 3
The behaviourist approach

SPECIFICATION

Approach	Assumptions and behaviour to be explained (including)	Therapy (one per approach)	Classic research	Contemporary debate
Behaviourist	• blank slate • behaviour learnt through conditioning • humans and animals learn in similar ways Learners will be expected to apply one of the given assumptions to the formation of a relationship	aversion therapy OR systematic desensitisation	Watson, J.B. and Rayner, R. (1920) Conditioned emotional reactions. *Journal of Experimental Psychology*, *3(1)*, 1–14.	using conditioning techniques to control the behaviour of children

CHAPTER CONTENT

'Give me a dozen healthy infants, well-formed, and my own specified world to bring them up in and I'll guarantee to take any one at random and train him to become any type of specialist I might select – doctor, lawyer, artist, merchant-chief and, yes, even beggar-man and thief, regardless of his talents, penchants, tendencies, abilities, vocations, and race of his ancestors.'

J.B. Watson (1930)
The father of behaviourism

Do you agree?

Can parents train any child to be any kind of specialist?

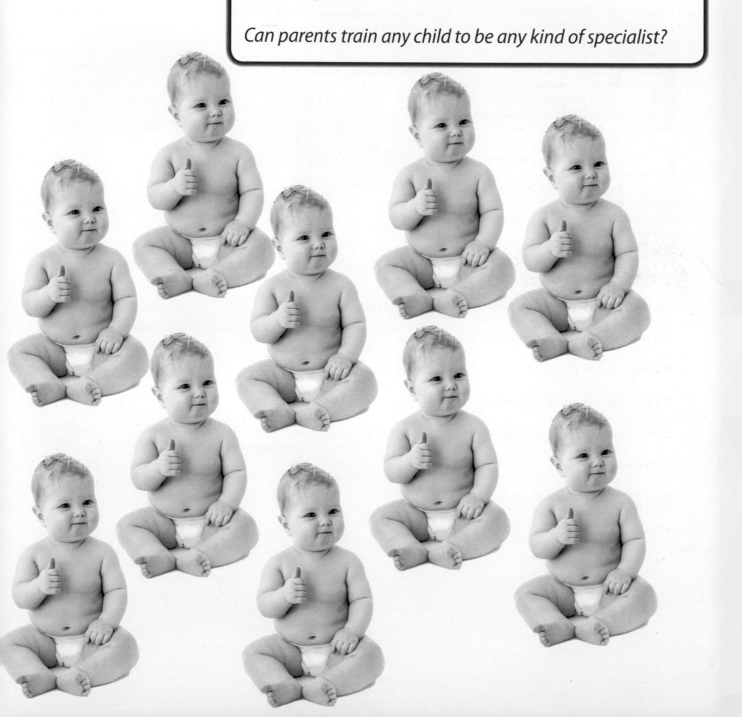

Behaviourist approach assumptions

SPECIFICATION REQUIREMENT

For each approach it will be necessary to:
- Know and understand the assumptions.
- Apply the assumptions to explain the formation of a relationship.

The essence of the **behaviourist approach** is the focus on the environment and learned behaviour. In the early 20th century an American psychologist, John B. Watson, proposed that psychologists should just study observable behaviour because this is the only way we would be able to measure human behaviour in a scientific way. Watson believed that, by adopting scientific methods, psychology could live up to the natural sciences. For the first half of the 20th century behaviourist psychology dominated psychology.

ASSUMPTION 1: HUMANS ARE BORN LIKE A BLANK SLATE

Behaviourists believe that when we are born our mind is a *'tabula rasa'*, which is the Latin term for blank slate. According to the traditional behaviourist approach, we are not born with in-built mental content; internal events such as thinking and emotion do not drive our behaviour. Instead, the belief is that all of our behaviour is learned from interactions with the environment; we do not think about our behaviour, we respond passively to environmental stimuli.

Central to this assumption is the support for the idea of **nurture** over **nature**, the view that social and environmental factors have the greatest influence on behaviour, over and above innate and biological factors.

Traditional behaviourist theory can be seen to lie at the extreme end of the **nature–nurture debate**, ignoring factors such as **genetics**, **physiology** and **evolution** (all examples of nature) in explaining behaviour.

This perspective is termed **environmental determinism** – our behaviour is determined by the environment that we grew up in. In other words, the associations we make early on in life (e.g. dentists = pain) and the early rewards/punishments provided by our environment (e.g. getting smacked for bad behaviour) pre-determine (heavily influence) our later reactions to other people and situations.

▲ A rat in a Skinner box. The rat might first be reinforced for pressing the lever, which over time should lead to a high frequency of lever-pressing. Then, we might begin to shock these rats after pressing the lever, which over time should lead to a reduced frequency of lever presses.

ASSUMPTION 2: BEHAVIOUR LEARNED THROUGH CONDITIONING

For the behaviourists, we learn through two types of conditioning: classical and operant.

Classical conditioning

In **classical conditioning**, new behaviours are learned through association. Ivan Pavlov first described the process of classical conditioning in 1902 from his observations of salivation in dogs.
- Before conditioning, food is an **unconditioned stimulus** (**UCS**) and salivation is the **unconditioned response** (**UCR**).
- During conditioning, a **neutral stimulus** (**NS**), such as the sound of a bell, is presented alongside the UCS, and this is repeated several times. This is where association occurs.
- After conditioning, the bell is now the **conditioned stimulus** (**CS**) which produces a new **conditioned response** (**CR**) – salivation.

Operant conditioning

In **operant conditioning**, new behaviours are learned through **reinforcement**. A reinforcer is something that will increase the chance that the behaviour will occur again. Reinforcement can be positive or negative and both will shape behaviour.

B.F. Skinner (1938) demonstrated via the Skinner box (see left) that an animal (e.g. pigeon or rat) can learn to behave in certain ways due to being rewarded (positively reinforced) with food. First, the animal may accidentally perform an action that results in a food pellet being given (e.g. pressing a lever).

As the behaviour has been reinforced (rewarded) it is likely that the animal will repeat this behaviour again. This is known as **positive reinforcement**, and any reinforcement will increase the chance that the behaviour will be repeated.

Negative reinforcement *strengthens* behaviour because it involves escaping something unpleasant. For example, completing your homework may result in you *avoiding* detention or *avoiding* making your teacher angry, so you will be more likely to complete your homework the next time.

In operant conditioning, behaviour is also learned through **punishment**. Punishment weakens behaviour and should decrease the likelihood that the behaviour will reoccur again – the opposite of reinforcement. For example, if Skinner's rats received a shock following pressing the lever rather than a food pellet, they were less likely to press the lever again.

Watch Pavlov conditioning animals and children: *https://www.youtube.com/watch?v=N5rXSjld0q4*

B.F. Skinner (1904–1990, named Burrhus Frederic, but Fred to his friends) started out as an English specialist but changed to psychology and became the strongest proponent of behaviourism. He believed that society could provide reinforcements in order to shape behaviour in the most desirable direction. He showed how that could be done in his novel describing a utopian world, *Walden Two*.

Thinking along these lines he created an aircrib for his baby daughter which created reinforcement opportunities. The environment was heated so she could play safely and unhindered.

ASSUMPTION 3: HUMANS AND ANIMALS LEARN IN SIMILAR WAYS

The laws of learning are the same for both humans and non-human animals. It therefore follows that we are able to study animal learning in a **laboratory** environment and make *generalisations* about human behaviour.

Pavlov, for example, developed the principles of classical conditioning with dogs, where he showed how they could be conditioned to salivate at the sound of a bell, applying the principles to humans. These same principles have been applied in **behaviourist therapies**, to help people overcome problems such as **phobias**. In **systematic desensitisation**, for example, the client will learn to *associate* the phobic object (e.g. having an injection) with feelings of relaxation, instead of anxiety.

Similarly, operant conditioning principles that were developed in the confinements of a laboratory with animals (e.g. Skinner's research with rats) are applied in many contexts to help shape human behaviour, for example in education and in prisons. **Token economy systems** are a classic example of this, whereby desirable behaviour is reinforced with tokens that can be exchanged for rewards such as sweets and cigarettes (see page 60).

BEHAVIOURIST EXPLANATION FOR RELATIONSHIP FORMATION

As behaviourists believe that all behaviour is learned from the environment, they would believe that external factors will be most influential in the formation of our relationships. They might explain relationship formation in the following ways.

Operant conditioning

According to operant conditioning principles, reinforcements and punishments drive our behaviour. A new relationship may be positively reinforcing in many ways, for example the attention someone gives us, their compliments or even having the company of someone we like is rewarding. For these reasons, we are likely to repeat the behaviour, i.e. spend more time with them. Also, being with somebody else may help us avoid feelings of loneliness and rejection, and successfully avoiding these feelings is also reinforcing (negative reinforcement). We may also feel punished if we are not in a relationship, for example being on the receiving end of nasty comments from others or excluded from events where only couples are invited. This type of punishment will decrease the likelihood that we will want to be alone and increase the likelihood we will want to form a relationship.

Classical conditioning

As well as liking people with whom we share a pleasant experience, we also like people who are *associated* with pleasant events. If we meet someone when we are feeling happy (positive mood), we are much more inclined to like them than if we meet them when we are feeling unhappy (negative mood). In this way, a previously neutral stimulus (e.g. someone we had not previously met and therefore have no real feelings about) can become positively valued because of their association with a pleasant event (i.e. we learn to like people through the process of classical conditioning). Liking leads to having a relationship.

Example: Explaining the formation of pet–owner relationships

The principles of operant conditioning are used in pet training and these help the formation of good pet–owner relationships. For example, training dogs usually involves rewarding good behaviour with a treat, such as waiting until a dog sits and then giving a reward, or walking without pulling on its leash. These rewards will increase contentment in both the owner and dog and so the good behaviour is likely to be repeated.

Studies have shown that pet owners are less likely to suffer from depression than those without pets, and that people with pets have lower blood pressure in stressful situations than those without pets. Thus the presence of a pet is generally *associated* with positive feelings such as companionship and loyalty (classical conditioning).

TRY THIS

The TV programme *Supernanny* shows nanny Jo Frost taming troublesome children – her techniques involve both direct and indirect reinforcement (positive and negative), as well as punishment.

Look for some examples of the programme on YouTube, and produce a list of examples of the behaviourist approach in action.

In particular, you should look for examples of direct reinforcement (both positive and negative).

TRY THIS

We have applied behaviourist explanations for relationships to pet–owner relationships, just one of the examples given in the specification.

Try to do the same for some of the other examples in the specification: siblings, mother and child, romantic partners and friends. Try to make each one different.

EXAM CORNER

For each assumption named in the specification, you need to be able to:
- Outline the assumption.
- Fully elaborate this assumption, drawing on examples in psychology.

In addition, you need to be able to:
- Use at least **one** assumption to explain the formation of **one** relationship.

Possible exam questions:
1. Describe the assumptions of the behaviourist approach. [12]
2. Outline the 'behaviour is learnt through conditioning' and 'humans are born as a blank slate' assumptions of the behaviourist approach. [4 + 4]
3. Explain how the behaviourist approach might explain relationship formation. [6]

Therapy 1: Aversion therapy

You only study one behaviourist therapy as part of your course – aversion therapy OR systematic desensitisation.

The **behaviourist approach** believes that we are born as a '*tabula rasa*', and that all our behaviour is learned. Learning occurs as a result of two main types of conditioning – **classical conditioning** (learning through *association*) and **operant conditioning** (learning through the *consequences* of our actions).

SPECIFICATION REQUIREMENT

For each approach it will be necessary to:
- Know and understand how the approach can be used in therapy (one therapy per approach).
- Know and understand the main components (principles) of the therapy.
- Evaluate the therapy (including its effectiveness and ethical considerations).

HOW BEHAVIOURIST ASSUMPTIONS APPLY TO AVERSION THERAPY

The main assumption of the behaviourist approach is that all behaviour is learned. Behaviourist therapies in general draw on the principles of classical and operant conditioning in order to help people 'unlearn' learned behaviour. The underlying principles of behavioural therapies are based on the notion that most forms of mental illness occur through maladaptive or faulty learning; therefore, a person can re-learn how to behave in a more functional, healthy way (behaviour modification).

In particular, **aversion therapy** uses the behaviourist assumption of classical conditioning to cause a patient to reduce or avoid an undesirable behaviour pattern. The patient currently has an undesirable behaviour pattern such as alcoholism, and the assumption of classical conditioning is that the patient has learned to *associate* drinking alcohol with pleasurable feelings. The aim of aversion therapy is therefore to condition the patient to associate alcohol (the undesirable behaviour) with an unpleasant or aversive stimulus (such as feeling sick). This should lead to the suppression of the undesirable behaviour.

Aversion therapy also uses another assumption of the behaviourist approach – operant conditioning. Modern forms of aversion therapy use drugs which reward patients for abstinence with feelings of calmness, i.e. **positive reinforcement**. The idea is that, if behaviour is rewarded, then it will be repeated, and so using operant conditioning principles, an alcoholic will repeat their abstinence from alcohol.

Exam advice…

Exam questions may require you to explain how the approach assumptions are applied to the therapy.

You can do this by starting with a general assumption, and applying this to the aims of the therapy.

Then select two specific assumptions and apply these to the therapy.

TRY THIS

One of the uses of aversion therapy is in the treatment of alcoholism. A drug is given to the individual that will make him or her feel very nauseous when having an alcoholic drink.
1. In the scenario above, work out which is the UCS, UCR, NS, CS and CR.
2. You can do the same for the use of electric shocks to treat a smoker.

MAIN COMPONENTS (PRINCIPLES) OF AVERSION THERAPY

How it works

Individuals are repeatedly presented with an aversive (i.e. unpleasant) stimulus, such as an electric shock or a drug that makes them feel nauseous, at the same time that they are engaging in the undesirable behaviour being treated. Note that the use of a shock is not the same as **electroconvulsive therapy** (**ECT**).

The aversive stimulus (the shock) is a **UCS**, which produces a **UCR**, such as avoidance. When the aversive stimulus (the shock) is repeatedly paired with the undesirable behaviour (such as drinking alcohol), the behaviour (e.g. violence, which was an **NS** and is now a **CS**) leads to the same consequences. As a result, clients lose their wish to engage in the undesirable behaviour.

Covert sensitisation

Covert sensitisation is a unique type of aversion therapy that follows the same basic principles, but the unwanted consequence is not actually present in the therapy. Instead the therapy relies on the client's ability to use their imagination rather than actually experiencing the negative consequences. For example, alcoholics are required to imagine upsetting, repulsive or frightening scenes while they are drinking. This form of therapy, called covert sensitisation, is used much less commonly than other forms of aversion therapy.

The therapist may verbally encourage the client to imagine scenarios that get progressively worse (e.g. from imagining feeling really sick after drinking alcohol, to imagining vomiting over someone on a first date because of too much alcohol), and so employs principles of **systematic desensitisation** too (discussed on the next spread).

New developments

Recent developments in the treatment of alcoholism have refined the use of traditional aversion therapy. Researchers have discovered drugs that make users sick if they mix them with alcohol, but also reward abstinence by inducing feelings of tranquillity and well-being (Badawy, 1999). These compounds (known as *tryptophan metabolites*) prevent alcohol from being properly converted within the body, turning it into a chemical that causes unpleasant effects such as nausea, vomiting and hot flushes. Unlike conventional aversion compounds, however, these also offer an incentive for staying with the treatment.

Operant conditioning

Aversion therapy employs principles of operant conditioning as well as classical conditioning. Once the *association* has been made between the once-pleasant stimulus (e.g. alcohol) and an unpleasant response (e.g. feelings of sickness), the person tends to avoid future contact with the stimulus, for example an alcoholic might avoid going into pubs or other social situations where people are drinking. Thus, negative reinforcement (avoidance of a what is now an unpleasant situation) is in operation, motivating the individual to continue to avoid these situations.

EXAM CORNER

For each therapy, you will need to be able to:
- Describe how the assumptions of the approach are applied in the therapy.
- Describe the main components (principles) of the therapy.
- Evaluate the therapy in terms of its effectiveness.
- Evaluate the therapy in terms of ethical considerations.

Possible exam questions:
1. Describe how the assumptions of the behaviourist approach are applied in aversion therapy. [8]
2. Describe the main components (principles) of aversion therapy. [10]
3. Evaluate aversion therapy in terms of its effectiveness and ethical considerations. [10]
4. Evaluate the ethical issues raised in aversion therapy. [6]

◄ Stanley Kubrick's film *A Clockwork Orange*, an adaptation of the novel by Anthony Burgess, is set in a violent near-future UK, and portrays the extreme use of aversion therapy as social control. Alex, a teenage hooligan, is captured by the police and jailed. There he undergoes aversion therapy to make him unable to commit further violence. Alex is strapped into a chair in front of a large theatre screen. His head is tied down and his eyes are forced open with metal clips. He is then injected with a drug that makes him feel violently ill, and is forced to watch images of horrific violence. After a few weeks of treatment, Alex is ready to return to society, now conditioned so that violence makes him feel ill.

EVALUATION: EFFECTIVENESS

Research

In a study of alcoholics, Miller (1978) compared the effectiveness of three types of treatment:
- Aversion therapy (using shocks).
- **Counselling** therapy plus aversion.
- Counselling alone.

One year later, recovery was the same for all groups, indicating that aversion therapy offered no benefit.

In contrast, Smith *et al.* (1997) found that alcoholics treated with aversion therapy (using shocks or a drug to induce nausea) had higher abstinence rates after one year than those treated with counselling alone. Smith (1988) also reported success with a group of 300 smokers: 52% of those treated with shocks maintained abstinence after one year.

Dropout

Aversion therapies often suffer from problems of patient dropout. Bancroft (1992) reported that up to 50% of patients either refuse treatment or drop out of aversion therapy programmes, which makes it difficult to evaluate such therapies if only willing patients engage in the therapy in the first place.

Are the effects long term?

Whether the positive effects of aversion therapy last long term is questionable. Many patients appear to be treated in the confinements of a therapist's office and may appear to recover. However, these effects are not likely to transfer to the outside world, when the punishing consequences of sickness-enhancing drugs or electric shocks have disappeared. Research on classical conditioning by Pavlov showed that a conditioned response is **extinguished** when the CS is no longer paired with the UCS.

Symptom substitution

Although therapies based on behaviourist assumptions can be effective in modifying behaviour, critics argue that the therapies fail to treat the possible underlying causes. This is because the behaviourist approach believes that the maladaptive behaviour *is* the disorder and therefore there are no underlying causes to be treated. One consequence of this is that the original symptoms may be removed (e.g. alcohol addiction), yet new symptoms appear in a different form (e.g. gambling addiction). This happens because there is an underlying cause that has not been identified. This is called **symptom substitution**.

TRY THIS

Expand your knowledge

In January 2014, Channel 4 aired a documentary in which the popular Dr Christian Jessen went undercover to explore the treatment of homosexuality using aversion therapy in the UK and USA.
www.channel4.com/programmes/undercover-doctor-cure-me-im-gay
You may want to watch this in order to increase your understanding of how the therapy was used, and to discuss some of the ethical issues involved in the treatment.

EVALUATION: ETHICAL ISSUES

The treatment of homosexuality

For many years aversion therapy was used in the UK and USA as a treatment to 'cure' homosexuality. Shockingly it wasn't until 2006 that the American Psychiatric Association (APA) considered this method too unethical. The method was used on men, and involved them being given drugs to make them feel nauseous as well as being placed in dirty surroundings while being shown pin-up pictures of males. It was thought that this would cause them to form an association between negative feelings and the images in order to 'turn them straight'.

In 1962 Billy Clegg-Hill died after he had undergone aversion therapy to 'cure' his homosexuality. At the time, it was claimed he had died of natural causes but he had in fact died from a coma and convulsions caused by *Apomorphine*, a vomit-inducing drug (BBC, 2009).

Control

Aversion therapy is seriously unpleasant for the patient, and for this reason has been branded unethical. Techniques which involve punishment in particular (e.g. electric shocks) have been criticised for exercising too much control over the patient, and 'brainwashing' them into treatment. However, this therapy cannot be administered without full patient consent, where all other attempts at treatment have failed. Also, new developments in aversion therapy (facing page) have resulted in more refined treatments.

In response to such ethical criticisms, some therapists will use covert sensitisation as an alternative 'milder' form of therapy (see facing page).

Therapy 2: Systematic desensitisation

You only study one behaviourist therapy as part of your course – aversion therapy OR systematic desensitisation.

SPECIFICATION REQUIREMENT

For each approach it will be necessary to:
- Know and understand how the approach can be used in therapy (one therapy per approach).
- Know and understand the main components (principles) of the therapy.
- Evaluate the therapy (including its effectiveness and ethical considerations).

The **behaviourist approach** believes that we are born as a '*tabula rasa*', and that all our behaviour is learned. Learning occurs as a result of two main types of conditioning – **classical conditioning** (learning through *association*) and **operant conditioning** (learning through the *consequences* of our actions).

Exam advice...

Exam questions may require you to explain how the approach assumptions are applied to the therapy.

You can do this by starting with a general assumption, and applying this to the aims of the therapy.

Then select two specific assumptions and apply these to the therapy.

HOW BEHAVIOURIST ASSUMPTIONS APPLY TO SYSTEMATIC DESENSITISATION

The main assumption of the behaviourist approach is that all behaviour is learned. Behaviourist therapies in general draw on the principles of classical and operant conditioning in order to help people 'unlearn' learned behaviour. The underlying principles of behavioural therapies are based on the notion that most forms of mental illness occur through maladaptive or faulty learning; therefore, a person can re-learn how to behave in a more functional, healthy way (behaviour modification).

In particular, **systematic desensitisation** is based mainly on classical conditioning principles, and the idea of stimulus–response association. It was developed by Joseph Wolpe in the 1950s and is used to treat **phobic disorders**, assuming that the client has learned to associate the phobic object with fear. It is based on the idea of **counterconditioning**, where the client learns to associate the phobic object with being relaxed rather than being anxious. This is the idea of **reciprocal inhibition** – that we cannot easily experience two contrasting states of emotion at the same time.

Operant conditioning principles also feature in this therapy. When the client successfully feels relaxed in the presence of the phobic object, this is rewarding, and such **positive reinforcement** encourages the client to move up the hierarchy to more feared situations.

How does it work?

▲ **Problem** – Patient is terrified whenever she sees a spider.

▲ **Result** – After SD, patient has overcome her fear of spiders and feels relaxed in their presence.

Step 1: Patient is taught how to relax their muscles completely. (A relaxed state is incompatible with anxiety.)

Step 2: Therapist and patient together construct a desensitisation hierarchy – a series of imagined scenes, each one causing a little more anxiety than the previous one.

Step 3: Patient gradually works his/her way through desensitisation hierarchy, visualising each anxiety-evoking event while engaging in the competing relaxation response.

Step 4: Once the patient has mastered one step in the heirarchy (i.e. they can remain relaxed while imagining it), they are ready to move onto the next.

Step 5: Patient eventually masters the feared situation that caused them to seek help in the first place.

CLASSICAL CONDITIONING AND COUNTERCONDITIONING

Pavlov's theory of classical conditioning explains how previously neutral stimuli (such as snakes, supermarkets, or even clocks) can provoke anxiety in some people because they have become associated with a different event that we naturally find distressing. A distressing event, e.g. being bitten (**UCS**), produces a natural fear response (**UCR**). An **NS**, e.g. the presence of a dog, becomes associated with the UCS, and thus the NS comes also to produce the UCR. They are now called the **CS** and the **CR**, respectively.

There is a reverse side to classical conditioning, called *counterconditioning*. This involves *reducing* a conditioned response (such as anxiety) by establishing an incompatible response (relaxation) to the same conditioned stimulus (e.g. snake, supermarket, or whatever).

MAIN COMPONENTS (PRINCIPLES) OF SYSTEMATIC DESENSITISATION (SD)

An individual may learn that their feared stimulus is not so fearful after all – if only they could re-experience the feared stimulus. However, this never happens because the anxiety the stimulus creates blocks any attempt to re-experience it. Joseph Wolpe developed a technique in the 1950s where phobics were *gradually* introduced to a feared stimulus.

Counterconditioning

The diagram on the left shows the steps of SD. The process begins with learning relaxation techniques. The eventual aim is to acquire a new stimulus–response link, moving from responding to a stimulus with fear, to responding to the feared stimulus with relaxation. This is called counterconditioning, because the client is taught a new association that runs counter to the original association. Wolpe also called this 'reciprocal inhibition' because the relaxation *inhibits* the anxiety.

Desensitisation hierarchy

The diagram on the left also shows how learning proceeds through a desensitisation hierarchy, a series of gradual steps that are determined at the beginning of therapy when the client and therapist work out a hierarchy of feared stimuli from least fearful to most fearful.

Different forms of SD

In the early days of SD, clients would learn to confront their feared situations directly (***in vivo*** desensitisation), by learning to relax in the presence of objects or images that would normally arouse anxiety. In more recent years, however, rather than actually presenting the feared stimulus, the therapist asks the subject to *imagine* the presence of it (***in vitro*** or **covert desensitisation**).

Research has found that actual contact with the feared stimulus is most successful, so *in vivo* techniques are more successful than covert ones (Menzies and Clarke, 1993). Often a number of different exposure techniques are involved – *in vivo*, covert and also modelling, where the client watches someone else who is coping well with the feared stimulus (Comer, 2002).

An alternative is self-administered SD. Humphrey (1973) reports that this has proved effective with, for example, social phobia.

EXAM CORNER

For each therapy, you will need to be able to:
- Describe how the assumptions of the approach are applied in the therapy.
- Describe the main components (principles) of the therapy.
- Evaluate the therapy in terms of its effectiveness.
- Evaluate the therapy in terms of ethical considerations.

Possible exam questions:
1. Describe **two or more** ways in which the assumptions of the behaviourist approach can be applied in systematic desensitisation. [8]
2. Describe the main components (principles) of systematic desensitisation. [12]
3. Assess the effectiveness of systematic desensitisation. [10]
4. Evaluate systematic desensitisation in terms of ethical considerations. [6]

TRY THIS

1. Think of your own example of a phobia (this could be an object or a situation).
2. Learn some relaxation techniques. For example, look at: *www.umm.edu/sleep/relax_tech.htm* (useful for exam stress!).
3. Develop a desensitisation hierarchy for your phobia.
4. Practise systematic desensitisation!

▲ American singer, actress and director Barbra Streisand developed a social phobia while giving a concert during which she forgot the words to several songs. For 27 years she avoided any public engagements. During an interview in 2006 with Oprah Winfrey, Barbra revealed that she had overcome her social phobia through the use of **antianxiety drugs** and by gradually exposing herself to more public performances, starting with a small warm-up show, then a national tour, and finally performing in front of a large television audience – a desensitisation hierarchy!

EVALUATION: EFFECTIVENESS

Research support

Generally SD has been proven to be successful when the problem is a learned one, for example specific phobias. For example, Capafóns *et al.* (1998) found that clients with a fear of flying showed less physiological signs of fear and reported lower fear levels whilst in a flight simulator following a 12–25-week treatment period, where both *in vitro* and *in vivo* techniques were used.

Not appropriate for all phobias

Some research suggests that SD is not effective for more generalised fears (e.g. agoraphobia). In addition, the therapy may not be suitable for 'ancient fears'. Martin Seligman (1970) argued that animals, including humans, are genetically programmed to rapidly learn an association between potentially life-threatening stimuli and fear. These stimuli are referred to as ancient fears – things that would have been dangerous in our **evolutionary** past (such as snakes, heights, strangers). It would have been **adaptive** to rapidly learn to avoid such stimuli.

This concept of **biological preparedness** would explain why people are much less likely to develop fears of modern objects such as toasters and cars that are much more of a threat than spiders. Such items were not a danger in our evolutionary past.

Research support for biological preparedness

Seligman's concept has been supported by research studies. For example, Bregman (1934) failed to condition a fear response in infants aged 8 to 16 months by pairing a loud bell with wooden blocks. It may be that fear responses are only learned with living animals, a link with ancient fears.

Symptom substitution

Behavioural therapies may not work with certain phobias because the symptoms are only the tip of the iceberg. If you remove the symptoms the cause still remains, and the symptoms will simply resurface, possibly in another form (**symptom substitution**).

For example, according to the **psychodynamic approach** phobias develop because of **projection**. Freud (1909) recorded the case of Little Hans who developed a phobia of horses. The boy's actual problem was an intense envy of his father but he could not express this directly and his anxiety was projected onto the horse. The phobia was cured when he accepted his feelings about his father. If the therapist had treated the horse phobia the underlying problem would have remained and resurfaced elsewhere.

Behavioural therapies may *appear* to resolve a problem but simply eliminating or suppressing symptoms can result in other symptoms appearing.

EVALUATION: ETHICAL ISSUES

Anxiety controlled

Generally SD is considered to be more **ethical** than other forms of behavioural therapies, such as 'flooding' techniques, which involve rapidly exposing the client to their most feared phobia.

In SD each step is conducted slowly and at a pace dictated largely by the client. Therefore the therapist is able to gauge whether the client is fully relaxed at each stage of the therapy. The therapist must only attempt to move up the hierarchy when the client is completely comfortable – therefore, anxiety should not be an issue.

Able to provide valid consent

SD is used mainly with phobias, and not with problems such as **depression** and **schizophrenia**. This means that clients are 'in touch' with reality and in a 'healthy' enough frame of mind to understand what the therapy will entail. This means they are able to provide **valid consent** to the therapy.

In addition, the client attends the therapy sessions at their own **free will** and so is able to choose to withdraw at any point. Some would argue that there is still an element of stress involved as the client is exposed in one way or another to an object/situation that they may have spent many years, or decades, feeling anxious about, and therefore avoiding mild levels of anxiety is impossible.

Classic evidence: Watson and Rayner (1920)

CONDITIONED EMOTIONAL REACTIONS

SPECIFICATION REQUIREMENT

For each approach it will be necessary to:
- Know and understand a classic piece of evidence (including methodology, procedures, findings and conclusions).

John B. Watson has been called the father of **behaviourism**. We mentioned him at the beginning of this chapter as the person who first proposed that psychologists should study only observable behaviour because this is the only way we would be able to measure human behaviour in a scientific way. He thus created the science of behaviourism.

Watson's work was concerned with **classical conditioning** (B.F. Skinner's **operant conditioning** was introduced a bit later). Pavlov had demonstrated that behaviour could be conditioned but Watson wondered if emotions could also be conditioned. He proposed that we learn responses such as fear, rage and love through conditioning. We are not born with such emotional responses but acquire them from experiences.

This study was an attempt to test whether it could be shown that our emotions can be acquired through classical conditioning.

CLASSICAL CONDITIONING

Before conditioning

White rat
NS
→
No response

Loud noise
UCS
→
Fear response
UCR

During conditioning

White rat + loud noise
NS + UCS
→
Fear response
UCR

After conditioning

White rat
CR
→
Fear response
CR

METHODOLOGY

This study involves one participant – a normal male infant aged nine months. In this study he was referred to as 'Albert B' but has since become known as 'Little Albert'.

This is not a **case study** because the focus was only on Little Albert's response to conditioning; a case study would involve a more in-depth analysis of the individual and aspects of their life.

The study is not an **experiment** because there was only one condition. It is simply an investigation to determine the effects of certain stimuli. Watson and Rayner call it an experiment but the use of that term has become more restricted. It was conducted in controlled conditions – in a well-lit dark room (i.e. a room where photographs were normally developed). Albert was placed on a mattress that was on top of a table.

The study could be described as a **controlled observation**.

PROCEDURES

Responses were recorded with a motion picture camera. The picture at the bottom of the facing page is from that record.

Emotional tests
To test Albert's emotional responses to certain objects he was confronted suddenly with a white rat, a rabbit, a dog, a monkey, masks with and without hair, cotton wool, burning newspapers, etc. (not all at the same time). In each instance this was the first time he had seen the objects.

Albert was then tested with a loud sound, made by striking a hammer upon a suspended steel bar. The bar was just over one metre in length and 2 cm in diameter. One experimenter got Albert's attention while the other used the hammer to strike the bar behind Albert's head.

Session 1: Establishing a conditioned emotional response
When Albert was 11 months 3 days old they brought him to their 'lab' again. A white rat was presented to him and Albert started to reach for it. At that moment the bar was struck just behind his head.

Session 2: Testing the conditioned emotional response
A week later Albert was returned for more testing, aged 11 months 10 days. He was shown the rat with no sound to see if the previous experience affected his behaviour with the rat.

After this Albert was exposed five times to the 'joint stimulation', i.e. he was shown the rat and the loud noise was made behind his head at the same time.

Session 3: Generalisation
At 11 months 15 days Albert returned for further testing. The research question at this time was whether the learned link between rat and noise would be generalised to other objects.

Albert was variously presented with the rat, wooden blocks, a rabbit, a dog, a seal fur coat, cotton wool and John Watson's hair.

Session 4: Changing the environment
At 11 months 20 days Albert's conditioned emotional response was 'freshened' up using some 'joint stimulation'. He was then taken to a new environment – a large well-lit lecture room with four people present. He was placed on a table in the centre of the room.

Session 5: The effect of time
At 12 months 21 days Albert was tested for one last time. He had been to the lab in the interim but no emotional tests had been conducted. The final tests involved a Santa Claus mask, a fur coat, the rat, the rabbit, the dog and the blocks.

FINDINGS

Emotional tests
Albert showed no fear response to the objects before conditioning. In fact hospital attendants and Albert's mother reported that they had never seen him in a state of fear or rage, and he practically never cried.

The first time the bar was struck behind his head the researchers recorded his response:

The child started violently, his breathing was checked and the arms were raised in a characteristic manner. On the second stimulation the same thing occurred, and in addition the lips began to pucker and tremble. On the third stimulation the child broke into a sudden crying fit. This is the first time an emotional situation in the laboratory has produced any fear or even crying in Albert. (Watson and Rayner, 1920, page 313)

Session 1: Establishing a conditioned emotional response
Albert was tested again, this time with a white rat. When the bar was struck he jumped and fell forward, burying his head on the table where he was sat, but did not cry. When the bar was struck a second time he fell forward again, this time whimpering a little.

Session 2: Testing the conditioned emotional response
When retested a week later Albert showed a new response to the rat. This time he did not reach for it, he just stared at it. When the rat was then placed nearer, he reached out carefully towards it but withdrew his hand when the rat started to nuzzle his hand.

Albert's cautious behaviour was tested by giving him some blocks to play with, which he did happily. This shows his cautious response was just to the rat and also shows that his general emotional state was normal.

After further 'joint stimulation' pairing the rat with the loud noise, Albert became more and more distressed. When he was again shown the rat he began to cry *'and began to crawl away so rapidly that he was caught with difficulty before reaching the edge of the table'* (1920, page 314).

Session 3: Generalisation
Albert played happily with the blocks but when shown the rat immediately responded with fear, indicating that he retained his conditioned emotional response to the rat.

His response to the rabbit was as extreme as to the rat. He burst into tears and crawled away. Neither the dog nor fur coat produced as violent a reaction as the rabbit.

The cotton wool was in a paper package which Albert played with, not touching the cotton wool at first but later being less cautious.

Albert played with Watson's hair, showing no fear response.

Session 4: Changing the environment
After being taken to the new environment Albert's responses to the rat, rabbit and dog were less extreme than before. After further 'freshening up' (exposure to rat plus loud noise) the conditioned fear response was stronger.

Even when the fear response was weak it was noticeably different from his reaction to the building blocks – he always played with those happily and never whimpered. This showed that a distinct learned response persisted towards the furry objects.

Session 5: The effect of time
Albert responded to the test objects in a clearly different way than to the control objects (the blocks). His reaction to the furry objects was not as extreme as previously but he clearly avoided them and whimpered. On occasions he cried.

CONCLUSIONS

This study demonstrated the ease with which a fear response can be created. Just two 'joint stimulations' in the first week were sufficient to create the conditioned emotional response. Just seven 'joint stimulations' were given to bring about the complete reaction.

This study also demonstrated that such learned (conditioned) responses generalise to similar stimuli – Albert maintained a fearful response to many different furry objects over the time he was studied.

Watson and Rayner suggest that 'it is probable' that many phobias are acquired in this way. However, they suspected that the persistence of early conditioned responses would only be found in persons who are 'constitutionally inferior'.

The Freudian position
At the time of this study (1920) Freudian explanations were favoured in psychology and Watson and Rayner addressed these specifically.

First of all they noted that Albert often started sucking his thumb when scared, possibly a form of sexual stimulation. Watson and Rayner therefore suggest that Freud may have been wrong in presuming that such stimulation is pleasure seeking. Instead it may be a form of compensation to block fear.

Second, Watson and Rayner describe a scene in the future where their Little Albert, now in his 20s, might seek help from a Freudian therapist for a phobia of furry objects. Such a therapist will analyse Albert's fear of a seal skin coat and might propose that young Albert had tried to play with the pubic hair of his mother and was scolded violently for it. This scolding would cause Albert to push the memory into his **unconscious** mind, where it would continue to exert an effect – leading to a phobia of furry objects.

Watson and Rayner suppose that a fear could actually be *conditioned* by the experience with a mother's pubic hair rather than the mistaken Freudian interpretation of what happened.

▲ Rosalie Rayner and John B. Watson conditioning fear in Little Albert.

TRY THIS

According to Watson and Rayner people acquire phobias because of a previous series of unpleasant experiences.

Ask people about their fears – do they recall a traumatic episode in the past when they might have been classically conditioned?

Exam advice...
A lot has been written about Watson and Rayner's research. It is good to read or watch secondary sources to help your understanding of this research, but be careful. The information about the method, procedures, findings and conclusions has to be taken only from the original article. Other sources may include 'myths' about Watson and Rayner's research, which would not receive credit in the exam.

Classic evidence: Watson and Rayner (1920) (continued)

SPECIFICATION REQUIREMENT

For each approach it will be necessary to:
- Make judgements on a classic piece of evidence including ethical issues and social implications.

TRY THIS

When researchers write a report of their study they usually write an **abstract**.

You can write an abstract for this study (and all the other classic studies in this book).

This abstract should contain brief details of the context and aims, procedures, findings and conclusions of this study – all in about 200 words.

THINGS TO DO

WWW
There are various video clips on YouTube, such as: *www.youtube.com/watch?v=Xt0ucxOrPQE*

You can see some of the original footage here: *www.youtube.com/watch?v=9hBfnXACsOI*

Original article
The full reference for this classic study is Watson, J.B. and Rayner, R. (1920) Conditioned emotional responses. *Journal of Experimental Psychology*, 3, 1–14.

The original article can be found at: *http://psychclassics.yorku.ca/Watson/emotion.htm*

Other resources
Learn about phobias at *www.phobias.about.com* or *www.nhs.uk/conditions/Phobias/Pages/Introduction.aspx*

You can see the criteria for specific phobias at: *www.behavenet.com/capsules/disorders/specphob.htm*

Read a Freudian account of how phobias develop – the case of Little Hans: *www.simplypsychology.org/little-hans.html*

▼ The **psychodynamic approach** would suggest that a fear of rats is caused by a traumatic experience that is buried in the **unconscious**. **Ego defence mechanisms** cause the trauma to be **displaced** onto a different object – a rat – so that we are afraid of the rat rather than the real trauma.

On this spread we are going to evaluate the classic study by looking at issues related to its methodology, and comparing the study to alternative evidence. When it comes to evaluation, you can make up your own mind. We have presented some evidence and statements, and invite you to use these to construct your own view of the classic study. You can use your knowledge of research methods as well.

EVALUATION: METHODOLOGY AND PROCEDURES

Controlled study

The study of Little Albert was carefully devised and run under controlled conditions. The study was conducted in a 'lab' of sorts (the dark room) where **extraneous variables** could be controlled.

There were other controls in place:
- There was a baseline condition where his pre-manipulation behaviour was established to show that he was not a fearful child.
- During the trials there was a **control condition** (the building blocks) which showed that Albert's fearful responses were exclusively to furry objects.
- Films were used to record Albert's behaviour so that the findings can be confirmed by others.

All of these controls enable us to conclude that the observed effects were due to the conditioning rather than other sources.

The sample

It was the researchers' intention to eventually study more than one participant. However, their dismissal from the University (see 'Meet the researchers' on facing page) meant they couldn't do this. Therefore any conclusions must be drawn from this one case. Watson and Rayner describe Albert as 'an extremely phlegmatic type', i.e. he was a calm and even-tempered baby. They suggest that, had he been emotionally unstable, he might have responded with even greater fear and the conditioned response might have persisted even longer.

Without any comparisons it is difficult to know whether the observed responses are unique to this individual or not.

EVALUATION: ALTERNATIVE EVIDENCE

The two-process theory

One of the criticisms of **classical conditioning** as an explanation for phobias is that it can't explain how they persist. Watson and Rayner talk about 'freshening' up Albert's conditioned response after a week. In other words, when Albert did not experience the rat and loud noise together the conditioned response lessened. If only classical conditioning was involved it might just disappear over time.

O.H. Mowrer (1947) explained why it doesn't disappear. In his two-process model, the first stage is classical conditioning and then, in a second stage, **operant conditioning** occurs. Classical conditioning explains how phobias are acquired and operant conditioning explains how they are maintained. Once a fear is learned an individual will avoid the situation producing the fear (e.g. Albert would avoid furry things in the future). The avoidance of (or escape from) the phobic stimulus reduces fear and is thus reinforcing. This is an example of **negative reinforcement** (escaping from an unpleasant situation). The fact that no anxiety is experienced from this avoidance behaviour is **positively reinforcing**. This reinforcement maintains the avoidance response.

Learning is not the only explanation

There are a number of other issues with conditioning as an explanation for phobias. First of all not all phobias are preceded by a conditioning episode – though it is possible that such traumatic incidents did happen, but have since been forgotten (Öst, 1987). It is also the case that some people who have experienced a traumatic incident, such as being bitten by a dog, do not develop a phobia (Di Nardo *et al.*, 1988). Therefore learning alone cannot explain all phobias.

One alternative explanation is **biological preparedness** (discussed on page 55). Martin Seligman (1970) argued that animals, including humans, are genetically programmed to rapidly learn an association between certain stimuli and fear. These stimuli are referred to as ancient fears – things that would have been dangerous in our **evolutionary** past (such as snakes, heights, strangers, even rats). It is **adaptive** to rapidly learn to avoid such stimuli.

When **John B. Watson** conducted this study he was 42 years old and had played a major role in the development of **behaviourism**. Rosalie Rayner (1896–1935) was his graduate student, who became his lover. As a consequence of their affair Watson left his wife and was asked to resign from the University where they both worked. He then took up an entirely new career as an advertising executive for a prestigious New York City firm, applying behaviourist principles to advertising.

Watson and Rayner married, had two sons and wrote the most popular child care guide of its time: *Psychological Care of Infant and Child*. As good behaviourists they believed that parents should focus on the environment in which they raised their children and also believed that parental affection was detrimental to independence, so their sons were not kissed or cuddled at home. One son later wrote:

▲ John B. Watson (1878–1958)

'I honestly believe the principles for which Dad stood as a behaviourist eroded both Bill's and my ability to deal effectively with human emotion…and it tended to undermine self-esteem in later life, ultimately contributing to Bill's [suicide] and to my own crisis. Tragically, that's the antithesis of what Dad expected from practicing these philosophies' (Smirle, 2013).

ETHICAL ISSUES AND SOCIAL IMPLICATIONS

The Watson and Rayner study often appears on lists of the most unethical studies in psychology. There are two main reasons: it involved creating fear in a young child and the effects were potentially long lasting, both of which are related to **psychological harm**.

Creating fear

Watson and Rayner seemed unsure about whether they had created excessive fear in Albert. Early in their article they say *'We felt that we could do him relatively little harm in the studies'*. However, later they say *'in order not to disturb the child too seriously no further tests were given for one week'*. This sounds like they were aware that what they were doing was distressing to Albert.

Psychologists determine what is or isn't ethically acceptable in psychological research by considering whether a research participant is experiencing distress greater than they would in everyday life. Watson and Rayner comforted themselves by saying that *'such attachments would arise anyway as soon as the child left the sheltered environment of the nursery for the rough and tumble of the home'*. In other words, they felt what Albert experienced in their study was fairly normal – but life in the hospital protected him.

More psychological harm

In addition to the **risk of harm** caused by creating fear in a young child, Watson and Rayner made the experience worse. They noted that one of Albert's responses, when frightened, was to start sucking his thumb. This had the effect of calming Albert down – but it also meant that it reduced the effect of the loud noise on conditioning Albert. Therefore, in order to observe the full effects of the fearful stimuli, they had to remove his thumb from his mouth so the conditioned response could be obtained. In other words they wanted to make sure he really was scared.

Lasting effects

Watson and Rayner did intend to remove Allbert's learned conditioned responses. However, Albert was suddenly removed from the hospital so this could not be done. Watson and Rayner believed that the responses they created would be likely to persist indefinitely in the home environment, unless an accidental method for removing them was hit upon. In other words they knew he would continue to be fearful of furry objects.

The researchers should have anticipated this issue at the beginning of the study and ensured that procedures were put in place to prevent the situation happening. For example, at the outset, the child's mother should have been fully informed of the procedures and the anticipated long-term consequences. The researchers should have ensured that 'unconditioning' took place.

See the next spread for a discussion of further ethical and social implications of this topic.

EXAM CORNER

You will need to be able to do the following with respect to the study by Watson and Rayner (1920):

Describe:
- The methodology of the study (describe and justify; includes characteristics of the sample but not the sampling technique).
- The procedures of the study (what the researcher did; includes the sampling technique).
- The findings of the study.
- The conclusions of the study.

Evaluate:
- The methodology of the study.
- The procedures of the study.
- The findings of the study (use methodology and/or alternative evidence).
- The conclusions of the study (use methodology and/or alternative evidence).
- The ethical issues and social implications.

Possible exam questions:
1. Outline the methodology of Watson and Rayner's (1920) research *'Conditioned emotional reactions.'* [3]
2. Outline the procedures used by Watson and Rayner's (1920) research *'Conditioned emotional reactions.'* [10]
3. *'Watson and Rayner's research was vital in showing that classical conditioning principles established in non-human animals could be applied to learning.'* Discuss the ethical issues and social implications that arose in Watson and Rayner's (1920) research *'Conditioned emotional reactions.'* [12]

THE REAL ALBERT B

In the article Watson and Rayner describe Albert B as a *'child reared almost from birth in a hospital environment; his mother was a wet nurse in the Harriet Lane Home for Invalid Children. Albert's life was normal: he was healthy from birth and one of the best developed youngsters ever brought to the hospital, weighing twenty-one pounds at nine months of age. He was on the whole stolid and unemotional. His stability was one of the principal reasons for using him as a subject in this test'* (2000, page 213).

A number of researchers have sought to discover who Albert B really was. Some lengthy detective work led researcher Hall Beck (2012) to conclude that Little Albert was Douglas Merritte, a baby who sadly died at a young age from hydrocephalus (water on the brain). If correct, this suggests that the baby may have had brain damage from birth and challenges the whole foundation of the study.

More recent research has identified someone else – William Albert Barger. Russ Powell and Nancy Digdon (2014) reported that their Albert died in 2007. They interviewed his niece who said Barger had a lifelong aversion to animals – family dogs had to be kept in a separate room whenever he visited. So it might appear that the conditioning had a lifelong effect after all!

Contemporary debate: Using conditioning techniques to control the behaviour of children

SPECIFICATION REQUIREMENT

For each approach it will be necessary to:
- Understand what is at the core of the debate.
- Refer to psychological studies and theories.
- Explore both sides of the contemporary debate from a psychological perspective (including the ethical, economic and social implications).

ETHICAL, SOCIAL AND ECONOMIC IMPLICATIONS

The impact of conditioning techniques have an important effect on society and thus economics.

Vulnerable children may especially benefit from conditioning techniques. By making their behaviour more 'normal' it should make them more likely to be accepted within society, thus allowing them to participate as fully as possible within society and rewarding employment.

However, the frequent use of rewards may actually lead to a society whereby some people are only motivated by extrinsic factors, meaning society may become less cohesive and more selfish.

Rewards or incentives are frequently used in education to improve outcomes. Levitt *et al.* (2010) reviewed a programme in Chicago, USA, where children were offered financial incentives to improve, resulting in modest gains in performance. This would ultimately benefit our society because school leavers would be better educated.

On the other hand Gneezy *et al.* (2011) claim that incentive programmes in education do not always offer the best return on investment. With many schools and education authorities having to operate on a diminishing budget, it is questionable whether it is **ethical** to pay or reward students for their performance, when that money could be better spent elsewhere.

▼ By rewarding household chores with pocket money are we creating a generation who are only motivated by money?

Using conditioning techniques is a highly contentious area because it involves the manipulation of someone else's behaviour – and not necessarily with their knowledge. Advocates believe such techniques offer a host of benefits to children, their parents, teachers, peers and society on the whole. Detractors believe they are creating a generation of selfish automatons.

CONDITIONING TECHNIQUES ARE APPROPRIATE

At home

Supernanny Jo Frost used the 'naughty step' to correct inappropriate behaviour. When a child is naughty, their mother may shout. This kind of attention, even though it is unpleasant, is **positively reinforcing**. The way to deal with this is to resist any kind of reinforcement. 'Supernanny Team' (*www.supernanny.co.uk*) techniques such as the naughty step work best when parents make a fuss of what their child does right, i.e. giving positive reinforcement at appropriate times.

Parental control over pocket money has long been used to increase positive behaviours, such as washing the car or tidying a child's bedroom. Gill (1998) asked parents to encourage chore completion by the payment of pocket money (positive reinforcement) or the postponement of pocket money (**punishment**). The researcher concluded that these strategies were successful because children ended up performing 20% of the household chores.

In school

Education has been a major user of **operant conditioning** techniques to control the behaviour of children. Gold stars, merits and even house points are positive reinforcers, the aim of which is obviously to reward good behaviour and performance. Praise is also reinforcing. McAllister *et al.* (1969) looked at inappropriate talking in high school English classes and found that the increased use of 'teacher praise' and 'teacher disapproval' led to a decrease in 'inappropriate talking'. In a **control condition** there was no decrease.

LeFrançois (2000) suggests that **classical conditioning** can be used to improve student performance. For example, he proposes that teachers should maximise the pleasant stimuli in their classrooms (including attractive wall displays, nice smells and laughter) and minimise the unpleasant stimuli (such as shouting, negative comments). This means students have more positive feelings about the work environment and their behaviour and/or academic performance will improve.

Peers

A child's peers are children who are similar in age and development. We may start off being influenced by our parents, but when we move to nursery and later to school, the influence of our peer group starts to grow. In order to reduce the negative sanctions of a peer group (such as exclusion and criticism) and increase positive sanctions (such as praise and acceptance), children imitate the behaviours and actions of their peers. We are conditioned by our peers.

Vulnerable groups of children

Psychologists use conditioning techniques with various psychological and medical conditions. For example, Lovaas (1987) developed **applied behaviour analysis (ABA)** to increase the frequency and quality of social interactions for children with **autistic spectrum disorder**. Target behaviours might include language difficulties or problems with self-care. One-on-one therapy shapes the behaviour of the child; initially the child is rewarded for most behaviours but over time the rewards are reduced and are only issued if the behaviour is close to the ideal target behaviour.

Robinson *et al.* (1981) showed how the use of **token economies** can improve performance in reading and vocabulary-related tasks of children with hyperactivity issues. In a token economy students are given rewards (tokens) for desirable behaviours, which then they get to collect and exchange for rewards. Students may periodically exchange the tokens for rewards, which are items or activities desirable to them.

Chaney *et al.* (2004) reported on the use of a 'Funhaler' with children with asthma, basically an inhaler which is fun to use and thus reinforcing. After two weeks of using the Funhaler, parents reported that their children had fewer problems when medicating and had a more positive response to treatment.

TRY THIS

- Think about all of the conditioning techniques you have been exposed to in secondary and primary schools. Do you think they have had any real impact on your behaviour?
- Watch an episode of *Supernanny*. What conditioning techniques are evident?
- Watch NAPCAN's community service video *Children see. Children do*. Discuss what psychological evidence they are basing this campaign message on.

Exam advice…

In preparation for this part of the exam it is really useful if you can actually hold debates about the issues being covered.

Don't limit your evidence to that included here. Collect evidence from other sources and ask people their opinions on the matter.

CONDITIONING TECHNIQUES ARE NOT APPROPRIATE

At home

Techniques such as the naughty step are frequently criticised by childcare experts. For example, Morris (2014) claims that the 'naughty step' can have long-term emotional effects. Children do not have the same ability as adults to reflect on their own behaviour and verbalise the feelings they experience from things like the naughty step experience. Without empathy and help with their feelings, the naughty step may ultimately have a negative effect on development.

A further issue is consistency. Parents may try to follow parenting gurus, like Jo Frost, and be calm and consistent whilst applying techniques such as the naughty step. However, the stressful life of a full-time parent means that even the most dedicated parent may slip up and demonstrate frustration and inconsistency in their applications of conditioning techniques. Therefore conditioning techniques are unlikely to be as effective in real life as experts promise.

In school

Some educational approaches, such as Montessori education, believe that the rewards and punishments advocated by conditioning techniques are actually harmful to a child's development and that they interfere with a child's internal drives to learn. Lepper *et al.* (1973) conducted research that supports this criticism. Nursery children were asked to draw some nice pictures. When children were promised a reward they spent half as much time drawing as children who were not promised a reward, suggesting that their own motivation had been destroyed by the expectation of extrinsic rewards.

A similar critical issue relates to how rewards may create a form of 'learned helplessness'. Dweck (1975) found that children who were praised for doing good work on a maths test did worse on a later, more difficult test than children who had been told they were lazy. The second group had learned task persistence whereas the 'praised' group gave up easily. This shows that rewards don't always lead to better performance.

Reward systems are not evident in schools from different cultures. Lewis (1995) conducted observations of Japanese elementary schools and found the use of reward systems or praise was rarely used, but also that the children seemed to be internally motivated.

Peers

Peer group influences may not be desirable ones. For example, Bricker *et al.* (2006) found that children as young as 10 years old were more likely to try smoking if members of their peer group smoked. This demonstrates that a child's need for positive reinforcement from their peer group is not always a healthy option.

Vulnerable groups of children

Critics of the use of the Lovaas method believe that the technique has many problems. First, the treatment is mainly supported by Lovaas's (1987) research and this contained many methodological flaws including not randomly allocating children to be part of the control or experimental group. This means any conclusions drawn about the effectiveness of the treatment may not be entirely valid. Second, Lovaas indicates the treatment is intensive, approximately 40 hours per week. Apart from being incredibly costly, Anderson *et al.* (1987) found that an average of 20 hours per week was enough contact to allow for a significant improvement.

As conditioning techniques only treat symptoms, some believe the undesirable behaviours may re-emerge once the reinforcement has been removed.

EXAM CORNER

You will need to be able to:

- Discuss the argument and evidence in favour of conditioning techniques being appropriate.
- Discuss the argument and evidence against conditioning techniques being appropriate.
- Present a conclusion to the debate.
- Include discussion of the ethical, economic and social implications of this debate.

Possible exam questions:

1. 'Using conditioning techniques to control the behaviour of children does more harm than good'.
   Using psychological evidence, discuss the extent to which you agree with this statement. [20]
2. 'Without the use of conditioning techniques, children in the UK would be out of control'.
   Discuss the use of conditioning techniques to control the behaviour of children. [20]

Exam advice…

In the possible exam question 1 above the statement is proposing just one side of this debate.

However, the actual question is asking you to 'discuss the extent to which you agree'. It is completely up to you what to conclude – you will not get points awarded or removed because you agreed or because you disagreed with the statement.

It may be wise to think about what your conclusion will be and then think about what evidence you are going to use to support your conclusion. Remember, in this kind of question it is probably best to consider evidence from both sides of the debate.

CONCLUSION

Parents, schools, peers and other agencies all have an obligation to ensure that children grow up able to function within the society in which they live. This process of socialisation inevitably involves conditioning as that is one of the basic routes to learning and teaching.

However, the issue is, first of all, whether such techniques are the most effective ways to manage behaviour, for example reward systems may be ineffective. Second, there are important **ethical** considerations related to the manipulation of behaviour, for example in vulnerable groups of children.

We mentioned B.F. Skinner's ideal world on page 51. In his book *Walden Two* he showed how society could provide reinforcements in order to shape behaviour in the most desirable direction. Such an approach may create an 'ideal' society but whose ideal is it? And at what price to **free will** and individuality?

Evaluating the behaviourist approach

SPECIFICATION REQUIREMENT

For each approach it will be necessary to:
- Evaluate the approach (including strengths, weaknesses and comparison with the four other approaches).

You have studied the main assumptions of the **behaviourist approach** and considered how some of these assumptions might explain the formation of relationships and how they apply to one therapy. You have further considered the behaviourist approach in the context of a classic study and a debate.

It is now time to use your understanding of the behaviourist approach to consider the strengths and weaknesses of this approach, and also to consider how the approach compares with the other approaches.

STRENGTHS OF THE BEHAVIOURIST APPROACH

1. Scientific approach

Behaviourism was first introduced by John B. Watson at the beginning of the 20th century. He recognised that Pavlov's work on conditioned reflexes could be used to create a really objective, and therefore scientific, psychology. Behaviourism continues to embody the truly scientific approach, seeking to study behaviour that is observable and directly measurable. Intangible concepts such as feelings and thoughts are **operationalised** in terms of stimulus and response behaviours. Behaviourists believe that, through the use of the **scientific method**, we can analyse, quantify and compare behaviour.

Such a scientific approach is advantageous because it enables us to distinguish mere beliefs from real facts. For example, people may believe that wearing a gold token around your neck will ward off evil spirits, but how would we know this to be true without conducting **experiments**? When it comes to treatments for mental disorders, people want evidence to show that such treatments have been successful rather than just being asked to believe that they work. Therefore the scientific approach is desirable.

2. Focus on the here and now

The behaviourist approach is not concerned with events in a person's past. Other approaches in psychology seek to explain a person's behaviour in terms of things that happened in childhood or in terms of **innate** factors. The behaviourist approach means that the treatment of mental disorders does not have to look for complicated causes but just focuses on the current symptoms and trying to remove them.

For example, **aversion therapy** is used to treat alcoholism by teaching the person a new stimulus–response link between alcohol and nausea, thus reducing the undesirable behaviour. The treatment does not seek to understand why the person may have turned to alcohol.

Systematic desensitisation also seeks to treat undesirable behaviour, such as a fear of social situations, by teaching a new stimulus–response link between the feared situation and relaxation. No attempt is made to understand why the phobia might have developed in the first place; removal of the symptoms is the sole aim of the treatment.

Some people prefer such a direct approach, and the success of such therapies suggests that it is not always necessary to look for deep meanings. On the other hand, the approach does not work for all people or all disorders. This suggests that a focus on the here and now is not always sufficient.

3. Successful applications

Behaviourist principles have been successfully applied in the real world, most notably in the treatment of mental disorders and in education. For example, **classical conditioning** principles are applied in aversion therapy to help people with addictions, and they have also been applied in systematic desensitisation to help people suffering from **phobias**.

In education, **operant conditioning** underlies successful teaching strategies. **Positive reinforcement** and punishment have helped shape behaviour in the classroom, as well as in the school environment in general.

B.F. Skinner specifically applied the principles of operant conditioning to teaching, designing a mechanical programmed instruction device (Skinner, 1954). Skinner believed that classroom teaching was often ineffective because different students learn at different rates, and reinforcements are therefore too variable to be effective. Reinforcements are also delayed due to the lack of individual attention. Skinner's concept of a teaching machine meant that each student could work at his/her own pace and receive reinforcements that would encourage future learning. Every time an answer is correct, the student is reinforced; and every time the answer is wrong, further explanation is offered. Feedback is immediate and therefore more effective. Feedback is also positive, which is more encouraging than negative feedback. The machine breaks down the learning process into small steps so that the student receives frequent rewards.

▲ The principles of behaviourism (such as reinforcement and punishment) are successfully used to train animals, for example training lions to perform in circuses or training dogs in the TV programme *Dog Borstal*. But to what extent are the same principles applicable to humans?

Exam advice…
You will never be asked to describe a specific strength or weakness in the exam, as they are not named on the specification. You are, however, expected to know at least two strengths and two weaknesses. A question might ask you to offer one or two or it may ask you for two or more. If the question does ask you for two or more, you could either write about two in depth or three in less depth. This is what examiners call a 'breadth/depth trade-off'.

WEAKNESSES OF THE BEHAVIOURIST APPROACH

1. Emphasis on nurture

The behaviourist approach focuses exclusively on the surrounding environment as a means of shaping behaviour. Therefore, in terms of the **nature–nurture debate**, the role of **nature** is ignored. For example, behaviourists would not consider how our genetic make-up could influence personality and behaviour.

In addition, the role of external factors (i.e. **nurture**) is exaggerated within this approach. If learning was all that mattered, then everyone could become a surgeon or a rocket scientist. Our behaviour is governed by many internal factors, such as motivation, emotion and innate abilities.

2. Determinist approach

Behaviourists believe that behaviour is influenced almost exclusively by the associations we make between certain environmental stimuli (classical conditioning), or the rewards/punishments provided by our environment (operant conditioning). Thus people are controlled by external (environmental) factors.

This **determinist** approach does not consider the thought processes that occur before we behave in a certain way, and suggests that we are not making a choice when we behave. This view that our environment determines how we act undermines the choice or **free will** that we have as human beings when making such decisions. It means that people cannot make choices and have no personal or moral responsibility for their behaviour. The implications of this are that people cannot be held responsible for any wrongdoing – instead they should simply be punished in order to change their behaviour rather than being taught to think responsibly.

3. More relevant to animals than humans

It is worth remembering that behaviourism has its roots in experiments with non-human animals, such as the research by Pavlov and Skinner. Systematic desensitisation was also initially developed in research with animals. Wolpe (1958) created a phobia in cats by placing them in cages and administering repeated electric shocks. He then found he could reduce this learned anxiety response by placing food near a cage that was similar to the original. The act of eating apparently diminished their anxiety response (**reciprocal inhibition**), and gradually the cats could be placed in cages that were more and more similar to the original cages without symptoms of anxiety.

Human anxiety may not always respond in the same way. Wolpe (1973) treated one woman for a fear of insects and found SD did not cure her phobia. It turned out that her husband, with whom she had not been getting along, was nicknamed after an insect. So her fear was not the result of conditioning, but a means of representing her marital problems; Wolpe recommended marital **counselling**, which succeeded where SD failed.

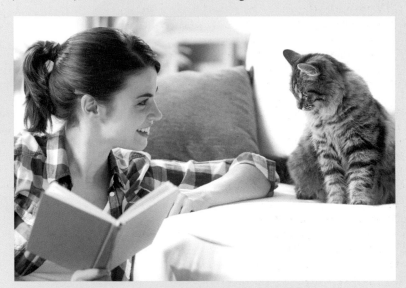

▲ Can we really assume that animals and humans learn in similar ways? If not, how can behaviourist principles be used to successfully treat human problems?

COMPARING APPROACHES

You have now studied three approaches: the biological, psychodynamic and behaviourist approaches. Working in pairs, complete the table below where one of you compares the behaviourist with the biological and the other compares it with the psychodynamic approach. Explain to your partner your comparison and see if they agree with you.

Issue/debate	Biological approach	Behaviourist approach	Similar or different?
Nature–Nurture			
Scientific–Non-scientific			
Reductionism–Holism			
Determinism–Free will			

The issues and debates listed in the table above are explained in the introductory chapter on page 7.

The issues and debates listed in the table above are explained in the introductory chapter on page 7.

EXAM CORNER

To evaluate the approach you need to be able to:
- Fully discuss the strengths (at least **two**).
- Fully discuss the weaknesses (at least **two**).
- Compare and contrast the approach with the four other approaches in terms of key issues and debates.

Possible exam questions:
1. Evaluate **two** strengths of the behaviourist approach. [6]
2. Evaluate **one** weakness of the behaviourist approach. [3]
3. Compare and contrast the behaviourist approach with the psychodynamic approach. [12]
4. A therapist is discussing what therapy to recommend to a patient – would a therapy from the biological approach be better than one from the behaviourist approach? Using your knowledge of both approaches compare and contrast the biological and behaviourist approaches and their therapies. [10]

Some activities for you

ANSWERS ON PAGE 172

ASSUMPTIONS

Key terms

Without looking back, try to explain the following terms:
- Classical conditioning
- Operant conditioning
- *Tabula rasa*
- Environmental determinism
- Generalisation

Guide dogs

One fascinating area for you to look into is how guide dogs are trained. On YouTube there are numerous videos explaining this process.

Watch several clips and write a short summary, relating behaviourist principles to training guide dogs.

Sally

ANSWERS ON PAGE 172

Sally has always owned dogs, and forms a very close bond with them. In fact, she prefers spending time with dogs compared to people.

Using behaviourist assumptions, explain Sally's close relationship with her dogs.

Relationship formation

Copy out the text below and try to fill in the blanks without looking back at the text. See how much you remember. The answers are shown below.

> Both _____ and _____ conditioning can be used to explain relationship formation.
>
> In operant conditioning, we are likely to _____ any behaviour that leads to a desirable outcome. This is known as positive _____. For example, stimuli that produce positive feelings in us are _____ (they make us feel happy). So we may enter into a relationship because that person creates _____ feelings in us and it is therefore rewarding and likely to be _____.
>
> In classical _____, we may _____ pleasant people with pleasant experiences. For example, if we meet someone when we are in a _____ _____, we are much more likely to like them, as we have formed an _____ between that person and feeling good. Liking can lead to _____ where relationship formation is concerned.

classical loving repeat positive
reinforcement associate rewarding reinforced
positive mood conditioning operant association

ANSWERS ON PAGE 172

CLASSIC EVIDENCE

Methodology and findings

Match the first half of the sentence on the left with the correct second half on the right to test your knowledge of Watson and Rayner (1920).

1. This study involves …	A. the focus was on conditioning rather than a more in-depth analysis examining a number of things.
2. To test emotional responses to certain objects …	B. they tested to see if Albert had learned the conditioned response.
3. In session 2 …	C. before conditioning began.
4. This is not a case study because …	D. a normal male infant aged 9 months.
5. In session 1 …	E. Albert started violently and raised his arms.
6. Responses were recorded with …	F. Albert was suddenly confronted with a rat, rabbit, dog, monkeys and masks.
7. Albert showed no fear …	G. Albert's reaction to the rat, rabbit and dog was less extreme.
8. The first time the bar was struck behind his head …	H. the ease with which a fear response can be created.
9. When taken to a new environment …	I. a motion picture camera.
10. This study demonstrates …	J. create the conditioned emotional response.
11. Just two 'joint stimulations' in the first week were sufficient to …	K. they established a conditional emotional response.

DEBATE

Survey opinions

In small groups, conduct a survey of parents and/or teachers.
- Find out if they use conditioning techniques when parenting or teaching.
- Find out their opinions as to whether they think such techniques are effective in controlling the behaviour of children.
- Find out if they think there are any advantages or disadvantages of using conditioning techniques for parenting or teaching.

On completion of your survey, report your findings to the rest of your class using appropriate descriptive statistics, such as a bar chart.

THERAPIES

Drawing

Depending which therapy you have studied, either:

Draw an anxiety hierarchy outlining the in-vitro and in-vivo steps that a client with a phobia of horses may need to work through.

Or

Using the following terms, UCS, UCR, CS, NS and CR, create an illustration to explain how a person with an addiction to using fruit machines may be treated using aversion therapy.

You can use some of the review activities described at the ends of the other chapters. For example, you could produce some sticky notes for revision (see page 85).

You should certainly list again the key words in this chapter and make sure you understand them.

Multiple choice questions

Working on your own or in groups, write multiple choice questions and answers related to the material in this chapter. Then pool your questions with the rest of the class. You can answer the questions individually or in teams.

Make a mobile

Write key terms on pieces of cardboard and arrange them in some meaningful way on a mobile. Decorate the classroom.

EVALUATION

ANSWERS ON PAGE 172

Match up

Match up the strengths/weaknesses on the left-hand side with the correct elaboration sentences on the right-hand side:

	Strength/weakness		Explanation
1	One strength of the behaviourist approach is that it is scientific…	A	Unlike other approaches (e.g. psychodynamic), it is not concerned with the past as a means of explaining the present.
2	Another strength of the behaviourist approach is that it has successful applications…	B	It views behaviour as being the result of our environment and upbringing and doesn't take into account biological factors.
3	Another strength of the behaviourist approach is that it focuses on the here and now…	C	It uses objective methods to measure observable behaviour, adopting scientific methodology and quantitative methods.
4	One weakness of the behaviourist approach is that it only focuses on nurture…	D	Research has focused on animal learning, for example studies into classical conditioning; these principles have been applied to human learning.
5	Another weakness of the behaviourist approach is that it is more relevant to animals than humans…	E	According to this approach the environment shapes our behaviour, through classical and operant conditioning.
6	Another weakness of the behaviourist approach is that it is determinist…	F	For example, classical and operant conditioning principles have been used in education and therapy.

Are behaviourists SANE?

The acronym SANE may help you when you have to evaluate the behaviourist approach.

S = Scientific
A = Applications
N = Nurture
E = Environmental determinism

Write a short paragraph for each of these four topics. As always, try first to do this without looking at your notes.

Extension activity

Effective evaluation includes explanation of why something is a strength or weakness, using relevant examples. In pairs, elaborate each of the strengths/weaknesses above using examples.

Exam questions and answers

QUESTION ON ASSUMPTIONS

Outline **two** assumptions from the behaviourist approach. [4 + 4]

Mark scheme for this question

Mark	Description
4	Description of assumption **well detailed** and clearly linked to human behaviour.
3	Description of assumption is **detailed** and linked to human behaviour. There may be some minor inaccuracies.
2	Description of assumption is **limited** with some link to human behaviour.
1	Description of assumption is **superficial** with no links to human behaviour.
0	**No response / inappropriate** response.

TRY THIS

Using the mark scheme on the left, mark Bob and Megan's answers.

Identify two ways in which each answer could be improved.

TRY THIS

Use 'CARDS' to reflect on one of the answers on the facing page (question on a therapy).

- **C**oherence = Does what is written make sense?
- **A**ccuracy and **A**ppropriateness = Are the facts accurate and relevant to the question being asked?
- **R**ange = Does the answer contain a number of evaluation points?
- **D**epth = Are the issues covered addressed in detail?
- **S**pelling and grammar = Is the correct terminology used and has the candidate expressed themselves well?

Use these CARDS to write an improved answer.

Bob's answer

Assumption 1 – Behaviourists believe that behaviour can be learned through conditioning, e.g. classical conditioning was suggested by Pavlov through his research on salivation in dogs. Pavlov said that food was an unconditioned stimulus (UCS) to a dog in that when given food the dog will always salivate (UCR). He then introduced a bell and he called this the neutral stimulus (NS) to condition the dog. He rang the bell (NS) every time the dog was fed (UCS). Over time the bell became the conditioned stimulus (CS) and produced a conditioned response (CR) which was salivation. This is classical conditioning.

Another example of conditioning is, e.g., operant conditioning. Skinner says that behaviour can be learned through reinforcement, something that encourages you to repeat a behaviour, like a reward. Skinner proved this with his research on rats and pigeons as he gave them a food pellet each time they pressed a lever. Over time they learnt to press the lever on demand. Punishment can also be used.

Assumption 2 – Behaviourists believe that humans and animals learn in the same way, therefore you can do research on animals and then apply the findings to humans. An example of this is when Skinner did his research on rats and developed operant conditioning. This was then used and applied to humans through token economy schemes in prisons and hospitals to encourage and reinforce positive behaviours as tokens are given out that can be exchanged for individual rewards like sweets or TV time. Pavlov used animals to develop classical conditioning; this has also been applied to humans when treating phobias.

265 words

Megan's answer

The behaviourist approach says we are born as a *tabula rasa*, i.e. a blank slate, and all our behaviour is shaped by the environment and nothing to do with our biology or internal things. This means that behaviourists believe in nurture and reject nature, e.g. all our behaviour comes from the environment as this is what shapes us.

The behaviourist approach says that conditioning causes our behaviour and that there are two types of conditioning. Classical conditioning is when we learn behaviour through association and Pavlov showed this with dogs. Firstly, he gave his dogs food and this made them salivate/dribble. He then started ringing a bell every time he fed them and they still salivated/dribbled. Over time the bell and the food got fused in the dog's mind until eventually the dog salivated/dribbled when Pavlov rung the bell. The other type of conditioning is reinforcement which is when we learn through rewards and punishments, e.g. giving children sweets to encourage them to do something good like tidy their room will make them want to tidy their room again in the future. Where as if you shout at them and punish them when they do something bad they are unlikely to do it again. Skinner showed reinforcement with his study on the rats where he taught them to press a button using rewards.

223 words

Using the mark scheme at the top of the page what mark would you give to each answer?

How effectively do Bob and Megan use research to illustrate the assumption?

Who has the best-structured answer, Bob or Megan?

Are both Bob and Megan's assumptions equally detailed?

How do the two answers compare in terms of terminology?

Examiner comments and marks on page 173

QUESTION ON A THERAPY

Evaluate **one** behaviourist therapy in terms of its effectiveness. [12]

Mark scheme for this question

Mark	Description
10–12	**Thorough** and **well-detailed** discussion of issues, arguments well balanced and reaches appropriate conclusion.
7–9	**Effective** and **reasonably detailed** discussion of issues, arguments well balanced and reaches appropriate conclusion.
4–6	**Limited** discussion of issues and arguments may be one sided.
1–3	**Very basic** and **superficial** discussion of issues and evaluation **muddled**; no conclusion drawn.
0	**No response / inappropriate** response.

Food for thought

This is an AO3 question with the command term being 'evaluate' – candidates should be reminded that no credit can be given for descriptions of therapy. Does this criticism apply to Bob and/or Megan?

To achieve top marks, candidates need to provide 'balanced arguments' – this means they need to consider what works well as well as what doesn't. Are Bob's and/or Megan's arguments balanced?

Does Bob and/or Megan's answers contain a range of evaluation points, i.e. 3+, and are they discussed in appropriate depth/detail?

A feature of weaker answers is that conclusions are not drawn, i.e. a direct reference to effectiveness after each evaluation point. Do Bob and/or Megan do this?

Systematic desensitisation – Megan's answer

Systematic desensitisation (SD) is a therapy used by the behaviourist approach to treat people with phobias. It uses the principles of classical conditioning to countercondition a maladaptive response and replace it with more functional learning. Practically, SD involves three key stages; firstly the patient has to learn breathing techniques to help them relax, secondly they work with the therapist to construct an anxiety hierarchy, and lastly they work their way up the hierarchy using the relaxation techniques until eventually they feel calm when faced with their phobia, e.g. spiders.

SD has been studied to see how effective it is at treating phobias. Capafóns (1998) found that people with a fear of flying reported feeling less afraid and had less biological symptoms of fear after completing a 25 week treatment of *in vivo* and *in vitro* SD and this was compared to a control group. This shows it is an effective therapy for this type of phobia. However, it was also found that one person in the control group showed improvement even though they didn't have SD and two people who had SD showed no improvement at all. This shows SD is not 100% effective. Other research by McGrath shows SD is reasonably effective because he found that 75% of patients with a specific phobia respond. Some researchers say that *in vivo* techniques are more effective than *in vitro* techniques.

Some research suggests that SD is a better treatment for some phobias rather than others, e.g. it is less effective for agoraphobia as it is a more complex illness. Also, it is not very good for ancient fears, e.g. fears of things that would be a threat to our ancestors such as snakes as it would have been essential for our survival to fear these creatures in the past.

Something called symptom substitution is the biggest weakness of SD because sometimes the fears we display are just the tip of the iceberg and if you remove the symptoms through SD the cause will still be there. A classic example of this is Little Hans who had a horse phobia. Freud found that his fear of horses was actually caused by intense envy of his father and if he had been given SD it would have cured him of his phobia of horses but his intense envy would remain and still cause him issues. SD does not get to the root of the problem and questions where the phobia came from in the first place; this means it is not a highly effective treatment as symptoms will just show themselves in another way.

432 words

Aversion therapy – Bob's answer

Aversion therapy (AT) is a type of therapy used to help treat people with addictions such as alcoholism. It uses the principles of classical conditioning and aims to break down maladaptive learning, e.g. the association of alcohol and pleasure, and replace it with more adaptive learning, e.g. the association of alcohol with displeasure. They do this by giving the alcoholic a drug that makes them violently sick when it is mixed with alcohol so that the addict associates the alcohol with sickness and does not want to do it again. AT has been used over the years to treat a range of disorders such as homosexuality, drug addictions, etc. and was famously used as a treatment for George Best.

AT has had mixed results in terms of its effectiveness. Miller (1978) looked at how well aversion therapy worked compared to counselling and used three groups – patients just having aversion therapy (electric shocks), just counselling, and the last group had aversion therapy and counselling. He found that one year later recovery rates were the same from all groups and this shows aversion therapy isn't that effective. However, Smith (1997) says it is more effective as he found that after a year alcoholics who had been given AT had better recovery rates than those given counselling. He also showed AT worked well for smokers because 52% of smokers who had been given AT using electric shocks had given up smoking. This shows it can work well.

One big problem with AT is that because it is really unpleasant (e.g. having electric shocks or being given drugs that make you sick) lots of people will drop out of this therapy or even refuse it in the first place. This was shown by a researcher who showed 50% drop out rates. This means it is hard to see how good the therapy really is.

Another key weakness of AT is something called symptom substitution. Psychologists believe that things like addictions are just a symptom of a deeper underlying problem, e.g. people may drink because of a trauma they have experienced in childhood. AT treats the alcoholism but it doesn't treat why the person turned to drink, so you may get rid of the drinking but not the underlying problem and as a result the problem will manifest itself in a different way, e.g. gambling. Because of this AT has a limited effectiveness as it doesn't get to the root of the problem, it simply offers a plaster rather than a cure. It is also really only useful for things like addictions and wouldn't be appropriate for many other mental disorders so has a limited use as well.

443 words

Examiner comments and marks on page 173

Chapter 4
The cognitive approach

SPECIFICATION

Approach	Assumptions and behaviour to be explained (including)	Therapy (one per approach)	Classic research	Contemporary debate
Cognitive	<ul><li>computer analogy</li><li>internal mental processes</li><li>schemas</li></ul>Learners will be expected to apply one of the given assumptions to the formation of a relationship	cognitive-behavioural therapy OR rational emotive behaviour therapy	Loftus, E. and Palmer, J.C. (1974) *Reconstruction of automobile destruction: An example of the interaction between language and memory. Journal of Verbal Learning and Verbal Behaviour*, 13, 585–589.	reliability of eye-witness testimony (including children)

Chapter 4 **The cognitive approach**

'In real life, as well as in experiments, people can come to believe things that never really happened'.

Elizabeth Loftus (1979a)

Memory is an important cognitive process.

Is our memory for events always accurate?

CHAPTER CONTENT

Cognitive approach assumptions

SPECIFICATION REQUIREMENT

For each approach it will be necessary to:
- Know and understand the assumptions.
- Apply the assumptions to explain the formation of a relationship.

Unlike the **behaviourist approach**, the **cognitive approach** is concerned with internal, mental processes in explaining behaviour, rather than external observable actions. Cognitive psychology was largely influenced by Wilhelm Wundt in the late 19th century. Wundt founded the first psychological laboratory in Germany. He wanted to develop ways in which internal mental processes could be studied scientifically and systematically. Like the behaviourist approach, the cognitive approach believes that behaviour should be studied experimentally and objectively.

The cognitive approach is concerned with how our thinking affects our behaviour. It assumes that the internal processes of the mind are of prime importance in understanding behaviour.

ASSUMPTION 1: COMPUTER ANALOGY

The notion of the 'computer analogy' has become well accepted within the cognitive approach. Cognitive psychologists have often compared the human mind with a computer. In very basic terms, they compare how we take in information (*input*), change it/store it (*process*), and then recall it when necessary (*output*). During the process stage, we actively use the cognitive processes of perception, attention, memory and so on. Thus the mind is compared with the hardware of a computer and the cognitive processes with a computer's software.

One example of this approach is the **multistore model** of memory (Atkinson and Shiffrin, 1968). In this model (see below), it was proposed that information is *input* to the brain through the senses (eyes, ears, etc.) and moves to the short-term memory (STM) store and then to the long-term memory (LTM) store. It is *output* when required.

ASSUMPTION 2: INTERNAL MENTAL PROCESSES

This approach sees human beings basically as information processors, where essential cognitive processes all work together to enable us to make sense of, and respond to, the world around us. Some of the most well-studied cognitive processes include perception, attention, memory and language. These processes all relate to each other, and constantly work together to help individuals understand their environment.

It is possible to see how these processes work if you consider the experience of recognising a dog. When we see a dog, what enables us to know it is a dog? We have to pay attention to it, perceive its features (e.g. four legs, tail, fur) and search through our memory store to see if there is a 'match' with something we have already seen/experienced. In order to be able to name it, we use our knowledge of language. Our mental processes work together within a split second to allow us to respond to the world around us. This is also known as information processing.

Investigating internal mental processes

One question that some people ask is: how can we measure our internal processes? That is, how do we know what is going on inside the mind? Cognitive psychologists have to infer what is going on inside your head and use processes such as **introspection**, a technique developed by Wilhelm Wundt (often thought of as the father of psychology).

Wundt opened the first experimental psychology laboratory in Germany in 1879. He tried to investigate thinking in a scientific and systematic way. Highly trained research assistants would be given a stimulus (e.g. a ticking metronome) and would report what that stimulus made them think and feel.

While some psychologists question the **validity** of introspection as an objective scientific tool, it is still used today (see study by Griffiths on gambling, below).

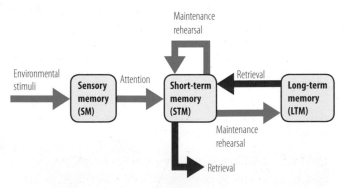

▲ The multistore model (Atkinson and Shiffrin, 1968).

USING INTROSPECTION TO INVESTIGATE GAMBLING

Introspection was used in a study of gambling behaviour (Griffiths, 1994). The study investigated the thought processes of people who gambled regularly versus non-regular gamblers, proposing that the thought processes of regular gamblers would be more irrational. To assess irrational thinking the participants were asked to 'think aloud' while playing a fruit machine. In order to do this the participants were given a list of instructions, such as:
- Say everything that goes through your mind. Do not censor any thoughts even if they seem irrelevant to you.
- Keep talking as continuously as possible, even if your ideas are not clearly structured.
- Do not hesitate to use fragmented sentences if necessary.
- Do not try to justify your thoughts.

The study found that gamblers used more irrational verbalisations, for example 'I lost because I wasn't concentrating' or 'this machine likes me'.

Exam advice...

You may be asked to identify/outline/describe an assumption. As a rough guide, follow the format below:

- *Identify (one sentence stating the assumption; one sentence giving an example).*
- *Outline (one sentence stating the assumption; one sentence elaborating this; one sentence giving an example).*
- *Describe (one sentence stating the assumption; two sentences elaborating the assumption; at least one other sentence with an example).*

TRY THIS

Define the five cognitive processes of perception, attention, memory, language and thinking.

In pairs, select an item from the classroom (e.g. a pen), and explain how each of the five cognitive processes allows you to identify the object.

▲ A man and his son were in a car crash. The father died, but the son was critically injured and rushed to hospital.

Medics decided he needed surgery immediately. When he reached the operating table, the surgeon on duty looked at him and said 'I can't operate because it's my son'.

How can you explain this? It is to do with schemas. See below left for the solution.

EXAM CORNER

For each assumption named in the specification, you need to be able to:
- Outline the assumption.
- Fully elaborate this assumption, drawing on examples in psychology.

In addition, you need to be able to:
- Use at least **one** assumption to explain the formation of **one** relationship.

Possible exam questions:

1. Describe the assumptions of the cognitive approach. [12]
2. Describe the formation of **one** relationship using **one** of the assumptions of the cognitive approach. [4]
3. Outline the 'computer analogy' and 'schemas' assumptions of the cognitive approach. [4 + 4]
4. Identify **three** assumptions of the cognitive approach. [3]

ASSUMPTION 3: SCHEMAS

The concept of **schemas** is one of the most important introduced by the cognitive approach. Schemas are organised packets of information that are built up through experience, and stored in our long-term memory. For example, our 'dog schema' (the packet of information we have stored about dogs) might contain 'four legs', 'furry', 'bark', 'tail', etc.

Generally, schemas are derived from past experiences, but can be refined through further interactions with people and the world around us. Schemas do not necessarily represent reality as they are often built up via social exchanges (e.g. conversations with others, the media) rather than personal interactions.

Take the example of our 'burglar' schema. Most people have probably never witnessed a burglary, yet their 'burglar' schema would probably be a male, fairly young and possibly with a balaclava over his face! Schemas can take different forms, for example we have event schemas which are known as scripts (e.g. going to a restaurant), and role schemas which tell us about different roles (e.g. nurse).

TRY THIS

Each student thinks of a word related to 'going to a restaurant'. Write it on a Post-it Note and stick it on your forehead. See if you can find others in the class with the same words.

Were there many with the same words, and if so, what does this tell us about our schemas?

COGNITIVE EXPLANATION FOR RELATIONSHIP FORMATION

As the cognitive approach focuses on how our internal, mental processes affect feelings and behaviour, they might explain relationship formation in the following ways.

Schemas

The packets of knowledge we have about other people (our schemas) may govern how we feel and act towards them. For example, Dion *et al.* (1972) demonstrated that people believe that physically attractive people also have attractive personal qualities. This is a schema called the **halo effect**. Therefore, if we perceive a person to be physically attractive, we may also think of them having good qualities (e.g. kind, caring) and we may become interested in forming a relationship with them. Self-schemas refer to how we feel about ourselves and these are important in relationship formation (see below).

Internal mental processes

Internal, mental processes, or cognitive processes, are essential in relationship formation, particularly perception – self-perception (the beliefs we have about ourselves) and perception of others. The way we believe others to be will determine whether we desire to enter into a relationship with them. For example, if you start talking to a stranger at a party, your perceptions, based on first impressions of them, will influence whether you want to be in their company again, possibly for a date.

Memory is another important internal mental process in relationship formation. If we have positive memories of past relationships (e.g. romantic relationships) we may be driven to forming new relationships. If, however, our memories are negative and we remember being hurt, we may be very reluctant to form new relationships even with people who we like.

Example: Explaining the formation of romantic relationships

The concept of schemas can explain why romantic relationships are formed with some people and not others. Self-schemas refer to how we feel about ourselves and govern our self-concept (how we perceive ourselves). Self-schemas are particularly important in the **matching hypothesis** – an explanation for relationship formation. According to the matching hypothesis, how we perceive ourselves in terms of physical attractiveness will influence who we want to engage in relationships with. In particular, we are attracted to those we feel match us in terms of physical attraction. So, if our self-concept is strong, and we perceive ourselves to be highly attractive, we will 'try our luck' with highly attractive others. If, however, our perception of our attractiveness is low, we will not go for those we perceive to be attractive for fear of rejection.

TRY THIS

We have applied cognitive explanations for relationships to romantic relationships, just one of the examples given in the specification.

Try to do the same for some of the other examples in the specification: siblings, mother and child, pet and owner, and friends. Try to make each one different.

Therapy 1: Cognitive-behavioural therapy (CBT)

Cognitive psychologists explain all behaviour in terms of thoughts, beliefs and attitudes, i.e. they look at the internal processes of the mind. Central to this approach is the belief that our perceptions of the world around us, and how we react to our environment, is largely driven by **schemas** – organised packets of knowledge that are built up from experiences.

You only study one behaviourist therapy as part of your course – CBT OR REBT.

SPECIFICATION REQUIREMENT

For each approach it will be necessary to:
- Know and understand how the approach can be used in therapy (one therapy per approach).
- Know and understand the main components (principles) of the therapy.
- Evaluate the therapy (including its effectiveness and ethical considerations).

CHAPTER 4 The cognitive approach

HOW COGNITIVE ASSUMPTIONS APPLY TO CBT

The overall assumption of the **cognitive approach** is that our thoughts influence our emotions and the behaviours that follow. Cognitive psychologists believe that psychological disorders, for example **depression** and anxiety, stem from faulty or irrational thinking, and if a person is to be cured of these disorders, their thinking patterns need to change. **CBT** is a form of therapy that relates to this main assumption, and works by helping change these thinking patterns as well as behaviour.

The assumption that internal processes, such as perception, impact on our behaviour underlies the principles of CBT as it is the role of the therapist to help the client change their perceptions of the world around them (e.g. nobody likes me), as these are causing their illness. This can be achieved through **cognitive restructuring**, where the therapist questions the evidence base for the client's perceptions (e.g. where is the evidence that nobody likes you?). Often, the client will see for themselves that their perceptions are not based on any real evidence, and this can elicit change.

Another important aspect of CBT relates to the assumption that schemas influence how we respond to the world around us. Aaron Beck proposed that depressed people have developed negative schemas of three things – themselves, the world around them and their futures (**cognitive triad**). In CBT, the client is helped to change these negative schemas, resulting in a change in how they respond to the world around them.

MEET THE RESEARCHER

Aaron Beck (1921–) trained as a psychoanalyst but found, through his research with depressed patients, that **psychodynamic** explanations were inadequate and that he could better explain his patients' experiences in terms of negative thoughts. This led to him being one of the first to develop cognitive therapy. He now runs the *Beck Institute for Cognitive Therapy and Research* in Philadelphia, USA, with his daughter, Dr Judith Beck.

MAIN COMPONENTS (PRINCIPLES) OF CBT

CBT combines both cognitive and **behaviourist** techniques in order to help clients – thus 'cognitive-behavioural'.
- The cognitive element – the therapist works with the client to help them identify negative thoughts that are contributing to their problems.
- The behavioural element – the therapist encourages the client to engage in reality testing, either during the session (e.g. role play) or as homework.

Both the client and the therapist play an active role in the therapy, and in particular the client will have to work on various things outside of the therapeutic setting in order to aid their recovery.

Some of the techniques that are used are described below.

THE COGNITIVE TRIAD

Beck believed that depressed people have a negative cognitive triad. This is where they have unrealistic thoughts about:
- The self (I am a bad person).
- The world (my life is terrible).
- The future (things will not improve).

Beck's theory has been used to inform techniques used in CBT, to help clients change these pessimistic views.

Dysfunctional thought diary

As 'homework', clients are asked to keep a record of the events leading up to any unpleasant emotions experienced. They should then record the automatic 'negative' thoughts associated with these events and rate how much they believe in these thoughts (on a scale of 1–100%). Next, clients are required to write a rational response to the automatic thoughts and rate their belief in this rational response, again as a percentage. Finally, clients should re-rate their beliefs in the automatic thoughts.

Cognitive restructuring

Once the client has revealed more about their thought patterns to the therapist, they can then work together on identifying and changing negative thinking patterns. This is done collaboratively and is also known as 'therapy during therapy'.

A client may feel distressed about something they have overheard, assuming that another person (person X) was talking about them. During CBT, that client is taught to challenge such dysfunctional automatic thoughts, for example by asking themselves: 'Where's the evidence that X *was* talking about me? What is the worst that can happen if X was?' By challenging these dysfunctional thoughts, and replacing them with more constructive ones, clients are able to try out new ways of behaving.

Pleasant activity scheduling

This technique involves asking the client to plan for each day (say, over the period of a week) one pleasant activity they will engage in. It could be something that gives a sense of accomplishment (e.g. going to a new class in the gym) or something that will involve a break from a normal routine (e.g. eating lunch away from the office desk).

It is thought that engaging in these pleasant activities will induce more positive emotions, and that focusing on new things will detract from negative thinking patterns. This is an example of a **behavioural activation** technique – helping clients change their *behaviour*.

The technique involves asking clients to keep a record of the experience, noting how they felt and what the specific circumstances were. If it didn't go as planned, the client is encouraged to explore why and what might be done to change it. By taking action that moves toward a positive solution and goal, the patient moves further away from negative thinking and maladaptive behaviour.

EXAM CORNER

For each therapy, you will need to be able to:
- Describe how the assumptions of the approach are applied in the therapy.
- Describe the main components (principles) of the therapy.
- Evaluate the therapy in terms of its effectiveness.
- Evaluate the therapy in terms of ethical considerations.

Possible exam questions:
1. Describe how the assumptions of the cognitive approach are applied in **one** therapy. [6]
2. Describe the main components (principles) of CBT. [12]
3. 'Cognitive restructuring' is one principle of CBT. Describe **two** other principles of CBT. [8]
4. Evaluate ethical issues raised in CBT. [8]

▲ 'Beauty is in the eye of the beholder'. This sums up the cognitive approach – there is no 'reality', what matters is the way you think about reality.

EVALUATION: EFFECTIVENESS

Research support

There is a large body of evidence to suggest that CBT is highly effective in treating depression and anxiety-related problems in particular. A number of studies have compared the effectiveness of CBT with **drug therapy** in terms of treating severe depression. For example, Jarrett *et al.* (1999) found that CBT was as effective as some **antidepressant** drugs when treating 108 patients with severe depression over a 10-week trial. However, Hollon *et al.* (1992) found no difference in CBT when compared with a slightly different kind of antidepressant drug in a sample of 107 patients over a 10-week trial. This suggests that CBT is not superior to all antidepressants.

Therapist competence

One factor influencing the success of CBT appears to be therapist competence. Competencies in CBT include: ability to structure sessions, ability to plan and review assignments (homework), application of relaxation skills, and the ability to engage and foster good therapeutic relations. Kuyken and Tsivrikos (2009) claim that as much as 15% of the **variance** in outcomes of CBT effectiveness may be attributable to therapist competence.

Individual differences

As with all therapies, CBT may be more suitable for some people compared to others, so individual differences need to be taken into consideration when examining effectiveness. For example, CBT appears to be less suitable for people who have high levels of irrational beliefs that are both rigid and resistant to change. It also appears to be less suitable in situations where high levels of stress in the individual reflect realistic stressors in the person's life that therapy cannot resolve (Simons *et al.*, 1995).

Empowerment

CBT empowers clients to develop their own coping strategies and recognises that people have **free will** to do this. CBT has become an increasingly popular alternative to drug therapy and **psychoanalysis**, particularly for people who could not cope with the **determinist** principles of these approaches, i.e. they dislike the idea that their behaviour is caused by your biological make-up/the past. Partly for this reason, CBT has become the most widely used therapy by clinical psychologists working in the NHS.

EVALUATION: ETHICAL ISSUES

Patient blame

The cognitive approach to therapy assumes that the client is responsible for their disorder. While this is a positive thing in that they are empowered to change the way they think (i.e. they have free will), there are also disadvantages to this approach. For example, important situational factors may be overlooked which are contributing to their disorder, such as family problems or life events that the client is not in a position to change. Therefore 'blaming' the individual for the way they think/feel/behave is not necessarily helpful because it may take other aspects of their life to change in order to help them feel better.

What is rational?

Another **ethical** debate concerns who judges an 'irrational' thought. While some thoughts may seem irrational to a therapist, resulting in the client feeling they must change them, they may in fact not be that irrational. Alloy and Abrahamson (1979) suggest that depressive realists tend to see things for what they are, and normal people have a tendency to distort things in a positive way (through rose-coloured glasses). They found that depressed people display the *sadder but wiser effect*, that they were more accurate in their estimates of the likelihood of 'disaster' than non-depressed individuals. The ethical issue is that CBT may damage self-esteem, an example of **psychological harm**.

TRY THIS

How much are self-defeating beliefs affecting your life? Try a questionnaire yourself at: *www.testandcalc.com/Self_Defeating_Beliefs*

   Correlate your score on this with some other measure, such as happiness (make up your own scale for this or find one on the web – happiness is the topic for Chapter 5).

Therapy 2: Rational emotive behaviour therapy (REBT)

You only study one cognitive therapy as part of your course – CBT OR REBT.

SPECIFICATION REQUIREMENT

For each approach it will be necessary to:
- Know and understand how the approach can be used in therapy (one therapy per approach).
- Know and understand the main components (principles) of the therapy.
- Evaluate the therapy (including its effectiveness and ethical considerations).

Cognitive psychologists explain all behaviour in terms of thoughts, beliefs and attitudes, i.e. they look at the internal processes of the mind. Central to this approach is the belief that our perceptions of the world around us, and how we react to our environment, are largely driven by **schemas** – organised packets of knowledge that are built up from experiences.

HOW COGNITIVE ASSUMPTIONS APPLY TO REBT

One overall assumption of the **cognitive approach** is that the key influence on behaviour is how the individual *thinks* about a situation. Albert Ellis focused on how faulty thinking affects behaviour, in particular irrational beliefs lead to mental disorders such as **depression**. Thus the route to treat mental disorders is to turn irrational beliefs into rational ones.

Ellis first called his approach 'rational therapy' to emphasise the fact that, as he saw it, psychological problems occur as a result of irrational thinking. He later named his therapy 'rational emotive therapy' (RET) because he realised that the focus was on resolving emotional problems. Even later, this therapy was renamed '**rational emotive behaviour therapy (REBT)**' because the therapy also resolves behavioural problems. This relates to the assumption that we use our internal mental processes (thoughts) to direct how we respond to the world around us (behaviour).

The second relevant assumption is that behaviours can be explained in terms of schemas. For example, a depressed client may have developed negative schemas relating to the self ('I am a worthless person') or the world around them ('Nobody likes me'). During REBT, the therapist helps the client to alter these negative schemas by challenging their perceptions of themselves and the world around them. This challenge includes asking for evidence for their ways of thinking, so that the therapist can encourage the client to see that they haven't built up a *realistic* schema of themselves or the world around them. For example, their 'work' schema may be that they will never get promotion as their boss doesn't like them, but during therapy it could be established that there has never been any real evidence that their boss doesn't like them!

Negative event (A) → Rational belief (B) → Healthy negative emotion (C)

Negative event (A) → Irrational belief (B) → Unhealthy negative emotion (C)

▲ We experience negative events all the time, such as being given a low grade on an essay or seeing a sad movie. Such negative events lead to negative emotions only if they are followed by an irrational belief instead of a rational one.

📌 DISPUTING

- **Logical disputing** – Self-defeating beliefs do not follow logically from the information available (e.g. 'does thinking this way make sense?').
- **Empirical disputing** – Self-defeating beliefs may not be consistent with reality (e.g. 'where is the proof that this belief is accurate?').
- **Pragmatic disputing** – This emphasises the lack of usefulness of self-defeating beliefs (e.g. 'how is this belief likely to help me?').

The effect of disputing is to change self-defeating beliefs into more rational beliefs. The individual can move from *catastrophising* ('no one will ever like me') to more rational interpretations of events ('my friend was probably thinking about something else and didn't even see me'). This, in turn, helps the client to feel better and, eventually, to become more self-accepting.

MAIN COMPONENTS (PRINCIPLES) OF REBT

The ABC model

Ellis (1957) proposed that the way to deal with irrational thoughts was to identify them using the ABC model. (**A**) stands for the activating event – a situation that results in feelings of frustration and anxiety. Such events are quite real and will have caused genuine distress or pain. These events may lead to irrational beliefs (**B**), and these beliefs lead to self-defeating consequences (**C**). For example:
- **A** (activating event): friend ignores you in the street.
- **B** (belief): he obviously doesn't like you; no one likes you and you are worthless.
- **C** (consequences): avoid social situations in future.

ABCDE – disputing and effects

The ABC model was extended to include **D** and **E** – disputing beliefs and the effects of disputing (see box on left). The key issue to remember is that it is not the activating events that cause unproductive consequences, it is the *beliefs* that lead to the self-defeating consequences. REBT therefore focuses on challenging or disputing the beliefs and replacing them with effective, rational beliefs (see left).

Musturbatory thinking

The source of irrational beliefs lies in musturbatory thinking – thinking that certain ideas or assumptions *must* be true in order for an individual to be happy. Ellis identified the three most important irrational beliefs:
- *I must* be approved of or accepted by people I find important.
- *I must* do well or very well, or I am worthless.
- The world *must* give me happiness, or I will die.

Other irrational assumptions include:
- Others *must* treat me fairly and give me what I need, or they are absolutely rotten.
- People *must* live up to my expectations or it is terrible! An individual who holds such assumptions is bound to be, at the very least, disappointed; at worst, depressed.

An individual who fails an exam becomes depressed not because they have failed the exam but because they hold an irrational belief regarding that failure (e.g. 'If I fail people will think I'm stupid'). Such 'musts' need to be challenged in order for mental healthiness to prevail.

Unconditional positive regard

Ellis (1994) came to recognise that an important ingredient in successful therapy was convincing the client of their value as a human being. If the client feels worthless, they will be less willing to consider changing their beliefs and behaviour. However, if the therapist provides respect and appreciation regardless of what the client does and says (i.e. **unconditional positive regard**), this will facilitate a change in beliefs and attitudes.

For each therapy, you will need to be able to:
- Describe how the assumptions of the approach are applied in the therapy.
- Describe the main components (principles) of the therapy.
- Evaluate the therapy in terms of its effectiveness.
- Evaluate the therapy in terms of ethical considerations.

Possible exam questions:
1. Describe how the assumptions of the cognitive approach are applied in **one** therapy. [6]
2. Describe the main components (principles) of REBT. [12]
3. Outline **two** components (principles) of REBT. [4 + 4]
4. Evaluate the effectiveness of REBT. [6]

MEET THE RESEARCHER

Albert Ellis (1913–2007) held open audiences demonstrating his ABC approach until his death at the age of 93 in 2007. Every Friday night, there were lively sessions with audience volunteers at the Albert Ellis Institute in New York for only $5.00 including cookies and coffee!

Like many psychologists, Ellis became interested in an area of behaviour that was personally challenging. His own experiences of unhappiness (for example his parents divorced when he was 12) led him to develop ways to help others. Initially, he trained as a psychoanalyst, but gradually became disillusioned with the Freudian approach and started to develop his own methods. Over the course of half a century, he wrote 54 books and published 600 articles on RET/REBT, as well as advice on good sexual relationships and good marriage.

EVALUATION: EFFECTIVENESS

Research evidence

REBT has generally been shown to be effective in outcome studies (i.e. studies designed to measure responses to treatment). For example, in a **meta-analysis** Engels *et al.* (1993) concluded that REBT is an effective treatment for a number of different types of disorder, including **social phobia**. Ellis (1957) claimed a 90% success rate, taking an average of 27 sessions.

Silverman *et al.* (1992) conducted a review of 89 studies into the effectiveness of REBT. It was shown to be either more effective or equal to other types of therapy (such as **systematic desensitisation**) for a wide range of disorders including anxiety, depression, stress and alcohol abuse. In summary:
- 49 studies showed REBT to be more effective than other treatments.
- 40 showed no difference between REBT and other treatments.

Appropriateness

A particular strength of REBT is that it is not only useful for **clinical** populations (i.e. people suffering from mental disorders or phobias), but it is also useful for **non-clinical** populations (e.g. people who might suffer from lack of assertiveness or examination anxiety).

Not suitable for all

Like all psychotherapies, REBT does not always work. Ellis (2001) believed that sometimes people who *claimed* to be following REBT principles were not putting their revised beliefs into action and therefore the therapy was not effective. Ellis also explained lack of success in terms of suitability – some people simply do not want the direct sort of advice that REBT practitioners tend to dispense. They prefer to share their worries with a therapist, without getting involved with the cognitive effort that is associated with recovery (Ellis, 2001).

Irrational environments

REBT fails to address the very important issue that the irrational environments in which clients exist continue beyond the therapeutic situation, e.g. marriages with bullying partners, or jobs with overly critical bosses. As a result, these environments continue to produce and reinforce irrational thoughts and maladaptive behaviours. REBT may help individuals to cope with such situations but there is a limit to the effectiveness of just 'thinking differently'.

EVALUATION: ETHICAL

Client distress

REBT is a forceful therapy, in which the therapist may quite aggressively challenge the client's thinking using direct and confrontational methods. For this reason, it is deemed unethical by some, who feel that this causes unnecessary anxiety to the client.

Furthermore, there are issues when client and therapist beliefs differ. For example, very little attention has been given to the unique **ethical** problems that arise when REBT therapists treat devoutly religious clients. Disputing what appears to be an irrational belief *to the therapist* may create moral problems for the client for whom this 'irrational' belief is based on fundamental religious faith.

What is rational?

Another ethical debate concerns who judges an 'irrational' thought. While some thoughts may seem irrational to a therapist, resulting in the client feeling they must change them, they may in fact not be that irrational. Alloy and Abrahamson (1979) suggest that depressive realists tend to see things for what they are, and normal people have a tendency to distort things in a positive way (through rose-coloured glasses). They found that depressed people display the *sadder but wiser effect*, that they were more accurate in their estimates of the likelihood of 'disaster' than non-depressed individuals.

A film was produced of Albert Ellis interviewing a client named Gloria, which you can see on YouTube in four segments (search YouTube for 'Albert Ellis Gloria'). It provides useful insights into the process of REBT.

TRY THIS

1. Think of a situation where you feel frustrated or unhappy.
2. Identify the *activating event*, *self-defeating thoughts* and *consequences* of this irrational thinking.
3. How might REBT be used to change this irrational thinking and bring about more productive consequences for you?

CHAPTER 4 **The cognitive approach**

Classic evidence: Loftus and Palmer (1974)

RECONSTRUCTION OF AUTOMOBILE DESTRUCTION: AN EXAMPLE OF THE INTERACTION BETWEEN LANGUAGE AND MEMORY

SPECIFICATION REQUIREMENT

For each approach it will be necessary to:
- Know and understand a classic piece of evidence (including methodology, procedures, findings and conclusions).

Elizabeth Loftus and John Palmer's research is concerned with the inaccuracy of **eyewitness testimony** (**EWT**). One explanation offered for the inaccuracy of EWT is that questioning by the police or other officials after a crime may alter witnesses' perception of the events and thus affect what they subsequently recall. Some questions are more 'suggestive' than others. In legal terms, such questions are called **leading questions** – a question that, 'either by its form or content, suggests to the witness what answer is desired or leads him to the desired answer' (Loftus and Palmer, 1974, page 585).

Loftus and Palmer aimed to investigate the effect of leading questions on the estimate of speed. Estimates of speed were selected because people are quite poor at judging the numerical details of traffic accidents, such as speed and distance, and therefore would be more easily affected by leading questions.

▲ Participants were shown film clips of different traffic accidents and asked to estimate the speed the cars had been travelling at before the accident. The form of the question varied, so that some participants were asked how fast the cars were travelling when they hit each other, whereas others were asked the same question using the word smashed, collided, bumped or contacted.

WHAT IS EYEWITNESS TESTIMONY?

The term eyewitness testimony (EWT) is actually a legal term, referring to the use of eyewitnesses (or earwitnesses) to give evidence in court concerning the identity of someone who has committed a crime. Psychologists tend to use the term 'eyewitness memory' instead of 'testimony' when carrying out research to test the accuracy of eyewitness testimony.

Eyewitness memory can be described using the computer analogy:

- The witness encodes into LTM details of the event and the persons involved. Encoding may be only partial and distorted, particularly as most crimes happen very quickly, frequently at night, and sometimes accompanied by rapid, complex and often violent action.
- The witness retains the information for a period of time. Memories may be lost or modified during retention (most forgetting takes place within the first few minutes of a retention interval) and other activities between encoding and retrieval may interfere with the memory itself.
- The witness retrieves the memory from storage. What happens during the reconstruction of the memory (e.g. the presence or absence of appropriate retrieval cues or the nature of the questioning) may significantly affect its accuracy.

METHODOLOGY

This study consists of two **experiments** conducted in a **laboratory** using an **independent groups design**. Each experiment was conducted with a different set of participants:
- In Experiment 1 there were 45 student participants.
- In Experiment 2 there were 150 student participants.

PROCEDURES

Experiment 1

The participants were shown seven film clips of different traffic accidents. The length of the film segments ranged from 5–30 seconds. The clips were originally made as part of a driver safety film. After each clip, participants received a **questionnaire** in which they were asked to give an account of the accident they had just seen, and were also asked a series of specific questions about the accident. Among these questions was one 'critical' question which asked the participants: 'About how fast were the cars going when they _____ each other?' The word used in the blank space varied from group to group. In total there were five groups with nine participants in each. The questions were:
- About how fast were the cars going when they *hit* each other?
- About how fast were the cars going when they *smashed* into each other?
- About how fast were the cars going when they *collided* with each other?
- About how fast were the cars going when they *bumped* into each other?
- About how fast were the cars going when they *contacted* each other?

Participant estimates of speed in each group were recorded in miles per hour.

Experiment 2

The second experiment investigated whether leading questions simply *bias* a person's response or actually *alter* the memory that is stored.

Part 1

The participants were shown a film of a multiple car crash. The actual accident lasted less than four seconds. They were then asked a set of questions including the critical question about speed. The participants were divided into three groups, each of 50 participants.
- **Group 1** was asked: 'How fast were the cars going when they *smashed* into each other?'
- **Group 2** was asked: 'How fast were the cars going when they *hit* each other?'
- **Group 3** This was the **control group** and its members were not exposed to any question.

Part 2

One week later the participants were asked to return to the psychology laboratory and were asked further questions about the filmed accident. The critical question that all participants were asked was: 'Did you see any broken glass?' There was no broken glass in the film but, presumably, those who thought the car was travelling faster might expect there to have been broken glass.

Exam advice...

In an exam question where you might need to describe Loftus and Palmer's findings, you would be expected to refer to both Experiment 1 and Experiment 2. You would receive credit if you 'wrote them out in full' or if you drew appropriately labelled tables of results – drawing a table may also be quicker to do!

FINDINGS

Experiment 1

The mean speed estimate was calculated for each **experimental group**, as shown in the table on the right and graph below. The group given the word 'smashed' estimated a higher speed than the other groups (40.8 mph). The group given the word 'contacted' estimated the lowest speed (31.8 mph).

Verb	Mean speed estimate
smashed	40.8
collided	39.3
bumped	38.1
hit	34.0
contacted	31.8

▲ Speed estimates for the different verbs.

▲ Showing data from the table above.

Experiment 2

Part 1

The findings of Experiment 2 are shown in the table on the right. Participants gave higher speed estimates in the 'smashed' condition, just like the participants in Experiment 1.

	Verb condition		
	Smashed	Hit	Control
Yes	16	7	6
No	34	43	44

▲ 'Yes' and 'No' responses to the question about broken glass.

Part 2

Participants returned a week later and answered further questions about the filmed accident. The findings are shown in the bar chart below. Participants in the 'smashed' condition were more than twice as likely to report seeing broken glass than those in the group given the word 'hit' or in the control condition.

- **Group 1 ('smashed' condition):** 16 reported having seen broken glass; 34 reported not having seen broken glass.
- **Group 2 ('hit' condition):** 7 reported having seen broken glass; 43 reported not having seen broken glass.
- **Group 3 (control condition):** 6 reported having seen broken glass; 44 reported not having seen broken glass.

▲ 'Yes' and 'No' responses to the question about broken glass in Experiment 2.

CONCLUSIONS

The findings indicate that the form of a question (in this case, changes in a single word) can markedly and systematically affect a witness's answer to that question.

Loftus and Palmer propose two explanations for this result:

1. **Response-bias factors** – The different speed estimates occur because the critical word (e.g. 'smashed' or 'hit') influences or biases a person's response.
2. **The memory representation is altered** – The critical word changes a person's memory so that their perception of the accident is affected. Some critical words would lead someone to have a perception of the accident having been more serious.

If the second conclusion is true, we would expect participants to 'remember' other details that are not true. Loftus and Palmer tested this in their second experiment. In the 'smashed' condition, the two pieces of information combine to form a memory of an accident that appears quite severe and therefore generates certain expectations, for example that there is likely to be broken glass.

The findings from Experiment 2 suggest that the effect of leading questions is not the result of response-bias but because leading questions actually alter the memory a person has for the event.

These findings can be understood in relation to research on the effects of verbal labels on to-be-remembered forms, such as in the classic study by Carmichael *et al.* (1932) (see below). Verbal labels cause a shift in the way information is represented in memory in the direction of being more similar to the suggestion given by the verbal label.

STUDY BY CARMICHAEL *ET AL.* (1932)

This study by Carmichael *et al.* provided evidence for the effect of verbal labels. Participants were shown a set of drawings (central column) and then provided with a verbal description (either the column on the left or the one on the right). When participants were later asked to redraw the image, the resulting object was typically affected by the verbal label.

Reproduced Figures	Word List 1	Stimulus Figures	Word List 2	Reproduced Figures
	Curtains In A Window		Diamond In A Rectangle	
	Bottle		Stirrup	
	Crescent Moon		Letter 'C'	
	Beehive		Hat	
	Eye-glass		Dumb-bells	
	Seven		Four	
	Ship's Wheel		Sun	
	Hour Glass		Table	
	Kidney Bean		Canoe	
	Pine Tree		Trowel	
	Gun		Broom	
	Two		Eight	

TRY THIS

Design a study similar to the one by Loftus and Palmer.
- Find a TV clip of a car accident (look on YouTube).
- Decide on a set of questions to use with your participants, one of which will be the critical question about speed.
- Decide on how you will divide your participants into groups – each group gets a different critical question.

Classic evidence: Loftus and Palmer (1974) (continued)

SPECIFICATION REQUIREMENT

For each approach it will be necessary to:
- Make judgements on a classic piece of evidence including ethical issues and social implications.

TRY THIS

What do you conclude about the ecological validity of the study by Loftus and Palmer?

Hold a 'mock trial'. One team has the task of arguing that this study has ecological validity and another team has to present the opposite case. You might do some extra research first.

What does your class conclude?

THINGS TO DO

WWW

There is a great video on YouTube about the accuracy of memory, 'False memory and eyewitness testimony', at: *www.youtube.com/watch?v=bfhIuaD183I&feature=PlayList&p=743 ADEA0 6B23C9A7&index=0&playnext=1*

Original article

The full reference for this classic study is Loftus, E.F. and Palmer, J.C. (1974) Reconstruction of automobile destruction: an example of the interaction between language and memory. *Journal of Verbal Learning and Verbal Behavior*, 13, 585–589.

You can read this article in full at: *https://webfiles.uci.edu/eloftus/LoftusPalmer74.pdf*

Other resources

A classic book by Elizabeth Loftus is *Eyewitness Testimony* (1996, a revision of her 1979 book).

She has also written two books with Katherine Ketcham:
- *The Myth of Repressed Memory: False Memories and Allegations of Sexual Abuse* (1996).
- *Witness for the Defense: The Accused, the Eyewitness and the Expert Who Puts Memory on Trial* (1992).

Research by Elizabeth Loftus is discussed in a chapter of *Opening Skinner's Box: Great Psychological Experiments of the Twentieth Century* by Lauren Slater (2004), a book that contains the background to a number of key studies in psychology, although it has received some serious criticism (search Google).

On this spread we are going to evaluate the classic study by looking at issues related to its methodology, and comparing the study to alternative evidence. When it comes to evaluation, you can make up your own mind. We have presented some evidence and statements, and invite you to use these to construct your own view of the classic study. You can use your knowledge of research methods as well.

EVALUATION: METHODOLOGY AND PROCEDURES

Controlled experiment

Loftus and Palmer conducted their research using **experiments**. One advantage of experimental research is that it demonstrates a causal relationship. By deliberately manipulating the **independent variable** (the verb used to describe the impact) we can see the causal effect on the **dependent variable** (estimate of speed) and draw a causal conclusion.

This is especially true in a **laboratory** study where potentially **confounding variables** are carefully controlled so that any change in the dependent variable is due to the independent variable and not other factors. In field experiments or real-life examples other factors may influence behaviour.

Ecological validity

In this study participants watched film clips of accidents, which is not the same as witnessing a real accident. People don't take the task seriously and/or they are not emotionally aroused in the way that they would be in a real accident. This means that the findings may not represent real life, i.e. they lack **ecological validity**.

In real life EWT may be more accurate. For example, Foster *et al.* (1994) found that if participants thought they were watching a real-life robbery, and also thought that their responses would influence the trial, their identification of a robber was more accurate.

Yuille and Cutshall (1986) also found evidence of greater accuracy in real life. Witnesses to an armed robbery in Canada gave very accurate reports of the crime four months after the event even though they had initially been given two misleading questions. This suggests that misleading information may have less influence on real-life EWT.

In contrast, Buckout (1980) also conducted a 'real life' study involving 2,000 participants. A very short film (13 seconds) was shown on prime-time TV. Later, an identity parade was shown on TV and viewers were invited to phone in their choice of suspect. Only 14% got it right!

The sample

The participants in this study were US college students. Other groups of people may be more (or less) prone to being affected by misleading information than others. For example, there may be age differences. This may be a consequence of **source monitoring**. An eyewitness typically acquires information from two sources: from observing the event itself and from subsequent suggestions (misleading information). A number of studies (e.g. Schacter *et al.*, 1991) have found that, compared to younger subjects, elderly people have difficulty remembering the source of their information, even though their memory for the information itself is unimpaired. As a result, they become more prone to the effect of misleading information when giving testimony.

EVALUATION: ALTERNATIVE EVIDENCE

There has been considerable support for research on the effect of misleading information. For example, Loftus conducted a memorable study involving a cardboard cut-out of Bugs Bunny (Braun *et al.*, 2002). College students were asked to evaluate advertising material about Disneyland. Embedded in this material was misleading information about either Bugs Bunny or Ariel (neither character could have been seen at Disneyland because Bugs is not Disney and Ariel hadn't been introduced at the time of their childhood).

Participants were assigned to the Bugs, Ariel or a **control condition** (no misleading information). All had visited Disneyland. Participants in the Bugs or Ariel group were more likely to report having shaken hands with these characters than the control group. This shows how misleading information can create an inaccurate (false) memory.

Elizabeth Loftus (1944–) is Distinguished Professor at the University of California, Irvine. She is probably one of the best known living psychologists, famous for her extensive research on eyewitness testimony and, more recently, false memory. She is often called as an expert witness in court cases to testify about the unreliability of memory, such as in the Michael Jackson case, and she has received countless awards such as the 2001 William James Fellow Award from the American Psychological Society (for 'ingeniously and rigorously designed research studies . . . on difficult and controversial questions').

John Palmer (1954–) was a student studying psychology when he was given the chance to work with Elizabeth Loftus on this study. He has gone on to focus on visual attention and is a Research Professor at the University of Washington, USA.

ETHICAL ISSUES AND SOCIAL IMPLICATIONS

Lack of valid consent

Loftus and Palmer did not gain **valid consent** from their participants. If participants had been aware of the aims of the study this would have affected their behaviour. They would have been aware that the questions were 'leading' and more careful in the responses they gave. Thus their behaviour would not reflect EWT in everyday life and would not provide useful insights.

The issue is whether such **deception** is acceptable. The researchers can justify it in terms of the importance of this research. It had a profound effect on our understanding of the inaccuracy of EWT.

From the participants' point of view the deception could be considered 'mild'. They were not psychologically or physically harmed and it is unlikely that knowing the true purpose of the study would have led to refusing to take part.

Psychological harm

One of the criticisms of this study is that the participants did not witness a real accident but, instead, watched film clips of an accident. This meant that they may not have responded to the task in the way that an eyewitness would in a real accident.

One alternative might have been to expose participants to a real accident. However, this might have been very distressing, leading to **psychological harm** which would not necessarily be diffused by debriefing. The emotional impact might have been long lasting.

So, this study avoided the **ethical** issue of psychological harm by using film clips.

See the next spread for a discussion of further ethical and social implications of this topic.

See the next spread for a discussion of further ethical and social implications of this topic.

TRY THIS

Elizabeth Loftus (1975) investigated leading questions by asking people the question: '*Do you get headaches frequently?*'

People who were asked this question reported an average of 2.2 headaches per week, whereas those who were asked 'Do you get headaches occasionally, and, if so, how often?' reported an average of 0.7 headaches! The *way* the question was asked had a significant effect on the answer given.

Try it out for yourself.

EXAM CORNER

You will need to be able to do the following with respect to the study by Loftus and Palmer (1974):

Describe:
- The methodology of the study (describe and justify; includes characteristics of the sample but not the sampling technique).
- The procedures of the study (what the researcher did; includes the sampling technique).
- The findings of the study.
- The conclusions of the study.

Evaluate:
- The methodology of the study.
- The procedures of the study.
- The findings of the study (use methodology and/or alternative evidence).
- The conclusions of the study (use methodology and/or alternative evidence).
- The ethical issues and social implications.

Possible exam questions:
1. 'The methodology used in Loftus and Palmer's (1974) research "*Reconstruction of automobile destruction: An example of the interaction between language and memory*" offers us a valuable, scientific insight into eyewitness testimony'. Discuss the extent to which you agree with this statement. [8]
2. Outline the findings and conclusions of Loftus and Palmer's (1974) research '*Reconstruction of automobile destruction: An example of the interaction between language and memory*'. [10]
3. '*However interesting or valuable the findings offered in Loftus and Palmer's research are, the research is limited by both methodological and ethical problems*'. Evaluate Loftus and Palmer's (1974) research '*Reconstruction of automobile destruction: An example of the interaction between language and memory*'. [16]

"Do the words 'huff and puff' mean anything to you, Mr Wolf?"

Contemporary debate: The reliability of eyewitness testimony (including children)

SPECIFICATION REQUIREMENT

For each approach it will be necessary to:
- Understand what is at the core of the debate.
- Refer to psychological studies and theories.
- Explore both sides of the contemporary debate from a psychological perspective (including the ethical, economic and social implications).

In 1969, Laszlo Virag was convicted in Bristol of stealing from parking meters and using a firearm. Despite having an alibi and other contradictory evidence, Virag was identified by eyewitnesses as the perpetrator. Whilst serving his prison sentence it was found that another person had committed the crime and Virag was eventually pardoned. Lord Devlin investigated this and other cases and in his 1976 report he recommended that

'*The trial judge be required to instruct the jury that it is not safe to convict on a single eyewitness testimony alone, except when there is substantial corroborative evidence*'.

Devlin's recommendation was never made law, so is **eyewitness testimony** reliable enough to be used in today's justice system?

ETHICAL, SOCIAL AND ECONOMIC IMPLICATIONS

Exonerated is a term used to describe people who have been found guilty and convicted of a crime, but are later found to be innocent. In fact, Huff *et al.* (1986) reported that nearly 60% of 500, mainly American, cases of wrongful convictions involved eyewitness identification errors. This suggests that too much reliance on eyewitness testimony has major **ethical** implications.

On the other hand, there may be dangers inherent in becoming too sceptical of such evidence. Greene (1990) reports that when mock juries were asked to make decisions about the guilt or innocence of a perpetrator based on eyewitness testimony, some jurors mentioned their knowledge of mis-identification mistakes. They knew about such mistakes from items on the news and this knowledge made them more sceptical about the testimony of eyewitnesses. As eyewitnesses are a major source of information in any crime scene it is important to pay *some* attention to the evidence.

A balance can be struck. In the UK, there are safeguards that are 'built in' to the Justice System. The Police and Criminal Evidence Act (PACE), introduced in 1984 (revised 1995), offered a code of practice that needs to be adhered to with regard to the conduct of identification attempts. However, it is still permissible to secure a conviction on the uncorroborated evidence of a single eyewitness.

Unreliable eyewitness testimony has big costs in terms of retrials and compensation to those wrongly convicted. The economic costs of crime in the UK are vast. Recent estimates indicated about £124 billion per year (Institute for Economics and Peace, 2013); this equates to 7.7% of the UK's GDP.

However, perhaps the biggest implication for unreliable eyewitness testimony is not financial, but rather the risk society faces as the real perpetrator of the crime has been allowed to remain free.

EYEWITNESSES ARE NOT RELIABLE

Post-event information

In Loftus and Palmer's classic (1974) research (see previous two spreads), the information 'suggested' after the event became incorporated into the original memory.

Loftus and Zanni (1975) also demonstrated the effects of such **post-event information**. They found that 7% of those asked 'Did you see <u>a</u> broken headlight?' reported seeing one, whereas 17% of those asked 'Did you see <u>the</u> broken headlight?' reported seeing a headlight. The post-event information was the word 'a' or 'the'. This research clearly demonstrates that even subtle changes in the wording used in questions can influence the recollection of the participant. This suggests that whenever a witness is questioned, either by the police, lawyers, friends, etc., their recollection of the actual event may be distorted.

Crimes are emotive experiences

Eyewitnesses may not be reliable because the crimes they witness are unexpected and emotionally traumatising. Freud argued that extremely painful or threatening memories are forced into the unconscious mind. This process, **repression**, is an **ego-defence mechanism**. Nowadays, psychologists might call this 'motivated forgetting', but in either form perhaps eyewitnesses are not reliable because the memory of the crime is too traumatising.

Child witnesses are not reliable

Children as eyewitnesses are often regarded as unreliable because they are prone to fantasy and their memories may be especially affected by the suggestions made by others. Therefore, researchers have been interested in finding out if children are accurate eyewitnesses, for example when identifying a perpetrator from a line-up.

Line-ups do not always include the *target* individual because otherwise a suspect could be selected because he/she fits an erroneous description. Therefore eyewitnesses are now often told that the line-up may or may not include the *target* (target-present or target-absent). A meta-analysis by Pozzulo and Lindsay (1998) drew data from a number of studies that, between them, had tested over 2,000 participants. The researchers found that children under the age of 5 were less likely than older children or adults to make correct identifications when the target was present. Children aged 5–13 years did not differ significantly from adults in the target-present condition, but were more likely to make a choice (which was inevitably wrong) in the target-absent condition. It was thought that this was due to children being more sensitive about doing what they are asked to do – they feel they can't say 'no' and have to give some answer; in this case, a false positive.

Memory is reconstructive

Schemas are used to help us process information quickly. However, one drawback with schemas is that the information already held in our schemas may distort our memory of an event. For example, in your 'criminal' schema you will have an expectation of what a criminal will look like. These expectations may be derived from news reports, movies and television programmes. When we later have to recall the information, these expectations may have become incorporated into our memory, leading to inaccurate recall.

Yarmey (1993) asked 240 students to look at videos of 30 unknown males and classify them as 'good guys' or 'bad guys'. There was high agreement amongst the participants, suggesting that there is similarity in the information stored in the 'bad guy' and 'good guy' schemas.

In the same way any preconceived ideas about the facial features of criminals may influence us when making decisions on suspects in a line-up or photo array. This suggests that eyewitnesses may not select the actual criminal, but the individual who looks most like a criminal.

Watch the TED talks by Elizabeth Loftus, 'The fiction of memory', and by Scott Fraser, 'Why eyewitnesses get it wrong' (see TED.com).

You could then produce your own TED talk either advocating eyewitness reliability or advocating that eyewitnesses are not reliable. These could be a great revision device for you and your classmates!

Picking Cotton
- Find out about the case of Ronald Cotton and Jennifer Thompson.
- What factors resulted in Jennifer mistakenly identifying Ronald?
- What was the impact of the wrongful conviction on Ronald and Jennifer?

EYEWITNESSES ARE RELIABLE

Post-event information

Eyewitness research is misleading as it tends to focus on details that are tricky for us to estimate (e.g. speed) or details that are not central to the incident, and thus may be more susceptible to corruption.

In addition, not all research suggests that post-event information is misleading. Loftus (1979b) showed participants slides of a man stealing a large, bright red purse from a woman's bag. The participants were later exposed to information containing subtle errors or a more obvious one, purporting that the purse was brown. Although participants were often wrong about 'peripheral' items, 98% of the participants correctly remembered the purse they had seen was red. This suggests that eyewitness recollection for central or key details may be more resistant to distortion from post-event information than previously suggested.

Crimes are emotive experiences

Some psychologists believe that when we experience events which are very emotionally shocking and/or which hold personal significance we create a particularly accurate and long-lasting memory, called a **flashbulb memory**. There is evidence that the **hormones** associated with emotion, such as **adrenaline**, may enhance the storage of memories (Cahill and McGaugh, 1995). This suggests that the emotion surrounding a crime may actually lead to more, rather than less, reliable memories.

Child witnesses are reliable

Davies *et al.* (1989) reviewed the literature discussing children used as witnesses and came to some interesting conclusions. Children between the ages of 6 and 7, and 10 and 11, are fairly accurate in their memories of an event, they do not usually 'make things up', and they do not deliberately lie when giving testimony. In addition, their memory for important details is not significantly altered by adult suggestion after the event. These conclusions challenge many of the claims made by other researchers.

Also, is it really fair to claim child eyewitnesses are unreliable when much of the research uses adults as the 'target' individual? Anastasi and Rhodes (2006) found that all age groups are most accurate when recognising an offender from their own age group. This may mean that if the child witnesses had observed children committing staged crimes, perhaps they would be more reliable in their identifications.

Memory may be reconstructive, but that doesn't mean it is unreliable

In many crimes, eyewitnesses know the perpetrator of the crime and as such they don't need to refer to their schemas. For example, RapeCrisis reports that 90% of rapists are known to their victims. This means that the eyewitness's ability to identify the assailant is likely to be very reliable, even when the crimes themselves are incredibly traumatic.

As we can see in Yuille and Cutshall's research (see previous spread), when research is conducted with eyewitnesses to real-life crimes (rather than laboratory-based 'crimes') their accuracy is much higher than that suggested by laboratory-based research. If memory was reconstructive, you would have expected the eyewitness recollections to have faded over time and to have been susceptible to leading questions; however, this was not the case in Yuille and Cutshall's research.

CONCLUSION

It is difficult for psychologists to definitively prove that eyewitnesses are, or are not, reliable. This area of research has been helpful in that it has led us to be more critical of the recollection of eyewitnesses. As a result, we have developed methods which mean eyewitness recollection is less susceptible to distortion, such as **cognitive interviews** (a method of questioning that aims to increase the amount and accuracy of information recalled) and **sequential line-ups** (eyewitnesses see people in the line-up one-by-one, rather than all at the same time). The increasing use of CCTV systems in the UK means that the unreliability of eyewitnesses is likely to become less of a problem in the future.

▲ Eyewitness recall is often influenced by their schema. An eyewitness may recall the features of a hooded figure based on their expectations rather than anything they actually saw.

EXAM CORNER

You will need to be able to:
- Discuss the argument and evidence in favour of eyewitnesses not being reliable.
- Discuss the argument and evidence in favour of eyewitnesses being reliable.
- Present a conclusion to the debate.
- Include discussion of the ethical, economic and social implications of this debate.

Possible exam questions:
1. *'The reliability of eyewitnesses is so poor that no conviction should happen if the only evidence is eyewitness testimony'.*
   With reference to the quote, discuss the extent to which you agree with this statement. [20]
2. Discuss the view that eyewitnesses are reliable. [20]

Exam advice...
In question 1 above the statement is proposing the view that eyewitnesses are not reliable. Therefore to answer this question you would need to summarise the points and evidence that support this view to gain 10 marks of the AO1 credit.

To gain the other 10 marks of the AO3 credit, you will need to present points and evidence that challenge this statement.

You would also be expected to come to some sort of conclusion based on the evidence you have presented.

CHAPTER 4 **The cognitive approach**

81

Evaluating the cognitive approach

SPECIFICATION REQUIREMENT

For each approach it will be necessary to:
- Evaluate the approach (including strengths, weaknesses and comparison with the four other approaches).

THE VALUE OF RETRIEVAL CUES

Can't remember something? If someone gives you a clue the memories might come flooding back.

Research has shown that people can remember more than they think they know – if they are given the right cue. Tulving and Psotka (1971) conducted an experiment that demonstrated this.
- They gave participants six different word lists to learn, each containing 24 words.
- Each list was divided into six different categories (so over the six lists there were 36 categories, such as kinds of tree and names of precious stones).
- After all the lists had been presented, the participants were asked to write down all the words they could remember (called 'free recall').
- Then they were given cues – the names of the different categories (e.g. 'trees' or 'precious stones') – and asked to recall the words again (called 'cued recall').

The key finding was that people remembered about 50% of the words when initially tested in the free recall condition, but this rose to 70% when given cued recall. It shows that there is often more in your head than you think there is, if someone would just give you the right cues!

▲ PET scans (see text) are usually shown as a coloured picture where the 'hot' colours, such as orange and red, are used to represent the areas where there is greatest activity, and the 'cold' colours, such as green and blue, represent the areas with least activity. PET scans tell us which bits of the brain are busy but not what they are doing. These PET scans show the difference between 'normal' brain activity (on the left) and that in a person with Alzheimer's disease (on the right). There is much less activity in the brain of the Alzheimer's patient.

You have studied several assumptions of the **cognitive approach** and have gained an insight as to how this approach might explain behaviour. You have also studied how the cognitive approach applies in therapies such as **CBT** and **REBT**. You have further considered the cognitive approach in the context of a classic study and a debate.

It is now time to use your understanding of the cognitive approach to consider the strengths and weaknesses of this approach, and also to consider how the approach compares with the other approaches.

TRY THIS

Before reading the text on this spread try to think of some strengths and weaknesses of the cognitive approach.

Draw on your knowledge of the cognitive assumptions, and how they apply in therapy, as well as drawing on your familiarity with some key evaluation terms (e.g. reductionism, scientific, applications).

STRENGTHS OF THE COGNITIVE APPROACH

1. Mediational processes

One major advantage of the cognitive approach, especially when compared with **behaviourism**, is the focus on the important 'processes' that occur between stimulus and response. Whereas behaviourists did not attempt to investigate what goes on inside the 'black box', cognitive psychologists have gone some way to explaining how important *mediational* processes, such as perception and memory, affect the way we respond to the world around us.

This has helped explain practical elements of human behaviour. For example, cognitive psychologists look at ways of improving memory using retrieval cues (see study on the left). Such research can show us why we need to make shopping lists before going to the local supermarket.

2. Important contributions

The cognitive approach has influenced many areas of psychology. As well as being usefully applied in therapy, such as in CBT, to successfully treat disorders such as **depression**, it has also been applied to the field of developmental psychology. For example, theories about how children's thinking develops have guided teaching practices in schools. Piaget (1970) developed one such theory, suggesting that children's thinking is not the same as that of adults. He suggested, for instance, that children aged around eight or nine years old cannot think in the abstract. If they want to solve a mathematical problem, they need to see it in a concrete form, such as manipulating counting sticks. Piaget's ideas had a major effect on teaching in primary schools because teachers realised it was important to use concrete examples with younger children.

Additionally, cognitive psychology has advanced memory research, and one such application is in the field of eyewitness testimony. For example, the work of Elizabeth Loftus has shown how eyewitnesses' accounts can be easily distorted by post-event information and this had had an impact on police interviewing techniques, such as the abolishment of leading questions during interviewing.

3. Scientific approach

Like many of the approaches, another strength of the cognitive approach is that it lends itself to objective and controlled scientific research. For example, memory research has in the main been conducted under strict **laboratory** conditions, and in more recent times this has involved using **brain scanning** techniques (e.g. **PET scans**, **MRI scans**; see page 141) to pinpoint specific areas of the brain that are involved in short- and long-term memory.

This field is known as **cognitive neuroscience**, and it is a field devoted to pinpointing the exact biological mechanisms involved in our cognitive processes. Therefore, in a scientific, objective manner, researchers are able to establish the exact responsibilities of different areas of the brain in relation to our cognitive process. Cognitive neuroscience is also useful in trying to understand what the brain does when it is 'at rest' (i.e. not performing any tasks), effectively studying 'mid-wandering'.

The cognitive approach has thus emerged as an extremely scientific field in psychology, in which causal relationships between emotions, cognitions and behaviours can be confidently predicted.

▶ Twin studies

If nature is the major influence on behaviour (rather than nurture) then we would expect identical (monozygotic) twins to be more similar than non-identical (dizygotic) twins in terms of a target behaviour such as intelligence or personality.

Research tends to find a **concordance** of about 86% for identical twins for IQ and about 60% for non-identical twins. Even though 80% is not a perfect correlation, it suggests that a large part of intelligence appears to be inherited.

WEAKNESSES OF THE COGNITIVE APPROACH

1. Nature and nurture

While the cognitive approach does consider the influence of both internal and external factors on behaviour (e.g. processes within the mind are 'internal' and the role of experience in the formation of **schemas** is 'external'), it fails to consider important elements of **nature** and **nurture**. For example, the role of **genes** in human cognition is ignored, yet research into intelligence has consistently looked at the influence of genes, through the use of **twin studies**.

Additionally, important social and cultural factors (nurture) are often ignored, which seems unrealistic. For example, within the field of cognitive development, key theorists such as Piaget (see facing page) failed to consider the role of culture and gender on the development of thinking in children.

2. Determinist approach

As we have seen, 'schemas' are an important assumption of the cognitive approach (see page 71). People acquire such schemas through direct experience. For example, Piaget suggested that cognitive development is essentially the development of schemas. At a young age a child might call everything with four legs and hair a 'dog'. Later the child learns various related schemas – one for a dog and one for a cat and so on.

Another important way in which we acquire schemas is through our social interactions. We acquire **stereotypes** about people and situations, such as the belief that women with blonde hair are stupid but fun, or that people with glasses are intelligent. These are cultural stereotypes, and such stereotypes (or schemas) may *determine* the way that we interpret situations.

3. Mechanistic approach

Another criticism of the cognitive approach is that it is 'mechanistic' – it portrays human behaviour as being like that of a machine. Indeed, the cognitive approach is based on the 'behaviour' of computers, so it is inevitable that the outcome would be a rather mechanistic view of human behaviour. This raises other, more philosophical, issues such as whether a computer could ever perform like a human brain.

The main objection to such mechanistic explanations is that they ignore social and emotional factors. This can be illustrated in the cognitive perspective on mental illness. For example, a depressed person may have faulty thinking patterns that can be changed; however, the cause of the depression may lie in significant life events (e.g. going through a divorce). Whilst changing thinking patterns may help the person, this doesn't change the environmental stimuli or the social situation causing the emotions that they feel.

This mechanical view also ignores the important role that emotions play in influencing cognitive processes, and this is a problem with humans being likened to computers. A computer is not influenced by emotion, a computer will recall information exactly as it is inputted; this is not the same for human beings.

Exam advice...
When answering a 'compare and contrast' question, remember that in order to gain marks, you must explain the similarities and differences between the two approaches using the key issues and debates discussed in the introduction to this book (see page 7).

COMPARING APPROACHES

So far, you have learned to compare and contrast the approaches in terms of key issues and debates. In order to improve your analytical skills, you should also consider the therapies attached to each approach, as this will provide an additional point for comparison. Try to fill in the table below:

	Biological	Cognitive
What types of therapies are used in this approach?		
How does the therapy aim to help people with problems?		
Is it a physically invasive therapy?		
Does the therapy require much effort on behalf of the patient?		
Is it a successful therapy, and what sort of problems is it used to treat?		

Hopefully you can see how comparing and contrasting the approaches in terms of their therapies can be used to help you in your answers to 'compare and contrast' questions!

EXAM CORNER

To evaluate the approach you need to be able to:

- Fully discuss the strengths (at least **two**).
- Fully discuss the weaknesses (at least **two**).
- Compare and contrast the approach with the four other approaches in terms of key issues and debates.

Possible exam questions:

1. Evaluate **two** strengths and **two** weaknesses of the cognitive approach. [12]
2. Discuss the weaknesses of the cognitive approach. [8]
3. *'In order to change human behaviour we need to understand conscious thinking patterns, and this can be achieved through scientific observation'.* With reference to this quote, compare and contrast the cognitive and psychodynamic approaches in psychology. [12]

Some activities for you

ASSUMPTIONS

The jigsaw technique

In the jigsaw technique each person is responsible for a piece of the jigsaw and then, as a group, you put the pieces of the jigsaw together.

Divide your class into groups with four members in each group. It is best if the groups are not 'friendship groups'. Give each person in your group a letter – A, B, C or D. Each person has to perform the task specific to the letter they have been assigned – possible examples are listed below.

Person A = Computer analogy
Person B = Internal mental processes
Person C = Schemas
Person D = Explanation for relationship formation

For example, people with the letter A must prepare material on the assumptions of the cognitive approach. They can do this by meeting with all the other As in the class. They must:

a. Prepare a set of brief and memorable notes on their topic.
b. Brief the group on their topic.
c. Write three (or more) questions for a test on their topic.

Your teacher should collect all the questions that have been written and use them to produce a class test. Each person will take the test individually – your performance will depend on how well you were briefed by your group members!

CLASSIC EVIDENCE

Be Elizabeth Loftus for the day

Find a clip on YouTube of a car accident. You should get footage from 'Police, Camera, Action' type programmes.

Watch the clip and write some questions relating to the clip, including one with misleading information or which might influence the memory of those who watch the clip.

Gather a sample of students and ask them to watch the clip, then give them the questions.

Analyse the responses and see how many were influenced by the leading question.

ANSWERS ON PAGE 172

CLASSIC EVIDENCE

True or false?

Check the statements below related to the study by Loftus and Palmer.

Statement	T or F
In Experiment 1, the mean speed estimate for the 'smashed' group was 40.8 mph.	T or F
In Experiment 1, the mean speed estimate for the 'collided' group was 33.9 mph.	T or F
In Experiment 1, the mean speed estimate for the 'bumped' group was 38.1 mph.	T or F
In Experiment 1, the mean speed estimate for the 'hit' group was 30.4 mph.	T or F
In Experiment 1, the mean speed estimate for the 'contacted' group was 31.8 mph.	T or F
In Experiment 1, Loftus and Palmer concluded the form of a question can markedly and systematically affect a witness's answer to that question.	T or F
In Experiment 2, in the 'smashed' condition – 16 reported seeing broken glass and 34 reported that they didn't see broken glass.	T or F
In Experiment 2, in the 'hit' condition – 43 reported seeing broken glass and 7 reported that they didn't see broken glass.	T or F
In Experiment 2, in the control condition – 6 reported seeing broken glass and 44 reported that they didn't see broken glass.	T or F
In Experiment 2, Loftus and Palmer concluded it must be due to an alteration of the memory representation and the participants believed there wasn't any broken glass.	T or F

DEBATE

Conduct an interview

There are numerous US TV news segments about eyewitness testimony. Use these as an inspiration to create your own!

You and your classmates can use information relevant to eyewitness testimony and interview pretend 'experts' in the field. Record your interviews.

THERAPIES

Illustrate the techniques

Bob has struggled with negative thoughts for the last few years. He has no self-confidence and believes he is losing friends, and that he may lose his job in the future. Bob's thoughts are affecting his behaviour; he struggles to go into work and avoids any social activities.

In groups, prepare a poster which illustrates how the techniques used in either CBT or REBT may help Bob, and share your thoughts with the rest of the group.

Extension activity

Divide the class into two groups. Each group must prepare material for a class debate into whether cognitive therapies are more ethical than behaviourist therapies, using key research and issues to support their ideas.

You can use some of the review activities described at the ends of the other chapters. For example, you could produce rolling shows or write exam advice (see page 105).

You should certainly list again the key words in this chapter and make sure you understand them.

Sticky note fun

Each student should have a pile of sticky notes. Think of all the specialist terms you have learned when studying the cognitive approach and write each one on a sticky note.

Each class member should then place their sticky notes on one wall in the classroom so that the notes are organised in some way. For example, all sticky notes related to assumptions should go together, and all sticky notes on the therapy you studied should go together. Within each of these you can further organise the sticky notes. In the end, you will have created a mind map of the chapter!

EVALUATION

Compare and contrast therapies

In order to improve your understanding of how the cognitive approach compares with the other approaches, write a few sentences in response to the following statements.

First state whether you think each of them is true or false (there is no right answer), then fully justify your answer:

Statement	True or false?	Justify your answer
The cognitive approach is more scientific than the behaviourist approach.		
The cognitive approach is less reductionist than the biological approach.		
Like the psychodynamic approach, the cognitive approach can be seen to be interactionist (i.e. it considers internal and external factors in explaining behaviour).		
The cognitive approach is nomothetic like the biological approach.		
The cognitive approach is more successful as a therapy compared to the other approaches.		
The cognitive approach employs both nomothetic **and** idiographic methods unlike the behaviourist and psychodynamic approaches.		

Compare your answers to your classmates. Did you have the same ideas?

Using idiographic methods

Research the case of Clive Wearing (you can look at this on YouTube). This case of brain damage is often used to illustrate the use of the **case study** method (see page 139) in cognitive psychology, and specifically to find out more about how our memory works.

Case studies are part of the idiographic approach to studying behaviour.

Using your research of this case, write as many pros and cons of using the idiographic approach in cognitive psychology as you can think of.

Exam questions and answers

QUESTION ON CLASSIC EVIDENCE

Describe the findings of Loftus and Palmer's (1974) research 'Reconstruction of automobile destruction: An example of the interaction between language and memory'. [6]

Mark scheme for this question

Mark	Description
5–6	Findings from **both** experiments are provided. There will be **no** major inaccuracies and up to **two** minor inaccuracies.
4	Findings from both experiments are provided. There is **one** major inaccuracy and up to **two** minor inaccuracies.
3	Accurate findings from **one** of the experiments is provided OR findings from **both** experiments are provided but there are **two** major inaccuracies and up to **two** minor inaccuracies.
1–2	Findings from only **one** experiment are provided. There are **major** inaccuracies throughout.
0	**Inappropriate** answer / **no response**.

Bob's answer

In Experiment 1 Loftus and Palmer found that the mean estimate for each condition was:

*   Smashed = 40.8 mph
*   Collided = 39.3 mph
*   Hit = 38.1 mph
*   Bashed = 34.0 mph
*   Contacted = 31.8 mph

In Experiment 2 they found participants gave higher speed estimates in the 'smashed' condition. They also found that 1 week later:

*   6 out of 50 participants reported seeing broken glass when the verb smashed had been used the week before.
*   7 out of 50 participants reported seeing the glass when the verb hit had been used the week before.
*   6 out of 50 participants reported seeing broken glass when no question was asked the week before.

From these findings Loftus and Palmer concluded that leading questions can alter or distort people's recall of an event.   126 words

> Bob has presented his answer as a list/table – this is appropriate and a useful strategy to employ on this type of question.

> Bob has a number of minor inaccuracies – can you spot what they are?

Megan's answer

Loftus and Palmer showed 45 participants a video of a car crash and asked them to estimate the speed at which the cars hit each other.

The 45 people were split into 5 groups and each was asked the question using a different verb.

Group 1 were asked 'How fast were the cars going when they smashed into each other?' The participants said 40 mph.

Group 2 were asked 'How fast were the cars going when they collided?' They said 39.3 mph. Group 3 were asked 'How fast were the cars going when they bumped each other?' They said 38 mph. Group 4 were asked 'How fast were the cars going when they hit each other?' They said 34 mph. The last group were asked 'How fast were the cars going when they made contact?' They said 31 mph.

They also did a follow up study where participants were once again shown a video and were split into 3 groups. They were asked to give a speed estimate and then return a week later to answer questions about what they had seen.

The 3 groups were asked a critical question about whether they had seen broken glass or not. Group 1 were the smashed condition and 25 out of 50 of them saw glass. Group 2 were the hit condition and only 2 out of 50 of them saw glass. Group 3 were a control group and had not been asked to estimate speed the week before and 1 out of 50 saw glass.

This was the most surprising finding.   248 words

> Megan has included elements of the procedure – this is not creditworthy.

> Megan's findings are less specific than Bob's and none of the findings offered for Experiment 2 are correct.

> Examiner comments and marks on page 174

TRY THIS

Reflect on the examiner's comments in the table below and decide if they relate to Bob, Megan or both.

Major inaccuracy present	Findings covered in detail
Less accurate and less detailed.	Some findings are very accurate and detailed.
An excellent way to present findings concisely.	Minor inaccuracies.
Appropriate coverage of both experiments.	Well structured and highly relevant.
Irrelevant and not creditworthy.	Repetitive and less concise.
Mark = 2/6	Mark = 4/6

QUESTION ON THE DEBATE

'The reliability of eyewitnesses is so poor that no conviction should happen if the only evidence is eyewitness testimony'.

Using your psychological knowledge, discuss the extent to which you agree with this statement. [20]

Megan's answer

In about 1980 Ronald Cotton was convicted of the rape of Jennifer Thompson. He was found guilty on the basis of Jennifer's eyewitness testimony, which many years later was disproved and proven to be inaccurate and unreliable. The consequence of this is that Ronald spent over ten years behind bars whilst the real perpetrator was free to commit further crimes. Because of cases like this I don't think eyewitness testimony should be used in court cases and feel it cannot be trusted.

After witnessing a crime you are exposed to a lot of post-event information, e.g. news reports, talking about it with family and friends, questions from the police and in the end when questioned in court. This can have a bad effect on the accuracy of your own memory. Loftus has done lots of research on this and has scientifically proven that you can alter someone's memory of, e.g., a traffic accident. She did this by using leading questions, whereby the participants watched a clip of a car crash and then asked them the following questions: 'Did you see a broken headlight?', 7% reported seeing one; whereas when they asked 'Did you see the broken headlight?', 17% reported seeing one. This is a very subtle difference in post-event questioning, 'a' or 'the', yet the difference in memory is astounding. This study clearly shows how easy it is to alter someone's memory of an event and could be applied to when the police question you – if they did this your testimony would not be accurate and may result in an incorrect conviction.

Children are also witnesses in crimes and it is quite obvious that their memory may not be fully accurate. Children are more susceptible to fantasy and pressure from others to say the 'right' thing. Pozzula (1998) showed in his research that children were more likely to give an incorrect answer because they feel they have to give an answer. They should not be trusted.

Freud would suggest that being a victim of crime or actually just observing a violent crime would be a highly distressing event and would be traumatising. He suggests that when we experience things like that we are likely to repress the information. Repression means pushing the memory deep into the unconscious mind where you have no awareness of it so that it cannot cause you stress and anxiety. Often the only way to retrieve it is to get something like hypnosis. As a result any recall may not be reliable.

Lastly, the final reason why eyewitness testimony is unreliable is because of something called reconstructive memory. Reconstructive memory involves using all of your existing knowledge, e.g. schemas, to help you make sense of the world around you. Schemas are packets of knowledge we keep in our memory regarding objects, events, etc. They help us process information quickly and we rely on them a lot. Unfortunately our schemas may distort our memory of an event, for example, for most people their 'criminal schema' may be made up of expectations based on films, news reports and others' experiences so you would build up a schema based on that information. If you were then to become a victim of crime you would call upon your schema to help you fill in any gaps and understand what had happened to you, this would mean you are not recalling exactly what actually happened but rather details of the schema. A researcher proved this with his good guy/bad guy study where he used around 250 students and showed them 30 videos of males they did not know. The students then had to categorise the males into being a good guy or a bad guy. There was high agreement which provides evidence that people had very similar schemas for the good guy and the bad guy.

I believe that the evidence I have presented shows we should not trust eyewitness testimony as evidence in court. It is obvious it is flawed and psychologists need to do more research to fully understand why as well as looking at the consequences wrong eyewitness testimony can have. Unreliable eyewitness testimony can have big costs in terms of retrials and compensation, as well as for society as a whole, as every person that is wrongly convicted means that the real criminal is free to commit further crimes as I said earlier about Ronald Cotton and Jennifer Thompson.

739 words

Mark scheme for this question

Mark	AO1	AO3
10	Examples of research/theory are well chosen to exemplify points made. **Depth** and **range** of material included. Effective use of terminology.	**Sophisticated** and **articulate analysis** of the debate. **Balanced arguments** with evaluative commentary. Excellent structure. **Appropriate conclusion** reached.
7–9	Examples of research/theory are appropriate to support points made. There is **depth** and **range** of material used but not in equal measure. Good use of terminology.	**Good analysis** of the debate. Arguments made are well supported and **balanced**. Evaluative commentary is clearly relevant to the context. Logical structure and **appropriate conclusion**.
4–6	Examples may not always be appropriate. **Depth or range** of material used. Some inaccuracies.	**Reasonable analysis** of the debate. Arguments may be **one sided** and evaluative commentary is generic and not contextualised. Reasonable structure but **no conclusion** or generic statement.
1–3	Examples **not made relevant**. Details **muddled/inaccurate**.	**List like** commentary, answer lacks clarity. **No conclusion**.
0	**No response / inappropriate** response.	**No response / inappropriate** response.

TRY THIS

What mark would you give Megan? Use the questions below to help you decide.

Tip: You could go through the answer with a highlighter and highlight conclusions and research/theory offered – this will help you comment and give a final mark.

Conclusions from research – has Megan explained what the research suggests about the reliability of eyewitness testimony?

The range of research/theory covered – has Megan used a range (three or more pieces) of research/theory?

The quality of the arguments presented – has Megan provided balanced arguments and considered that eyewitness testimony may or may not be unreliable?

The use of terminology – has Megan used psychological terminology to good effect?

Overall conclusion – has Megan drawn a meaningful conclusion based on the evidence she has presented with regard to whether eyewitness testimony should be trusted or not?

Balance of skills – has Megan got equal amounts of AO1 and AO3 in this answer?

There is an answer from Bob on page 174, which you can also mark.

Examiner comments and marks on page 174

CHAPTER 4 **The cognitive approach**

Chapter 5
The positive approach

SPECIFICATION

Approach	Assumptions and behaviour to be explained (including)	Therapy (one per approach)	Classic research	Contemporary debate
Positive	• acknowledgement of free will • authenticity of goodness and excellence • focus on 'the good life' Learners will be expected to apply one of the given assumptions to the formation of a relationship	mindfulness OR quality of life therapy	Myers, D.G. and Diener, E. (1995) Who is happy? *Psychological Science, 6(1)*, 10–17.	relevance of positive psychology in today's society

CHAPTER CONTENT

Identify three things that have made you happy in the last 24 hours.

Compare your three experiences with the people sitting around you.

How did it make you feel talking about the things that made you happy?

Did talking about the things that made you happy actually make you happy?

Positive approach assumptions

SPECIFICATION REQUIREMENT

For each approach it will be necessary to:
- Know and understand the assumptions.
- Apply the assumptions to explain the formation of a relationship.

The **positive approach** in psychology was officially introduced by Martin Seligman towards the end of the 20th century, and its primary focus is on the positive aspects of human nature – the good qualities that people have and how they can be nurtured. Positive psychology's approach to understanding human behaviour is based on the belief that people wish to enhance their lives, to make them more meaningful, and to increase their levels of happiness to achieve greater fulfilment. Many researchers believe that, as a discipline, psychology has been dominated by a focus on pathology – understanding mental illness – and that a 'shift' is needed in order to understand how people may flourish as individuals.

ASSUMPTION 1: ACKNOWLEDGEMENT OF FREE WILL

The positive approach believes that humans are in charge of their own emotions and have the **free will** to change how they direct their emotions. The assumption is that, as humans, we are self-directing and adaptive, and that a good life can be experienced if we use our strengths and virtues to enhance our lives. According to Seligman, happiness is not a result of good **genes** or luck, it is a result of recognising our own strengths and working on developing these in order to make our lives better, and to minimise negativity.

This assumption stands in contrast to some other approaches in psychology which have been labelled **determinist** in some way. For example, the **biological approach** suggests that our thoughts and feelings are determined by our physiological make-up, the **psychodynamic approach** proposes that childhood experiences determine adult behaviour and the **behaviourist approach** attributes our behaviour to the influence of environmental stimuli.

The free will assumption is supported by the work of Ed Diener, who has carried out research into why people are happy. Diener has devoted much research time to finding out about the factors that increase well-being and happiness. Research carried out by Diener and Seligman (2002) looked at the ties that students had to friends and family, measured in terms of the amount of time they invested in these relationships. The researchers found that the students who had the strongest ties to friends and family were happier and there was also a **negative correlation** between level of happiness and **depression**. This highlights the fact that we are in control of our happiness in that we can choose to engage in activities that are known to make us happy, and which alleviate feelings of low mood.

ASSUMPTION 2: AUTHENTICITY OF GOODNESS AND EXCELLENCE

This assumption states that feelings of happiness and goodness are as natural as feelings of anxiety and stress, and therefore psychologists need to assign these positive states of mind equal attention. According to Seligman (2002), the belief that traits such as virtue and happiness are less **authentic** than negatives traits and states (e.g. anxiety and depression) has been an obstacle in psychological research.

Seligman believes that we have inherent traits, which he calls 'signature strengths', such as kindness, generosity and humour. We need to nurture these traits in order to transform our lives.

Traditionally, psychology as a discipline has focused on disorders (i.e. mental health problems) and negative states of mind, and the primary goal of the positive approach is to change this philosophy and practice. This involves focusing on celebrating the good things in life instead of magnifying the worst.

This assumption is influential in therapies which are based on the positive approach. Rather than trying to fix what is wrong, the role of a positive therapist is to facilitate positive well-being and help to achieve fulfilment. This approach offers a different way of alleviating mental illnesses such as depression. It can be achieved by focusing on traits that produce goodness and excellence in the individual (e.g. altruistic behaviour and/or the individual's competencies), and helping people understand that these natural, valuable traits can be further developed.

The positive approach believes that such understanding will act as a buffer to protect the individual from future mental health problems, as well as being important in its own right.

ASSUMPTION 3: FOCUS ON 'THE GOOD LIFE'

One of the primary focuses of positive psychology is on the good life, i.e. those factors that contribute most predominantly to a well-lived life. Seligman (2003) distinguishes between three desirable lives:
- The pleasant life – happiness comes from pursuing positive emotions in relation to the past, present and future.
- The good life – happiness comes from pursuing activities that positively absorb and engage us.
- The meaningful life – happiness comes from a deep sense of fulfilment by living for a purpose much greater than oneself.

The pleasant life is a starting point. The next step is the good life which is a place of happiness, good relationships and work. However, Seligman encourages people to go further than 'the good life' and seek a meaningful life in their continuing quest for happiness.

In order to achieve the good life, we need to develop our strengths and virtues (e.g. wisdom and knowledge, courage, spirituality, love) as these are the natural routes to gratification, and help us function in the face of adversity. Seligman suggests the good life is the combination of three elements:

1. Positive connection to others – this encompasses our ability to love, trust, enjoy happiness, forgive and develop spiritual connections with the self and others.
2. Positive individual traits – these may include personal qualities such as a sense of integrity, morality, creativity, bravery, courage and humility.
3. Life regulation qualities – these are qualities that we need to develop to regulate, monitor and control our behaviour in order to accomplish our goals. They may include a sense of autonomy, independence, faith in our decision making and wisdom to guide our behaviour.

POSITIVE EXPLANATION FOR RELATIONSHIP FORMATION

According to the positive approach, positive relationships contribute to healthy well-being, and this includes friendships, relationships with family as well as romantic relationships. Positive psychology is firmly focused on the conditions in which happiness thrives, and therefore the topic of relationships is of utmost importance.

Authenticity of goodness and excellence

For positive psychologists, feelings of love, kindness, generosity and forgiveness and other positive qualities are authentic, and this can explain why relationships are formed. Entering into, and maintaining, a relationship allows individuals to develop and express their 'signature strengths', as Seligman calls them. In turn, individuals will strive toward a happier and more contented life whereby, through their relationships, they are able to nurture these qualities (e.g. practise generosity, kindness and forgiveness). According to the positive approach, we are socially programmed to work hard to find and build relationships with others. In turn, these relationships, if positive, contribute substantially to happiness.

The good life

Positive psychology would advocate that as individuals we strive toward 'a good life', which is a place of happiness, good relationships and work. Seligman suggests that one of the elements of a good life is 'positive connection to others' and this can explain relationship formation. 'Positive connection to others' encompasses our ability to love, trust, enjoy happiness and forgive, and these are all essential ingredients in healthy relationship formation and maintenance.

For Seligman, happiness and the good life comes from pursuing activities that absorb and engage us. For many people, social and romantic relationships, as well as relationships with one's family, help achieve this. For example, many people become besotted and totally absorbed in the other person when they first enter into a romantic relationship. This absorption and engagement in the relationship may lead them to feel they are experiencing the good life!

This idea is supported by research that shows that people in relationships are happier than those who are not, with some psychologists claiming that marriage is the single most reliable happiness indicator. Indeed research carried out by the Pew Research Center in 2005 reported 43% of married respondents to be 'very happy' compared with 24% of unmarried respondents.

Example: Explaining the formation of friendships

As humans, we seek friendship for a number of reasons. First, friendship encourages expression of many authentic emotions such as kindness, generosity and altruism for both parties involved.

Second, the rewards from friendship act as a buffer during difficult challenges in life, helping to prevent negative states such as depression and anxiety developing.

Finally, positive psychology would see friendships as one of the key ingredients to happiness. Using our signature strengths to promote mutually useful and altruistic friendships assures physical, emotional and mental well-being. Overall, people feel happier when engaging in activities which increase their connection to a friend (Howell *et al.,* 2009).

TRY THIS

We have applied positive explanations for relationships to friendships, just one of the examples given in the specification.

Try to do the same for some of the other examples in the specification: siblings, mother and child, pet owner, and romantic partners. Try to make each one different.

Have a look at this blog on the happiness approach:
www.blogpsicopositiva.com/en

MEET THE RESEARCHER

Martin Seligman (1942–) is a professor at the University of Pennsylvania in America. His early research in psychology focused on different kinds of learning. You can read about his research on biological preparedness on page 55. This is a way of explaining the rapid learning that takes place on some occasions, such as learning the link between Pernod and nausea after one bad experience.

Seligman also conducted research on learned helplessness, a syndrome that develops when an individual persistently feels unable to control events in their life, and which leads to permanent feelings of helplessness and ultimately depression. This approach is related to the cognitive view of depression (see pages 72 and 74).

In the 1980s he was in the vanguard of the new Positive Psychology movement and has been referred to as its founding father. Listen to him on *www.ted.com*

TRY THIS

Take the happiness test at:
http://psychologytoday.tests.psychtests.com/take_test. php?idRegTest=1320
What areas do you need to work on to make you happier?

EXAM CORNER

For each assumption named in the specification, you need to be able to:
- Outline the assumption.
- Fully elaborate this assumption, drawing on examples in psychology.

In addition, you need to be able to:
- Use at least **one** assumption to explain the formation of **one** relationship.

Possible exam questions:
1. Describe **two** assumptions of the positive approach. [8]
2. Explain the positive assumption 'authenticity of goodness and excellence'. [3]
3. Describe the formation of relationships using **one or more** assumptions of the positive approach. [6]

▲ A positive action from a friend like a hug (or *cwtch* in Wales) can make you feel better!

Therapy 1: Mindfulness

You only study one positive therapy as part of your course – mindfulness OR QoLT.

SPECIFICATION REQUIREMENT

For each approach it will be necessary to:

- Know and understand how the approach can be used in therapy (one therapy per approach).
- Know and understand the main components (principles) of the therapy.
- Evaluate the therapy (including its effectiveness and ethical considerations).

▲ Not focusing on that kind of present.

MINDFUL BREATHING

Below is an example of how mindful breathing can be achieved:

1. Settle into a comfortable and balanced sitting position on a chair or the floor in a quiet room.
2. Keep your spine straight and close your eyes.
3. Bring your awareness to your body sensations and become aware of your body's movements (e.g. breathing at the chest and abdomen).
4. Maintain your awareness as you breathe in and out from one breath to the next.
5. Allow the breath to flow without trying to change or control it. Notice the sensations that go with every movement.
6. As soon as you notice your mind wandering, bring back your awareness to the movement of your abdomen. Do this over and over again.
7. Be patient with yourself, it will develop.

The **positive approach** focuses on the study of topics such as happiness, optimism and subjective (perceived) well-being. It is concerned with three issues: positive emotions, positive individual traits and positive institutions. Unlike other psychological approaches, its focus is not to provide explanations or treatment for psychological illness, but instead to celebrate individual happiness and contentment via the development of the individual's natural positive traits, which will then lead to overall greater well-being.

HOW POSITIVE ASSUMPTIONS APPLY TO MINDFULNESS

The overall aim of the positive approach in psychology is to promote human flourishing, and this is where it matches the goals of **mindfulness** training. Mindfulness cultivates human characteristics that are central to positive psychology, including core character strengths and virtues, and psychological well-being.

One of the assumptions of the positive approach is that positive human traits are as authentic as negative ones (the assumption of **authenticity** of goodness and excellence), and that individuals strive to achieve greater life fulfilment by developing their natural strengths and virtues. In line with this, mindfulness aims to enhance a person's positive characteristics (e.g. optimism) through 'acceptance-based methods' which encourage the individual to develop core virtues such as gratitude and flexibility as well as optimism.

Another assumption of the positive approach is the acknowledgement of **free will**. Central to practising the art of mindfulness is becoming consciously aware of one's present thoughts and feelings, which involves self-regulation of attention. Therefore, mindfulness enhances self-regulation, and encourages people to gain control of their thoughts and emotions, in order to develop a more productive attitude towards them, and to control the amount of time spent on negative thinking. This free will-based therapy is in line with the positive approach – taking control of our feelings is central to increasing life satisfaction and contentment.

MAIN COMPONENTS (PRINCIPLES) OF MINDFULNESS

Mindfulness has its roots in ancient Buddhist practice. It is a way of teaching people to control their own mind by paying attention to, and increasing awareness of, their present thoughts. Although mindfulness may sound obvious, it is the antithesis of our mental habits, whereby our mind is usually on auto-pilot, focused on the past or the future.

Gaining control of thoughts

Being mindful trains us to focus on our present thoughts, emotions and feelings. Normally our minds are too focused on the past (going over old feelings) or too busy contemplating the future (worrying needlessly). Mindfulness teaches us to focus on the present, to become aware of all incoming thoughts and feelings and also to accept them. The goal of focusing on the present is to gain greater awareness of unhelpful or negative thoughts that often dominate us in order to can gain control over them and spend less time dealing with them.

Negative automatic thinking can lead to anxiety and **depression** – thus mindfulness practice will help an individual notice when these automatic processes are occurring and to alter their reaction to be more of a reflection.

Meditation and mindful breathing

Central to mindfulness is the art of meditation. Formal training by way of sitting meditation is most effective for developing mindfulness skills as it physically removes an individual from their daily interactions with life, so that it is easier to focus the mind. Meditation is usually learned through a mixture of guided instruction and personal practice. Guided meditation will involve getting the client to sit in a comfortable position, keeping the spine straight and asking them to direct their attention to their breathing. They will then be encouraged to pay attention to their body sensations, to their thoughts and emotions. This alone prevents the intrusion of unhelpful, negative thoughts. Meditation helps people reprocess their internal experiences and helps them to accept that thoughts (and the emotions that follow) are impermanent – they come and go. In this way, an individual learns not to react in an automatic way to their thoughts.

Informal practices of mindfulness

Once learned, mindfulness can be practised throughout our daily life, amid other activities such as driving, cleaning or having a shower. Informal mindfulness practice is the opposite of multi-tasking – it is making the conscious decision to focus on one single task. Informal practice simply involves paying attention to your surroundings; for example, if in the shower, noticing your body sensations as the water hits your skin, listening to the sound of the falling water and so on. When an individual's attention begins to wander, they should bring their attention back to these sensations. Such informal mindfulness practices can be incorporated into daily life to give us a break from our normal thought processes.

EXAM CORNER

For each therapy, you will need to be able to:
- Describe how the assumptions of the approach are applied in the therapy.
- Describe the main components (principles) of the therapy.
- Evaluate the therapy in terms of its effectiveness.
- Evaluate the therapy in terms of ethical considerations.

Possible exam questions:
1. Describe how the assumptions of the positive approach are applied in **one** therapy. [6]
2. Describe the main components (principles) of mindfulness. [12]
3. Evaluate the effectiveness of mindfulness. [6]
4. Evaluate mindfulness in terms of ethical issues. [6]

MEET THE RESEARCHER

Jon Kabat-Zinn is a Professor Emeritus of Medicine, a writer and a meditation teacher who is devoted to bringing mindfulness into mainstream medicine as well as society. Born in 1944, Kabat-Zinn studied molecular biology. During his studies, he was introduced to the concepts of mindfulness and meditation and then focused his research on mind–body interactions for healing.

In 1979 he founded the Stress Reduction Clinic at the University of Massachusetts Medical School, where he combined Buddhist teachings of mindfulness with stress reduction and relaxation in order to relieve physical symptoms. His therapy is known as *Mindfulness-Based Stress Reduction* (MBSR). More than 250 medical centres and clinics worldwide now use the MBSR model. In 1998, Kabat-Zinn received the Art, Science and Soul of Healing Award from the Institute for Health and Healing California Pacific Medical Center.

EVALUATION: EFFECTIVENESS

Integration with other therapies

The techniques of mindfulness practice are becoming increasingly incorporated into other therapies, such as **psychoanalysis** and **cognitive-behavioural therapy** (**CBT**), offering a new and alternative perspective in therapy. For example, mindfulness-based CBT (MiCBT) is a four-stage therapeutic approach which incorporates mindfulness with CBT. While traditional CBT attempts to modify people's unrealistic thoughts and beliefs, MiCBT helps to change the *process* of thinking, not just the *content* of our thoughts. Thus mindfulness is demonstrated to be an effective technique.

Application in Mindfulness-Based Cognitive Therapy (MBCT)

MBCT has been used to help prevent patients who suffer recurrent depression from relapse. Teasdale *et al.* (2000) evaluated the effectiveness of MBCT among 145 recurrently depressed patients. Patients were **randomly allocated** to receive treatment as usual (TAU) or TAU plus eight classes of MBCT. Relapse/recurrence to **major depression** was assessed over a 60-week period. Teasdale *et al.* reported that MBCT provided the greatest help to those who had suffered the most number of previous episodes. It did not have an effect on those who had only two episodes of depression in the past, but substantially reduced the risk of relapse in those who had three or more previous episodes of depression.

Application in Mindfulness-Based Stress Reduction (MBSR)

MBSR has been developed for use in general hospitals with patients suffering from conditions which may be painful, chronic, disabling or terminal (Kabat-Zinn, 1990). Reibel *et al.* (2001) reported that MBSR decreased levels of anxiety and depression in 136 patients who participated in an 8-week mindfulness programme, involving 20 minutes of meditation per day. These results were also seen after a one-year follow-up.

Group versus individual mindfulness

For certain psychological problems, there is some evidence to suggest that mindfulness meditation is more effective in group settings. For example, Mantzios and Giannou (2014) investigated group versus individual mindfulness among participants who were trying to lose weight. There were 170 participants who were randomly assigned to practise meditation for six weeks within a group or individually. The researchers found that participants in the group setting lost more weight and lowered their levels of cognitive-behavioural avoidance (e.g. avoiding social activities/invitations), concluding that the benefits of individual mindfulness meditation need to be viewed with caution.

EVALUATION: ETHICAL ISSUES

A 'positive' approach to therapy

Unlike other therapies (e.g. psychoanalysis), mindfulness does not involve dragging up the past as a means of offering an explanation for present behaviour – therefore client anxiety is avoided. Mindfulness does not involve attributing current issues to past events; this lack of a **determinist** stance is extremely positive for the individual. Further, mindfulness therapy does not focus on helping change the process of thinking, rather it encourages an acceptance of the process of thinking, and for this reason is less frustrating for clients compared with other therapies such as CBT. Cognitive-based therapies can result in the individual feeling guilty about their thought processes; however, mindfulness teaches clients acceptance.

Mindfulness and morality

For those who practise mindfulness, it is seen as essential in maintaining moral and **ethical** standards. Mindfulness is being taught in organisations to enhance leadership skills, because at the heart of this practice lies decision-making.

Ruedy and Schweitzer (2010), for example, demonstrated how individuals who were high in mindfulness were less likely to cheat on a task, and more likely to uphold ethical standards (e.g. moral identity). Put simply, improving our state of mind through mindfulness will result in us becoming more moral in many facets of life.

Exam advice…
To demonstrate your understanding of the effectiveness of therapies, you should be able to describe the procedure and/or findings of research evidence – but then, most importantly, form conclusions relating to the therapy.

TRY THIS

Does meditation improve concentration? Divide the class in half. With one half, give them 10 minutes to conduct the mindful breathing exercise (see facing page), while the other half go out of the room and chat. After 10 minutes give all individuals a wordsearch task to complete and time how long it takes each individual to complete it. You can use the data to find out the **mean/standard deviation** and whether there are between-group differences.

Therapy 2: Quality of Life Therapy (QoLT)

SPECIFICATION REQUIREMENT

For each approach it will be necessary to:
- **Know and understand how the approach can be used in therapy** (one therapy per approach).
- **Know and understand the main components (principles) of the therapy.**
- **Evaluate the therapy** (including its effectiveness and ethical considerations).

QoLI

The 16 areas of life assessed by the inventory are:
1. Health
2. Self-esteem
3. Goals and values
4. Economical standards of living
5. Work satisfaction
6. Play, recreation and leisure
7. Learning
8. Creativity
9. Help and civic action
10. Love
11. Friendship
12. Relationships with children
13. Relationships with relatives
14. Home
15. Good relationships with neighbours
16. Community

▲ Put the Three Pillars together with CASIO and QoLT and you're sorted.

The **positive approach** focuses on the study of topics such as happiness, optimism and subjective (perceived) well-being. It is concerned with three issues: positive emotions, positive individual traits and positive institutions. Unlike other psychological approaches, its focus is not to provide explanations or treatment for psychological illness, but instead to celebrate individual happiness and contentment via the development of the individual's natural positive traits, which will then lead to overall greater well-being.

You only study one positive therapy as part of your course – mindfulness OR QoLT.

HOW POSITIVE ASSUMPTIONS APPLY TO QoLT

In line with the main assumptions of the positive approach, QoLT focuses on helping the individual to experience greater life satisfaction through the promotion of their **authenticity**. Thus there is a central focus on increasing happiness and optimism (natural traits) as a means of improving a person's quality of life, while having the same goal as other therapies – to decrease worry and dysfunction.

Positive therapies such as QoLT also work on the underlying assumption that human beings have the **free will** to change their thoughts, feelings and behaviours. This is also related to the belief that, often, people with mental health issues feel a lack of control over their self/destiny, and so it follows that helping them regain feelings of control will lead to greater life satisfaction. The positive approach believes that as humans we are self-regulating and 'in charge' of our happiness because we can develop our unique strengths and virtues to lead an enhanced life. In line with this, QoLT teaches clients that happiness is a choice, and that as humans we are in control of our emotions. Its basic aim is to help people increase their happiness, which in turn will lead to better relationships, success and better health.

In line with another assumption of the positive approach, that positive emotions are as important as negative ones, QoLT encourages clients to develop their natural strengths and virtues. It is believed they are then better equipped to deal with life's challenges, instead of merely attacking problems when they occur. In other words the therapy works on the assumption that our natural positive emotions can provide resilience and coping strategies during difficult times.

MAIN COMPONENTS (PRINCIPLES) OF QUALITY OF LIFE THERAPY (QoLT)

QoLT was developed by Michael Frisch in 2006 and advocates a whole life goal/perspective. QoLT integrates principles drawn from Beck's **cognitive-behavioural therapy** (see page 72) combined with the principles of positive psychology, i.e. the promotion of happiness in order for people to live a life of contentment and satisfaction.

The Quality of Life Inventory (QoLI)

Quality of life therapy starts with an assessment of the client's life using the QoLI. This is used to identify problem areas, plan intervention and measure the effects of intervention. The QoLI assesses 16 areas of life, deemed by Frisch to have the most influence on our quality of life. These are listed on the left.

The inventory enables the therapist/client to identify the areas of life that are personally important (i.e. those areas which they wish to focus on to increase their life satisfaction). Intervention can then begin to increase contentment and overall well-being in the target areas of life.

CASIO Model

Central to QoLT is the 'CASIO' Model, which is a five-fold model of life satisfaction. This model proposes that satisfaction in any given area of life is made up of:
C – *circumstances* or characteristics of an area of life;
A – the person's *attitude* with respect to that area of life;
S – the person's evaluation or fulfilment in that area of life, based on their *standards*;
I – the *importance* the person places on that life area; and
O – *overall* satisfaction with other areas in life that are not of immediate concern.
During therapy, clients are encouraged to follow this model to review the areas of life that they feel dissatisfied with, and to increase their overall level of life satisfaction by focusing on other areas of life that they may be overlooking. For example, a person may be so fixated on problems at work that they may be neglecting their personal relationships.

The 'Three Pillars' of QoLT

During QoLT, the therapist may also focus on the Three Pillars. The first pillar involves helping the client foster feelings of strength or inner abundance (feeling calm, rested and ready to meet new challenges). This means that the client has the energy to live beyond the moment and strive toward a better quality of life.

Next, the second pillar involves finding a meaning in life. This helps the client identify and articulate a goal for each of the valued areas of life (identified in the QoLI).

Finally, the third pillar is quality time, where the client is encouraged to spend time for rest, reflection and problem solving.

Introduction to the Three Pillars occurs at the same time as the client begins intervention (the CASIO Model) on the 16 areas of life, and this forms the basis of QoLT and coaching.

EXAM CORNER

For each therapy, you will need to be able to:
- Describe how the assumptions of the approach are applied in the therapy.
- Describe the main components (principles) of the therapy.
- Evaluate the therapy in terms of its effectiveness.
- Evaluate the therapy in terms of ethical considerations.

Possible exam questions:
1. Describe how the assumptions of the positive approach are applied in **one** therapy. [6]
2. Describe the main components (principles) of Quality of Life Therapy. [12]
3. Evaluate the effectiveness of Quality of Life Therapy. [10]
4. Evaluate Quality of Life Therapy in terms of ethical considerations. [6]

EVALUATION: EFFECTIVENESS

QoLT for adolescents

Toghyani *et al.* (2011) investigated the effectiveness of QoLT on the subjective well-being of Iranian male adolescents. 20 male students aged 15–17 with low scores on the subjective well-being **questionnaire** were randomly assigned to the **experimental** or **control groups**. Those in the experimental group participated in eight QoLT sessions, and showed a significant improvement in subjective well-being compared with the control group in a follow-up assessment.

QoLT for depression

Grant *et al.* (1995) looked at the effectiveness of QoLT for those with **depression**, with participants who had shown an aptitude for, and interest in, bibliotherapy (a type of therapy that draws on the subject's interest in books to help overcome mental health issues). 16 clinically depressed volunteers participated in a weekly meeting to discuss a manual on quality of life. By the end of the treatment, all participants showed significant increases in quality of life and self-efficacy (a person's belief in their own competence).

QoLT for patients suffering with multiple sclerosis

Aghayousefi and Yasin Seifi (2013) examined the impact of QoLT on 30 patients with multiple sclerosis. The patients were **matched** and **randomly allocated** to the experimental or control groups. Those in the experimental group underwent 10 sessions of QoLT focused around the CASIO Model. The researchers reported a significant decrease in depression and anxiety amongst the experimental group following treatment.

QoLT versus 'other' positive psychology therapies

There is no evidence to suggest that participating in QoLT is any more effective than adopting positive psychology principles and virtues in one's daily life, such as practising gratitude (counting one's blessings). For example, Emmons and McCullogh (2003) found that college students who kept a daily gratitude journal reported higher levels of the positive states of alertness, enthusiasm and determination, whilst those who wrote a gratitude journal on a weekly basis exercised more regularly, felt better about their lives as a whole and were more optimistic about the upcoming week than those who recorded hassles or neutral life events.

MEET THE RESEARCHER

Michael B. Frisch (1955–) is a Professor at Baylor University in Waco, Texas. He is unusual in that he both teaches and works as a therapist and life coach. He has been described as 'a disciplined researcher, a passionate clinician, and a fervent educator'. You can see this in the video of Mike singing about all the happy people to the tune of The Beatles' *Eleanor Rigby* on YouTube: *www.youtube.com/watch?v=FimEHZgh988*

TRY THIS

'Be your own therapist'
Choose two areas of your life that you feel least satisfied with from the 16 identified in Frisch's QoLI. Now apply the CASIO Model to these areas and be honest! Can you see ways to improve your life satisfaction overall? If so, how?

EVALUATION: ETHICAL ISSUES

A 'positive' approach to therapy

Unlike other therapies, such as those based on **psychodynamic** principles, positive therapies do not involve dragging up the past as a means of offering explanations for present behaviour, and from this stance, client anxiety is avoided. In contrast to some **cognitive** therapies, such as **REBT**, there is no blame laid on the client and the reason for this is that negative states of mind are not the focus. The recognition that positive traits are authentic and we all possess them, and can develop them totally acknowledges the free will of individuals instead of offering a determinist stance of some other therapies (e.g. psychoanalysis).

Moving too fast?

Critics argue that the field of positive psychology is moving too fast, and the danger of this is that therapists may be 'jumping the gun' in the strategies they use to help well-being. Techniques employed in QoLT therapies assume that all positive states are essential to well-being and should be encouraged; however, this is a subjective judgement. Azar (2011), for example, cites research which has shown that optimism and positivity may not benefit everyone, and in fact 'defensive pessimists' (those that deal with anxiety by thinking about everything that could go wrong) can have their performance damaged if optimism and other positive emotions are forced upon them.

Exam advice…
To demonstrate your understanding of the effectiveness of therapies, you should be able to describe the procedure and/or findings of research evidence – but then, most importantly, form conclusions relating to the therapy.

Classic evidence: Myers and Diener (1995)

SPECIFICATION REQUIREMENT

For each approach it will be necessary to:
- Know and understand a classic piece of evidence (including methodology, procedures, findings and conclusions).

WHO IS HAPPY?

Happiness is at the core of the **positive approach**. The approach doesn't just seek to improve people's lives (make them happier) but also to find evidence that indicates how this can be done – the positive approach is a psychological approach and therefore aims to be scientific and evidence based.

David Myers and Ed Diener took on the task, in this classic study, of looking at the evidence for what makes people happy. Such an approach is in contrast with the traditional psychological emphasis on what causes negative emotions.

There aren't really any of the usual 'procedures' in this study – except that the researchers searched for articles related to their aim of finding out 'who is happy?'

METHODOLOGY AND PROCEDURES

This article is a **review** of research on the topic of happiness. In the 1980s and early 1990s there was a flood of research exploring people's sense of well-being, so this is a look at what had, up to this point, been revealed.

Interviews and questionnaires

One way to assess happiness is to consider a person's sense of their own happiness or well-being – called **subjective well-being (SWB)**.

This is done by **interviewing** people using a simple **closed question**: '*How satisfied are you with your life as a whole these days?*' – Are you very satisfied? / Not very satisfied? / Not at all satisfied?

Alternatively a multi-item scale (basically a **questionnaire**) can be used which includes a number of questions related to happiness.

In both cases a **quantitative** measure (numerical value) is produced to represent happiness.

Observation

One way to discover what people are doing is asking them to report what they are doing at selected times (a kind of **observation** of their behaviour). Researchers use beepers to remind a participant to send a message saying what they are doing and/or thinking at a particular moment. This is a way to **sample** people's behaviour.

Correlations

Another way to understand happiness is to consider what factors co-vary with it. Some of these factors may contribute to making a person happy whereas other factors are a consequence of being happy. It is not always clear which is cause and which is effect. For example, people with high SWB tend to have a positive appraisal of life events around them. However, it could be the other way around – if a person tends to see events around them in a rose-coloured way, this may create a higher SWB.

Reviews

This study is a review of other research, and some of the research referred to is also based on multiple studies. Some of these are reviews and some are **meta-analyses**.

FINDINGS

The myths of happiness

Who are the happy people?

Is happiness related to age?

A survey of almost 170,000 people of all ages in 16 different countries found no differences. People of all ages were equally happy – the mean score was 80% satisfaction with life (Inglehart, 1990).

However, at different ages, different factors contribute to happiness. For example, social relations and health become more important factors with age (Herzog *et al.*, 1982).

People do experience crises but these are not restricted to a particular age such as the supposed mid-life crisis in one's early 40s (McCrae and Costa, 1990).

Is happiness related to gender?

Inglehart's survey of people in 16 different countries found that 80% of men and 80% of women said they were 'fairly satisfied' with life.

In another study it was calculated that a person's gender accounted for 1% of global well-being (Haring *et al.*, 1984).

However, research has also found that women are twice as vulnerable as men to depression (Robins and Regier, 1991).

Is happiness related to race or culture?

African-Americans report nearly twice as much happiness as European-Americans (Diener *et al.*, 1993).

There are notable differences between countries. In Portugal 10% of people reported that they were happy compared with 40% in the Netherlands (Inglehart, 1990).

People in **individualist cultures** report greater SWB than in **collectivist cultures** – in an individualist culture people are more concerned with their individual needs whereas in collectivist cultures people focus on the needs of the group. It probably makes sense that, in individualist cultures, individual happiness matters more.

Is happiness related to money?

A survey in 1993 found that 75% of American college students selected 'being well off financially' as an essential life goal, compared with 39% in 1970 (Astin *et al.*, 1987). Not everyone agrees that money buys happiness but most agree that having more money would make them a little happier.

However, the **correlation** between income and happiness is only modest. Diener *et al.* (1993) found a correlation of +.12 between income and happiness.

People who are rich do not report greater happiness – a survey of people on the Forbes rich list found that 37% were *less* happy than the average American (Diener *et al.*, 1985). People who win the lottery only report brief increases in their happiness (Argyle, 1986).

On the other hand, the lack of importance of money does not apply to situations where people are poor. For example, in a poor country such as Bangladesh, people with money report higher SWB than those without money. So affluence does increase happiness but only up to a point. Once a certain level of comfort is reached (basic needs for food and warmth are met) increased wealth makes little difference (see graph on facing page).

TRY THIS

Conduct your own investigation of happiness.

1. Assess a person's happiness using a rating scale. You can use one devised by Diener (see *http://internal.psychology.illinois. edu/~ediener/SWLS.html*).

2. Assess some other aspect(s) of each participant such as their age and/or gender, or assess psychological traits such as self-esteem and/or personality. There are many tests available on the internet for measuring psychological characteristics.

3. Draw a bar chart or a scatter diagram to analyse your findings.

Happy people

It seems that some people are simply happier than others, regardless of life's ups and downs. Costa *et al.* (1987) found the people who reported being happy in 1973 tended to be the happy ones a decade later.

The traits of happy people

The key characteristics of happy people are listed below. It is not clear whether these traits make people happier or the traits develop because a person is happy:

- *High self-esteem* – such individuals like themselves and typically agree with statements such as 'I'm a lot of fun to be with' and 'I have good ideas'.
- *Sense of personal control* – people who feel empowered rather than helpless do better at school, cope better with stress and are typically happier.
- *Optimism* – such people agree with a statement such as 'When I undertake something new, I expect to succeed'.
- *Extraversion* – people who are more outgoing are happier when with other people and also when alone.

The relationships of happy people

For some people relationships create more stress and unhappiness than happiness; as the philosopher Jean-Paul Sartre (1973) said: '*Hell is other people*'.

For most people the benefits of relationships outweigh the strains. Research shows that people who can name several close friends are healthier and happier than people who can't name such friends (Burt, 1986).

Married people are happier than non-married people – in one study the rates were 39% versus 24% (Lee *et al.,* 1991). In a meta-analysis of 93 studies, women and men reported similar levels of happiness for marriage and non-marriage (Wood *et al.,* 1989).

Work and the 'flow' of happy people

Work satisfaction affects happiness. People who are out of work are less happy than those in work. Work provides a personal identity, a sense that one's life matters and also a sense of community (working with other people).

However, work can be unsatisfying and/or stressful and is then associated with unhappiness. Mihaly Csikszentmihalyi (MEE-hy CHEEK-sent-me-HY-ee) introduced the concept of 'flow', the extent to which we become caught up in an activity so that other things matter less. Csikszentmihalyi used beepers to question people throughout their day about what they were doing and whether they were happy. He found that people were happiest when they were engaged in mindful challenge and experiencing flow.

The faith of happy people

In North America and Europe people who are religious report higher levels of happiness (Poloma and Pendleton, 1990). People with a high 'spiritual commitment' were twice as likely to say they were very happy, i.e. people who agree with statements such as 'My religious faith is the most important thing in my life' (Gallup, 1984).

Happiness is also associated with strength of religious affiliation and frequency of worship attendance (Witter *et al.,* 1985).

CONCLUSIONS

Three elements can be identified that are a part of a theory of happiness.

1. The importance of adaptation

The effects of positive and negative events fade over time. For example, people who win the lottery only experience short-term increases in happiness. Conversely, people who go through psychological trauma, such as those who survived horrific experiences in concentration camps, recover their hope and happiness. A recent **longitudinal study** found that it is only events in the last three months that influence SWB. This is all due to the human capacity to adapt to life circumstances.

2. Cultural world view

Cultural attitudes predispose people to interpret life events differently. Some cultures construe the world as a benevolent and controllable place whereas other cultures emphasise negative emotions such as anxiety, anger and guilt.

3. Values and goals

People with a high sense of SWB have goals – ambitions and things they are striving to achieve. All the other factors, such as money or intelligence, only matter if they are relevant to your goals. This explains why money matters more in a poor country – because it is relevant to one's goals. In a more affluent society money matters less because that is not the prime factor in achieving one's goals.

The future

A person's happiness is not predictable from their age, gender or affluence. It does appear to be associated with race and culture. People who are happy possess certain traits, tend to have close relationships, enjoy their work and are religious.

The importance of such understanding is that psychologists can help build a world that enhances human well-being.

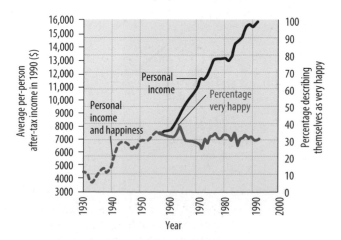

▲ Graph showing the relationship between increased income and happiness.

Americans have become wealthier since 1930 and up to a certain point happiness increased as wealth increased. However, after 1960 the percentage of happy people remained fairly constant.

Classic evidence: Myers and Diener (1995) (continued)

SPECIFICATION REQUIREMENT

For each approach it will be necessary to:
- Make judgements on a classic piece of evidence including ethical issues and social implications.

On this spread we are going to evaluate the classic study by looking at issues related to its methodology, and comparing the study to alternative evidence. When it comes to evaluation, you can make up your own mind. We have presented some evidence and statements, and invite you to use these to construct your own view of the classic study. You can use your knowledge of research methods as well.

THINGS TO DO

WWW

Watch David G. Myers on YouTube; for example: 'The scientific pursuit of happiness' (*https://www.youtube.com/watch?v=y3huf9nArhY*).

Watch Ed Diener on YouTube; for example: 'The new science of happiness' at Happiness & Its Causes 2013 (*www.youtube.com/watch?v=EdxbmVbr3NY*).

Original article

The full reference for this classic study is Myers, D.G. and Diener, E. (1995) Who is happy? *Psychological Science*, 6(1), 10–17.

You can read this article at: *www.echocredits.org/downloads/2794689/Who.is.Happy.pdf*

Other resources

Mihaly Csikszentmihalyi on TED: 'Flow, the secret to happiness' (*www.ted.com/talks/mihaly_csikszentmihalyi_on_flow?language=en*).

▼ In the film *Happy* (made 2011), filmmaker Roko Belic travels to more than a dozen countries in search of what really makes people happy, combining real-life stories of people from around the world. The cast includes Ed Diener, Mihaly Csikszentmihalyi, Sonja Lyubomirsky and the Dalai Lama.

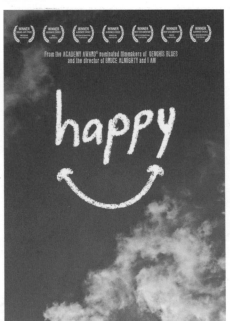

EVALUATION: METHODOLOGY AND PROCEDURES

Self-report

The data collected about **subjective well-being (SWB)** is inevitably subjective. When someone reports they are very happy we have no way of confirming or challenging that.

It may be that respondents are not telling the truth. On **questionnaires** people often provide socially desirable answers because they want to appear in a good light. Research has found that **social desirability** scores correlate reasonably with happiness scores, i.e. people who represent themselves as happy also tend to give socially desirable answers. However, when friends are asked to rate the happiness of the same people, their ratings also **correlate** with the target individual's social desirability scores. This confirms the **validity** of the original answers.

Another possibility is that people only think they are happy but are actually **repressing** their true feelings of unhappiness (a **psychodynamic** view). However, this is unlikely since research has found that those people who describe themselves as happy and satisfied with life are described in the same way by family and friends.

So overall, there is reason to believe that we can trust subjective reports of happiness.

Correlations

Many of the findings are **correlational**. This means that we cannot assume that a particular factor is a *cause* of happiness. There may be important **intervening variables**. For example, the link between marriage and happiness may be due to other things in a marriage rather than the relationship. It might be that married people have more disposable cash than single people because they have two incomes but only need one house and one car and so on, and this makes them happier.

A further issue with correlational data is that we do not know the direction of the relationship. For example, if we consider marriage again, research shows that happy people are more appealing as marriage partners (Mastekaasa, 1992). Therefore it could be that happiness makes marriage more likely than vice versa.

The samples

A lot of the data is based on Western samples as the researchers are American and have conducted much of their research in the USA. The roots of happiness may be different in other cultures. There is a hint of this in the article when comparing **individualist** and **collectivist** cultures. People in the former report higher levels of happiness – but it may be that people in collectivist cultures are equally happy but just don't express it as happiness. Their pleasure comes from the success of the group rather than the individual.

EVALUATION: ALTERNATIVE EVIDENCE

One of the emergent ideas in this classic study is that happiness stays at a fairly steady level through life, with occasional highs or lows. Some researchers call this your *happiness set-point* and believe that it could be at least partly due to **genetics**. One gene has been linked to happiness, the 5-HTT gene, which controls levels of the **neurotransmitter serotonin**. Some people have a form of this gene and report higher instances of life satisfaction (Schinka *et al.*, 2004).

However, not all psychologists agree with this view. For example, Sonja Lyubomirsky (2013) argues that happiness is 50% due to genetics and 10% due to circumstances. The remaining 40% is caused by 'self-control', i.e. factors the individual themselves is able to have influence over. Lyubormirsky arrived at these percentages from a review of studies that asked people about their happiness – studies comparing happiness levels in twins and family members (to estimate genetic factors) and studies comparing people who had 'easy' lives and 'more difficult' ones (to estimate the role of circumstantial factors).

MEET THE RESEARCHER

Ed Diener (1946–) has been called Dr Happiness because he is one of the main researchers interested in the topic of subjective well-being. He has published over 300 articles and books on the topic and was recently awarded the Distinguished Scientist Lifetime Career Award by the American Psychological Association. He held the Smiley Chair in Psychology at the University of Illinois – not because he smiles a lot, but because the position was funded by Joseph R. Smiley.

Before he became focused on positive psychology one of his areas of research was on the effects of deindividuation; for example, how does behaviour change when you're wearing a Halloween costume and can't be identified? Diener and his co-researchers watched to see what trick-or-treaters would do when left alone with a bowl of money. They found that 57% of those children who were with a group of friends and hadn't stated their name stole money when given the opportunity.

ETHICAL ISSUES AND SOCIAL IMPLICATIONS

Psychological harm

One of the benefits of this kind of research is that there is very little **risk of harm** to participants because behaviour is not being manipulated.

However, it is possible that some people, who are unhappy, may not welcome being asked about their happiness and in fact may feel more **depressed** after being asked about their sense of well-being. Therefore researchers must be sensitive to participants' needs and **debrief** them appropriately.

One important point to note is that the **ethical guidelines** (such as the British Psychological Society's code of ethics) advise psychologists to practise within the boundaries of their competence. This means that they should not try to help someone who might, for example, start to discuss their depression during a debriefing session. It would be the psychologist's duty to recommend a good source of professional help.

Socially sensitive research

One reason why some research is classed as 'socially sensitive' is that it might make us more likely to think (positively or negatively) about a certain group of people, such as a particular culture, in a particular way.

Research cited by Myers and Diener (1995) draws conclusions about the happiness of particular cultural groups, such as Inglehart's (1990) findings that in Portugal 10% of people reported that they were happy compared with 40% in the Netherlands. This may lead people to assume that any Portuguese people they meet will be unhappy and that you are more likely to meet a happy Dutch person.

Also we may need to be cautious about statistics such as this because we do not know if the sample used was a fair representation of the Portuguese and Netherlands populations.

See the next spread for a discussion of further ethical and social implications of this topic.

EXAM CORNER

You will need to be able to do the following with respect to the study by Myers and Diener (1995):

Describe:
- The methodology of the study (describe and justify; includes characteristics of the sample but not the sampling technique).
- The findings of the study.
- The conclusions of the study.

Evaluate:
- The methodology of the study.
- The findings of the study (use methodology and/ or alternative evidence).
- The conclusions of the study (use methodology and/or alternative evidence).
- The ethical issues and social implications.

Possible exam questions:
1. *'The methods used in Myers and Diener's (1995) research 'Who is happy?' allow the researchers to be confident in the conclusions that they draw'.* To what extent do you agree with this statement? [8]
2. Outline the conclusions of Myers and Diener's (1995) research *'Who is happy?'* [6]
3. Outline the methodology used in Myers and Diener's (1995) research *'Who is happy?'* [6]

TRY THIS

On the previous spread a study was described using beepers to collect data at regular intervals. You could try this yourself. Set an alarm on your mobile phone to go off, say once an hour.

At that time just write down what you are feeling. Alternatively, when the beeper goes off, you could just rate your happiness on a 5-point scale.

You could also record what you are doing.

Keep a record over the period of a week and draw some conclusions about what made you happy or not happy. Share your findings with others in your class.

"Money can't buy happiness, but if I had a big house, fancy car and a giant plasma TV, I wouldn't mind being unhappy."

Contemporary debate: Relevance of positive psychology in today's society

SPECIFICATION REQUIREMENT

For each approach it will be necessary to:

- Understand what is at the core of the debate.
- Refer to psychological studies and theories.
- Explore both sides of the contemporary debate from a psychological perspective (including the ethical, economic and social implications).

ETHICAL, SOCIAL AND ECONOMIC IMPLICATIONS

Can creating happiness, as positive psychology suggests, have an economic impact? There is evidence to suggest that it does.

First, looking at unhappiness and stress, there is evidence of high costs to businesses and the economy in general. Staff sickness, 'presenteeism' and staff turnover were estimated to be costing the UK economy £26 billion per year (Foresight Mental Capitala and Wellbeing Project, 2008).

Second, in recent laboratory research conducted by Oswald *et al.* (2009), happy workers were found to be 12% more productive. This suggests a direct link between happiness and productivity.

Third, measures that increase happiness may appear to cost a lot but, in the long term, may produce overall savings. For example, the Boorman Review (2009) estimated the NHS could save £555 million with healthier work environments. In the private sector, Google (which frequently tops the charts in the happiest places to work) found that the costs of increasing their standard maternity leave from 3 months to a flexible 5-month system were outweighed by lower staff turnover. The number of female staff leaving the company dropped by 50% because they were happier with their working conditions.

The economic impact of monitoring and improving the well-being of the workforce seems to be evident on a small scale, but until positive psychology increases its profile and demonstrates these benefits on a wider scale, it is unlikely that employers will be willing or able to introduce such investment, especially in times of economic uncertainty.

Linley *et al.* (2006) suggest that positive psychology '*shines the light of scientific inquiry into previously dark and neglected corners*'. The main focus of positive psychology is really to ensure that all people lead productive and fulfilling lives. It is evident that members of our society are generally wealthier and healthier than they have ever been. This might lead us then to think that we should also be happier and more content with our lives, but this is not the case for many. In fact, in 2014, the *Gallup and Healthways Well-Being Index* identified the United Kingdom as only 76th in the world in terms of happiness. Look up the report and you may be surprised at the society that was considered to be the happiest.

POSITIVE PSYCHOLOGY IS RELEVANT IN TODAY'S SOCIETY

Education

Can what or how we learn in school really be beneficial to our happiness? Martin Seligman, one of the leading proponents of the positive psychology movement, proposed that a positive psychology curriculum (PPC) can: (1) promote skills and strengths that are valued by most, including parents; (2) produce measurable improvements in students' well-being and behaviour; and (3) facilitate students' engagement in learning and achievement (Seligman *et al.*, 2009).

One positive psychology curriculum, the Penn Resiliency Program (PRP), has provided support for Seligman's claims. Students on this programme showed reduced symptoms of **depression** compared to a **control group** (Gillham *et al.*, 1995). In fact, at 24 months after the intervention, only 22% of the PRP group showed symptoms compared to 44% of the control group.

Seligman *et al.* (2009) also conducted research. They **randomly assigned** 347 ninth grade students to a PPC class or a non-PPC class. Students, their parents and teachers completed standard **questionnaires**. The study found that the PPC students were more cooperative and had better social skills. Seligman *et al.* claim that '*increasing the skills of well-being does not antagonise the traditional goals of classroom learning, but rather enhances them*'.

Work

Mihaly Csikszentmihalyi's research has shown that work can be the major source of our happiness. His 'flow' theory (see page 97) posits that our experiences will be most positive when both challenges and skills are high; the person is not only enjoying the moment, but is also stretching their capabilities with the likelihood of learning new skills and increasing self-esteem. Surprisingly, Csikszentmihalyi and LeFevre (1989) found that most people experience 'flow' situations more than three times as much at work than during leisure. This suggests that our working environments generally offer more opportunity for positive experiences, which is probably contrary to what many people claim.

Csikszentmihalyi and LeFevre went on to comment that if workers admitted to themselves that work can be as or more enjoyable than most of their leisure time, they might work more effectively and in the process also improve the quality of their own lives.

Leisure and lifestyle advice

Csikszentmihalyi and LeFevre (1989) advocate that people increase their experience of flow and the quality of their lives by being more conscious of and more active in their use of leisure time. Positive psychology is evident in many online 'projects' that aim to make life in UK society better, such as Action for Happiness (*www.actionforhappiness.org*). Action for Happiness claim they are 'a movement for positive social change. We're bringing together people from all walks of life who want to play a part in creating a happier society for everyone'. Although the site offers support for those struggling with problems and depression, the majority of the site offers content such as '10 keys to happier living'.

Health

Kubzansky and Thurston's (2007) research followed more than 6,000 men and women aged 25 to 74 for 20 years. They found that those participants with high levels of 'emotional vitality' (a sense of enthusiasm, of hopefulness, of engagement in life, and the ability to face life's stresses with emotional balance) had a reduced risk of coronary heart disease. Medical professionals might treat patients with advice about how to increase their happiness, along with other lifestyle advice.

CONCLUSION

Positive psychology has re-focused psychology on research and advice that will help people improve their lives and the society in which they live, rather than being concerned with the negatives – such as aggressive behaviour or addiction. Such a focus has led to some interesting lines of research and new programmes in schools, work and leisure.

TRY THIS

- Think about the education you have received in schools or colleges. Have you ever been given any instruction about how to be happy?
- Keep a diary of the leisure activities you take part in during a week. Then reflect on whether they have offered you any opportunity for you to increase your 'flow'.
- After researching the content of websites such as *www.actionforhappiness.org* and *www.random actsofkindness.org* develop your own leaflet, poster or webpage that is offering advice to people about how to increase their happiness.

▲ Research shows that work is a major source of happiness and increases your self-esteem – love your job and love yourself.

POSITIVE PSYCHOLOGY IS NOT RELEVANT IN TODAY'S SOCIETY

Education

One issue concerns the lack of empirical evidence for most positive psychology programmes. Spence and Shortt (2007) argue that the research that does exist tends to be based on small-scale or short-term interventions. As such, the widespread dissemination of positive psychology in schools should not be taken without further, more long-term research. Seligman *et al.* (2009) have also admitted that further research needs to be conducted in order to ensure that such programmes are '*effective with students from a variety of socio-economic and cultural backgrounds*'.

A second issue is that adding positive psychology to the curriculum is likely to mean that other courses have to be dropped. Schools have limited budgets and have many curricular demands; they cannot add positive psychology techniques without subtracting other essential subjects. An editorial in the *Financial Times* (2007) suggested that this means society may end up paying more for students to leave school with fewer academic achievements.

Work

Although positive psychology may report research findings which support the concept of '*choose a job you love, and you will never have to work a day in your life*', it is not a new idea (some even attribute it to Chinese sage Confucius in 551 BC). Therefore we have to question whether positive psychology in the workplace has really offered us anything more than empirical support for something which much of society already know.

Work may make you happy, but the other aspect of work, having more money, does not appear to be relevant to happiness. On page 96 we reviewed research on the relationship between money and happiness. For example, Diener *et al.* (1993) found a modest correlation of +.12 between income and happiness.

However, in societies where people are poor, money is more important and work may be important for money rather than happiness. The Western, developed world may have the luxury of seeking happiness through work, a luxury not available elsewhere.

Leisure and lifestyle advice

Leisure activities that may increase flow experiences are likely to be prohibited to many, either because of a lack of dedicated leisure time or because of the financial costs that they incur.

It is difficult to assess the impact that movements such as *Action for Happiness* have on UK society. In order to conduct objective research all variables would need to be controlled. For example, it might be that wealthier people are attracted to such movements, and therefore beneficial outcomes might be due to their wealth rather than the programme itself causing happiness.

Health

It is difficult to prove a cause and effect relationship between happiness and health. Are people healthy because they are happy or happy because they are healthy? Positive psychology could be a significant influence in the health sector; however, it perhaps isn't taken as seriously because it has difficulty in conducting research that draws clear cause and effect conclusions.

However, such programmes may only be a small part of a person's life or only available to a small number of people, and thus have little impact. The positive approach may also be something relevant only to the Western, developed world.

The positive approach is relatively new and it may take time before its impact is felt. Perhaps the debate that really needs to be answered first is, *how can* positive psychology be made more relevant in today's society?

EXAM CORNER

You will need to be able to:

- Discuss the argument and evidence in favour of positive psychology being relevant in today's society.
- Discuss the argument and evidence against positive psychology being relevant in today's society.
- Present a conclusion to the debate.
- Include discussion of the ethical, economic and social implications of this debate.

Possible exam questions:

1. '*Positive psychology has yet to prove that it is as relevant in today's society as other psychological approaches*'. Discuss the extent to which the positive approach is relevant in today's society. [20]
2. '*Other approaches in psychology have had a much more significant impact on today's society than the positive approach*'. Discuss the extent to which you agree with this statement. [20]

TRY THIS

In 2014, Panama was ranked the happiest country in the world. Find out more about this country and compare it to the UK. A great place to start your investigation is the CIA's World Factbook (*www.cia.gov/library/publications/the-world-factbook*).

Evaluating the positive approach

SPECIFICATION REQUIREMENT

For each approach it will be necessary to:
• Evaluate the approach (including strengths, weaknesses and comparison with the four other approaches).

You have studied a 'new' approach in psychology, the **positive approach**, which has a different focus to traditional approaches. It believes that human goodness is natural and should be celebrated and enhanced. This perspective offers a different focus to the other approaches that you have studied in this book, and represents a 'shift' in psychology away from concentrating on pathological disorder.

With this in mind, you should be able to offer some evaluation in terms of the strengths and weaknesses of this approach, which many psychologists see as refreshing for psychology as a whole. Below are some evaluation points you may wish to consider.

STRENGTHS OF THE POSITIVE APPROACH

1. A shift in focus for psychology

One of the strengths of positive psychology is that it moves the focus of psychology beyond explaining and treating disorder and illness to celebrating the human character, and how our **authentic strengths** can be developed to ensure that we experience greater life contentment. In short, the positive approach shifts attention from an interest in negative states (e.g. anxiety and depression) to positive states (e.g. happiness, optimism). This focus is underpinned by the belief that focusing on only disorder and disease results in a limited understanding of the human condition.

Sheldon and King (2001) note that psychology has traditionally failed to encourage human growth. Instead it has had a negative bias: '*when a stranger helps another person, psychologists are quick to find the selfish benefit in the act*'. Instead of studying weakness and damage, and trying to fix what is wrong, psychology needed to build on what is right about human nature.

The traditional psychological approaches have also involved a **determinist** view of abnormality, looking at the past instead of the individual's future. In contrast, positive psychology recognises that people want to think about their future, to become proactive in changing their destiny, and understanding they have the **free will** over their emotions to achieve this.

Martin Seligman (2000) was extremely keen to bring about this shift in thinking, believing: '*The aim of positive psychology is to begin to catalyse a change in focus of psychology from preoccupation only with repairing the worst things in life, to also building positive qualities*'.

2. Applications

The fundamental assumptions of positive psychology have been applied in many fields of life in order to help individuals, organisations and communities to flourish. Examples can be seen in education, stress management, occupational psychology and, of course, therapy.

One notable application of this approach has been in resilience training for the US Army following extended campaigns in Afghanistan and Iraq in recent years. The aim of the specialised training is to improve different aspects of resilience (e.g. emotional, spiritual), and to try to reduce the incidence of stress symptoms and suicide. Employing techniques drawn from positive psychology, the programme focuses on building mental toughness by identifying and developing signature strengths (e.g. humour, courage, perseverance) as well as preventing pathology, so that soldiers can return home without serious mental health issues.

Another popular area for the application of positive psychology is in education. In the USA, in particular, a growing number of schools are embracing positive psychology curricula (PPCs), which involve intentional activities to increase overall well-being through the development of positive cognitions, feelings and behaviours. In 2002, the US Department of Education awarded a 2.8 million dollar grant for positive psychology to be taught to ninth graders.

In 2007, the UK Department for Children, Schools and Families set 10 new targets to improve children's well-being by 2020, so it is anticipated that schools in the UK will start to implement positive psychology strategies into their curriculum, following in the footsteps of Wellington College, Berkshire, which, in 2006 took the decision to timetable positive psychology and happiness lessons as part of its core curriculum.

3. Free will approach

One of the strengths of the positive approach is that, unlike other approaches (e.g. **biological**, **psychodynamic**, **behaviourist**), it does not propose a determinist account of human behaviour. Positive psychology is based on the notion that individuals are neither pre-determined nor restricted. They have the personal freedom to grow and develop their natural signature strength and virtues. Psychology has long been criticised for its determinist view of human behaviour, and positive psychology questions the **validity** of some traditional approaches, which display hard determinism – a determinism which treats the individual as a victim of his or her own biological and environmental characteristics. Traditional psychological approaches have postulated the view that the past determines the present and the future, and Seligman believes that such pessimism obstructs proper development.

Positive psychologists recognise that humans are self-regulating and are not 'victims' of their past. Instead, they possess character strengths and virtues which can be developed to enhance life and result in greater fulfilment. This control of developing our authentic strengths results in control over our mental health and well-being, leading to a contented, happy life. In positive psychology, free will is not only an option but a necessity for leading a more contented life. According to this approach, in order for humans to flourish, they must have the motivation to develop their authentic strengths; they will only achieve this when they recognise they have the free will to elicit change.

◄ The Army has used methods developed by positive psychologists – developing resilience by focusing on signature strengths such as humour and courage.

WEAKNESSES OF THE POSITIVE APPROACH

1. Not a new idea

While many celebrate the positive psychology movement as a new, fresh approach to enhancing human behaviour, such claims of novelty are false. The positive potential of human beings was first celebrated by Abraham Maslow and the **humanistic psychology** movement in the late 1950s and early 1960s. Some critics of positive psychology maintain that figures like Seligman ignore the work of psychologists such as Abraham Maslow, Carl Rogers and Carl Jung who were among the first to criticise existing approaches in psychology as being rooted in negativity. In fact, the humanistic movement emerged as a backlash to predominant psychological theories of behaviourism and **psychoanalysis**, and Maslow urged people to think about addressing their higher needs, recognising that individuals are internally directed and motivated to fulfil their human potential.

Therefore, positive psychology is neither unique nor novel in recognising the deficit in psychological research. A further clash between these two approaches comes from positive psychology's desire to separate itself from humanistic psychology on the grounds of methodological inquiry. Whereas positive psychology claims to be an advance on humanistic psychology because it has adopted a 'scientific' study of well-being, humanistic psychologists are critical of their successors, believing that ignorance of **qualitative** methods will result in narrow explanations of human behaviour.

Whether the two approaches will reconcile remains to be seen; however, it cannot be denied that positive psychology has its roots in humanistic psychology, and in order to understand the positive movement, we need to understand where it has come from.

2. Can happiness be measured?

One of the most fundamental questions in positive psychology is whether we can define and measure happiness scientifically. Defining happiness has proved challenging in itself, as each individual will have a different idea about what happiness means to them. When two people say they are happy, they could be referring to two completely different states of mind. This may not be an issue in its own right; however, it is a problem when it comes to measuring happiness and developing 'scientific' measurements for this subjective state of mind.

Advances in **neuroscience** have, however, allowed researchers to objectively measure the emotional experience of happiness. For example, according to a **meta-analysis** by Wager *et al.* (2003), positive emotions were found to be more likely to activate the **basal ganglia** than negative emotions.

Neuroscientific research into happiness raises a new question about whether happiness is a discrete emotion that can be measured in a confined time in a laboratory setting, or whether it runs along a continuum with other emotions.

3. Ignoring individual differences

The positive psychology approach has been criticised for ignoring individual and cultural differences, and proposing a 'one size fits all' philosophy and its conclusions about the power of the positive.

Christopher and Hickinbottom (2008) suggest the approach is **ethnocentric**, based on culture-bound Western ideas centred on individual autonomy and fulfilment. They claim that America is a culture preoccupied with the idea that positive emotions, attitudes and thoughts are obligatory for a 'good life', where negative emotions are generally considered to be something to be avoided or controlled. They point out that **collectivism** as opposed to **individualism** is the dominant outlook in 70% of the world's population, and cultural context should not be overlooked when determining positive qualities (complaining).

The work of Julie Norem (2001) further highlights the danger in ignoring individual differences in the assumption that all positive qualities are beneficial and should be universally developed. Norem studies people who she calls 'defensive pessimists' who deal with anxiety by thinking of everything that could go wrong in a particular situation (i.e. negative thinking). Her studies show that, by processing all the realistic possibilities, defensive pessimists deal with their anxiety and work harder to avoid anticipated pitfalls. Studies by Norem and others suggest that forcing optimism or a positive mood on an anxious defensive pessimist can actually damage performance.

◄ Maslow's hierarchy of needs is an example of the humanistic approach in psychology. This approach sought, like the positive approach, to be more holistic and looking beyond the basic elements of human behaviour. For example, Maslow's higher needs were aesthetic and self-actualisation.

COMPARING APPROACHES

For the exam, you will be required not only to evaluate positive psychology, but to compare it with any of the other approaches in terms of key issues and debates.

In pairs/small groups, revisit the assumptions of the positive approach. Next write a couple of sentences for each issue/debate, explaining how the approach fits in with each issue/debate. Then choose one other approach (each individual can choose a different approach) and try comparing it with the positive approach using the table below.

Issue/debate	Positive approach	Other approach	Similar or different?
Nature–Nurture			
Scientific–Non-scientific			
Reductionism–Holism			
Determinism–Free will			

The issues and debates listed in the table above are explained in the introductory chapter on page 7.

EXAM CORNER

To evaluate the approach you need to be able to:
- Fully discuss the strengths (at least **two**).
- Fully discuss the weaknesses (at least **two**).
- Compare and contrast the approach with the four other approaches in terms of key issues and debates.

Possible exam questions:
1. Describe **two** strengths of the positive approach. [6]
2. 'The positive approach is different to traditional psychological approaches in a number of ways'. With reference to this quote, discuss the strengths and weaknesses of the positive approach compared to the other approaches you have studied. [12]
3. Evaluate **two** weaknesses of the positive approach. [8]
4. Compare and contrast the psychodynamic and positive approaches in psychology. [10]

Some activities for you

ASSUMPTIONS

ANSWERS ON PAGE 172

True or false?

Are the following statements true or false in relation to the assumptions of the positive approach? Circle the correct answer.

1	Seligman refers to three desirable lives: the pleasant life, the great life, and the meaningful life.	T or F
2	In the good life, happiness comes from activities that positively absorb and engage us.	T or F
3	In order to achieve the good life, we need to develop our strengths and virtues.	T or F
4	The positive approach assumes that happiness and goodness are less natural states than anxiety and stress.	T or F
5	'Signature strengths' are our inherent traits, such as kindness and generosity.	T or F
6	Psychology has predominantly studied positivity and happiness.	T or F
7	The positive approach denies humans as having free will.	T or F

Develop your own 'Happiness' questionnaire. Discuss some of the problems you face in doing this with the rest of your class.

Authenticity

List all the possible emotions you feel when you are in the following scenarios:
1. In a relationship
2. Just come out of an exam
3. Had an argument with a friend

Now tick which emotions were the quickest to emerge (i.e. they came most naturally). Are these emotions generally the positive or negative ones?

Discuss your answers with respect to the positive assumption of 'Authenticity of goodness and excellence'.

DEBATE

Who is best?

Hold a good old-fashioned debate!

Using two small teams (2–4 people in each), respond to the following motion:

'This house believes that the positive approach is a useful addition to psychological approaches.'

One team will argue for the motion, the other team will argue against the motion.

Host the debate in front of a small audience and have them vote on the issue after they have listened to both sides of the debate.

CLASSIC EVIDENCE

Findings

Review the work of Myers and Diener (1995) and create a mind map highlighting the key findings.

Use the headings Age, Gender, Money, Relationships, Happy people, Work and Faith, and give each a separate colour.

THERAPIES

PowerPoint

In groups, prepare a PowerPoint presentation which explains the main components of either mindfulness therapy or quality of life therapy.

Your challenge is to explain the main components to the rest of the group, using only images in your presentation.

EVALUATION

Not a new idea

One of the criticisms of the positive approach is that its assumptions are based on humanistic psychology, and it is therefore not a new approach (as some would claim).

Find out more about humanistic psychology, for example use the following website: *www.simplypsychology.org/maslow.html*

1. What is meant by the 'humanistic approach'?
2. How is the humanistic approach different to other approaches?
3. What is personal agency and how does this relate to the humanistic approach?
4. According to Rogers and Maslow, what is an important basic human motive?
5. What methodology is used by humanistic psychologists?
6. Summarise Maslow's 'Hierarchy of Needs'.
7. What is meant by self-actualisation?

EVALUATION

In groups

Discuss the similarities between the humanistic approach and the positive approach. Are there any differences. If so, what?

EVALUATION

Key phrases

1. For each key phrase, try to write a whole sentence. Try to do this without looking at your notes.
2. For each sentence, try to write a further sentence, explaining why this is a strength/weakness.

Shift in focus   *Free will*   *Applications*

Individual   Differences

Subjective measurement   Not a new idea

You can use some of the review activities described at the ends of the other chapters. For example, you could produce a key words game or mind maps (see page 25).

You should certainly list again the key words in this chapter and make sure you understand them.

Rolling shows

A rolling show* is a series of images, each placed on one PowerPoint slide, that automatically changes after a period of time (such as five seconds). Working in groups, students can produce a rolling show about the positive approach (or just one of the topics in this chapter), and then show this to students in other groups, who have to guess what the images represent.

* Thanks to Mike Griffin and Cath Gellis for this idea from *Psychology AS: The Teacher's Companion for AQA*, published by OUP.

Written exam advice

Several possible exam questions are listed below:

- **Describe** the assumptions of the positive approach. [12]
- Identify a therapy that belongs to the positive approach. **Discuss** how the assumptions of the positive approach apply to the therapy you identified. [8]
- **Evaluate two** strengths and **two** weaknesses of the positive approach. [20]

1. Imagine that you are writing a book for students studying psychology. Write down **four** (or more) top tips for students about how to answer these questions in order to get maximum marks.
2. When you have finished writing the advice, select one of the questions and prepare **two** example answers for it:
   - An answer that *does not* follow your advice.
   - A model answer that does follow the advice.
3. After you have written both versions, give them to someone else to read and ask them to identify which is the better one, and explain to them why the essays are different. (Mark schemes for the different kinds of exam answers are shown at the end of each chapter.)
4. Write notes for the model answer highlighting what makes it a model answer.

Create a 'happy board' in your classroom

Everybody in your group needs to bring in an image of an activity that makes them happy. (Please note this board should have a PG rating.)

They then need to explain to the rest of the group why that activity or image makes them happy; it might be linked to a hobby they have or to a memory of a great holiday.

Here are some images that make the authors happy…

Exam questions and answers

QUESTION ON THERAPIES

Answer either question (a) or (b):

(a) One principle used in mindfulness is meditation. Identify and explain **one** other principle that is used in mindfulness therapy. [4]

(b) One principle of quality of life therapy is the Three Pillars. Identify and explain **one** other principle of quality of life therapy. [4]

Bob's answer for (a)

The present is very important in this therapy, particularly our thoughts and emotions. As human beings we usually dwell on our past, especially if we feel negatively about something; furthermore we may spend a lot of time worrying about our futures too. This can lead us to automatically think negatively about situations which could lead to anxiety and depression. Mindfulness therapy makes us think about the here and now and teaches us to recognise past thoughts and reflect how useful they were. We can then reflect and adapt them to be more positive to help us in the here and now.   98 words

Megan's answer for (b)

The principle I am going to describe is the CASIO model. This is really important in QoLT and helps the therapist to understand what makes the patient satisfied and happy. They use CASIO to make you assess how satisfied you are and if you are not they pick the bits you're not happy with and help you to feel happier about them. They also make you realise that you are happy with certain bits of life so you concentrate on those bits rather than getting hung up on the bits you don't like.   93 words

Mark scheme for this question

Mark	Description
4	The principle is **clearly identified** and the explanation is **accurate** and **detailed**. Effective use of terminology.
3	The principle is **clearly identified** and the explanation is **reasonably accurate** and **detailed** OR **not named** but **accurate** and **detailed**. Good use of terminology.
2	The principle is **identified** and the explanation is **basic** OR **not named** but **reasonably detailed**. Some use of terminology.
1	The principle is **identified** only OR **superficial** explanation. Very little use of terminology.
0	**Inappropriate** answer / **no response**.

> Bob has not explicitly named the principle he is describing.

> Bob's explanation makes it clear he is describing the 'gaining control of thoughts', an important feature of this therapy.

> Megan's description is quite basic in that she has not explained what the CASIO factors are.

> Megan has explicitly identified what principle she is describing by naming it, i.e. CASIO.

TRY THIS

Have a go at being the examiner
Assess either Bob's (mindfulness therapy) or Megan's (QoLT) answer using the mark scheme above.

Examiner comments and marks on page 175

QUESTION ON EVALUATING THE APPROACH

'The positive approach is positively different to traditional psychological approaches in a number of ways'.

With reference to this quote, discuss the strengths of the positive approach. [8]

Bob's answer

The fact that the positive approach is 'positively different' can only be a good thing for psychology. Not only is it different, it has moved psychology forward and given us a new focus of research – this will help us understand more human behaviours. Its focus on our authentic strengths means it can help improve the lives of everyone, rather than only those suffering with mental illness, which is the focus of all other approaches, e.g. the biological approach. This is a bad thing because only focusing on disorders and disease results in a limited understanding of human behaviour, whereas if you focus on positive traits this can be applied to everyone in society and has better application and generalisation.

Furthermore, this approach is positively different and better than other approaches because it has a more free will perspective which puts the onus on the person to evaluate their life and think about the future and empower them to be proactive in changing their destiny and becoming happy and fulfilled. This is a very different philosophy to, e.g., the biological or psychodynamic approaches that are more determinist and see our lives as fait accompli as we can do very little about our genes or our early childhood experiences. As a result the positive approach allows humans to have more freedom and responsibility than the other approaches that encourage helplessness and a lack of personal responsibility over one's life.   238 words

Mark scheme for this question

Mark	Description
7–8	Evaluation is **well detailed** with **clear** reference to the quote. Depth and range displayed.
5–6	Evaluation is **reasonably detailed** with **some** reference to the quote. Depth or range displayed.
3–4	Evaluation is **basic** with **little** reference to the quote.
1–2	Evaluation is **superficial** with **no** reference to the quote.
0	**Inappropriate** answer / **no response**.

TRY THIS

Reflect on the examiner's comments in the table below and decide which relate to Bob (on left), Megan (facing page) or both.

Evaluation is accurate and relevant to the positive approach.	Evaluation makes clear reference to the quote provided.
Well-developed evaluation.	Evaluation makes little reference to the quote provided.
Terminology is used well.	Depth and range.
Mark = 7/8	Mark = 4/8

QUESTION ON THE DEBATE

To what extent does positive psychology benefit society today? [20]

Mark scheme for this question

Mark	AO1	AO3
10	Examples of research/theory are well chosen to exemplify points made. **Depth** and **range** of material included. Effective use of terminology.	**Sophisticated** and **articulate analysis** of the debate. **Balanced arguments** with evaluative commentary. Excellent structure. **Appropriate conclusion** reached.
7–9	Examples of research/theory are appropriate to support points made. There is **depth** and **range** of material used but not in equal measure. Good use of terminology.	**Good analysis** of the debate. Arguments made are well supported and **balanced**. Evaluative commentary is clearly relevant to the context. Logical structure and **appropriate conclusion**.
4–6	Examples may not always be appropriate. **Depth or range** of material used. Some inaccuracies.	**Reasonable analysis** of the debate. Arguments may be **one sided** and evaluative commentary is generic and not contextualised. Reasonable structure but **no conclusion** or generic statement.
1–3	Examples **not made relevant**. Details **muddled/inaccurate**.	**List like** commentary, answer lacks clarity. **No conclusion.**
0	**No response / inappropriate** response.	**No response / inappropriate** response.

Megan's answer

The positive approach has three key strengths, these are free will, its application, and the fact that it looks at positive behaviours over negative ones.

Positive psychology suggests that our behaviour is not pre-determined nor is it restricted. We have the power to be what we want to be, e.g. if we want to be happy and feel fulfilled it is up to us to focus on our strengths and take joy in this rather than spending our time focusing on the negatives in life. They encourage us to be the best that we can be and empower us to do this.

Positive psychology has also been praised for its application to the real world, e.g. the Army has used positive principles in its training programmes in order to make soldiers more resilient and suffer less from post traumatic stress disorder. The Army increase the mental toughness of soldiers and help them develop positive behaviours such as humour and courage. It has also been used in education. An approach is good if it is actually useful in real life.

Lastly, the positive approach is good because it concentrates on positive rather than negative traits. This is more generalisable to society as only a few have negative behaviours such as mental illness which seems to be the focus of other approaches. Seligman believes that we should be concerned with not only repairing the worst things in life but building the good things too and this approach does that.

248 words

Examiner comments and marks on page 175

TRY THIS

Have a go at being the examiner

Assess the answer below and write an examiner's comment highlighting what has been done well and what could be improved for AO1 and AO3, before giving it a final mark.

Bob's answer

The assumptions of the positive approach have been applied in many fields of life in order to help individuals, organisations and communities to flourish. I plan to discuss how this has been done in the military, education and leisure time. Positive psychology has shied away from traditional areas of research which have focused more on the dark side of human nature and instead favouring to examine all things good. Their overwhelming philosophy is that research should be done to see how productivity and happiness can be promoted and encouraged.

One application that has adopted positive psychology is the military. The US Army has developed specialist training to improve and build soldiers' resilience by building mental strength by getting recruits to recognise their own signature strengths such as courage and humour, and how they can be developed to act as a buffer to the horrors of war. This is a classic way the assumptions of the positive approach have helped us in today's society.

> Bob has clearly used a range of examples to illustrate how the positive approach has been applied to society today.

Another application is education, where some schools have timetabled positive psychology and happiness lessons for the learners.

> Describing research studies that have examined the effectiveness of the application is a good way to boost your AO1 mark.

Seligman (2009) conducted research to see the effectiveness of initiatives like these. He used 350 students that were randomly assigned to either classes that contained a positive psychology curriculum (PPC) or did not contain PPC – this was the control group. All stakeholders, e.g. students, teachers and parents, completed a questionnaire. Seligman found that students given PPC were more cooperative and had better social skills than those in the control group. Seligman concluded that PPC was not a threat to traditional education but could enhance and promote traditional education.

Education does not end in school and adults can benefit from positive psychology in the workplace as well. Employers that provide challenges and opportunities to develop new skills enable employees to enjoy work, stretch their capabilities and increase their self-esteem and self-worth. Csikszentmihalyi identified something called flow and suggested that work provided lots of opportunity for flow to occur which in turn increases positive experiences.

The final application that positive psychology has is in terms of our leisure time and interests. Self-help groups, charities and online projects all aim to try and promote users' happiness and understanding of their strengths over weaknesses.

> Bob is only describing the ways the positive approach has been used, rather than engaging in a debate, e.g. is the approach useful and beneficial or not?

An example of this is the Action for Happiness online project which publishes information on how to make your life happier.

It is clear to see from these applications, e.g. military, education and leisure time, that positive psychology is useful for people today.

417 words

See page 175 for Megan's answer
Examiner comments and marks on page 175

Chapter 6
Investigating behaviour

What are the rules to your favourite board game?

Explain them briefly to a person sitting next to you.

Now think about a psychological question that has always bugged you, such as: 'If a child's parents get divorced, is the child more likely to get divorced when they become an adult?'

How could you investigate this question?

Research methods are really just the rules to playing Psychology! Knowing these rules *allows psychologists to investigate the questions that bug them too.*

The experimental method

Your study of psychology should be fun(!) and relevant to your life. So a good way to begin understanding the research process is to investigate something about human behaviour that interests you. However, before you get too excited, you can't study anything that would be unethical!

Psychologists use a number of different methods and techniques to conduct research and that's what this chapter focuses on. Many people think it is all experiments – in fact people quite often use the phrase 'They conducted an experiment on…' when they actually mean 'They conducted an investigation on…' An experiment has some very specific rules and this is where we are going to begin our exploration of research methods.

ETHICAL ISSUES

Whenever you conduct research, you must always consider **ethical issues** and related matters carefully.
- Never use anyone under the age of 16 as a participant (or in fact any people who may be described as 'vulnerable' in any way).
- Always obtain **valid consent** from all participants – tell your participants what they will be expected to do and allow them to refuse to take part.
- **Debrief** your participants after the study to tell them of any **deception** and to allow them to **withdraw** their data if they object, on reflection, to having taken part. Before beginning any study, consult with others on the 'script' you will use for the valid consent and the debrief.

In this chapter we have defined some of the key terms on the page because research methods are so tied to the meaning of the specialist vocabulary.

TRY THIS

Observations of everyday life
You might think up your own idea but here is one possibility. Many students do their homework in front of the TV. Cara's daughter thinks she does it just as well in front of the TV as when working at a desk with no distractions. As you might imagine, Cara doesn't think this is true.

Research aim
To investigate whether people work just as well with the TV on, or whether their work will suffer as a result.

1. Work with a small group of other students and discuss the following questions:
   - How could you find out whether people can work just as well with the TV on as in a quiet room?
   - What will you need to measure?
   - Will you have two different conditions? What will you change across the two conditions?
   - How many participants will you need? Will everyone take part in both conditions, or will you have two groups of participants?
   - What will you expect to find?
   - What will the participants do?
   - What do you need to control?
2. When you have worked out what you will do, join with another group and explain your ideas to each other. The other group may ask useful questions that will help you refine your ideas.
3. Conduct your study. You may be able to do this in class or each member of your group could go away and collect some data.
4. Pool the data collected by your group and prepare a poster to present your results and conclusions.

KEY TERMS

Aims A statement of what the researcher(s) intend to find out in a research study.

Confounding variable Any variable which varies systematically with the independent variable that might potentially affect the dependent variable and thereby confound the results.

Debrief To inform the participants of the true nature of the study and to restore them to the same state they were in at the start of the study. Debriefing is not an ethical issue; it is a means of dealing with ethical issues.

Dependent variable The variable measured by the experimenter.

Ethical issues concern questions of right and wrong. They arise in research where there are conflicting sets of values between researchers and participants concerning the goals, procedures or outcomes of a research study.

Experiment A research method where causal conclusions can be drawn because an independent variable has been deliberately manipulated to observe the causal effect on the dependent variable.

Hypothesis A precise and testable statement about the assumed relationship between variables. Operationalisation is a key part of making the statement testable.

Independent variable (IV) Some event that is directly manipulated by an experimenter in order to test its effect on another variable – the dependent variable (DV).

Operationalise Ensuring that variables are in a form that can be easily tested. A concept such as 'educational attainment' needs to be specified more clearly if we are going to investigate it. For example it might be operationalised as 'GCSE grade in Maths'.

Standardised procedures A set of procedures that are the same for all participants in order to be able to repeat the study. This includes standardised instructions – the instructions given to participants to tell them how to perform the task.

Valid consent Participants must be given comprehensive information concerning the nature and purpose of the research and their role in it, in order that they can make an informed decision about whether to participate.

ABOUT EXPERIMENTS

You have just done what psychologists do – conducted a systematic study of human behaviour. You followed the **scientific method**: observe → explain → state expectations → design a study → see if your expectations were correct.

Psychologists use special words to identify aspects of the research process. We have used some of the terms already in this book, and most of them are probably familiar to you from using them in science classes.

- **Question**: *What will you measure?* This is called the **dependent variable** (**DV**). When you decided exactly what you would measure, you **operationalised** the DV – it isn't enough just to get people to do 'some work' – you should have made sure that all participants were doing the same task and would have specified what that task was (such as a memory test).

- **Question**: *What are your two conditions?* This is called the **independent variable** (**IV**). There are often two conditions of the IV – in this case having the TV on or having the TV off.

  In order to conduct an experiment we need to compare one condition (studying with the TV on) with another condition – studying with the TV off. These two conditions are described as different *levels* of the IV. A good study should always have two (or more) levels of the IV. If we don't have these different conditions or levels, we have no basis for comparison.

- **Question**: *What will you expect to find?* This is your **hypothesis**, a statement of what you believe to be true. A good hypothesis should always include the two (or more) levels of the IV. So the hypothesis might be:

  > *Students who do a memory task with the TV on produce work which gets fewer marks than those who do the same task without the TV on.*

  This is different to the **aims** of the experiment – the aims would be to investigate the effect of TV on the work a student produces. Aims are intentions or possibly a research question ('Does noise affect the quality of work?'), whereas a hypothesis is a statement of the relationship between the independent and dependent variable.

- **Question**: *What will the participants do?* You worked out a set of **standardised procedures**. It is important to make sure that each participant did exactly the same thing in each condition, otherwise the results might vary because of changes in procedure rather than because of the IV. Such identical procedures are described as 'standardised'.

- **Question**: *What do you need to control?* You will have tried to control some **confounding variables** such as time of day (people might do better on a test in the morning than in the afternoon, so all participants should do the test at about the same time of day).

This study you just did is an **experiment**. The main characteristic of an experiment is that there is an IV which is deliberately changed (TV on or not) to see if this has any effect on the DV (quality of work). This permits us to draw *causal conclusions* – we can make a statement about whether having the TV on or off *causes* a change in the quality of work that is done because we can compare the effect of the two levels of the IV that have been deliberately manipulated.

▶ Ivy Deevy.
Many students find it difficult to remember which is the IV and which is the DV – think of the silly woman. The thing that comes first (Ivy) is the IV which leads to a change in the DV (Deevy).

EXAM CORNER
Practice for novel scenarios

Four experiments are described below. For each experiment, answer the following questions:

1. Identify the IV and DV (including both levels of the IV). [2]
2. Explain how you could operationalise the IV and DV. [2]
3. Identify **one** possible confounding variable. [1]

Study A In order to study the effects of sleep deprivation, students are asked to limit their sleep to five hours a night for three nights and then sleep normally for the next night. Each day the students' cognitive abilities are assessed using a memory test.

Study B Participants volunteer to take part in a study. They are told the study is about public speaking but the real aim is to see how people respond to encouragement by others. Some participants speak in front of a group of people who smile at them, while others talk to a group who appear disinterested.

Study C Marathon runners are assessed on how much sleep they have the night before and the night after a race to see what the effects of exercise are on sleep.

Study D A teacher is doing a psychology course and decides to try a little experiment with her class of eight-year-olds. She gives half the class a test in the morning, and half of them do the same test in the afternoon to see if time of day affects their performance.

EXAM CORNER

1. Identify the key features of an experiment. [2]
2. Explain the difference between the aims of a study and a hypothesis. [2]
3. Explain what is meant by *operationalisation*. [3]
4. Explain why standardisation is important in research procedures. [2]

Validity: Control of variables

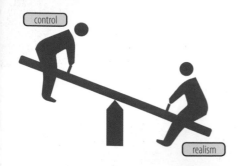

control

realism

Invariably, studies in psychology involve a trade-off between **control** and realism. The greatest control can be achieved in a **laboratory**. However, it is debatable to what extent findings from the laboratory can be generalised to other environments, especially the less controlled environments in which everyday life is lived.

Some psychologists argue that we can only discover things about behaviour if we uncover cause-and-effect relationships in highly controlled laboratory experiments.

Others argue that studies in the natural environment are the only real option for psychologists who are interested in how life is actually lived.

KEY TERMS

Confounding variable A variable that is not the independent variable (IV) under study but which varies systematically with the IV. Changes in the dependent variable may be due to the confounding variable rather than the IV, and therefore the outcome is meaningless. To 'confound' means to cause confusion.

Control Refers to the extent to which any variable is held constant or regulated by a researcher.

External validity The degree to which a research finding can be generalised: to other settings (**ecological validity**); to other groups of people (**population validity**); over time (**historical validity**).

Extraneous variables do not vary systematically with the IV and therefore do not act as an alternative IV but may have an effect on the dependent variable. They are nuisance variables that muddy the waters and make it more difficult to detect a significant effect.

Internal validity The degree to which an observed effect was due to the experimental manipulation rather than other factors such as confounding/extraneous variables.

Mundane realism Refers to how a study mirrors the real world. The research environment is realistic to the degree to which experiences encountered in the research environment will occur in the real world.

Validity Refers to whether an observed effect is a genuine one.

CONTROL

Confounding variables

Consider our experiment on the previous spread: A class of psychology students conducted the study with the **aim** of finding out whether participants could do their homework effectively while in front of the TV. The **independent variable** (IV) was whether the TV was on or not. The **dependent variable** (DV) was the participants' score on the memory test. If TV is a distraction, the 'TV off' group should do better on the test.

But consider this: Suppose it happened that all the participants in the 'TV off' condition did the memory test in the morning and all the participants in the 'TV on' condition did the memory test in the afternoon.

People (generally) are more alert in the morning and this might mean that it was the time of day rather than the lack of noise that caused the change in the DV. Time of day may then be regarded as a **confounding variable**.

The experimenter may claim that the IV caused a change in the DV but in fact this may not be the case – changes in the DV may actually be caused by a confounding variable(s). *Consequently the experimenter may not have actually tested what he (or she) intended to test.* Instead, the influence of a different variable has been tested.

The experimenter must be careful to control any possible confounding variable. In the case of our experiment participants in both conditions should do the test at the same time of day.

Extraneous variables

Some students will have better memories than others. It is unlikely that all the people with better memories would end up in the 'TV off' group. If they did, this would act as a confounding variable, but it is more likely that this variation is a nuisance variable because we can never be sure that people with good (or bad) memories are likely to be distributed evenly across the two conditions. The extraneous variable of memory ability just makes it more difficult to detect an effect because other factors have an influence.

These nuisance variables are called **extraneous variables** because they may affect the DV but not in a systematic way. They are 'extra'. They also should be controlled if possible. For example, controlling distractions such as noise.

REALISM

The aim of any psychological study is to provide information about how people behave in 'real life' – the everyday settings in which life is lived. If the set-up of a study is too artificial or contrived then the participants will not act as they would normally.

For example, the study by Loftus and Palmer (see page 76) investigated eyewitness testimony by showing participants a film of a car accident and asking questions about the speed of a car. But how realistic is this? Is watching the film the same as seeing a real accident?

Many things affect the *realism* of a psychological study. The term **mundane realism** refers to how an experiment mirrors the real world. 'Mundane' means 'of the world' – commonplace, ordinary. So lack of mundane realism means something is not like everyday experience. Watching a car accident on film lacks mundane realism because it is not like everyday experience, and this means that the results of the study may not be very useful in terms of understanding behaviour in the real world.

Generalisation

The point of realism in psychological research is to be able to *generalise* the results beyond the particular unique research setting – in particular to be able to understand behaviour in everyday life (the 'real world').

- If the *materials* used in the study are contrived (such as film clips) then the behaviour observed may lack realism.
- If the *environment* in which a study is conducted is contrived and especially if participants are aware they are being studied, the participants' behaviour may lack realism.
- Even if the environment and materials are 'natural' or real (i.e. high realism) a study can still lack generalisability. For example, if all the participants in a study are American university students, it may not be reasonable to generalise the findings to the behaviour of all people because Americans (and students) have unique characteristics that may set them apart in some way from other people.

The question psychologists are always asking themselves is: 'To what extent can I generalise these findings to everyday life?'

The scientific cycle

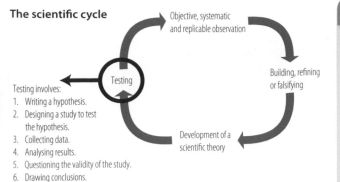

Testing involves:
1. Writing a hypothesis.
2. Designing a study to test the hypothesis.
3. Collecting data.
4. Analysing results.
5. Questioning the validity of the study.
6. Drawing conclusions.

VALIDITY

The term **validity** refers to how true or legitimate something is as an explanation of behaviour. It involves the issues of control, realism and generalisability.

Students often believe that validity is about 'being correct'. This is both right and wrong. It is right because a researcher seeks to find out whether their **hypothesis** is true, i.e. correct, but it is wrong if you think that being correct means finding out that the predicted expectations have been confirmed. Validity is not about confirming your expectations.

Validity can be separated into **internal validity** and **external validity**. Internal validity is about control and realism. External validity is about being able to generalise from research participants to other people and situations.

Internal validity

Internal validity concerns what goes on inside a study. It is concerned with things such as:

- Whether the IV produced the change in the DV (or did something else affect the DV, such as a confounding variable?).
- Whether the researcher tested what she or he intended to test. For example, if you want to find out whether watching TV affects the quality of homework, you cannot be certain you are testing 'watching the TV' by just having the TV on (the person may not be watching it).
- Whether the study possessed (or lacked) mundane realism.

To gain high internal validity researchers must design the research carefully, controlling confounding and extraneous variables, and ensuring that they are testing what they intended to test.

External validity

External validity is affected by internal validity – you cannot generalise the results of a study that was low in internal validity because the results have no real meaning for the behaviour in question.

External validity also concerns:

- The place where the research was conducted (**ecological validity**). It may not be appropriate to generalise from the research setting to other settings, most importantly to everyday life.
- The people who are studied (**population validity**). If a research study involved just students or all men or only Americans, etc., then it may not be appropriate to generalise the findings to all people.
- The historical period (**historical validity**). If a study was conducted in the 1950s it may not be appropriate to generalise the findings to people today because many other factors affect behaviour now.

TRY THIS

Learning about research methods is a bit like learning a foreign language. When you learn a foreign language you have to learn a new set of words and, more especially, you have to learn what they mean. One of the best ways to do this is to *speak* the language.

The same is true for research methods. Don't hold back, don't be scared – use the words. Talk the talk.

To help you learn the language you could create your own **Research Methods Vocabulary Book** to record all the terms used, their meanings and their advantages and disadvantages.

You can include a copy of the specification for research methods in your book and tick off each term when you have recorded the details and again when you feel you understand it.

EXAM CORNER
Practice for novel scenarios

1. An area of study that has interested psychologists is *massed versus distributed practice*, i.e. whether learning is better if you practise something repeatedly all in one go (massed) or space your periods of practice (distributed). This topic has been studied in different settings; for example:

    Study 1: Participants were required to recall nonsense syllables on 12 occasions spread over either 3 days or 12 days (Jost, 1897). Recall was higher when spread over 12 days. This finding has been supported by subsequent research.

    Study 2: Post office workers had to learn to type postcodes either using massed or distributed practice (Baddeley and Longman, 1978). Distributed practice was again found to be superior.

    Present arguments for why each of these studies could be viewed as having high and low external validity.

2. Select **one or more** studies that you are familiar with and explain why you think the study might be:
    - High in internal validity
    - Low in internal validity
    - High in external validity
    - Low in external validity

EXAM CORNER

1. Give an example of a confounding variable in the context of a named study. [2]
2. Explain why it is important to control extraneous variables in a study. [2]
3. Distinguish between extraneous variables and confounding variables. [3]

Return to hypotheses and other things

A **hypothesis** is a statement of what the researcher believes to be true. Strictly speaking it is not a research *prediction*. It should not be stated in the future tense (i.e. 'this will happen…'). At the end of a study the researcher decides whether the evidence collected supports the hypothesis or not.

A hypothesis is also not the same as the **aims** of a research study. Aims are an initial statement of what the researcher plans to investigate, whereas the hypothesis is a formal and testable statement of the relationship between variables.

That's a recap of what you know so far, so you are ready for the next instalment on hypotheses…

► Babies who sleep more do better than babies who sleep less – a directional hypothesis – but how would you operationalise it?

DIRECTIONAL AND NON-DIRECTIONAL HYPOTHESES

Let's consider a different experiment to our TV on/off study – we might consider the effects of lack of sleep on school performance. That is our research aim, i.e. to see if lack of sleep affects school performance.

We might propose the following hypothesis: People who have plentiful sleep (an average of 8 hours or more per night over a period of one month) have better marks in class tests than people with a lower sleep average. (Note that this hypothesis has been **operationalised**.)

The hypothesis above is a **directional hypothesis** – it states the expected *direction* of the results, i.e. you are stating that people who sleep well do *better* on class tests.

If you changed the hypothesis to 'People who have plentiful sleep (an average of eight hours or more per night) have *lower* marks in class tests than people with a lower sleep average' this is still a directional hypothesis – you are then stating that the results are expected to go in the opposite direction.

A **non-directional hypothesis** states that there is a difference between two conditions but does not state the direction of the difference: People who have plentiful sleep (an average of eight hours or more per night over a period of one month) have *different* marks on class tests than people with a lower sleep average. We may well have a hunch that lack of sleep will affect performance but have no real evidence to suggest whether this would be a positive or a negative effect.

Here are two more examples:

Directional hypothesis	People who do homework without the TV on produce *better* results than those who do homework with the TV on.
Non-directional hypothesis	People who do homework with the TV on produce *different* results from those who do homework with no TV on.

Note that the IV and DV haven't been operationalised in the above examples.

Which should you use?

Why do psychologists sometimes use a directional hypothesis instead of a non-directional one (or vice versa)? Psychologists use a directional hypothesis when past research (a theory or a study) suggests that the findings will go in a particular direction. It makes sense then to frame the hypothesis in the direction indicated.

Psychologists use a non-directional hypothesis when there is no past research or past research is contradictory. Non-directional hypotheses may be more appropriate if the study is exploring a new area, where informed expectations about how people might behave have yet to be established through research.

KEY TERMS

Alternative hypothesis Any hypothesis except the null hypothesis. It is the alternative to the null hypothesis.

Confederate An individual in a study who is not a real participant and has been instructed how to behave by the investigator.

Directional hypothesis states the direction of the predicted difference between two conditions or two groups of participants.

Experimental hypothesis The term used to describe the alternative hypothesis in an experiment.

Non-directional hypothesis predicts simply that there is a difference between two conditions or two groups of participants, without stating the direction of the difference.

Null hypothesis The assumption of no relationship (difference, association, etc.) between variables being studied.

Pilot study A small-scale trial run of a study to test any aspects of the design, with a view to making improvements.

ALTERNATIVE, EXPERIMENTAL AND NULL HYPOTHESES

Just when you thought you understood hypotheses, we have some further distinctions to make:

The **null hypothesis (H_0)** is a statement of no effect. For example:
  There is no difference in the marks on class tests between people who sleep an average of 8 hours or more per night and those with a lower sleep average.

The **alternative hypothesis (H_1)** is the alternative to the null hypothesis – it is the hypothesis we wrote earlier:
  People who have plentiful sleep (an average of 8 hours or more per night) have better marks in class tests than people with a lower sleep average.

In the case of an experiment, this alternative hypothesis is called an **experimental hypothesis**. We will be explaining the null hypothesis later in this chapter (see page 150).

▲ The woman on the left (a confederate) talks 'blirtatiously' (loudly and effusively) to see what effect this has on the person who is studying.

A FEW OTHER THINGS

Pilot studies and the aims of piloting

If you conducted the study on page 110 (or any other studies) yourself you are probably aware that there were flaws in your research design. Did you realise that there would be flaws beforehand? Or did some of the flaws become apparent during or after conducting the experiment?

Scientists deal with this problem by conducting a **pilot study** first. A pilot study is a small-scale trial run of a research design before doing the real thing. It is done in order to find out if aspects of the design do or don't work. For example, participants may not understand the instructions or they may guess what an experiment is about. They may also get bored because there are too many tasks or too many questions.

If a researcher tries out the design using a few typical participants they can see what needs to be adjusted without having invested a large amount of time and money in a full-scale study.

Note that the results of any such pilot study are irrelevant – the researcher is not interested in what results are produced but is simply seeing to what extent the procedures need fine tuning.

Confederates

Sometimes a researcher has to use another person to play a role in an experiment or other investigation. For example, you might want to find out if people respond differently to orders from someone wearing a suit compared with someone dressed in casual clothes.

In this experiment the IV would be the clothing worn by a person who has been briefed to behave in a certain way by the experimenter. The experimenter would arrange for this person to give orders either dressed in a suit or dressed casually. This person is called a **confederate**.

The study on obedience by Milgram (see page 162) involved a confederate playing the role of the 'experimenter'.

Exam advice...

Exam questions about pilot studies rarely ask you to explain what a pilot study is – you are more likely to be asked how a researcher would conduct one or why a researcher might conduct a pilot study. Make sure you deal with 'how' or 'why' in such questions.

EXAM CORNER

1. Explain what a pilot study is. [2]
2. Explain why a researcher might use a pilot study. [2]
3. Briefly explain how a pilot study might be conducted. [2]
4. Distinguish between a directional and non-directional hypothesis. [2]
5. The alternative hypothesis for a study is 'Boys are better than girls at Maths'. What would the null hypothesis be for this study? [2]
6. Explain why a researcher would choose to use a non-directional hypothesis rather than a directional hypothesis. [2]

EXAM CORNER

Practice for novel scenarios

1. Read the statements below and identify which are aims and which are hypotheses.
   a. Younger people have better memories than older people. [1]
   b. To see if blondes have more fun than brunettes. [1]
   c. Do people who sleep with a teddy bear sleep longer than people who don't? [1]
   d. Positive expectations lead to differences in performance. [1]
   e. Men with beards are more attractive. [1]
   f. Lack of sleep may affect schoolwork. [1]
2. For each of the following, decide whether it is a directional or non-directional hypothesis or a null hypothesis.
   a. Boys score differently on aggressiveness tests than girls. [1]
   b. There is no difference in the exam performance of students who have a computer at home compared with those who don't. [1]
   c. People remember the words that are early in a list better than the words that appear later. [1]
   d. People given a list of emotionally charged words recall fewer words than participants given a list of emotionally neutral words. [1]
   e. Hamsters are better pets than budgies. [1]
   f. Words presented in a written form are recalled differently from those presented in a pictorial form. [1]
3. Now write your own. Below are research aims for possible experiments. For each one identify and operationalise the IV and DV and then write **three** hypotheses: a directional one, a non-directional one and a null hypothesis.
   a. Do girls watch more television than boys? [1]
   b. Do teachers give more attractive students higher marks on essays than students who are less attractive? [1]
   c. A researcher believes older people sleep more than younger people. [1]
   d. Do people rate food as looking more attractive when they are hungry? [1]
   e. A teacher wishes to find out whether one maths test is harder than another maths test. [1]
4. Select **one** of the experiments from question 3.
   a. Explain *why* you would conduct a pilot study for this experiment. [2]
   b. Describe *how* you would do it. [2]

Experimental design

On this spread we are going to find out a little more about experiments. As you know by now an experiment has an **independent variable (IV)** and a **dependent variable (DV)**. In order to find out whether the IV did affect the DV we always need a comparison condition – a condition where there is a different level of the IV.

For example, consider the sleep experiment. If you only got data on people who slept eight or more hours a night that wouldn't help you to know anything about their performance unless you have another condition to compare them with (people who slept less than eight hours). The two levels of the IV are therefore: (1) 'sleep eight hours or more' and (2) 'sleep less than eight hours'.

The same is true for the experiment looking at the effects of watching TV while doing your homework – the two levels of the IV are 'TV on' and 'TV off'.

The way that the two levels of the IV are delivered is called **experimental design**.

TYPES OF EXPERIMENTAL DESIGN

Type of experimental design	Disadvantages	Method of dealing with the disadvantages
Repeated measures All participants receive all levels of the IV; for example: • Each participant does the task with the TV on, e.g. does a memory test. • Then, perhaps a week later, each participant does a similar test without the TV on. We compare the performance (DV) of the participant on the two tests.	1. The order of the conditions may affect performance (an **order effect**). For example, participants may do better on the second test because of a **practice effect** or because they are less anxious. In some situations participants may do worse on the second test because of being bored with doing the same test again (**boredom effect**). 2. When participants do the second test they may guess the purpose of the experiment, which may affect their behaviour. For example, some participants may purposely do worse on the second test because they want it to appear as if they work less well in the afternoon.	Researchers may use two different tests to reduce a practice effect – though the two tests must be equivalent. This can be done by constructing a test of 40 items and randomly allocating items to Test A and Test B. The main way that order effects are dealt with is use of **counterbalancing** (see facing page). In order to avoid participants guessing the aims of a study, a cover story can be presented about the purpose of the test.
Independent groups Participants are placed in separate (independent) groups. Each group does one level of the IV; for example: • Group A does the task with the TV on (one level of the IV). • Group B does the task with no TV (the other level of the IV). We compare the performance (DV) of the two groups.	1. The researcher cannot control the effects of **participant variables** (i.e. the different abilities or characteristics of each participant). For example, participants in Group A might happen to have better memories than those in Group B. This would act as a **confounding variable**. 2. Independent groups design needs more participants than repeated measures design in order to end up with the same amount of data.	**Randomly allocate** participants to conditions which (theoretically) distribute participant variables evenly. Random allocation can be done by putting the participants' names in a hat and drawing out the names so that every other person goes in Group A. See random techniques on page 125.
Matched pairs A compromise is to use two groups of participants but match participants on key characteristics believed to affect performance on the DV (IQ or time spent watching TV). Then one member of the pair is allocated to Group A and the other to Group B. The procedure is then the same as for independent groups. It is important to realise that the characteristics for matching *must* be relevant to the study. In other words you wouldn't need to match participants on gender if you were testing memory – unless there was some evidence that women had better memories.	1. It is very time consuming and difficult to match participants on key variables. The researcher probably has to start with a large group of participants to ensure they can obtain matched pairs on key variables. 2. It is not possible to control all participant variables because you can only match on variables known to be relevant, but it could be that others are important. For example, in a memory experiment you might match on memory abilities but later find that some of the participants had been involved in a teaching programme to boost memory skills and you should have matched on this.	Restrict the number of variables to match on to make it easier. Conduct a **pilot study** to consider key variables that might be important when matching.

ADVANTAGES

You can work out the advantages of each experimental design by looking at the disadvantages of the other designs.

For example, one disadvantage of repeated measures is that participants do better on one condition because of a practice effect. Therefore one advantage of independent groups and matched pairs designs is that these designs avoid such order effects, i.e. there would be no practice effect because each participant only does one condition.

Identify **two** advantages for each design listed in the table above.

In a repeated measures design there are two (or more) levels of the IV. Each level is called a 'condition'. Instead of levels there may be an experimental condition and a control condition.

In an independent groups or matched pairs design each group does one condition – the experimental group does the experimental condition and the control group does the control condition.

KEY TERMS

Counterbalancing An experimental technique used to overcome order effects when using a repeated measures design. Counterbalancing ensures that each condition is tested first or second in equal amounts.

Experimental design A set of procedures used to control the influence of factors such as participant variables in an experiment.

Independent groups design Participants are allocated to two (or more) groups representing different levels of the IV. Allocation is usually done using random techniques.

Matched pairs design Pairs of participants are matched in terms of key variables such as age and IQ. One member of each pair is allocated to one of the conditions under test and the second person is allocated to the other condition.

Order effect In a repeated measures design, an extraneous variable arising from the order in which conditions are presented, e.g. a practice effect or fatigue effect.

Random allocation Allocating participants to experimental groups or conditions using random techniques.

Repeated measures design Each participant takes part in every condition under test, i.e. each level of the IV.

COUNTERBALANCING

Counterbalancing ensures that each condition in a repeated measures design is tested first or second in equal amounts. If participants do the same memory test first in the morning and then in the afternoon, we might expect them to do better on the second test because they have had some practice – or they might do worse because they are bored with the task. These are called order effects, which can be dealt with using counterbalancing.

There are two ways to counterbalance order effects. In each case, we have two conditions:
- Condition A – test done in the morning.
- Condition B – test done in the afternoon.

Way 1. AB or BA

Divide participants into two groups:
- Group 1: each participant does A then B.
- Group 2: each participant does B then A.

Note that this is still a repeated measures design even though there are two groups of participants, because comparison will be made for each participant on their performance on the two conditions (morning and afternoon).

Way 2. ABBA

This time, all participants take part in each condition twice.
- Trial 1: Condition A (morning)
- Trial 2: Condition B (afternoon)
- Trial 3: Condition B (afternoon)
- Trial 4: Condition A (morning)

Then we compare scores on trials 1 and 4 with trials 2 and 3. As before, this is still a repeated measures design because we are comparing the scores of the same person.

EXAM CORNER
Practice for novel scenarios

1. For each of the following experiments a–f, identify the experimental design that has been used.
   When trying to decide, it might help you if you ask yourself:
   - Would the findings be analysed by comparing the scores from the same person or by comparing the scores of two (or more) groups of people?
   - If it is two or more groups of people then ask: 'Are the people in the different groups related (i.e. matched) or not?'

   a. Boys and girls are compared on their IQ test scores. [1]
   b. Hamsters are tested to see if one genetic strain is better at finding food in a maze than another. [1]
   c. Reaction time is tested before and after a reaction time training activity to see if test scores improve after training. [1]
   d. Students are put in pairs based on their GCSE grades and then one member of the pair is given a memory test in the morning and one in the afternoon. [1]
   e. Three groups of participants are given different word lists to remember, in order to find out whether nouns, verbs or adjectives are easier to recall. [1]
   f. Participants are asked to give ratings for attractive and unattractive photographs. [1]

2. Construct scenarios whereby a researcher might use each of the three types of experimental design.
   Describe your scenarios to a partner; can they identify which experimental design(s) you thought would be appropriate to use?

Exam advice…

Exam questions often ask you to identify the experimental design used in a particular study. When students see the phrase 'experimental design' in an exam question they often can't remember what 'experimental design' means.

Here's one way to remember – in the middle of the word 'experimental' are the letters RIM, which stand for repeated, independent and matched pairs.

EXAM CORNER

1. Explain what is meant by independent groups design. [2]
2. Name **one** other type of experimental design and explain how it might be used. [2]
3. Explain **one** disadvantage of using a matched pairs design. [3]

Location of research

The location that a psychologist chooses to conduct their research is one which can depend on the sort of method they are using, or it might rely on the approach or area of psychology that they are studying.

Experiments are traditionally conducted in laboratories, but they are also conducted in the field and online; the **biological**, **behaviourist** and **cognitive approaches** generally prefer lab-based experiments, whereas the **psychodynamic** and **positive approaches** tend to use non-experimental methods outside the lab.

▲ A psychology lab might look like the room above. The main characteristic of a lab is that it is an environment where variables can be easily controlled – the independent variable can be easily manipulated, the dependent variable can be easily measured and extraneous/confounding variables can be controlled.

Just because a research study is conducted in such an environment does not mean it is a laboratory experiment. It might not be an experiment. It might even be a natural or a quasi-experiment, something you will study on the next spread.

CONDUCTING RESEARCH...

...in a laboratory

Conducting research in a **laboratory** is the most scientific way to conduct research. Although when thinking of a laboratory you may think of a room with lots of test tubes, machines and of course a scientist in a white lab coat, a psychology laboratory does not really look like this.

A laboratory is really just a room equipped to allow scientific research and measurement. Most psychological research that gets conducted in a laboratory tends to be experimental in nature, but this is not always the case. Many researchers conduct **observational** research in a laboratory setting. Ainsworth's *Strange Situation* is an example of this (see picture below).

...in the field

Conducting research in **the field** is where psychologists conduct and collect research data outside of a laboratory, in a more natural setting. Field research can happen in many locations, such as shopping centres, trains, hospitals, etc. Such environments may be new to participants, i.e. they are not the participants' natural environments but, in general, the setting is more natural.

A hospital might seem like quite a controlled environment, making it difficult to distinguish between a laboratory and the field – one way to do this is to think of whether the participants have gone to the research (laboratory) or the researcher has gone to the participants (field).

...online

This method of conducting research has only arisen in the last couple of decades. Being **online** allows researchers to be able to access participants via the internet or on social networking tools. Websites such as *www.onlinepsychresearch.co.uk* or *www.socialpsycology.org/expts.htm* allow anybody to visit the site and become a participant in a piece of psychological research. The kind of research is often **questionnaires** or maybe experimental.

KEY TERMS

Laboratory An environment which can be controlled by the researcher. In particular a researcher wishes to control extraneous variables and, in an experiment, needs to manipulate the independent variables. This is easy in a controlled environment.

Online Refers to being connected via the internet to another source. You may be connected to a website or could be using an app on a mobile phone. Data can be collected from individuals.

The field This is not the same as 'a field'. Conducting research in 'the field' usually means working with participants in an environment that is more familiar to them.

EXAM CORNER

1. Explain what is meant by a *laboratory* environment. Give an example in your answer. [2]
2. Explain what is meant by *field research*. [2]
3. Explain what is meant by *online research*. [2]

▲ Ainsworth's *Strange Situation* is a research technique used to assess an infant's attachment type. It is conducted in an observation laboratory with video cameras so as to record the behaviour of mothers and their children. The laboratory contains two easy chairs, a low table and a set of toys.

EVALUATION...

...in a laboratory

Advantages

Laboratories allow researchers to measure research variables more easily, making it easier to control **confounding** or **extraneous variables**, and also easier for other researchers to replicate the research.

Some psychologists need to utilise equipment that isn't very portable in their research. **PET** machines, as used by Raine *et al.* (see page 18), are very large and aren't especially robust.

Disadvantages

Laboratories may cause participants to demonstrate artificial behaviour because the laboratory surrounding they are in reminds them that they are taking part in a piece of research and as such participants may be on their best behaviour.

Some research really cannot be conducted in a laboratory because of the nature of the behaviour being researched. Some behaviours may occur in small, inaccessible populations, such as observing the breeding habits of dugongs (Great Barrier Reef), or some behaviour may take an impractically long time to demonstrate, such as the 22-month gestation period of an African elephant.

...in the field

Advantages

Field research is especially useful if you want to minimise the artificial nature of research. When people are in a real, everyday environment they are less likely to be aware of their participation in research and as a result may behave more naturally.

Field research allows psychologists to examine behaviour in a huge range of contexts that would be difficult to accommodate in a laboratory. If I want to investigate how happiness rates increase after spending some time in an area of outstanding natural beauty, such as Yosemite National Park, then field research allows me to do this. In a laboratory a researcher would only be able to offer pictures or, at best, a virtual reality representation of the park.

Disadvantages

Although it is not impossible, it is more difficult to measure research variables and it also makes it more difficult to control for confounding or extraneous variables. A second researcher replicates the research and they may not find the same findings because of differences in the settings.

It is difficult for researchers to utilise a full complement of equipment. Brain scanning machines, as previously stated, are not very portable and as such are not easily used by field researchers. However, it must be noted that improvements in technology, such as the use of eye tracking glasses, show how researchers are continually updating their ability to use equipment in the field.

...online

Advantages

The researcher has the ability to access a large group of participants; in fact Nosek *et al.* (2002) collected 1.5 million completed responses to their research. This therefore allows the researcher to seek out a diverse sample that may be less culturally biased than if they just conducted research on their own undergraduates.

Conducting research online is cost effective. Researchers frequently use free, cheap software which allows them to quickly put research onto the internet. The costs of this activity are generally less than the costs of posting surveys, or having a research assistant complete telephone interviews. Data analysis is generally quicker as participants have already transcribed their responses and analysis can be conducted.

Disadvantages

Methods used in online research tend to be limited, with most being surveys or questionnaires. There is some experimental research being conducted online, but this tends to be infrequent.

Ethical issues, such as **consent** and protection of participants from any **risk of harm**, may become more difficult to deal with. Most internet users are asked to simply tick a box to indicate they've read the terms and conditions, so can online researchers be sure that participants have given valid consent? It also makes it difficult to appropriately **debrief** the participants if the need arises. The British Psychological Society do offer guidance on how to conduct online research in an ethical manner.

AN EXPERIMENT IN THE FIELD

Piliavin *et al.* (1969) conducted some very famous field experiments in the New York Subway. They wanted to investigate 'helping behaviour'. Laboratory research published in the previous year by Darley and Latané (1968) had suggested that people were less likely to help if they believed others were also able to offer help. However, Piliavin *et al.* thought that people might behave differently in more everyday settings, especially when they were face-to-face with the person needing help.

So, during a 7½-minute journey between Harlem and the Bronx in New York City, **confederates** played the role of 'victims' who were either drunk or ill, black or white. In the drunk condition, the victim smelled of alcohol and carried a brown paper bag. In the ill condition, the victim carried a black cane. In both conditions, the victim was dressed identically and collapsed in a train compartment. There were 40–45 passengers in the compartment and eight or nine close to the victim each time the confederate collapsed.

Help for the victim was provided by one or more passengers in 81 of the 103 trials. This was much higher than the level of help suggested by laboratory research.

EXAM CORNER

Practice for novel scenarios

1. Consider the following research scenarios; which location could a researcher use – laboratory, the field or online?
   a. The alcohol consumption rates of underage adults. [1]
   b. Commuters are less helpful on their way to work than on their return home. [1]
   c. Do students misbehave more in the lessons of experienced or inexperienced teachers? [1]
   d. Is there a difference in the reaction times of gamers and non-gamers to visual stimuli? [1]
   e. Do females prefer to meet friends in a coffee shop or a bar? [1]
   f. People rate films more favourably if they watch the film with their friends. [1]
2. Afterwards discuss your answers with a partner. There may be more than one suitable location for each research study.

Quasi-experiments

A **quasi-experiment** is not a 'true' experiment because the **independent variable** (**IV**) is not deliberately manipulated. This means that it is not possible to claim that changes in the **dependent variable** (**DV**) are caused by the independent variable.

However, in some circumstances using a quasi-experiment is the only way to study behaviour.

▲ What is natural?

Natural means 'derived from nature, not made or caused by humankind'.

In a natural experiment the thing that is natural is the IV. In a natural experiment the environment may not be natural – for example, the DV may be tested in a lab.

KEY TERMS

Difference studies A kind of quasi-experiment. The independent variable is actually not something that varies at all – it is a condition that exists. The researcher records the effect of this 'quasi-IV' on a dependent variable (DV). As with a natural experiment, the lack of manipulation of the IV and the lack of random allocation means that causal conclusions can only tentatively be drawn.

Quasi-experiment Studies that are 'almost' experiments. A research method in which the experimenter has not manipulated the independent variable (IV) directly. The IV would vary whether or not the researcher was interested. The researcher records the effect of the IV on a dependent variable (DV) – this DV may be measured in a lab. Strictly speaking, an experiment involves the deliberate manipulation of an IV and random allocation to conditions by the experimenter, neither of which apply to a quasi-experiment, and therefore causal conclusions can only tentatively be drawn.

QUASI-EXPERIMENTS

There are two kinds of quasi-experiments – those with an IV (**natural experiments**) and those with no IV (**difference studies**).

Natural experiments

A natural experiment is conducted when it is not possible, for ethical or practical reasons, to deliberately manipulate an IV. Therefore it is said that the IV varies 'naturally' (and thus the term 'natural experiment' is used). The DV may be tested in a **laboratory**.

Consider these examples:

- **Effects of watching violence** Berkowitz (1970) compiled monthly FBI crime statistics on the frequency of violent crimes from January 1960 to December 1966. He reported a steep increase in the number of violent crimes being recorded following November 1963. This, he proposed, was the result of the American population being exposed to television footage of John F. Kennedy's assassination. In this study the IV was exposure to television footage of Kennedy's assassination.
- **Effects of TV** Before 1995 people living on the small island of St Helena in the middle of the Atlantic had no TV. The arrival of TV gave researchers a chance to see how exposure to Western programmes might influence behaviour – overall Charlton et al. (2000) found no difference in either pro- or anti-social behaviour after the introduction of Western TV. In this study the IV was no TV and later exposure to TV.

In both of these examples, the IVs were not controlled by the researchers – they took advantage of something which would be practically and ethically quite difficult to control.

Difference studies

In a difference study the apparent IV is also naturally occurring and the DV may be measured in a laboratory. The key feature is that the IV has not been made to vary by anyone. It is simply a difference between people that exists. So it isn't actually a variable at all. Such 'difference studies' are included as quasi-experiments.

Consider these examples:

- **Gender differences** Sheridan and King (1972) tested obedience by asking male participants to give genuine electric shocks of increasing advantage to a puppy. They found that 54% of male participants delivered the maximum (non-fatal) shock, but the obedience rate for females was a staggering 100%! The IV in this study was gender – a difference that cannot be manipulated and thus not a 'true' IV.
- **Olfactory abilities of non-sighted individuals** Rosenbluth et al. (2000) compared the olfactory (smell) abilities of sighted and non-sighted children. One group of 30 non-sighted children were **matched** to 30 sighted children in terms of their age, sex and ethnicity. The researchers found that although the two groups of children did not differ significantly in their olfactory abilities, the non-sighted children scored higher (12.1 out of a maximum of 25) compared to the sighted children (10.4) when labelling smells.

In both of these examples the characteristics of people, gender or visual ability, is being investigated and hence is the IV of the research.

◄ Many studies in psychology compare the behaviour of older and younger people, for example on the accuracy of their eyewitness testimony. In such studies the IV is age. This is a 'condition' of the individual and therefore such studies are considered to be quasi-experiments.

It is not age that has caused the behaviour but characteristics that vary with age such as, for example, the likelihood that some participants may have dementia or are less skilled on the task being tested.

EVALUATION

There are several reasons why researchers cannot draw cause-and-effect conclusions from quasi-experiments.

Manipulation of the IV

The lack of control over the IV means that we cannot say for certain that any change in the DV was caused by the IV. For example, if there were uncontrolled **confounding variables** then observed changes in the DV might not be due to the IV. (Remember that poor experimental design may make causal conclusions unjustified in a laboratory or field experiment – so causal conclusions are not guaranteed.)

Random allocation

In an experiment with an **independent groups design** participants are **randomly allocated** to conditions. This is not possible in natural or quasi-experiments. This means that there may be biases in the different groups of participants.

For example, in the study that investigated the olfactory abilities of non-sighted individuals (see facing page), the non-sighted participants were matched with sighted individuals. Although this was done with the best intention of removing possible biases, it may still mean that the individuals included in the two conditions are very different.

This means that, due to the lack of random allocation, there may be uncontrolled confounding variables.

Unique characteristics of participants

The sample studied may have unique characteristics. For example, in the St Helena study (on the facing page), the people were part of a particularly helpful and pro-social community, and this might explain why violence on TV didn't affect their behaviour whereas, in other studies, the advent of TV did have an effect.

The unique characteristics of the sample mean that the findings can't be generalised to other groups of people (i.e. the study may be described as having low **population validity**).

Different kinds of experiment

Some experiments are conducted in a laboratory whereas others are conducted in the field. The third kind of experiment is a quasi-experiment, which sounds like it is quite 'natural'. Consider the table below.

	IV	DV, measured by an experimenter
Lab	Manipulated by the researcher.	In lab. Participants are probably aware that their behaviour is being measured.
Field	Manipulated by the researcher.	In natural environment.
Quasi	Would vary even if experimenter not interested.	Probably in lab (or a controlled environment), though it may be measured in the field. Participants are probably aware that their behaviour is being measured.

Here's a study to think about. Cognitive psychologist Alan Baddeley conducted a study on memory, showing that context helps recall. He used underwater divers as his participants.

- Group 1 learned words underwater and then were asked to recall them underwater (same content).
- Group 2 learned words underwater and then were asked to recall them on land (different context).
- Group 3 learned words on land and then were asked to recall them on land (same context).
- Group 4 learned words on land and then were asked to recall them underwater (different context).

Participants recalled word lists better when the context was the same.

This sounds like a very 'natural' study because it was conducted in a natural environment – but it used word lists (contrived) and tested people underwater (an unusual environment).

EXAM CORNER

1. Explain what is meant by a *quasi-experiment*. [2]
2. Discuss the use of quasi-experiments in psychological research. Give examples in your answer. [6]

Exam advice…

In preparation for the exam, you may want to devise a decision tree using your knowledge of the different types of experiments (laboratory, field, quasi/natural).

EXAM CORNER
Practice for novel scenarios

Six studies are described below. For each study: (a) identify the IV and DV [2]; (b) identify whether it is a laboratory, field or quasi-experiment [2]; (c) explain your decision [2]; and (d) explain why you think the study would have high or low validity [2].

1. Two primary schools use different reading schemes. A psychological study compares the reading scores at the end of the year to see which scheme was more effective.
2. Children take part in a trial to compare the success of a new maths programme. The children are placed in one of two groups – a group receiving the new maths programme or a group receiving the traditional one – and taught in these groups for a term.
3. The value of using computers rather than books is investigated by requiring children to learn word lists, either using a computer or with a book.
4. People who score highly on the authoritarian personality scale are compared with people low on the authoritarian personality scale in terms how willing they are to obey orders.
5. The effect of advertisements on gender stereotypes is studied by asking participants to look at adverts with women doing feminine tasks or neutral tasks and then asking them about gender stereotypes.
6. A study investigates the anti-social effects of TV by monitoring whether people who watch a lot of TV (more than five hours a day) are more aggressive than those who don't.

Threats to validity and dealing with them

There are a number of problems that arise in experiments that threaten the **internal validity** of an experiment. We have considered **extraneous** and **confounding variables** already. On this spread we consider more issues that may act as extraneous or confounding variables.

▲ Participants may want to offer a helping hand. If they know they are in an experiment they usually want to please the experimenter and be helpful, otherwise why are they there? This sometimes results in them being over-cooperative – and behaving artificially.

However, some participants react in the opposite way – the 'screw you' effect where a participant deliberately behaves in a way that spoils an experiment.

PARTICIPANTS OR SUBJECTS?

In early psychological research the people in the studies were called 'subjects'. In the 1990s there was a move to use the term 'participant' instead of 'subject'.

One reason for the change of terminology is that the term 'participant' reflects the fact that such individuals are not passive members of a study but are actively involved. They search for cues about what to do and this may mean that they behave as researchers expect rather than as they would in everyday life. The use of the term 'participant' acknowledges this active involvement.

A further reason for the change is that the term 'subject' implies that those involved must be obedient and are powerless whereas, in fact, psychologists owe them a great deal for their willingness to take part – it is an equal partnership.

DEMAND CHARACTERISTICS

Participants want to be helpful and therefore they pay attention to cues in the experimental situation that may guide their behaviour. Consider this study by Martin Orne:

> Participants had to sit in a room on their own for four hours. One group of participants were asked at the beginning of the study to sign a form releasing the experimenter from responsibility if anything happened to them during the experiment. They were also given a panic button to push if they felt overly stressed. The other group were given no information to arouse their expectations. The first group showed extreme signs of distress during isolation. This can only be explained in terms of expectations created by the situation. (Orne and Scheibe, 1964)

Orne invented the term **demand characteristics** to describe the effect of expectations and defined them in the folllowing way:

> The totality of cues that convey the experimental hypothesis to the [participant] become determinants of the [participant's] behaviour.
> (Orne, 1962)

Everyday demand characteristics

Watching a football game at home you sit relatively quietly, but at a football ground you would chant and jump up and down. These different situations create different expectations and 'demand' different behaviours.

Experimental demand characteristics

In an experiment, participants are often unsure about what to do. They actively look for clues as to how they should behave in that situation. These clues are demand characteristics – which collectively convey the experimental hypothesis to participants. For example:

- A participant is given two memory tests (**repeated measures**), one in the morning and one in the afternoon. Participants might try to guess why they are being given two tests and correctly work out that the study is looking at the effects of time of day on performance. This might lead the participant to try to perform the same on each test.
- Boys and girls are compared to see who is more friendly. A questionnaire is used to assess friendliness. It is quite apparent that the questions are about friendships. This leads participants to guess the purpose of the questionnaire. The girls want to help and give answers showing how friendly they are. The boys are a bit contrary and give answers that show how unfriendly they are. In both cases the result is that participants do not behave as they would usually. They have altered their behaviour as a consequence of cues in the research situation. Thus demand characteristics may act as an extraneous (confounding) variable.

RESEARCHER BIAS

Researcher bias refers to information (other than the IV) from a researcher that encourages certain behaviours in the participant which might lead to a fulfilment of the investigator's expectations. Such cues act as extraneous or confounding variables.

Consider this study by Robert Rosenthal and Kermit Fode (1963):

> Students were asked to train rats to learn the route through a maze. The students were told that there were two groups of rats: one group consisted of 'fast learners' having been bred for this characteristic, while the other comprised 'slow learners'. In fact, there were no differences between the rats. Despite this, the findings of the study showed that the supposedly brighter rats actually did better. When the students were asked about their rats afterwards those with 'fast learning' rats described them as smarter, more attractive and more likeable than the descriptions given by the other group of students. The only explanation can be that the students' expectations affected the rats' performance.

So even rats were affected by the investigator's expectations. How?

Investigators unconsciously encourage participants by, for example, spending more time with one group of participants or being more positive with them. For example, research has found that males are more pleasant and friendly with female participants than with other male participants (Rosenthal, 1966).

Alternatively (with human participants) the way in which an investigator asks a question may *lead* a participant to give the answer the investigator 'wants' (similar to **leading questions**; see page 76).

Indirect investigator effects

There are also indirect investigator effects, such as the *investigator experimental design effect*. The investigator may **operationalise** the measurement of variables in such a way that the desired result is more likely, or may limit the duration of the study for the same reason.

The *investigator loose procedure effect* refers to situations where an investigator may not clearly specify the **standardised instructions** and/or **standardised procedures**, which leaves room for the results to be influenced by the experimenter.

▲ An example of demand characteristics.

Clever Hans (full name Hans Von Osten) was a stallion owned by Wilhelm Von Osten. Hans demonstrated an astonishing ability with arithmetic. Someone would ask a simple arithmetic question, for example 'What is 7 plus 4?', and they would then start counting aloud. When they reached 28 the horse would start stamping its hooves. However, rigorous testing showed that he was not adding, he was responding to subtle unconscious cues from his owner – Wilhelm was communicating expectations which acted as demand characteristics. The reason the horse did as expected was because of the cues, not his ability. Fulfilling expectations is the outcome of demand characteristics.

DEALING WITH THESE PROBLEMS

Single blind design

In a **single blind design** the participant is not aware of the research aims and/or of which condition of the experiment they are receiving. This prevents the participant from seeking cues about the aims and reacting to them.

Double blind design

In a **double blind design** both the participant *and* the person conducting the experiment are 'blind' to the aims and/or hypothesis. Therefore the person conducting the investigation is less likely to produce cues about what he/she expects.

Experimental realism

If the researcher makes an experimental task sufficiently engaging the participant pays attention to the task and not the fact that they are being observed.

OTHER EXTRANEOUS VARIABLES (EVS)

Participant variables

A **participant variable** is any characteristic of individual participants. Participant variables are not the same as **participant effects**. Demand characteristics are an effect of participants' behaviour (participant effect), whereas a participant variable is a characteristic of participants.

Participant variables act as extraneous variables only if an independent groups design is used. When a repeated measures design is used, participant variables are controlled. In a matched pairs design participant variables are hopefully controlled.

Participant variables include age, intelligence, motivation, experience, gender and so on. Students often identify gender as an extraneous variable and it may be. For example Alice Eagly (1978) reported that women may be more **conformist** than men. This means that if there are more women than men in one condition of an experiment this might mask the effects of the IV. However, it is important to realise that gender only acts as an EV in some circumstances. For example, we would not control gender in a memory experiment unless we had a reason to expect that it would matter. When considering participant variables as EVs we need only focus on those that are relevant to the task.

Situational variables

Situational variables are those features of a research *situation* that may influence participants' behaviour and thus act as EVs or confounding variables. One example of a situational variable is **order effects**, which were described on page 116. Improved participant performance may be due to practice (a confounding variable) rather than the IV.

Situational variables are only confounding if they vary systematically with the IV, for example if all members of one group are tested in the morning and all members of the second group are tested in the afternoon.

EXAM CORNER
Practice for novel scenarios

1. Orne's panic button study (see facing page) is an example of demand characteristics. Identify the demand characteristics in this study. [2]

2. Consider Piliavin *et al.*'s (1969) research (see page 119). Are participants in this research likely or unlikely to suffer from demand characteristics? Explain why. [3]

3. In the two studies listed below give an example of a possible: (a) demand characteristic; (b) investigator effect; (c) participant variable; and (d) situational variable. [1 mark each]
   For each one, if you can, suggest how the problem might be dealt with.

   Study 1 Participants' memory was tested in the morning and in the afternoon, to see if there was any difference in their ability to recall numbers.

   Study 2 Participants were given a list of adjectives describing Mr Smith. One group had positive adjectives first, followed by negative adjectives. The other group had the adjectives in reverse order. They were all then asked to describe Mr Smith.

KEY TERMS

Demand characteristics A cue that makes participants unconsciously aware of the aims of a study or helps participants work out what the researcher expects to find.

Researcher bias Anything that an investigator does that has an effect on a participant's performance in a study other than what was intended. This includes direct effects (as a consequence of the investigator interacting with the participant) and indirect effects (as a consequence of the investigator designing the study). Investigator effects may act as a confounding or extraneous variable.

EXAM CORNER

1. Explain what is meant by *demand characteristics*. [2]

2. Explain what is meant by *researcher bias*. Use an example in your answer. [2]

3. Explain how a researcher might deal with the effects of demand characteristics. [2]

Sampling

By now you realise that the people who are studied in a research investigation are called participants. This is generally a small group of people, maybe only 20 or 30 people. How does a psychologist select this group of people? The process is called **sampling** and there are a variety of techniques that can be used to obtain the sample of people actually used in the study.

TARGET POPULATIONS AND SAMPLES

In any study the **target population** is the group of individuals a researcher is interested in, for example 'babies in the Western world', 'people in the UK' or 'young people living in Bristol'. At the end of the study the researcher wants to be able to make a statement about this target population of people.

The researcher obviously cannot study all the people in the target population. Instead the researcher starts by identifying a smaller group, called the **sampling frame**. For example, if the researcher was interested in 'all the babies in the Western world', he might select babies born in two hospitals in London in January 2015.

The researcher then draws a **sample**. Ideally this sample will be representative of the target population so that **generalisations** about the target population can be made.

Sampling method	Advantage; why would you use this method?	Disadvantage
Opportunity sampling How? Recruit those people who are most convenient or most available, for example people walking by you in the street or students at your school.	The easiest method because you just use the first suitable participants you can find, which means it takes less time to locate your sample than if using one of the other techniques.	Inevitably **biased** because the sample is drawn from a small part of the target population, for example if you selected your sample from people walking around the centre of a town on a Monday morning then it would be unlikely to include professional people (because they are at work) or people from rural areas.
Random sampling How? See 'random techniques' on facing page.	Unbiased; all members of the target population have an equal chance of selection.	Need to have a list of all members of the target population and then contact all of those selected, which may take some time.
Snowball sample How? Current participants recruit further participants from among people they know. Thus the sample group appears to grow like a snowball.	Enables a researcher to locate groups of people who are difficult to access, such as drug addicts.	The sample is not likely to be a good cross-section from the population because it is friends of friends.
Self-selected sampling How? Advertise in a newspaper or on a noticeboard or on the internet.	Gives access to a variety of participants (e.g. all the people who read a particular newspaper), which may make the sample more representative and less biased.	Sample is biased in other ways because participants are likely to be more highly motivated to be helpful, and/or with extra time on their hands. This results in a **volunteer bias**.
Stratified and quota sampling How? Subgroups (or strata) within a target population are identified (e.g. boys and girls, or age groups: 10–12 years, 13–15, etc.). Participants are obtained from each of the strata in proportion to their occurrence in the target population. For a stratified sample selection from the strata is done using a random technique. For a quota sample selection is done using a non-random technique.	Likely to be more representative than other methods because there is a proportional representation of subgroups.	Very time-consuming to identify subgroups and then select participants and contact them.
Systematic sampling How? Use a predetermined system to select participants, such as selecting every 6th, 14th, 20th (or whatever) person from a phonebook. The numerical interval is applied consistently.	Unbiased as participants are selected using an objective system.	Not truly unbiased/random unless you select a number using a random method and start with this person, and then select every nth person.

A sampling method is about how participants are identified, NOT about who eventually takes part. Whatever the sampling method, it may be that some participants refuse to take part, which then leaves the researcher with a biased sample – a sample of only those who are willing participants.

However, this doesn't apply in most field experiments – when participants aren't aware they are being studied, they can't refuse.

KEY TERMS

Bias A systematic distortion.

Generalisation Applying the findings of a particular study to the target population.

Opportunity sampling A sample of participants produced by selecting people who are most easily available at the time of the study.

Quota sampling Similar to a stratified sample except participants are not selected from strata using a random sampling technique.

Random sampling A sample of participants produced by using a random technique such that every member of the target population being tested has an equal chance of being selected.

Sampling The selection of participants from the sampling frame with the aim of producing a representative selection of people from that group.

Sampling frame The source material from which a sample is drawn.

Self-selected sampling A sample of participants that relies solely on volunteers to make up the sample. Also called a self-selected sample.

Snowball sample Relies on referrals from initial participants to generate additional participants.

Stratified sampling A sample of participants produced by identifying subgroups according to their frequency in the target population. Participants are then selected randomly from the subgroups.

Systematic sampling A sample obtained by selecting every *n*th person (where *n* is any number). This can be a random sample if the first person is selected using a random method; you then select every *n*th person after that.

Target population The group of people that the researcher is interested in. The group of people from whom a sample is drawn. The group of people about whom generalisations can be made.

Exam advice...
Mathematical skills
About 10% of your exam questions (at AS or A Level) will relate to mathematical concepts. There is a full list of these on page 142. The list includes the principles of sampling as applied to scientific data, for example explaining how a random or stratified sample could be obtained from a target population.

RANDOM TECHNIQUES

People tend to use the word 'random' to mean 'whatever comes into my head'. In science the word random has a very specific meaning – it means that each item in a target population has an equal chance of being selected. There are various random techniques that are used to obtain a **random sample** (or also to achieve random allocation of participants to groups).

The lottery method

The easiest way to obtain a random selection is to draw numbers or names 'out of a hat'. This is sometimes called the **lottery method**. There are three important steps:
1. Obtain a list of all the people in the target population. This may simply be the names of all the people in your school.
2. Put all the names in a lottery barrel or hat.
3. Select the number of names required.

If a researcher is using this method for the random allocation of participants to groups then they might put the first 10 names drawn in group A and the second 10 names in group B.

Random number generators

Calculators have functions that generate random numbers, as do computers and apps on phones.
1. Number every member of the target population.
2. Using, for example, Microsoft Excel, type =RAND(100) to get a random number between 1 and 100.

EXAM CORNER
Practice for novel scenarios

Identify the sampling method in each of the studies below and in each case identify **one** advantage in using that sampling method for that study.
1. A researcher wishes to study memory in children aged between 5 and 11. He contacts the headmaster of his local primary school and arranges to test the children in the school. [3]
2. A study on sleep habits identifies various subgroups in the target population and then randomly selects members from each subgroup. [3]
3. A university department conducts a study of mobile phone use in adolescents, using a questionnaire. The questionnaire is given to a group of students in a local comprehensive school. The sample is selected by placing all the students' names in a container and drawing out 50 names. [3]
4. A class of psychology students conducts a study on memory. They put up a notice in the sixth-form common room asking for participants who have an hour to spare. [3]
5. A researcher wants to interview teenagers about the appeal of the latest boy band. After interviewing one teenager, the psychologist asks the teenager to contact other teenagers that they know are fans and ask them to be interviewed. [3]

TRY THIS

- Get a bag of sweets which has a variety of different colours (e.g. *Skittles* or *Smarties*).
- Tip the contents of the packet into a cup. Make a note of the total number of sweets and the number of sweets of each colour.

- Practise selecting a sample (approximately 10% of the total number of sweets in the packet).
- Using some of the different sampling techniques noted on this spread, keep a record of the number of different-coloured sweets offered in each sampling method.

Do any of the samples you choose offer a true representation of the characteristics of the sweets when you opened the packet?

EXAM CORNER

1. Explain the difference between a target population and a sample. [3]
2. Identify **one** sampling method used in psychological research and explain how a sample would be obtained using this method. [3]
3. Explain how bias is a problem in opportunity sampling. [2]
4. Explain what is meant by *generalisation*. [2]
5. Give **one** disadvantage of using a self-selected sample. [2]

Ethical issues

What is an *issue*? It is a conflict between two points of view. In psychology, an **ethical issue** is a conflict between:

1. what the researcher needs to do in order to conduct useful and meaningful research, and
2. the rights of participants.

Ethical issues are conflicts about what is acceptable. Everyone conducting psychological research, including psychology students, is expected to be aware of their responsibility to ensure participants are treated in an ethically appropriate manner. Whenever you conduct any research you must ensure that you deal properly with all ethical issues.

Risk to the participants' values, beliefs, relationships, status or privacy

This ethical issue requires psychologists to not just consider the research participant as part of a research study, but to make a broader consideration of the impact that their research may have on the participant. Researchers have to make provision to ensure that research participants' attitudes and opinions are not demeaned, or that their associations with other people are not damaged by their participation in the research. Finally, their position within an organisation or society in general should not be jeopardised by participating. Most of the elements in this issue can be easily dealt with by ensuring that the privacy of the research participant is maintained through adequate confidentiality arrangements.

Working with vulnerable individuals (including children)

Special ethical considerations need to be paid when conducting research with vulnerable individuals. The BPS considers vulnerable populations to include *'children under the age of 16, people with learning or communication difficulties, patients in care, people in custody or on probation, and people engaged in illegal activities, such as drug abuse'* (BPS, 2009). Valid consent needs to be obtained from the person legally responsible for the individual, such as a parent or guardian. Researchers may be encouraged to seek this consent because it is considered that the vulnerable individual may not be able to fully understand the reasons for the research and therefore not really be able to give 'informed' consent to participate.

Working with animals

Research is governed by legislation, such as the Animals (Scientific Procedures) Act 1986. In addition there are strict requirements for the ethical treatment of animals. Members of the BPS, for example, are *'reminded of their general obligation to avoid or at least minimise discomfort to living animals'* (Guidelines for Psychologists Working with Animals, 2012). Researchers are asked to consider alternatives to using animals, such as computer simulations. If using animals is unavoidable, there are strict recommendations about factors such as the species type, care requirements, etc. that need to be met by the researcher.

ETHICAL ISSUES

	From the researcher's point of view
Valid consent	Valid consent means revealing the true **aims** of the study – or at least telling participants what is actually going to happen. However, revealing the details might cause participants to guess the aims of a study. For example, a psychologist might want to investigate whether people obey a male teacher more than a female teacher. If the participants are told the aim of this experiment before the study takes place, it might change the way they behave – they might try to be equally obedient to both. Researchers therefore may not always want to reveal the true aims or even the full details of what is going to happen.
Deception	It can be necessary to deceive participants about the true aims of a study otherwise participants might alter their behaviour and the study could be meaningless. A distinction, however, should be made between withholding some of the details of the research aims (reasonably acceptable) and deliberately providing false information (less acceptable).
Risk of harm (stress, anxiety, humiliation or pain)	Studying some of the more important questions in psychology may involve a degree of risk of harm (psychological or physical) to participants. It is also difficult to predict the outcome of certain procedures (such as in the Milgram obedience study; see page 162) – therefore it is difficult to guarantee protection from any risk of harm.
Confidentiality	It may be difficult to protect confidentiality because the researcher wishes to publish the findings. A researcher may guarantee **anonymity** (withholding participants' names), but even then it may be obvious who has been involved in a study. For example, knowing that a study of children in hospital was conducted on the Isle of Wight could permit some people to be able to identify participants because the target group has been narrowed down.
Privacy	It may be difficult to avoid invasion of privacy when studying participants without their awareness, for example in a **field experiment**.

KEY TERMS

Confidentiality Concerns the communication of personal information from one person to another, and the trust that the information will be protected.

Deception A participant is not told the true aims of a study (e.g. what participation will involve) and thus cannot give valid consent.

Privacy A person's right to control the flow of information about themselves.

Risk of harm During a research study, participants should not experience negative physical or psychological effects, such as physical injury, lowered self-esteem or embarrassment – beyond what would be normal for them to experience.

Valid consent Participants are given comprehensive information concerning the nature and purpose of the research and their role in it, in order that they can make an informed decision about whether to participate.

From the participants' point of view

Participants should be told what they will be required to do in the study so that they can make an informed decision about whether they wish to participate. This is a basic human right, established during the Nuremberg war trials. In the Second World War Nazi doctors conducted various experiments on prisoners without their consent and the war trials afterwards decided that consent should be a right for participants involved in any study.

Even if researchers have obtained valid consent, that does not guarantee that participants really do understand what they have let themselves in for. Epstein and Lasagna (1969) found that only a third of participants volunteering for an experiment really understood what they had agreed to take part in.

Another problem is the requirement for the researcher to point out any likely benefits or risks of participation. Researchers are not always able to accurately predict the risks or benefits of taking part in a study.

Deception is unethical – the researcher should not deceive anyone without good cause. Perhaps more importantly, deception prevents participants being able to give valid consent. They may agree to participate without really knowing what they have let themselves in for and they might be quite distressed by the experience.

Deception can also lead people to see psychologists as untrustworthy. It might further mean that a participant may not want to take part in psychological research in the future.

Nothing should happen to them during a study that causes harm. There are many ways harm can be caused to participants, some physical (e.g. getting them to smoke, or drink coffee excessively) and some psychological (e.g. making them feel inadequate, or embarrassing them). It is considered acceptable if the risk of harm is no greater than a participant would be likely to experience in ordinary life, and if participants are in the same state after a study as they were before, unless they have given their valid consent to be treated otherwise.

The Data Protection Act makes confidentiality a legal right. It is only acceptable for personal data to be recorded if the data are not made available in a form that identifies the participants.

People do not expect to be observed by others in certain situations, for example when in the privacy of their own homes, while they might expect this when sitting on a park bench in public.

EXAM CORNER

1. One ethical issue is 'risk of harm'. Explain situations where apparent harm might be considered acceptable. [4]
2. Identify **one** other ethical issue in psychological research and explain why it is an issue. [2]
3. Explain what specific issues arise when conducting research with children. [3]
4. Discuss ethical issues in the design and conduct of psychological studies. Refer to examples of studies in your answer. [10]

▲ Middlemist *et al.* conducted a field experiment in a men's urinal. There were three conditions: a **confederate** stood either immediately next to a participant, one urinal away, or there was no confederate. An observer recorded the onset of micturation times (how long participants took before they started to urinate) as an indication of how comfortable the participant felt. Some psychologists regard this as an important study of personal space.

Confidentiality and privacy – what's the difference?

The words 'confidentiality' and 'privacy' are sometimes used interchangeably, but there is a distinction between them. Confidentiality concerns the communication of personal information from one person to another, and the trust that this information will then be protected. Privacy refers to a zone of inaccessibility of mind or body, and the trust that this will not be 'invaded'.

In other words, we have a right of privacy. If this is invaded, confidentiality should be respected.

EXAM CORNER
Practice for novel scenarios

Ethical issues are *issues* because there are no easy answers. On the right are descriptions of various studies. When considering them it might be useful to discuss your thoughts in small groups and then present your views to the class. In each study:

1. Identify any ethical issues raised in the study. [2]
2. Consider to what extent they are acceptable from the researcher's point of view. [2]
3. Consider to what extent they are acceptable from the participants' point of view. [2]
4. Decide whether you think the study was ethically acceptable, or not, giving your reasons. [2]
5. Suggest what you think the researcher might have done to make the study more ethically acceptable. [3]

Study A Middlemist *et al.* (1976) investigated personal space (see above).
Study B Piliavin *et al.* (1969) investigated the behaviour of bystanders in an emergency situation to see how quickly they would offer help to someone (a confederate) who collapsed on a New York Subway train (see page 119). The confederate either acted as if he was drunk or as if he was disabled. Observers recorded how long it took for anyone to offer help. There was no opportunity to debrief participants.
Study C Orne (1962) observed that people behave in quite unusual ways if they think they are taking part in a psychology experiment. For example, he asked participants to add up columns of numbers on a sheet of paper and then tear the paper up and repeat this again. Some were willing to continue the task for over six hours!

Dealing with ethical issues

Embedded in any discussion of **ethical issues** (see previous spread) are ways of dealing with these issues. For example, the issue of **valid consent** is dealt with by asking participants to give their valid consent; the issue of **risk of harm** is dealt with by ensuring that people are in the same state after a study as they were before, unless they have consented. The BPS code of practice (see page 5) identifies issues and at the same time suggests how these issues are dealt with. Therefore there are some overlaps between the previous spread and this one.

The most obvious way of dealing with ethical issues is through the use of codes of practice (guidelines) produced by a professional organisation. Psychologists, like other scientists, have other ways of dealing with ethical issues.

Exam advice...
Issues versus guidelines
Issues are not the same as guidelines even though valid consent is both an issue and a guideline. An issue is a conflict; a guideline is a means of resolving this conflict.

Note that debriefing is not an issue, it is a way of dealing with ethical issues such as deception, psychological harm and lack of valid consent.

STRATEGIES TO DEAL WITH ETHICAL ISSUES

Ethical guidelines (code of conduct)

The BPS regularly updates its **ethical guidelines (code of conduct)**. The current version is the 'Code of Ethics and Conduct' (BPS, 2009). The intention of such guidelines is to tell psychologists which behaviours are not acceptable and give guidance on how to deal with ethical dilemmas.

Right to withdraw

If a participant begins to feel uncomfortable or distressed they should be given the **right to withdraw**. This is especially important if a participant has been deceived about the aims and/or procedures. However, even if a participant has been fully informed, the actual experience of taking part may turn out to be rather different, so they should be able to withdraw.

Debriefing

At the end of a study participants are given various kinds of information about the study they took part in. The aim of such **debriefing** is to inform the participants of the true nature of the study and to restore them to the same state they were in at the start of the study. Debriefing is not an ethical issue; it is a means of dealing with ethical issues such as deception and psychological harm and any unforeseen **psychological harm** that may have arisen in the research.

If participants were deceived about the true aims of the study, they are told what the aims were during the debriefing. Participants may not have been deceived but might not have been told the *full* details of the study, for example there may have been several conditions in the study, such as a placebo condition. During the debriefing they should be given any other information about the study so they understand their role more fully. If the participants are harmed in any way (e.g. stressed or made to feel awkward or embarrassed), they should be offered reassurance that their behaviour was normal and, where necessary, be offered extra counselling.

Participants should be offered the right to withhold their data if they object to having participated.

Ethics committees

Most institutions where research takes place have an **ethics committee** which must approve any study before it begins. The committee looks at all possible ethical issues raised in any research proposal and at how the researcher suggests that the issues will be dealt with, weighing up the benefits of the research against the possible costs to the participants. Members of the committee often include lay people as well as experts in the field.

Punishment

If a psychologist does behave in an unethical manner, such as conducting unacceptable research, then the BPS reviews the research and may decide to ban the person from practising as a psychologist. It is not a legal matter (the psychologist won't be sent to prison).

EVALUATION

Ethical guidelines

This 'rules and sanctions' approach is inevitably rather general because of the virtual impossibility of covering every conceivable situation that a researcher may encounter.

The Canadians take a slightly different approach – they present a series of hypothetical dilemmas and invite psychologists to discuss these. The advantage of this approach is that it encourages debate, whereas the BPS approach tends to close off discussions about what is right and wrong because the answers are provided.

Guidelines also absolve the individual researcher of any responsibility because the researcher can simply say, 'I followed the guidelines so my research is acceptable'.

Right to withdraw

Participants may feel they shouldn't withdraw because it will spoil the study.

In many studies participants are paid or rewarded in some way, and may not feel able to withdraw.

Debriefing

Debriefing tries to redress the balance where harm may have been caused through deception of distress. However, it can't turn the clock back. Participants might still feel cheated if they were deceived, or still feel embarrassed by their behaviour despite reassurances. Therefore debriefing is, at best, a partial solution.

Stanley Milgram conducted arguably some of the most ethically contentious psychological research ever done (see page 162). However, what tends to get overlooked is that he was a pioneer in the use of techniques such as debriefing in a procedure he called a 'dehoax'. For example, he offered all of his participants the opportunity to discuss their actions in the research with an independent psychiatrist.

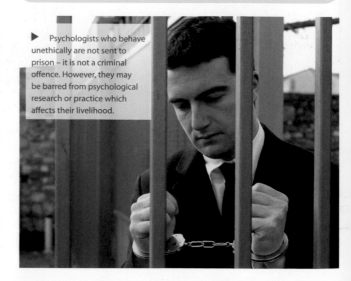

▶ Psychologists who behave unethically are not sent to prison – it is not a criminal offence. However, they may be barred from psychological research or practice which affects their livelihood.

THE BPS CODE OF ETHICS AND CONDUCT

The BPS code of ethics identifies ethical issues and gives psychologists advice on how to deal with these issues:

On valid consent

Failure to make full disclosure prior to obtaining valid consent requires additional safeguards to protect the welfare and dignity of the participants.

Research with children (under age 16), or with participants who have impairments that limit understanding and/or communication, to the extent that they are unable to give their consent, requires special safe-guarding procedures.

On deception

The central principle is the reaction of participants when deception is revealed; if this leads to discomfort, anger or objections from participants then the deception is inappropriate.

On risk of harm

If harm, unusual discomfort or other negative consequences for the individual's future life might occur, the investigator must obtain the disinterested approval of independent advisors, inform the participants, and obtain real, valid consent from each of them.

> **Valid consent**
> In this study you will be shown lists of words and later asked to recall them. All data will be confidential. You should not feel stressed at any time and, if you do, then ask the researcher if you can leave. There is no requirement for you to stay and you will still be paid for taking part. The aims of the study and the findings will be explained to you afterwards.
>
> Signed _____

▲ Participants are asked to sign a valid consent form to indicate they have been informed and are freely consenting to take part.

DEALING WITH SPECIFIC ETHICAL ISSUES

Ethical issue	How to deal with it	Disadvantages
Valid consent	Participants are asked to formally indicate their agreement to participate by, for example, signing a document which contains comprehensive information concerning the nature and purpose of the research and their role in it. An alternative is to gain **presumptive consent**. Researchers must also offer the right to withdraw.	If a participant is given full information about a study this may invalidate the purpose of the study. Even if researchers have obtained valid consent, that does not guarantee that participants really do understand what they have let themselves in for. The problem with presumptive consent is that what people expect that they will or will not mind can be different from actually experiencing it.
Deception	The need for deception should be approved by an ethics committee, weighing up benefits (of the study) against costs (to participants). Participants should be fully debriefed after the study. This involves informing them of the true nature of the study. Participants should be offered the opportunity to discuss any concerns they may have and to withhold their data from the study – a form of retrospective valid consent.	Cost–benefit decisions are flawed because they involve subjective judgements, and the costs and/or benefits are not always apparent until after the study. Debriefing can't turn the clock back – a participant may still feel embarrassed or have lowered self-esteem.
Risk of harm	Avoid any risks greater than experienced in everyday life. Stop the study if harm is suspected.	Harm may not be apparent at the time of the study and only judged later with hindsight.
Confidentiality	Researchers should not record the names of any participants; they should use numbers or false names.	It is sometimes possible to work out who the participants were using information that has been provided, for example the geographical location of a school. In practice, therefore, confidentiality may not be possible.
Privacy	Do not study anyone without their valid consent unless it is in a public place and public behaviour (e.g. it would exclude couples' intimate moments in a park).	There is no universal agreement about what constitutes a public place.

KEY TERMS

Debriefing A post-research interview designed to inform participants of the true nature of the study and to restore them to the state they were in at the start of the study. It may also be used to gain useful feedback about the procedures in the study. Debriefing is not an ethical issue; it is a means of dealing with ethical issues.

Ethical guidelines (code of conduct) A set of principles designed to help professionals behave honestly and with integrity.

Ethics committee A group of people within a research institution that must approve a study before it begins.

Presumptive consent A method of dealing with lack of valid consent or deception, by asking a group of people who are similar to the participants whether they would agree to take part in a study. If this group of people consents to the procedures in the proposed study, it is *presumed* that the real participants would also have agreed.

Right to withdraw Participants can stop participating in a study if they are uncomfortable in any way. This is especially important in cases where it was not possible to give valid consent. Participants should also have the right to refuse permission for the researcher to use any data they produced.

EXAM CORNER

Practice for novel scenarios

Re-examine the three studies on the previous spread and consider how a researcher might deal with the ethical issues in each case. [3 marks each]

EXAM CORNER

1. Describe **one** way that psychologists have dealt with ethical issues in psychological research. [3]
2. Discuss how psychologists deal with ethical issues in psychological research. Refer to examples of research studies in your answer. [12]

Observational techniques

In an observational study a researcher watches or listens to participants engaging in whatever behaviour is being studied. The observations are recorded.

One important aspect of observations worthy of note is that they are often used in an experiment as a means of measuring the **dependent variable**.
Therefore observations are less of a research method and more of a technique to use in conjunction with other research methods.

TRY THIS

Try this to understand how difficult observation actually is. Work with a partner and take it in turns to observe each other. One of you will be Person A and the other will be Person B.
- Person A should have a difficult task to do (e.g. answering one set of questions in this book).
- Person B should have a boring task to do (e.g. copying from a book).

Each person should spend five minutes on their task, while the other person observes them. The observer should note down everything their partner does.

KEY TERMS

Behavioural categories Dividing a target behaviour (such as stress or aggression) into a subset of specific and operationalised behaviours.

Covert observation When a participant is unaware of being observed. The observer may watch through a one-way mirror or be hidden in some other way.

Event sampling An observational technique in which a count is kept of the number of times a certain behaviour (event) occurs.

Inter-rater reliability The extent to which there is agreement between two or more observers involved in observations of a behaviour.

Non-participant observation The observer is separate from the people being observed.

Observer bias Observers' expectations affect what they see or hear. This reduces the validity of the observations.

Operationalisation Ensuring that variables are in a form that can be easily tested.

Participant observation Observations made by someone who is also participating in the activity being observed, which may affect their objectivity.

Social desirability bias A distortion in the way people answer questions – they tend to answer questions in such a way that presents themselves in a better light.

Time sampling An observational technique in which the observer records behaviours in a given time frame, e.g. noting what a target individual is doing every 15 seconds or 20 seconds or 1 minute. The observer may select one or more behavioural categories to tick at this time interval.

Exam advice...
Don't get confused about sampling procedures here and those discussed on page 124. It's really the same thing – using a method to select what to focus on. In the case of sampling on page 124 we are selecting participants. Here we are selecting which behaviours to record.

TYPES OF OBSERVATION

Participant and non-participant observation

In most cases an observer is merely watching (or listening to) the behaviour of others and acts as a **non-participant**. The observer observes from a distance and does not interact with the people being observed.

The alternative is **participant observation**. In this case the observer is part of the group being observed.

You might think that making observations is easy, but if you tried the activity on the left you should now realise it is difficult for two main reasons:

1. It is difficult to work out what to record and what not to record.
2. It is difficult to record everything that is happening.

Therefore it is usually helpful to have methods to help *structure* observations.

STRUCTURING OBSERVATIONS

Unstructured observations

The researcher records all relevant behaviour but has no system, as in the activity on the left. The most obvious problem with this is that there may be too much to record. Another problem is that the behaviours recorded will often be those which are most visible or eye-catching to the observer but these may not necessarily be the most important or relevant behaviours.

Structured observations

Observational techniques, like all research techniques, aim to be objective and rigorous. For this reason it is preferable to use **structured observations**, i.e. various 'systems' to organise observations. The two main ways to structure observations are using **behavioural categories** and **sampling** procedures.

Behavioural categories

One of the hardest aspects of the observational method is deciding how different behaviours should be categorised. This is because our perception of behaviour is often seamless; when we watch somebody perform a particular action we see a continuous stream of action rather than a series of separate behavioural components.

In order to conduct systematic observations, a researcher needs to break up this stream of behaviour into different behavioural categories. What is needed is **operationalisation** – breaking the behaviour being studied into a set of components. For example, when observing infant behaviour, we can have a list including things such as smiling, crying, sleeping, etc., or, when observing facial expressions, including different combinations of mouth, cheeks, eyebrows, etc.

Sampling procedures

When conducting an unstructured observation the observer should record every instance of the behaviour in as much detail as possible. This is useful if the behaviours of interest do not occur very often. However, in many situations, continuous observation is not possible because there would be too much data to record – therefore there must be a systematic method of sampling observations:

- **Event sampling** Counting the number of times a certain behaviour (event) occurs in a target individual or individuals, for example counting how many times a person smiles in a ten-minute period.
- **Time sampling** Recording behaviours in a given time frame. For example, noting what a target individual is doing every 30 seconds or some other time interval. At that time the observer may tick one or more categories from a checklist.

EVALUATION

Observational studies in general

What people say they do is often different from what they actually do, so observations give a different take on behaviour than other research methods. Such studies are also able to capture spontaneous and unexpected behaviour.

However, there is the serious issue of **observer bias**. It is difficult to be objective; what people observe is distorted by their expectations of what is likely or what they would hope to see. Using more than one observer may reduce the risk of observer bias affecting the **validity** of the observations.

Observations provide information about what people actually do but they don't provide information about what people think or feel.

Participant and non-participant observation

Non-participant observers are likely to be more objective because they are not part of the group being observed. However, participant observation may provide special insights into behaviour from the 'inside' that may not otherwise be gained.

Participant observation is more likely to be overt, i.e. participants will know they are being observed and thus have issues of participant awareness. In such situations participants adjust their behaviour to be seen in a 'better light'. This is called **social desirability bias**. It also might be that participants adjust their behaviour to fit in with the researcher's expectations, an example of **demand characteristics**.

Not all participant observations are overt (see 'Visitors from outer space' below). When observations are **covert** there are **ethical issues** because participants cannot give their consent and may feel their privacy has been invaded. In general it is regarded as acceptable to observe people in public places where they assume that others are observing them anyway.

Sampling procedures

Both of the observational sampling methods described on the facing page make the task of observing behaviour more manageable.

Event sampling is useful when behaviour to-be-recorded only happens occasionally. However, if there are too many things happening at once then the observer may miss events and this would reduce the validity of the observations.

Time sampling may not always represent what is happening because certain behaviours do not occur at the times sampled. The observer may miss important things.

EXAM CORNER

Practice for novel scenarios

1. In each of the studies described below, decide whether the study involved observations that were: (a) participant or non-participant [1]; and (b) ethically acceptable (explain your answer). [2]
   a. Mary Ainsworth studied infant attachment patterns using the Strange Situation (see page 118). Infants and a care-giver were placed in a room with a pre-determined and fixed set of toys. They were observed through a one-way mirror so that the infants wouldn't be disturbed by the observer's presence. Care-givers gave valid consent.
   b. Festinger *et al.* (1956) recorded the behaviour of a religious cult expecting visitors from outer space (see below left).
   c. Middlemist *et al.* (1976) observed men's behaviour in a toilet; see page 127.
   d. Moore (1922) spent weeks walking round New York, writing down everything he heard and uncovering some interesting exchanges between people he observed.
2. In each of the following observations state which behavioural sampling procedure would be most appropriate and explain how you would carry it out:
   a. Recording instances of aggressive behaviour in children playing in a school playground. [3]
   b. Vocalisations (words, sounds) made by young children. [3]
   c. Compliance to controlled pedestrian crossings by pedestrians. [3]
   d. Litter-dropping in a public park. [3]
   e. Behaviour of dog owners when walking their dogs. [3]
3. A group of students decided to study student behaviour in the school library.
   a. Suggest **one or more** hypotheses that you might investigate. [2]
   b. List **five** behavioural categories you might include in a behaviour checklist. [3]
   c. Identify a suitable sampling procedure and explain how you would do it. [3]
   d. How could you observe the students so that they were not aware that they were being observed? [2]
   e. What ethical issues might be raised in this observational study? [2]
   f. For each issue identified in your answer to (e), explain how you could deal with this issue and whether this would be acceptable. [3]
   g. Are the observations structured or unstructured? [1]

Visitors from outer space

In the 1950s the social psychologist Leon Festinger read a newspaper report about a religious cult that claimed to be receiving messages from outer space. These messages predicted that the end of the world would take place on a certain date in the form of a great flood. The cult members were going to be rescued by a flying saucer so they all gathered with their leader, Mrs Keech. Festinger was intrigued to know how the cult members would respond when they found their beliefs were unfounded, especially as many of them had made their beliefs very public.

In order to observe this first-hand, Festinger and some co-workers posed as converts to the cause and were present on the eve of destruction. When it was apparent that there would be no flood, the group leader Mrs Keech said that their prayers had saved the city. Some members didn't believe this and left the cult, whereas others took this as proof of the cult's power (Festinger *et al.*, 1956).

EXAM CORNER

1. Explain what is meant by *participant observation*. [2]
2. Explain what is meant by *event sampling*. [2]
3. Explain the difference between a participant observation and a non-participant observation. [4]
4. Identify and explain **one** ethical issue related to participant observations. [2]
5. Give **one** disadvantage and **one** advantage of using non-participant observation as a method of collecting data. [2 + 2]

Self-report techniques

Psychologists aim to find out about behaviour. One way to do this is to conduct experiments. Another method is by observation – called a non-experimental method. Another non-experimental method or technique is to ask people questions about their experiences and/or beliefs. These are called **self-report techniques** because the person is reporting their own thoughts/feelings. This includes questionnaires and interviews. A **questionnaire** can be given in a written form or it can be delivered in real-time (face-to-face or on the telephone), in which case it is called an **interview**.

A study may consist solely of a questionnaire or interview but often these techniques are used as a means of measuring the **dependent variable (DV)**. *Consider these two examples:*

The aims of a study may be to find out about smoking habits in young people. The researcher would design a questionnaire to collect data about what people do and why. In this case the whole study consists of a questionnaire. It is the research method.

On the other hand the aims of a study might be to see whether children who are exposed to an anti-smoking educational programme have different attitudes towards smoking than children not exposed to such a programme. The researcher would use a questionnaire to collect data about attitudes to smoking, but the analysis would involve a comparison between the two groups of children – an experimental study using a questionnaire as a research technique to measure the DV.

QUESTIONS

In questionnaires and interviews there are two types of question and each collects a specific kind of data.

Closed questions – the range of possible answers is fixed, such as listing five possible answers for respondents to choose from or asking a question with a yes/no/maybe answer. Such closed questions are easier to analyse but respondents may be forced to select answers that don't represent their real thoughts or behaviour.

Closed questions have a limited range of answers and produce **quantitative data**. Both of these aspects of closed questions make the answers easier to analyse using graphs and measures like the **mean**.

Open questions – there is an infinite range of possible answers. For example, for 'What do you like most about your job?' or 'What makes you feel stressed at work?' you may get 50 different answers from 50 people.

Open questions produce **qualitative data** (discussed on page 148) which are more difficult to summarise because there is likely to be such a wide range of responses. In any research study we are looking for patterns so we can draw conclusions about the behaviour being studied. If you have lots of different answers it is more difficult to summarise the data and detect clear patterns.

QUESTIONNAIRES AND INTERVIEWS

Questionnaires

A questionnaire is a set of written questions. It is designed to collect information about a topic or topics.

Questions permit a researcher to discover what people think and feel, a contrast to observations which rely on 'guessing' what people think and feel on the basis of how they behave. With a questionnaire you can ask people directly; whether they can and do give you truthful answers is another matter.

Structured and semi-structured interviews

Questionnaires are always pre-determined, i.e. structured, whereas an interview can be structured or unstructured.

A **structured interview** has pre-determined questions; in other words it is essentially a questionnaire that is delivered face-to-face (or over the telephone) with no deviation from the original questions. It is conducted in real-time – the interviewer asks questions and the respondent replies.

A **semi-structured interview** has less structure! Basically this 'structure' refers to the pre-determined questions. In an unstructured interview new questions are developed during the course of the interview. The interviewer may begin with general aims and possibly a few pre-determined questions but subsequent questions develop on the basis of the answers that are given.

This is sometimes called a *clinical interview* because it is a bit like the kind of interview you might have with a doctor. He or she starts with some pre-determined questions but further questions are developed as a response to your answers.

KEY TERMS

Closed questions Questions that have a pre-determined range of answers from which respondents select one. Produces quantitative data.

Interview A research method or technique that involves a face-to-face, 'real-time' interaction with another individual and results in the collection of data.

Interviewer bias The effect of an interviewer's expectations, communicated unconsciously, on a respondent's behaviour.

Open questions Questions that invite respondents to provide their own answers rather than select one of those provided. Tend to produce qualitative data.

Qualitative data Non-numerical data.

Quantitative data Data in numbers.

Questionnaire Data are collected through the use of written questions.

Semi-structured interview The interview starts out with some general aims and possibly some questions, and lets the respondent's answers guide subsequent questions.

Social desirability bias A distortion in the way people answer questions – they tend to answer questions in such a way that presents themselves in a better light.

Structured interview Any interview in which the questions are decided in advance.

Examples of open questions

1. What factors contribute to making work stressful?
2. How do you feel when stressed?

Examples of closed questions

1. Which of the following makes you feel stressed? (You may tick as many answers as you like.)

   ☐ Noise at work   ☐ Lack of control
   ☐ Too much to do   ☐ Workmates
   ☐ No job satisfaction

2. How many hours a week do you work?

   ☐ 0 hours
   ☐ Between 1 and 10 hours
   ☐ Between 11 and 20 hours
   ☐ More than 20 hours

3. Likert scale

   Work is stressful:
   ☐ Strongly agree   ☐ Agree   ☐ Not sure
   ☐ Disagree   ☐ Strongly disagree

4. Rating scale

   How much stress do you feel? (Circle the number that best describes how you feel.)

   At work:
   A lot of stress   5 4 3 2 1   No stress at all
   At home:
   A lot of stress   5 4 3 2 1   No stress at all
   Travelling to work:
   A lot of stress   5 4 3 2 1   No stress at all

5. Forced choice question

   Select one answer

   A   The worst social sin is to be rude
   B   The worst social sin is to be a bore

EVALUATION

Self-report techniques

There are a number of advantages and disadvantages that are common to all methods of self-report. The advantage is the access such techniques allow to what people think and feel, to experiences and attitudes.

One key disadvantage of questionnaires is that people may not supply truthful answers. Observations permit much more direct access to genuine behaviours. It's not a matter that people lie but they may simply answer in a socially desirable way (called a **social desirability bias**). For example, if asked whether you are a leader or a follower, many people would prefer not to class themselves as a follower even if they are.

In addition people sometimes simply don't know what they think or feel, so the answer they supply lacks **validity**.

A final issue relates to the **sample** of people used in any study using self-report. Such a sample may lack **representativeness** and thus the data collected cannot be generalised.

Questionnaire

Many students say that the advantage of a questionnaire is that they are easy – but this overlooks the fact that they actually take quite a lot of time to design. The advantage is that, once you have designed and tested a questionnaire, they can be distributed to large numbers of people relatively cheaply and quickly. This enables a researcher to collect data from a large sample of people.

A further advantage of a questionnaire is that respondents may feel more willing to reveal personal/confidential information than in an interview. In an interview the respondent is aware that the interviewer is hearing their answer and this may make them feel self-conscious and more cautious.

The impersonal nature of a questionnaire may also reduce social desirability bias as compared to an interview.

On the negative side, a disadvantage of questionnaires as a means of data collection is that they are only filled in by people who can read and write and who are also willing to spend time filling them in. This means that the sample is likely to be biased.

Structured interview

A structured interview (as well as a questionnaire) can be easily repeated because the questions are **standardised**. This means answers from different people can be compared. This also means that they are easier to analyse than an unstructured interview because answers are more predictable.

On the other hand, comparability may be a problem in a structured interview (but not a questionnaire) if the same interviewer behaves differently on different occasions or different interviewers behave differently (low **reliability**).

One disadvantage of both structured and unstructured interviews is that the interviewer's expectations may influence the answers the respondent gives (a form of investigator effect called **interviewer bias**). All interviewers have to be skilled to prevent interviewer bias as far as possible.

Semi-structured interview

In a semi-structured interview, more detailed information can generally be obtained from each respondent than in a structured interview. This is because the interviewer tailors the questions to the specific responses and can get deeper insights into the respondent's feelings and thoughts.

Unstructured interviews require interviewers with more skill than a structured interview because the interviewer has to develop new questions on the spot. Such questions may be more likely to lack objectivity than pre-determined ones because of their instantaneous nature, with no time for the interviewer to reflect on what to say.

The requirements for well-trained interviewers makes unstructured interviews more expensive to produce compared with structured interviews which don't require specialist interviewers.

● OTHER KINDS OF SELF-REPORT

Self-report methods are not just restricted to questionnaires and interviews. Diary studies are a research method traditionally used more by other social scientists, like sociologists; however, their use is growing more popular in psychology. The research participant is asked to complete a daily review of behaviours or events that occurred during a particular day. Research participants maintain this log and then are normally interviewed about the contents at the end of the research period.

This is advantageous as research participants are not having to recollect exact details from events that have occurred a long time ago and are hence not subject to problems with recall. The researcher can use entries in the diaries as a starting-off point for further questioning and understanding of the behaviour being investigated.

Diaries are problematic in that participants may not want to record their daily experiences for long periods of time. Such critics question the veracity of the content included in diaries in much the same way as other self-report methods such as interviews and questionnaires.

▲ Attractive female interviewer – not likely to affect his behaviour…

EXAM CORNER
Practice for novel scenarios

1. A group of students wishes to study mobile phone use in people aged 14–18. Why might it be preferable to:
   a. Conduct an interview rather than a questionnaire? [2]
   b. Conduct a questionnaire rather than an interview? [2]
2. Imagine instead that the students wished to find out about drug taking. Answer the same questions (a) and (b) above.
3. For each of the studies described in questions 1 and 2, suggest **two** ethical issues that should concern the students and suggest how they might deal with these. [2 + 2]

EXAM CORNER

1. Explain what is meant by *self-report techniques*. [2]
2. Explain the difference between a questionnaire and an interview. [3]
3. Explain the difference between a structured and a semi-structured interview. [3]
4. Give **one** disadvantage to using a questionnaire rather than a structured interview to collect data. [2]

Reliability

The concepts of **reliability** and **validity** are central to conducting good research. They are concepts that are interrelated and students easily get confused between them.

Reliability concerns consistency.

Validity concerns legitimacy, whether data collected in a study represents 'reality' – are the results really how people behave or are they an artefact of the research in some way?

▲ Validity and reliability.

▼ Different archers produce the following pattern of arrows:

Reliable, but not valid   Not reliable, not valid   Reliable and valid

Being reliable is being consistent, whereas being valid is being on target (related to what you are aiming to do).

A study that lacks reliability will therefore lack validity. For example, if an observer is inconsistent in the observations they make (e.g. recording some observations when they weren't sure what the target individual was doing), then the results are meaningless, i.e. lack validity.

You can, however, have a study that is reliable but not valid. For example, if an observer uses a coding system that is not very thorough, and sometimes the individual being observed does things that can't be recorded, the observations may be perfectly reliable but lack validity, because the behaviour checklist was poor.

EXAM CORNER
Practice for novel scenarios

1. A psychologist decided to observe the non-verbal behaviours between two people having a conversation. (Non-verbal behaviours are those that don't involve language, such as smiling, touching, etc.)
   a. Identify **one** issue of reliability in this research, and describe how you could deal with this issue of reliability. [3]
   b. Identify **one** issue of validity in this research, and describe how you could deal with this issue of validity. [3]
2. A group of students wishes to study mobile phone use in people aged 14–18. Answer questions (a) and (b) above.
3. A researcher is told his happiness questionnaire may lack validity. Explain how he could assess the validity of his questionnaire using concurrent validity. [3]

RELIABILITY

If you use a ruler to measure the height of a chair today and check the measurement again tomorrow, you expect the ruler to be reliable (consistent) and provide the same measurement. You would assume that any fluctuation was because the dimensions of the chair had somehow changed. If the fluctuation was due to some change in the ruler, it would be pretty useless as a measuring instrument – not dependable, consistent or reliable.

Any tool used to measure something must be reliable, such as a psychological test assessing personality, or an interview about drinking habits, or observations made by two observers of a target individual.

If the 'tool' is measuring the same thing, it should produce the same result on every occasion. If the result is different, then we need to be sure that it is the thing (chair or personality) that has changed or is different, and not the measuring tool.

Reliability of observations

In observational research, the issue is that observations should be consistent – we would expect two observers watching the same behaviour to produce exactly the same data. The extent to which two (or more) observers agree is called **inter-rater reliability**.

Inter-rater reliability is measured by **correlating** the observations of two or more observers. A general rule is that if there is more than 80% agreement on the observations, the data have inter-observer reliability:

Total agreement / total observations > 80%

Dealing with issues of reliability in observations

In order to improve reliability, observers should be trained in the use of a coding system/behaviour checklist. They should practise using it, and discuss their observations. The investigator can then check the reliability of their **observations**.

Reliability of self-report

Internal reliability is a measure of the extent to which something is consistent within itself. For example, all the questions on an IQ test (which is a kind of **questionnaire**) should be measuring the same thing. This may not be relevant to all questionnaires, because sometimes internal consistency is not important, for example a questionnaire about fear experiences might look at many different aspects of being fearful.

External reliability is a measure of consistency over several different occasions. For example, if an interviewer conducted an interview, and then conducted the same interview with the same interviewee a week later, the outcome should be the same – otherwise the interview is not reliable.

The **split-half method** is used to assess internal reliability. One group of participants is given a test once. The participants' answers to the test questions are divided in half and compared. This is done, for example, by comparing all answers to odd number questions with all answers to even number questions. The individual's scores on both halves of the test should be very similar. The two scores can be compared by calculating a **correlation coefficient** (see page 136).

The **test–retest method** is used to assess external reliability. A group of participants is given a test or questionnaire or interview once and then again some time later (when the participants have had the chance to forget it). The answers can be compared and should be the same. If the tests produce scores, these can be compared by calculating a correlation coefficient.

Note that the test must be given to the same person on the two separate occasions.

Dealing with issues of reliability in self-reports

In the case of low internal reliability, questions can be removed to see if the split-half test returns a high reliability score.

In the case of external reliability, it may be that poorly written questions are causing confusion and need to be rewritten. If an interview has low reliability the interviewer may need to be retrained in order to be more consistent.

A2 Level only: Types of validity

We have discussed internal and external validity on page 113.
On this page we will explain some further types of validity.

▲ **The psychomeasure of intelligence**

It has been suggested that the circumference of a person's head could be used as a measure of intelligence. This is likely to be a fairly RELIABLE measure of intelligence because adult head size is consistent from one year to the next.

You may even feel this is a VALID measure of intelligence. After all, if you have a bigger brain then you might have more intelligence. However, research doesn't bear this out. Intelligence is not related to brain or head size. This means this measure of intelligence lacks VALIDITY.

TYPES OF VALIDITY

A researcher decides to test whether men or women are more stressed. In order to do this he decides to measure stress using a questionnaire. We can assess the reliability of his measurements as discussed on the facing page. The questionnaire may be reliable – but is it valid? Does it actually measure stress?

There are a number of ways to assess the validity of our stress questionnaire:

Face validity concerns the issue of whether a self-report measure looks like it is measuring what the researcher intended to measure. For example, whether the questions on a stress questionnaire are obviously related to the stress. Face validity only requires intuitive measurement.

Content validity involves looking at your method of measurement and deciding whether it measures the intended content. You could ask an independent expert on the assessment of stress to evaluate the measurement to be used. The expert might suggest improvements, or might approve of the method, thus dealing with content validity.

Concurrent validity involves comparing the current method of measuring stress with a previously validated one on the same topic. To do this participants are given both measures at the same time and then their scores are compared. We would expect people to get similar scores on both measurements, thereby confirming concurrent validity.

Construct validity assesses the extent that a test measures the target construct. In the case of the stress measurement, we would look at a definition of stress and consider whether the questions were relevant to this construct.

Predictive validity is concerned with whether the scores on a test predict what you would expect them to predict! For example we would expect people who score high on a stress questionnaire to have higher blood pressure. Therefore, we can check this out as a means of assessing the predictive validity of a measurement.

Dealing with issues of validity

If measures of **internal validity** are low then the items on the questionnaire/interview/test need to be revised, for example to produce a better match between scores on the new test and an established one.

External validity is also an issue. For example, the **sampling** method used in a questionnaire may produce an unrepresentative sample and this can be improved.

PSYCHOLOGICAL TESTS

When discussing ways to assess validity we are mainly focusing on psychological tests. A psychological test is a task or set of tasks that measures some aspect of human behaviour. For example: IQ tests measure intelligence, personality tests assess personality type, and attitude scales report on people's feelings and opinions.

Strictly speaking, psychological tests and attitude scales are not self-report techniques but they do commonly involve filling in a questionnaire, so many of the issues discussed on the previous spread are relevant.

KEY TERMS

Concurrent validity A means of establishing external validity by comparing an existing test or questionnaire with the one you are interested in.

Construct validity Demonstrating the extent to which performance on the test measures an identified underlying construct; concerns internal validity.

Content validity Aims to demonstrate that the content (e.g. questions) of a test/measurement represents the area of interest; concerns internal validity.

External reliability The extent to which a measure varies from one occasion to another. Low external reliability would mean there is quite a bit of variation over time.

External validity The degree to which a research finding can be generalised to other situations and people.

Face validity A form of external validity, the extent to which test items look like what the test claims to measure.

Internal reliability A measure of the extent to which something is consistent within itself.

Internal validity The degree a study or test is measuring what was intended to be measured.

Predictive validity Correlating the results of a test with some other example of the behaviour that is being tested.

Reliability Consistency.

Validity Refers to whether an observed effect is a genuine one.

VALIDITY ISN'T JUST ABOUT MEASUREMENTS

In an experiment internal validity can be affected by poor control of **extraneous variables**, **demand characteristics** and **researcher bias**. These are discussed earlier in this chapter (see pages 122 and 123) along with ways to deal with such issues.

In observations internal validity may be affected by using poorly defined **behavioural categories** so that observations do not record what they see accurately.

In self-reports internal validity may be affected by **social desirability bias** or **leading questions**.

EXAM CORNER

1. Explain the difference between 'reliability' and 'validity'. [4]
2. Explain how you would assess the internal reliability of an IQ test. [4]
3. Identify **one** method used to assess validity and explain how you would do it. [3]

Correlational studies

The concept of a **correlation** should be familiar to you from GCSE maths. Strictly speaking, a correlation is a method used to analyse data, it is not a research method. A correlation is used to analyse the association between two variables, in this case **co-variables**.

A study that uses a correlational analysis should be called 'a study using a correlational analysis'. However, that's a bit of a mouthful so we generally just say 'a correlation' or 'a correlational study'.

▶ **Scatter diagrams**

The top scatter diagram illustrates a positive correlation. The middle scatter diagram shows a negative correlation. The bottom scatter diagram is a zero correlation.

The correlation coefficients for all three graphs are: (1) +.76; (2) −.76; (3) −.006. The plus or minus sign shows whether it is a positive or negative correlation. The coefficient (number) tells us how closely the co-variables are related: −.76 is just as closely correlated as +.76.

Scatter diagrams showing the relationship between age and beauty

"I MAY NOT LOOK IT BUT I'M ACTUALLY OLDER THAN I LOOK!"

▶ **Table of significance**

The table on the right gives an approximate idea of the values needed for a correlation to be considered significant. The more pairs of scores you have, the smaller the coefficient can be.

A coefficient of either −.45 or +.45 would be significant if there were 16 pairs of data, but not if there were 14 pairs.

The magnitude of the number informs us about significance, while the sign tells us which direction the correlation is in (positive or negative).

The coefficient must be equal to or greater than the number in the table to be significant.

Significance table $N =$	
4	1.000
6	0.829
8	0.643
10	0.564
12	0.503
14	0.464
16	0.429
18	0.401
20	0.380
22	0.361
24	0.344
26	0.331
28	0.317

CORRELATIONAL STUDIES

A correlation is a systematic association between two **continuous variables**. Age and beauty co-vary. As people get older they become more beautiful. This is a **positive correlation** because the two variables *increase* together.

You may disagree, and think that as people get older they become less attractive. You think age and beauty are systematically associated but it is a **negative correlation**. As one variable increases the other one decreases.

Or you may simply feel that there is no relationship between age and beauty. This is called a **zero correlation**.

Correlational hypothesis

When conducting a study using a correlational analysis we need to produce a correlational **hypothesis**. This states the expected association between the co-variables (in an experiment we were considering the difference between two conditions of an **independent variable**).

In our example, age and beauty are the co-variables, so possible hypotheses might be:

• Age and beauty are positively correlated (positive correlation, **directional hypothesis**).
• As people get older they are rated as more beautiful (positive correlation, directional hypothesis).
• As people get older their beauty decreases (negative correlation, directional hypothesis).
• Age and beauty are correlated (positive or negative correlation, **non-directional hypothesis**).
• Age and beauty are not correlated (zero correlation, non-directional hypothesis). [This is actually a **null hypothesis** because it states no relationship.]

Scatter diagrams

A correlation can be illustrated using a **scatter diagram**. For each individual we obtain two scores which are used to plot one dot for that individual – the co-variables determine the *x* and *y* position of the dot (*x* refers to the position on the *x* axis and *y* refers to the position on the *y* axis). The scatter of the dots indicates the degree of correlation between the co-variables.

Correlation coefficient

If you plot a scatter diagram, how do you know whether the pattern of dots represents a meaningful, systematic association? You can eyeball the graph and decide whether it looks like the dots form a line from top left to bottom right (strong negative correlation) or bottom left to top right (strong positive correlation). But this is a rather amateurish way of deciding whether there is a meaningful correlation.

Instead researchers use a **inferential test** to calculate the **correlation coefficient**, a measure of the extent of correlation that exists between the co-variables.

• A correlation coefficient is a number.
• A correlation coefficient has a maximum value of 1 (+1 is a perfect positive correlation and −1 is a perfect negative correlation).
• Some correlation coefficients are written with a minus sign (e.g. −.52), whereas others are written with a plus sign (e.g. +.52). The plus or minus sign shows whether it is a positive or negative correlation.
• The coefficient (number) tells us how closely the co-variables are related.

There is one final step and that is to find out if our correlation coefficient is **significant**. In order to do this we use tables of significance (such as the one on the left) which tell us how big the coefficient needs to be in order for the correlation to count as significant (meaningful).

EVALUATION

Difference between correlations and experiments

The unique feature of an experiment is that the investigator deliberately changes the **independent variable** in order to observe the effect on the **dependent variable**. Without this deliberate change no causal conclusions can be drawn.

In a correlation the variables are simply measured – no deliberate change is made. Therefore no conclusion can be made about one co-variable causing the other. Consider, for example, a study that showed that there was a positive correlation between students' attendance record at school and their academic achievement. A researcher could not conclude that the level of attendance *caused* the better achievement. Such causal conclusions are the special advantage of experiments.

Disadvantages

There are other disadvantages to correlational research. In the example above people jump to causal conclusions. This is a problem because such misinterpretation of correlations may mean that people design programmes for improvement based on false premises. For example, if a headteacher erroneously believed that higher attendance caused better academic achievement, he or she might mistakenly expect that improving attendance would improve exam results. Of course the causal connection might be true but not justified from correlational research, yet people often act on such spurious correlations.

In such cases what they have failed to consider are other, possibly unknown variables called **intervening variables** that can explain why the co-variables being studied are linked. In our example, it might be that students who do not attend are the ones that dislike school and their dislike of school also impacts on exam performance. Dislike of school is the more important intervening variable – and there are likely to be others.

A further disadvantage to consider is that, as with experiments, a correlation may lack **internal/external validity**, for example the method used to measure academic achievement may lack validity or the **sample** used may lack **generalisability**.

Advantages

Correlations have their own special value. They are used to investigate trends in data. If a correlation is significant then further investigation is justified. If a correlation is not significant then you can probably rule out a causal relationship.

As with experiments, the procedures in a correlation can usually be easily repeated again, which means that the findings can be confirmed.

LINEAR AND CURVILINEAR

The correlations we have considered are all **linear** – in a perfect positive correlation (+1) all the values would lie in a straight *line* from the bottom left to the top right.

However, there is a different kind of correlation – a **curvilinear** correlation. The relationship is not linear, but curved. There is still a predictable relationship. For example, stress and performance do not have a linear relationship. Performance on many tasks is depressed when stress is too high or too low; it is best when stress is moderate.

KEY TERMS

Continuous variable A variable that can take on any value within a certain range. Liking for football (on a scale of 1 to 10) is continuous whereas the football team a person supports isn't. The latter could be arranged in any order.

Correlation Determining the extent of an association between two variables; co-variables may not be linked at all (**zero correlation**), they may both increase together (**positive correlation**), or as one co-variable increases, the other decreases (**negative correlation**).

Correlation coefficient A number between −1 and +1 that tells us how closely the co-variables in a correlational analysis are associated.

Curvilinear correlation A non-linear relationship between co-variables.

Intervening variable A variable that comes between two other variables, which is used to explain the association between those two variables. For example, if a positive correlation is found between ice cream sales and violence this may be explained by an intervening variable – heat – which causes the increase in ice cream sales and the increase in violence.

Linear correlation A systematic relationship between co-variables that is defined by a straight line.

Scatter diagram A graphical representation of the association (i.e. the correlation) between two sets of scores.

Significance A statistical term indicating that the research findings are sufficiently strong for us to accept the research hypothesis under test.

EXAM CORNER

1. Explain what is meant by a *zero correlation*. [2]
2. Explain the difference between experiments and correlations. [4]
3. The data from a correlational study produces a scatter diagram with dots arranged in a line from bottom left to top right. What kind of correlation is this? [1]
4. A research study produced a negative correlation between two co-variables. What does this mean? [2]

EXAM CORNER

Practice for novel scenarios

Guiseppe Gelato always liked statistics at school and now that he has his own ice cream business he keeps various records. To his surprise he found an interesting correlation between his ice cream sales and aggressive crimes. He has started to worry that he may be irresponsible in selling ice cream because it appears to cause people to behave more aggressively. The table below shows his data.

All data rounded to 1000s	Jan	Feb	Mar	Apr	May	Jun	Jul	Aug	Sep	Oct	Nov	Dec
Ice cream sales	10	8	7	21	32	56	130	141	84	32	11	6
Aggressive crimes	21	32	29	35	44	55	111	129	99	36	22	25

1. Sketch a scatter diagram of Guiseppe's data. Make sure to label the axes and have a title for the scatter diagram. [3]
   a. What can you conclude from the data and the scatter diagram? (Conclusions are an interpretation of the findings.) [2]
   b. What intervening variable might better explain the relationship between ice cream and aggression? [1]
   c. Describe how you would design a study to show Guiseppe that ice cream does (or does not) cause aggressive behaviour. (You need to operationalise your variables, decide on a suitable research design and sampling method, etc.) [6]

Content analysis and case studies

There are a number of further research methods and techniques that psychologists use. We look at two of them on this spread.

SOMETIMES A STUDY IS JUST A STUDY

After reading this chapter you would be forgiven for thinking you had to classify every study you encountered as an experiment or an observation or a questionnaire and so on. This is not so – there are some occasions when a study doesn't fit into any of these categories. The study by Watson and Rayner on Little Albert (page 56) is an example of this. This study was very controlled but was not an experiment nor a case study. You will read about Milgram's study later in this chapter (page 162). This too is just a well-controlled investigation.

The multi-method approach

Another point to consider is that very few studies simply use one method. Many studies reported in this book use the *multi-method approach* – a combination of all sorts of different techniques and methods to investigate the target behaviour. For example, Bowlby's (1944) research (see page 36) was basically a collection of case studies; however, he obtained data using secondary sources like school reports, as well as primary sources such as observations, psychological tests, etc.

KEY TERMS

Case study A research investigation that involves a detailed study of a single individual, institution or event. Case studies provide a rich record of human experience but are hard to generalise from.

Content analysis A kind of observational study in which behaviour is observed indirectly in written or verbal material such as interviews, conversations, books, diaries or TV programmes.

CONTENT ANALYSIS

A **content analysis** is what it says – the analysis of the content of something. For example, a researcher might study the gender content of magazine advertisements and attempt to describe this content in some systematic way so that conclusions could be drawn.

Content analysis is a form of indirect observation, indirect because you are not observing people directly but observing them through the artefacts they produce. These artefacts can be TV programmes, books, songs, paintings, etc. The process involved is similar to any observational study the researcher has to make design decisions about:

- **Sampling method** – what material to sample and how frequently (e.g. which TV channels to include, how many programmes, what length of time).
- The **behavioural categories** to be used. In the example below the categories are 'product user', 'product authority' and so on. Numbers of males and females are counted so it is a **quantitative** content analysis. A content analysis can also be **qualitative** where examples in each category are described rather than counted. For example, when performing a content analysis of adolescent behaviour from letters in teen magazines, the researcher would provide quotes from different letters to illustrate the category.

Examples of content analysis

Manstead and McCulloch (1981) analysed adverts on British TV to look at gender stereotypes. They observed 170 adverts over a one-week period, ignoring those that contained only children and animals. In each advert they focused on the central adult figure and recorded frequencies in a table like the one on the right. For each advert there might be no ticks, one tick or a number of ticks (see table on right).

Cumberbatch and Gauntlett (2005) conducted a content analysis of the top ten programmes most watched by 10–15-year-olds in the UK. He found only 4% of the programmes contained no reference or portrayal of smoking or alcohol or drug use. The vast majority of scenes that included alcohol consumption or smoking portrayed it with a 'neutral' message (not saying it was a good or bad behaviour). However, the majority of the scenes depicting drug use contained a negative message.

	Male	Female
Credibility basis of central character		
Product user	☐	☐
Product authority	☐	☐
Role of central character		
Dependent role	☐	☐
Independent role	☐	☐
Argument spoken by central character		
Factual	☐	☐
Opinion	☐	☐
Product type used by central character		
Food/drink	☐	☐
Alcohol	☐	☐
Body	☐	☐
Household	☐	☐

EVALUATION OF CONTENT ANALYSIS

Content analysis has high **ecological validity** because it is based on observations of what people actually do: real communications which are current and relevant, such as recent newspapers or children's books in print.

When sources can be retained or accessed by others (e.g. back copies of magazines or videos of people giving speeches) findings can be **replicated**.

Observer bias reduces the objectivity and validity of findings because different observers may interpret the meaning of the behavioural categories differently.

CASE STUDIES

A **case study** involves the detailed study of a single individual, institution or event. It uses information from a range of sources, such as from the person concerned and also from their family and friends.

Many research techniques may be used – the people may be **interviewed** or they might be **observed** while engaged in daily life. Psychologists might use **IQ tests** or personality tests or some other kind of **questionnaire** to produce psychological data about the target person or group of people. They may use the **experimental** method to test what the target person/group can or can't do.

The findings are organised to represent the individual's thoughts, emotions, experiences and abilities. Case studies are generally **longitudinal**; in other words they follow the individual or group over an extended period of time.

On pages 36–37 we have described the classic study by John Bowlby, *Forty-four Juvenile Thieves: Their Characters and Home-life*. This study was essentially a series of case studies of children conducted over a period of many years.

EVALUATION OF A CASE STUDY

The method offers rich, in-depth data so information that may be overlooked using other methods is likely to be identified.

It is especially useful as a means of investigating instances of human behaviour and experience that are rare, for example investigating cases of people with brain damage or, in the case study of an event, how people responded to the London riots of 2011. It would not be ethical to generate such conditions experimentally.

The complex interaction of many factors can be studied, in contrast with experiments where many variables are held constant.

On the other hand, it is difficult to generalise from individual cases as each one has unique characteristics. Case studies also often involve the recollection of past events as part of the case history and such evidence may be unreliable. Case studies are also only identified *after* a key event has occurred (such as damage to the brain or a riot) and therefore we cannot be sure that the apparent changes observed actually were not present originally.

AN EXAMPLE OF A CASE STUDY: PHINEAS GAGE

Phineas Gage is probably the most famous patient to have survived severe damage to the brain. In 1848, Phineas was working on the construction of a railway track in Vermont, USA, blasting rock with gunpowder. He would fill a hole with dynamite, then cover the dynamite with sand and insert a tamping iron that was 109 cm long. This was then hammered into the hole to pack down the gunpowder. On one occasion he forgot to put in the sand, and as soon as he hammered the tamping iron in it exploded, driving the tamping iron right through his skull.

Not only did he survive, but he also was still able to speak, despite massive bleeding and substantial loss of brain tissue. After a short spell in hospital, he went back to work, and lived for a further 12 years. Some years after he died, his body was exhumed (along with the tamping iron, which he had kept), and his skull placed on display at Harvard University.

Phineas Gage was able to function fairly normally, showing that people can live despite losing large amounts of brain matter. However, the accident did affect Phineas's personality. Before the accident he was hard working, responsible and popular, whereas afterwards he became restless and indecisive, and swore a lot. His friends said he was no longer the same man.

This case was important in the development of brain surgery because it showed that parts of the brain could be removed without having a fatal effect. Thus surgeons started to remove brain tumours, no longer fearful that this would cause a patient's death. Phineas's injury also suggested that damage to the frontal lobe leads to personality change, which influenced the development of frontal lobotomies.

▲ Phineas's skull on display and an artist's impression of how the tamping iron would have passed through his head.

EXAM CORNER
Practice for novel scenarios

1. A hospital is interested to find out why some patients with head injuries recover faster than others.
   a. Why would you recommend using a case study for this research? [2]
   b. Suggest how you would conduct a case study in this situation. [3]
2. A university department was given funding to investigate the stereotypes presented in children's books (age stereotypes, gender stereotypes, etc.). They were to compare books that children read today with those from 20 years ago to see if and how stereotypes had changed.
   a. Suggest **three** items that could be used as behavioural categories in this study. [3]
   b. How might you ensure that two researchers were using the behavioural categories in the same way? [2]

EXAM CORNER

1. Describe **one** example of a case study you have studied. [2]
2. Explain **one** disadvantage of a case study. [2]
3. Explain what is involved in a case study. [3]
4. Explain what a content analysis is. [3]
5. Give **one** advantage of a content analysis. [3]

A2 Level only: Longitudinal and cross-sectional studies, and brain scans

On this spread we look at some further techniques and methods used in psychological research.

▲ Conducting a longitudinal study (Cara, above) eliminates participant variables (studying the same person over time). A cross-sectional study (below) can be conducted without waiting years for the individuals to get older. Cross-sectional studies may not just be related to age but could, for example, look at people from different professions.

LONGITUDINAL AND CROSS-SECTIONAL STUDIES

Longitudinal studies

A **longitudinal study** is research conducted over a long period of time in order to observe long-term effects, for example the difference between people of different ages.

Case studies are often longitudinal (but not always) – for example, the classic study by John Bowlby, *Forty-four Juvenile Thieves: Their Characters and Home-life*. This study was essentially a series of case studies of children conducted over a period of many years.

Developmental psychologists use longitudinal research to study how people change as they get older. For example, the Minnesota parent–child study (Sroufe *et al.*, 2005) has followed children from when they were infants to late adolescence and found continuity between early relationships and later emotional/social behaviour.

Cross-sectional studies

An alternative way to study the effects of age is to conduct a **cross-sectional study**. One group of participants of a young age are compared to another, older group of participants at the same point in time (e.g. in 2008) with a view to investigating the influence of age on the behaviour in question. This kind of cross-sectional study is sometimes called a *snapshot study* because a snapshot is taken at a particular moment in time.

Cross-sectional studies may look at other things rather than the effects of time. For example, a cross-sectional study might look at the behaviours of different professional groups (teachers, doctors, solicitors, etc.), i.e. different sections of society.

KEY TERMS

Brain scans A technique used to investigate the functioning of the brain by taking images of the living brain.

Cross-sectional study One group of participants representing one section of society (e.g. young people or working-class people) are compared with participants from another group (e.g. old people or middle-class people).

Longitudinal study A study conducted over a long period of time. Often a form of repeated measures design in which participants are assessed on two or more occasions as they get older. However, some longitudinal research is not experimental, for example people may simply be observed for a number of years, as in a case study.

EVALUATION

Advantages

Longitudinal studies control for **participant variables**. A longitudinal study often uses a **repeated measures design** – the same person is tested on a number of occasions and compared, so all other variables are controlled (such as the kind of child care they had or the number of children in their family). In a cross-sectional design the comparison is between two different individuals.

Cross-sectional studies have the advantage of being relatively quick. They can be conducted in less than a year, whereas longitudinal studies take many years and even decades.

Disadvantages

In a longitudinal study **attrition** is a problem. Some of the participants inevitably drop out over the course of a study. The difficulty is that the ones who drop out are more likely to have particular characteristics (e.g. be the ones who are less motivated or more unhappy or who have done less well), which leaves a biased sample or a sample that is too small.

In a longitudinal study participants are likely to become aware of the research aims and their behaviour may be affected (as in a repeated measures design).

Another problem is that such studies take a long time to complete, and therefore are difficult to finance.

In a cross-sectional study the groups of participants may differ in more ways than the behaviour being researched. For example, if a researcher is comparing teachers, doctors and solicitors, these groups differ in terms of profession but might also differ because teachers have less money. In other words, differences between groups are due to participant variables rather than the independent variable (like an **independent groups design**).

Cohort effects occur because a group (or cohort) of people who are all the same age share certain experiences, such as children born just before the First World War had poor diets in infancy because of rationing.

In a longitudinal study, findings that consider only one cohort may not be generalisable because of the unique characteristics of the cohort.

In a cross-sectional study, for example, the IQs of 20-somethings might be compared with 80-somethings, finding that the IQ of the latter group was much lower. This suggests that IQ declines with age. However, it might be that the 80-somethings had lower IQs when they were 20-something (due to poorer diet, for example). This is a cohort effect.

BRAIN SCANS

The main focus for understanding human behaviour is the brain. In the past the only way to study the brain was through **post-mortem** examination. For example, in the 19th century Paul Broca was able to identify a specific part of the brain – a language centre – by examining the brains of his patients after their death. One group of his patients had difficulty producing speech and he found that they all showed damage to a specific part of the brain (see page 10).

EEG

In the 1950s, the only method available for studying brain activity was the electroencephalogram (**EEG**). Electrodes are placed on the scalp, and electrical activity in different regions of the brain can be recorded. EEG was used in a classic study by Dement and Kleitman (1957) to detect different stages of sleep. As people go to sleep, their brain waves become slower. This can be detected by an EEG machine. During a night's sleep, this pattern occasionally changes to become very fast, accompanied by the eyes darting about under closed lids. This is called **rapid eye movement (REM)** sleep. Dement and Kleitman woke participants up at various points during sleep and found that the participants were much more likely to report having a dream if they were awoken during REM sleep.

The development of brain scanning techniques

In the past 30 years, much more precise methods of studying the brain have been developed. These are each described below.

▲ An MRI scanner. The patients lies on a table which slides through the circular chamber. At the bottom of the chamber is a magnet. The chamber contains receivers that pick up the radio signals emitted from the body's cells.

CAT scans
Computed axial tomography

These involve taking a series of x-rays and combining them to form a comprehensive two- or three-dimensional picture of the area being scanned. Usually, a dye is injected into the patient as a contrast material and then he or she is placed in the cylindrical CAT scan machine that takes the pictures.

Johnstone et al. (1976) used CAT scans to show that the brains of people with **schizophrenia** were different to normal brains – the fluid-filled spaces in the brain (called ventricles) were much larger.

MRI scans
Magnetic resonance imaging

These involve the use of a magnetic field that causes the atoms of the brain to change their alignment when the magnet is on and emit various radio signals when the magnet is turned off. A detector reads the signals and uses them to map the structure of the brain.

A classic study by Maguire et al. (2000) used MRI scans to demonstrate that taxi drivers had larger hippocampi than non-taxi drivers, supporting the view that this area of the brain is important in spatial memories.

Functional MRI (fMRI) provides both anatomical and functional information by taking repeated images of the brain in action.

PET scans
Positron emission tomography

This sort of scan involves administering slightly radioactive glucose (sugar) to the patient. The most active areas of the brain use glucose, and radiation detectors can 'see' the radioactive areas, so building up a picture of activity in the brain. The scans take between 10 and 40 minutes to complete and are painless.

Raine et al. (1997; see page 16) used PET scans to compare brain activity in murderers and normal individuals. They found differences in areas of the brain such as the prefrontal cortex and the amygdala, regions previously associated with aggressive behaviour. However, they pointed out that such brain differences do not demonstrate that violence is caused by biology alone.

Advantage: CAT scans are useful for revealing abnormal structures in the brain such as tumours, or structural damage. The quality of the images provided by the CAT scan is much higher than that of traditional x-rays.

Disadvantage: CAT scans require more radiation than traditional x-rays, and the more detailed and complex the CAT scan is, the more radiation exposure the patient receives. CAT scans only provide structural information.

Advantage: MRI scans give a more detailed image of the soft tissue in the brain than do CAT scans, and involve passing an extremely strong magnetic field through the patient rather than using x-rays. MRI is best suited for cases when a patient is to undergo the examination several times successively in the short term, because, unlike CAT, it does not expose the patient to the hazards of radiation.

Disadvantage: MRI scans take a long time and can be uncomfortable for patients.

Advantage: PET scans reveal chemical information that is not available with other imaging techniques. This means that they can distinguish between benign and malignant tumours, for example. PET scans can also show the brain in action, which is useful for psychological research.

Disadvantage: This is an extremely costly technique and therefore not easily available for research. Also, as the patient has to be injected with a radioactive substance, the technique can be used only a few times. Finally, PET scans are less precise than MRI scans.

Mathematical skills

The specification for both AS and A Level Psychology requires that, across all exams for each level, at least 25% of the marks will be from questions related specifically to research methods. Included in this 25% at least 10% of the marks must be related to mathematical skills.

▲ Maths is number 1.

The percentages given above indicate that research methods is NUMBER 1. It is considerably more important than any other of the psychological topics that you cover.

The contents of this chapter enable you to answer questions on parts B and C of the Unit 2 exam, worth just over one-third of your ENTIRE MARK FOR AS.

So, if you wish to do well in psychology, you need to embrace research methods.

Exam advice…
You will be allowed to use a calculator in the exam – just make sure you have one.

However, most mathematical skills won't require any calculation.

MATHEMATICAL REQUIREMENTS IN THE SPECIFICATION

Before you start to panic about maths skills read through this list of the skills that you will need for the 10% Maths questions at AS Level. There are others that you will need for A2.

	Skills	Where this is covered
Arithmetic and numerical computation	Recognise and use expressions in decimal and standard form.	See facing page.
	Use fractions, percentages and ratios.	See facing page.
	Estimate results.	See facing page.
Handling data	Use an appropriate number of significant figures.	See facing page.
	Find arithmetic means.	See page 145.
	Construct and interpret frequency tables and diagrams, bar charts and histograms.	See page 146.
	Understand simple probability.	See page 150. A2 Level only
	Understand the principles of sampling as applied to scientific data.	See pages 124–125.
	Understand the terms mean, median and mode.	See page 144.
	Use a scatter diagram to identify a correlation between two variables.	See page 136.
	Use a statistical test.	See pages 152–161. A2 Level only
	Make order of magnitude calculations.	See facing page.
	Know the characteristics of normal and skewed distributions.	See page 147. A2 Level only
	Understand measures of dispersion, including standard deviation and range.	See page 144.
	Understand the differences between qualitative and quantitative data.	See page 148.
	Understand the difference between primary and secondary data.	See page 149.
	Select an appropriate statistical test.	See page 151. A2 Level only
	Use statistical tables to determine significance.	See pages 153–161. A2 Level only
	Distinguish between levels of measurement.	See page 144.
Algebra	Understand and use the symbols: $=, <, <<, >>, >, \propto, \sim$.	See facing page.
	Substitute numerical values into algebraic equations using appropriate units for physical quantities.	See page 145.
	Solve simple algebraic equations.	See page 145.
Graphs	Translate information between graphical, numerical and algebraic forms.	See page 146.
	Plot two variables from experimental or other data.	See pages 136 and 146.

SOME BASIC MATHEMATICAL CONCEPTS

You are likely to have encountered at least some of the concepts outlined below in your Maths course – therefore only brief explanations are provided.

Fractions

A **fraction** is a part of a whole number such as $\frac{1}{2}$ or $\frac{3}{4}$. We may want to present the results from a study as a fraction. For example, if there were 120 participants in a study and 40 of them were in condition A, what fraction of the participants is this?

To calculate a fraction we divide 40 by 120 $= \frac{40}{120}$.

To make a fraction more comprehensible we reduce a fraction by dividing the top number (the numerator) and the bottom number (the denominator) by the lowest number that divides evenly into both (the lowest common denominator).

In this case that number is 40, which results in a fraction of $\frac{1}{3}$.

Percentages

The term 'per cent' means 'out of 100' (cent means 100). Therefore 5% essentially means 5 out of 100 or $\frac{5}{100}$. We have converted the **percentage** to a fraction.

We can reduce this fraction to $\frac{1}{20}$.

Or we can write $\frac{5}{100}$ as a decimal = 0.05, because the first decimal place is out of 10 and the second is out of 100.

The decimal 0.5 would be 5 out of 10, not 5 out of 100.

To change a fraction to a percentage, divide the numerator by the denominator. For example, for the fraction $\frac{19}{36}$, we divide 19 by 36 (using a calculator) and get 0.52777778. Next we multiply by 100 and get 52.777778%.

Ratios

A **ratio** says how much there is of one thing compared to another thing.

Ratios are used in betting, so if you are a betting man or woman you will be at home. Odds are given as 4 to 1 (4:1), meaning that out of a total of five events you would be expected to lose four times and win once.

There are two ways to express a ratio. Either the way above, which is called a part-to-part ratio; or a part-to-whole ratio, which would be expressed as 4:5, meaning four losses out of five occurrences.

A part-to-whole ratio can easily be changed to a fraction: 4:5 is $\frac{4}{5}$.

Ratios can be reduced to a lowest form in the same way that fractions are, so 10:15 would more simply be 2:3 (both parts of the fraction have been divided by 5).

Estimate results

When doing any calculations it helps to estimate what the result is likely to be because then you can detect if you make a mistake.

Consider the fraction $\frac{19}{36}$. It is fairly close to $\frac{18}{36}$, which is the same as half (50%) – therefore my answer should be slightly more than half.

The same thing could be done when dealing with big numbers. For example, to estimate the product of 185,363 times 46,208 I could round up 185,363 to 200,000 and round up 46,208 to 50,000.

Then I multiply 5×2 and add nine zeros = 10,000,000,000.

I know the actual answer will be smaller because I rounded both numbers up. The actual answer is 8,565,253,504.

Significant figures

In the example above there are a lot of digits, many of which are distracting! It would be a lot simpler if I told you that the answer was about eight billion (8,000,000,000). In this case I have given the answer to one **significant figure** and all the rest are zeros for less distraction.

Except that's not quite right. We can't just remove all the remaining figures without considering whether we have to round up. In our example, 8,500,000,000 would be half way between eight and nine billion and 8,565,253,504 should be rounded up to nine billion (1 significant figure). Two significant figures would be 8,600,000,000.

Let's consider the percentage on the left, 52.777778%, another awkward number. We might give that to two significant figures, which would be 53% (removing all but two figures and rounding up because the third figure is more than five). If we wanted to give this number to three significant figures it would be 52.8%. If the original number was 52.034267% then three significant figures would be 52.0% – we have to indicate three figures.

Order of magnitude and standard form

When dealing with very large numbers it is sometimes clearer to just give two significant figures and then say how many zeros there are, thus focusing on the **order of magnitude**. The convention for doing this for 8,600,000,000 is 8.6×10^9 where 9 represents how many places we have moved the decimal point. To convert 0.0045 we write 4.5×10^{-3} (this is **standard form**).

Mathematical symbols

And finally, you deserve a reward if you have got this far! The symbols you need to be able to use are in the table below.

= and ~	<	<< and >>	>	≤ ≥	∝
Equal and approximately equal	Less than	A lot less than and a lot more than	More than	Less than or equal to More than or equal to	Proportional to

---

KEY TERMS

Fraction, percentage, ratio Methods of expressing parts of a whole.
Order of magnitude is a means of expressing a number by focusing on the overall size (magnitude). This is done by expressing the number in terms of powers of 10.
Significant figure refers to the number of important single digits used to represent a number. The digits are 'important' because, if removed, the number would be quite different in magnitude.
Standard form A means of expressing very large or very small numbers, expressed as a number between 1 and 10 multiplied by 10 to the power of N, where N is the number of places the decimal point has moved.

EXAM CORNER

1. Represent $\frac{3}{8}$ as a percentage. Give your answer to two significant figures. [2]
2. A researcher wants to divide 4,526 by 42. Estimate what the result would be, explaining how you arrived at your answer. [2]
3. Express 0.02 as a fraction. [1]
4. Explain what the following expression means: 'The number of girls < number of boys'. [1]

Measures of central tendency and dispersion

The information collected in any study is called data or, more precisely, a 'data set' (a set of items). Data are not necessarily numbers; they could be words used to describe how someone feels. For the moment we are going to focus on numerical data, called **quantitative data**. Once a researcher has collected such data, it needs to be analysed in order to identify trends or to see the 'bigger picture'. One of the ways to do this is *describing* the data, for example by giving an average score for a group of participants. For this reason such statistics are called **descriptive statistics** – they identify general patterns.

▲ Finding the centre of your data – a measure of the centre or 'central tendency'.

LEVELS OF MEASUREMENT

Distinctions are made between different kinds of data.
- **Nominal** Data are in separate categories, such as grouping people according to their favourite football team (e.g. Liverpool, Inverness Caledonian Thistle, Oxford United, etc.).
- **Ordinal** Data are ordered in some way, for example asking people to put a list of football teams in order of liking. Liverpool might be first, followed by Inverness and so on. The 'difference' between each item is not the same, i.e. the individual may like the first item a lot more than the second, but there might only be a small difference between the items ranked second and third.
- **Interval** Data are measured using units of equal intervals, such as when counting correct answers or using any 'public' unit of measurement. Many psychological studies use 'plastic interval scales' where the intervals are arbitrarily determined and we can't therefore know for certain that there are equal intervals between the numbers. However, for the purposes of analysis, such data may be accepted as interval.
- **Ratio** There is a true zero point as in most measures of physical quantities.

NOIR – an acronym to help remember the four levels of measurement of data: nominal, ordinal, interval and ratio.

MEASURES OF CENTRAL TENDENCY

Measures of central tendency inform us about central (or middle) values for a set of data. They are 'averages' – ways of calculating a typical value for a set of data. The average can be calculated in different ways, each one appropriate for a different situation.

Mean

The **mean** is calculated by adding up all the data items and dividing by the number of data items. It is properly called the arithmetic mean because it involves an arithmetic calculation. It can only be used with **ratio** and **interval**-level data.

Median

The **median** is the middle value in an ordered list. All data items must be arranged in order and the central value is then the median. If there are an even number of data items there will be two central values. To calculate the median add the two data items and divide by two. The median can be used with ratio, interval and **ordinal** data.

Mode

The **mode** is the value that is the most common data item. With nominal data it is the category that has the highest frequency count. With interval and ordinal data it is the data item that occurs most frequently. To identify this the data items need to be arranged in order. The modal group is the group with the greatest frequency.
   If two categories have the same frequency the data have two modes, i.e. are bi-modal.

MEASURES OF DISPERSION

A set of data can also be described in terms of how dispersed or spread out the data items are. These descriptions are known as **measures of dispersion**.

Range

The **range** is the arithmetic distance between the top and bottom values in a set of data. It is customary to add 1, so with the first data set below, for example, the range would be $15 - 3 + 1$. The addition of 1 is because the bottom number of 3 could represent a value as low as 2.5 and the top number of 15 could represent a number as big as 15.5.

Consider the data sets below:

   3, 5, 8, 8, 9, 10, 12, 12, 13, 15   mean = 9.5, range = 13 $(15 - 3 + 1)$
   1, 5, 8, 8, 9, 10, 12, 12, 13, 17   mean = 9.5, range = 17 $(17 - 1 + 1)$

The two sets of numbers have the same mean but a different range, so the range is helpful as a further method of *describing* the data. If we just used the mean, the data would appear to be the same.

Standard deviation

There is a more precise method of expressing dispersion, called the **standard deviation**. This is a measure of the average distance between each data item above and below the mean, ignoring plus or minus values. It is usually worked out using a calculator. The standard deviations for the two data sets above are 3.69 and 4.45 respectively (worked out using a calculator).

◄ The mean number of legs that people have is 1.999. It would be better to use the mode to describe the average number of legs.

EVALUATION OF MEASURES OF CENTRAL TENDENCY

The mean

The mean is the most sensitive measure of central tendency because it takes account of the exact distance between all the values of all the data.

This sensitivity means that it can be easily distorted by one (or a few) extreme values and thus end up being misrepresentative of the data as a whole.

It cannot be used with nominal data nor does it make sense to use when you have discrete values as in average number of legs.

The median

By contrast, the median is not affected by extreme scores so can be useful under such circumstances. It is appropriate for ordinal data and can be easier to calculate.

On the negative side the median is not as 'sensitive' as the mean because the exact values are not reflected in the median.

The mode

The mode is also unaffected by extreme values and is much more useful for discrete data and is the only method that can be used when the data are in categories, i.e. nominal data.

It is not a useful way of describing data when there are several modes.

EVALUATION OF MEASURES OF DISPERSION

Range

The range is easy to calculate but is affected by extreme values.

It also fails to take account of the distribution of the numbers, for example it doesn't indicate whether most numbers are closely grouped around the mean or spread out evenly.

Standard deviation

The standard deviation is a precise measure of dispersion because all the exact values are taken into account.

It is not difficult to calculate if you have a calculator.

It may hide some of the characteristics of the data set (e.g. extreme values).

KEY TERMS

Mean The arithmetic average of a data set. Takes the exact values of all the data into account.

Measure of central tendency A descriptive statistic that provides information about a 'typical' value for a data set.

Measure of dispersion A descriptive statistic that provides information about how spread out a set of data are.

Median The middle value of a data set when the items are placed in rank order.

Mode The most frequently occurring value or item in a data set.

Quantitative Data measured in numbers.

Range The difference between the highest and lowest item in a data set. Usually 1 is added as a correction.

Standard deviation shows the amount of variation in a data set. It assesses the spread of data around the mean.

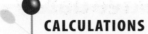

CALCULATIONS

You may be required to estimate or calculate the mean or median in an exam. The methods are described on the facing page.

The formula to calculate the mean can be given as: $\frac{\Sigma x}{n}$

'Σ' is pronounced as 'sigma' and means 'the sum of'. So the formula says 'add up all the values (x) and divide by the number (n) of data items.

You also may be required to estimate or calculate the standard deviation for a set of data, and can use a calculator. However, in the exam, you may be asked to substitute values in the formula. The formula is: $\sqrt{\frac{\Sigma(\bar{x}-x)^2}{n}}$

You have to subtract each data item (x) from the mean, which is written as ($\bar{x}$) (see table below using the data set from the facing page).

Then square the result (column 3) and add these up, divide by n and finally calculate the square root.

Data items	Subtract each data number from the mean	Square
3	$9.5 - 3 = 6.5$	42.25
5	$9.5 - 5 = 4.5$	20.25
8	$9.5 - 8 = 1.5$	2.25
8	$9.5 - 8 = 1.5$	2.25
9	$9.5 - 9 = 0.5$	0.25
10	$9.5 - 10 = -0.5$	0.25
12	$9.5 - 12 = -2.5$	6.25
12	$9.5 - 12 = -2.5$	6.25
13	$9.5 - 13 = -3.5$	12.25
15	$9.5 - 15 = -5.5$	30.25
$\Sigma x = 95$ $\frac{\Sigma x}{n} = 9.5$		$\Sigma(\bar{x}-x)^2 = 122.50$ Divide by n (which is 10) and calculate the square root = 3.50 (to two decimal places)

EXAM CORNER
Practice for novel scenarios

1. For each of the following data sets, where appropriate, first estimate and then calculate the mean, the median and/or the mode. [3 marks for each answer]
   a. 2, 3, 5, 6, 6, 8, 9, 12, 15, 21, 22
   b. 2, 3, 8, 10, 11, 13, 13, 14, 14, 29
   c. 2, 2, 4, 5, 5, 5, 7, 7, 8, 8, 8, 10
   d. cat, cat, dog, budgie, snake, gerbil

2. For each of the data sets (a–d) in question 1, state which of the three measures of central tendency would be most suitable to use and why. [2 marks for each]

3. Estimate the mean and standard deviation for the following data sets. [2 marks for each answer]
   a. 119, 131, 135, 142, 145, 147, 155, 156, 161, 163
   b. 0.15, 0.23, 0.28, 0.34, 0.34, 0.34, 0.36, 0.46

4. Look at the following two data sets. Which one do you think would have the smaller standard deviation? [1 mark for each answer]
   Data set A: 2 2 3 4 5 9 11 14 18 20 21 22 25
   Data set B: 2 5 8 9 9 10 11 12 14 15 16 20 25

5. Calculate the standard deviation for the data sets above. Give your answer to two significant figures. [2 marks for each answer]

EXAM CORNER

1. Identify **one** measure of central tendency and explain how to calculate it for a set of data. [1 + 2]

2. Explain **one** advantage and **one** disadvantage of using the mean to work out the central tendency of a data set. [2 + 2]

3. Identify **one** measure of dispersion and explain how to calculate it for a set of data. [1 + 2]

Display of quantitative data

A picture is worth 1,000 words! Graphs and tables provide a means of 'eyeballing' your data and seeing the findings at a glance. Using graphs and tables are a way of describing data and therefore are also **descriptive statistics**, like measures of central tendency and dispersion. In fact we often display measures of central tendency and dispersion in a graph because it is easier to grasp the significance of the statistics in visual form.

▲ Graph A – a bar chart showing the data in the table on the right on favourite pets.

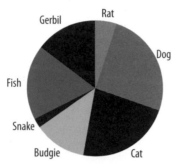

▲ Graph B – a pie chart showing favourite pets.

▲ Graph C – a histogram showing the mean memory scores for each year group in a school (maximum score is 40).

▲ Graph D – a line graph showing the same data as the histogram.

KEY TERMS

Bar chart A graph used to represent the frequency of data; the categories on the x-axis have no fixed order and there is no true zero.

Histogram Type of frequency distribution in which the number of scores in each category of continuous data are represented by vertical columns. There is a true zero and no spaces between the bars.

Negative skewed distribution Most of the scores are bunched towards the right. The mode is to the right of the mean because the mean is affected by the extreme scores tailing off to the left.

Normal distribution A symmetrical bell-shaped frequency distribution. This distribution occurs when certain variables are measured, such as IQ or the life of a light bulb. Such 'events' are distributed in such a way that most of the scores are clustered close to the mid-point; the mean, median and mode are at the mid-point.

Pie chart A circular graph divided into sections or 'slices' each representing the proportion of the total.

Positive skewed distribution Most of the scores are bunched towards the left. The mode is to the left of the mean because the mean is affected by the extreme scores tailing off to the right.

Skewed distribution A distribution is skewed if one tail is longer than another, signifying that there are a number of extreme values to one side or the other of the mid-score.

DISPLAY OF QUANTITATIVE DATA

Graphs and tables should be simple so they can be read easily.
- They should clearly show the findings from a study.
- There should be a short but informative title.
- In a graph both axes should be clearly labelled. The x-axis usually goes across the page. In the case of a bar chart or histogram, it is usually the independent variable. The y-axis is usually frequency.
- Always use squared paper if you are hand-drawing graphs.

Tables

The measurements you collect in a research study are referred to as 'raw data' – numbers that haven't been treated in any way. These data can be set out in a table and/or summarised using measures of central tendency and dispersion. Such summary tables are helpful for interpreting findings.

Frequency table

Frequency data is what it says – data that tells you how frequently certain items occurred. For example, a researcher might ask people to name their favourite pet and display this data in a table; see right.

Favourite pet	Frequency
Rat	10
Dog	51
Cat	45
Budgie	25
Snake	4
Fish	36
Gerbil	29

Bar chart

Frequency data can be represented in a **bar chart** (see Graph A on left). The height of each bar represents the frequency of each item. Bar charts are suitable for data that is not continuous, i.e. has no particular order such as Graph A on the left which is categorical or **nominal data**. In a bar chart a space is left between each bar to indicate the lack of continuity.

Histogram

A **histogram** is similar to a bar chart except that the area within the bars must be proportional to the frequencies represented (see Graph C). In practice this means that the vertical axis (frequency) must start at zero. In addition the horizontal axis must be continuous (therefore you can't draw a histogram with data in categories). Finally, there should be no gaps between the bars.

Line graph

A **line graph**, like a histogram, has continuous data on the x-axis and there is a dot to mark the top of each bar and each dot is connected by a line (see Graph D).

Pie chart

Pie charts are another way to represent frequency data or can be used to represent any proportion (see Graph B). Each slice of the 'pie' represents the proportion (or fraction) of the total. The size of each slice is calculated by working out the appropriate proportion out of 360 (since there are 360 degrees in a circle).

For the frequency data above we work out the total $(10 + 51 + 45 + 25 + 4 + 36 + 29 = 200)$. Then for each item we do the following calculation: rat $= 10/200 \times 360 = 18$.

That means that the 'rat' slice would be 18 degrees of the pie.

Scatter diagram

A **scatter diagram** is a kind of graph used when doing a **correlational** analysis (see page 136).

A2 Level only: Data distributions

DATA DISTRIBUTIONS

When we plot frequency data the *y*-axis represents frequency and the *x*-axis is the item of interest as in a histogram (see facing page). When doing this for large data sets we can see an overall pattern of the data called a distribution.

Normal distribution

The **normal distribution** has a classic bell-shaped curve. It is the predicted distribution when considering an equally likely set of results. For example, if a light bulb has a **mean** life time of 100 hours we would expect some light bulbs to last a little less than this and some to last a little more. If we plot the lifetime of 1,000 light bulbs we would get a normal distribution.

Many human characteristics are normally distributed, such as shoe sizes or intelligence. A normal distribution has certain defining features:

- The mean, median and mode are all in the exact mid-point.
- The distribution is symmetrical around this mid-point.
- The dispersion of scores or measurements either side of the mid-point is consistent and can be expressed in **standard deviations**.

For any set of data that is normally distributed, 34.13% of the people will lie within one standard deviation below the mean and 34.13% of the people will lie within one standard deviation above the mean. A total of 68.26% lie one standard deviation above or below the mean. Therefore a total of 95.44% of people lie two standard deviations above or below the mean, which means that only 4.56% lie in the area beyond this; 2.28% are at less than two standard deviations below the mean.

Skewed distribution

In some populations scores are not distributed equally around the mean. Consider a test of depression where 0–50 represents normal behaviour and 50+ represents **clinical** depression. If we plotted the distribution of scores for 100 people we would expect most scores to be towards the low end rather than the high end of this score range. This produces a **positive skewed distribution** as illustrated below right. The fact that there are a few extreme high scores has a strong effect on the mean, which is always higher than the median and mode in a positive skew.

The alternative is a **negative skewed distribution** (below left). This might happen if marks were plotted for an exam which was very easy so most people got a very high score.

Left-skewed (negative skewness)　　　Right-skewed (positive skewness)

Left Foot Negative Skew　　　Right Foot Positive Skew

▲ And to help you remember…

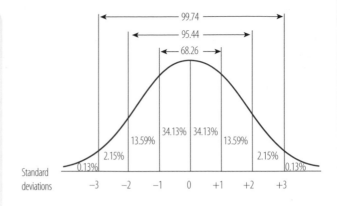

▲ The percentage of people in each part of the normal distribution curve is shown above.

Consider IQ. The mean score for IQ is 100 and one standard deviation is 15 points. If we tested a group of 1,000 people this is what we should find:

- Score between 85 and 115 (one standard deviation either side of the mean) = 683 people (68.26% of 1,000)
- Score between 70 and 130 = 954 people (95.44% of 1,000)
- Score less than 55 = 1 (0.13% of 1,000)

EXAM CORNER
Practice for novel scenarios

1. A psychologist conducted a study to look at whether watching certain films made children more helpful (one film was about being helpful, the other was neutral). Helpfulness was measured using a questionnaire. The mean score of children who watched the helpful film was 30.25 whereas the mean score for the neutral film was 24.62.
   a. Give each mean score to two significant figures. [2]
   b. Sketch a bar chart showing these results. Label the bar chart carefully. [3]
   c. The neutral film is described as a control condition. Explain why a control condition is used. [2]
2. There are four graphs on the facing page.
   a. For each graph state what conclusion you would draw. [1 mark each]
   b. What kind of data are displayed in each graph? [3]
3. Explain why the mean is always lower than the mode in a negative skew. [2]
4. What kind of skew would you get if a test had a ceiling effect? [1] (A ceiling effect occurs when all the items on a test are too easy and then everyone will do well and 'hit the ceiling'.)

EXAM CORNER

1. Explain **two** key differences between a bar chart and a histogram. [2]
2. Describe the characteristics of a normal distribution. [2]
3. Explain the difference between a normal and a skewed distribution. [3]

Types of data

We have already discussed **quantitative** and **qualitative data** (see page 132). On this spread we are going to discuss these two types of data in more depth and also consider two other types of data: **primary** and **secondary data**.

The opposite of quantitative data is qualitative data. The former is always numerical whereas the latter isn't. A different kind of distinction is made between primary and secondary data. The former is data collected by a researcher specifically for a current research project whereas the latter is data collected by someone else and/or for a different project than the current one.

▲ *The Kiss* by Gustav Klimt.

Many studies produce a mix of quantitative and qualitative data. For example Stanley Milgram, in his obedience research (see page 162), found that 65% of participants were fully obedient (quantitative data) but he also reported the comments of observers (qualitative data), providing additional insights into the experience of participants:

'I observed a mature and initially poised businessman enter the laboratory smiling and confident. Within 20 minutes he was reduced to a twitching, stuttering wreck, who was rapidly approaching a point of nervous collapse. He constantly pulled on his earlobe, and twisted his hands. At one point he pushed his fist into his forehead and muttered "Oh God, let's stop it". And yet he continued to respond to every word of the experimenter, and obeyed to the end.'

QUANTITATIVE AND QUALITATIVE DATA

Quantitative data

Quantitative data is data that represents how much or how long, or how many, etc., there are of something, i.e. behaviour is measured in numbers or quantities.

- The **dependent variable** in an **experiment** is quantitative.
- **Closed questions** in **questionnaires** collect quantitative data – numerical information about your age, how many hours you work in a week, how highly you rate different TV programmes.
- In an **observational** study a tally of **behavioural categories** is quantitative.

Qualitative data

Qualitative data can't be counted or quantified but it can be turned into quantitative data by placing the data in categories and then counting frequency. For instance, in the Milgram example at bottom left we might count how many participants described themselves as stressed.

Sometimes people define qualitative data as being about what people think and feel, but quantitative questions can also concern what people think and feel.

Open questions in questionnaires may collect qualitative data – data that express the 'quality' of things. This includes descriptions, words, meanings, pictures and so on.

In an observational study researchers can describe what they see and this would be qualitative.

Quantitative data	Qualitative data
• Quantity • Deals with numbers • Data which can be measured • Psychologists develop measures of psychological variables • Looking at averages and differences between groups	• Quality • Deals with descriptions • Data that is observed not measured • Observing people through the messages they produce and the way they act • Concerned with attitudes, beliefs, fears and emotions
***The Kiss* by Gustav Klimt**	
• Painted between 1907 and 1908, when the artist was 45 years old • Actual painting measures 180 × 180 cm • Bought for 25,000 crowns when it was first painted • It has 33% of surface covered in gold leaf • Listed as no. 12 on list of most popular paintings	• Representative of a style of art called Art Nouveau • Shows a couple locked in a kiss • Shows how bright, beautiful and golden everything is when you first kiss someone • Painted in oil and gold leaf on canvas • Probably his most famous work
A psychology class	
• 24 students • 18 girls, 6 boys • 72% gained Grade A on mock exam • 10 plan to go on to study Psychology at university • Most psychology teachers are female	• Very enthusiastic about psychology • Mixture of boys and girls • Hardworking students • School located in an innercity area • Teacher's name is Mrs Jones

EVALUATION OF QUANTITATIVE AND QUALITATIVE DATA

Quantitative data

Quantitative data are easy to analyse, using **descriptive statistics** and **inferential tests**. This enables conclusions to be easily drawn.

However, such data may oversimplify reality. For example a questionnaire with closed questions may force people to tick answers that don't really represent their feelings. Therefore the conclusions may be meaningless.

Qualitative data

Qualitative data provide detailed information which can provide unexpected insights into thoughts and behaviour because the answers are not restricted by previous expectations.

Of course the complexity makes it more difficult to analyse such data and draw conclusions.

PRIMARY AND SECONDARY DATA

Both primary and secondary data may be quantitative and/or qualitative.

Primary data

Primary data is information observed or collected directly from first-hand experience. In the case of psychological research it is data collected by the researcher for the study currently being undertaken. The collection of primary data would involve designing the study, gaining ethical approval, piloting the study, recruiting and testing participants, and finally analysing the data collected and drawing conclusions.

The study might be an experiment, possibly with a questionnaire and/or an observational element to measure the dependent variable. Or the study could just involve a questionnaire or just an observation. The data collected would be specifically related to the aims and/or hypothesis of the study.

Secondary data

Secondary data is information that was collected for a purpose other than the current one. The researcher could use data collected by themselves but for a different study or collected by another researcher. The researcher might make use of government statistics, such as information about the treatment of mental health, or make use of data held by a hospital or other institution.

A **correlation** study often uses secondary data and **review** studies use secondary data, conducting a **meta-analysis** on such data.

EVALUATION OF PRIMARY AND SECONDARY DATA

Primary data

The great advantage of generating primary data is the control the researcher has over the data. The data collection can be designed so it fits the aims and hypothesis of the study.

The disadvantage is that it is a very lengthy and therefore expensive process. Simply designing a study takes a lot of time and then time spent recruiting participants, conducting the study and analysing the data.

Secondary data

It is simpler to just access someone else's data and cheaper because significantly less time and equipment is needed.

Such data may have been subjected to statistical testing and thus it is known whether it is significant.

The disadvantage is that, for some studies, the data may not exactly fit the needs of the study.

EXAM CORNER
Practice for novel scenarios

1. On the facing page are descriptions of Klimt's painting *The Kiss* and of a hypothetical psychology class. Qualitative and quantitative descriptions are given of both. Try to do the same activity for the following:
   a. A television series. [6]
   b. The town or city you live in. [6]
   c. A major world event such as the London Olympics or the 9/11 bombing in New York. [6]
2. Based on your answers to question 1, consider what kind of data is 'better':
   a. Outline the advantages and disadvantages of using quantitative data in the examples above. [3 + 3]
   b. Outline the advantages and disadvantages of using qualitative data in the examples above. [3 + 3]
3. Evolutionary psychologists believe that there are sex differences in the characteristics sought in an ideal mate. They suggest that, because of evolutionary pressures, men look for youth and good looks, whereas women look for resources, ambition and industriousness.
   David Buss investigated this using a questionnaire issued in 36 countries.
   Robin Dunbar investigated this by conducting a content analysis of lonely hearts adverts.
   a. Which researcher collected primary data and which researcher used secondary data? [2]
   b. What advantages and disadvantages does each of the strategies used by these researchers offer? [2 + 2]

KEY TERMS

Primary data Information observed or collected directly from first-hand experience.

Qualitative data Information in words that cannot be counted or quantified. Qualitative data can be turned into quantitative data by placing them in categories and counting frequency.

Quantitative data Information that represents how much or how long, or how many, etc., there are of something, i.e. a behaviour is measured in numbers or quantities.

Secondary data Information used in a research study that was collected by someone else or for a purpose other than the current one. For example published data or data collected in the past.

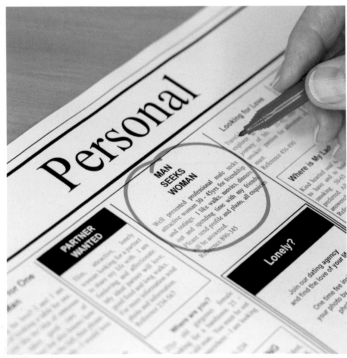

▲ What do men seek in a female partner? What do women look for? Robin Dunbar found answers by analysing the contents of lonely hearts adverts.

EXAM CORNER

1. Explain what is meant by quantitative data. Give examples in your answer. [3]
2. Give **one** advantage of producing qualitative data in a questionnaire. [2]
3. Distinguish between primary and secondary data. [3]

A2 Level only: Introduction to inferential statistics

We are about to continue our journey into **inferential statistics** land, looking in more detail at the concepts introduced on the previous spread – plus a new one, the **null hypothesis**. In fact it isn't new as we defined it on page 114. On this spread we will explain why it is used.

You may have heard the phrase 'statistical test' – for example, a newspaper might report that 'statistical tests show that women are better at reading maps than men'. If we wanted to know whether women are better at reading maps than men we could not possibly test all the women and men in the world, so we just test a small group of women and a small group of men. If we find that the sample of women are indeed better with maps than the sample of men, then we infer that the same is true for all women and men. We can only make such inferences using statistical tests (called inferential tests). Such statistical tests are based on probabilities.

THE NULL HYPOTHESIS

Until the 1930s scientists believed that their task was to find examples that would *confirm* their theories. Karl Popper, a philosopher of science, brought about a revolution in the way scientists thought about proof (confirming their theories). He pointed out: *'No matter how many instances of white swans we may have observed, this does not justify the conclusion that all swans are white'* (Popper, 1934).

This may sound familiar to you because we gave this example in Chapter 2 (page 43) when explaining **falsification**.

No number of sightings of white swans can prove the theory that all swans are white, whereas the sighting of just one black one will disprove it. This proposition led to the realisation that the only way to prove a theory correct was actually to seek *disproof* (falsification) – i.e. look for those black swans. Therefore, we start research with what is called a null hypothesis: 'Not all swans in the world are white, i.e. there are black swans.' We then go looking for swans and record many sightings, but if we see no black swans this leads us to be reasonably certain (we can never be absolutely certain) that the null hypothesis is false.

We therefore can reject the null hypothesis (with reasonable certainty). If the null hypothesis isn't true this means that the alternative must be true. The alternative to the null hypothesis is 'All swans are white' – called the **alternative hypothesis**. We can accept the alternative hypothesis, with reasonable certainty!

This is, in the present state of knowledge, the best approximation to the truth.

▲ The null hypothesis is a statement of no difference or no correlation. It is a statement that 'nothing is going on'. The null hypothesis isn't as strange as it sounds. Consider this example:

It's late at night and on your way home you happen to see your best friend's boyfriend with another girl, and he's doing more than talking. You think to yourself, 'How likely is it that he would be kissing her if there is nothing going on between them?'

- Null hypothesis: 'There is nothing going on, there is no relationship between them.'
- Alternative hypothesis: 'There is something going on between them.'

It isn't very likely that he would be kissing her if there was nothing going on; therefore you reject the null hypothesis and accept the alternative hypothesis – and tell your friend you are fairly certain that he is cheating on her.

PROBABILITY

In the example above about boyfriends and cheating, you might have worked out the *likelihood* that the cheating was real (e.g. you might have felt 'fairly certain'). In research we need to be a bit more precise than that. In order to work out whether a difference is or is not **significant** we use inferential tests. Such tests permit you to work out, at a given **probability**, whether a pattern in the data from a study could have arisen by chance or whether the effect occurred because there is a real difference/**correlation** in the **populations** from which the samples were drawn.

But what do we mean by 'chance'? Chance refers to something with no cause. It just happens. We decide on a probability that we will 'risk'. You can't be 100% certain that an observed effect was not due to chance but you can state how certain you are. In the kissing example you might say to your friend that you are 95% sure her boyfriend is cheating. Which means you are fairly confident that you are right but nevertheless have a little bit of doubt.

In general, psychologists use a probability of 95%. This expresses the degree of uncertainty. It means that there is a 5% chance (probability) of the results occurring if the null hypothesis is true (i.e. there is nothing going on). In other words, a 5% probability that the results would occur even if there was no real difference/association between the populations from which the **samples** were drawn. This probability of 5% is recorded as $p = 0.05$ (where p means probability).

In some studies psychologists want to be more certain – such as when they are conducting a replication of a previous study or considering the effects of a new drug on health. Then, researchers use a more stringent probability, such as $p < 0.01$ or even $p < 0.001$. This chosen value of 'p' is called the **significance level**, which we will discuss on the facing page.

KEY TERMS

Level of measurement Distinctions are made between different kinds of data. Nominal data are data in categories, ordinal data is ordered data. Interval data is data measured using units of equal intervals.

Null hypothesis The assumption of no relationship (difference, association, etc.) between variables being studied.

Observed (calculated) value The number (value) produced after applying an inferential test formula.

Critical value In an inferential test the value of the test statistic that must be reached to show significance, i.e. for the null hypothesis to be rejected.

SIGNIFICANCE

Consider the following example from the psychologist and statistician Hugh Coolican (2004):

At my local chippy I am convinced that they save money by giving some people rather thin chips (because they then can get more chips from each potato). There are two chip bins under the counter – the owner of the chippy claims the two bins contain the same kind of chips but I suspect they are different. So I (sadly) tried an experiment. I asked for one bag of chips from each of the chip bins, and I measured the width of the chips in each bag.

- *Belief 1 is 'The two bins contain chips of an equal average width'.*
- *Belief 2 is 'One bin has thinner chips on average than the other'.*

In fact I found a very small difference between the average width of the chips in each bag (as you can see in the bar chart below).

We would expect small differences between samples (bags of chips) just because things do vary a little – this is simply random variation or 'chance'. What we are looking for is a sufficiently large difference between the samples to be sure that the bins (the total population) are actually different. Otherwise we assume the bins are the same, i.e. the samples are drawn from a single population rather than from two different populations.

- The bins contain the populations – in the earlier example about gender differences in map reading, the population is all the map reading abilities of all the men and women in the world.
- The bags of chips are samples – in our other example, the 20 women and 20 men comprise our samples.
- The belief that the two bins contain chips of the same width or the belief that there is no gender difference in map reading is called the null hypothesis (H_0). This is a statement of no effect – the samples are not different.
- The alternative belief is that one bin has thinner chips or that women are better than men – this is called the alternative hypothesis (H_1). This is a statement that there is an effect – the samples are different.

Ultimately we are interested in making a statement about the population(s) from which the samples are drawn rather than just stating something about samples themselves.

USING INFERENTIAL TESTS

Inferential tests help us to draw inferences about populations based on the samples tested. These tests allow us to infer that a pattern in the data is likely (or not) to be due to chance.

Observed and critical values

Each inferential test involves taking the data collected in a study and doing some calculations to produce a single number called the test statistic. In the case of *Spearman's Rank Order Correlation Coefficient* that **test statistic** is called *rho* whereas for the *Mann–Whitney* test it is *U*. The *rho* or *U* value calculated for any set of data is called the **observed value** (because it is based on the observations made). This is sometimes alternatively called the **calculated value** because it is the value you calculate.

To decide if the observed value is significant this figure is compared to another number (the **critical value**), found in a **table of critical values**. There are different tables of critical values for each different statistical test, as you will see on the following spreads. The critical value is the number that a test statistic must reach in order for the null hypothesis to be rejected.

To find the appropriate critical value in a table you need to know four pieces of information:

- Degrees of freedom (*df*) In most cases you get this value by looking at the number of participants in the study (*N*).
- **One-tailed** or **two-tailed test** If the hypothesis was a **directional hypothesis**, then you use a one-tailed test; if it was **non-directional** you use a two-tailed test.
- Significance level selected, usually $p = 0.05$ (5% level).
- Whether the observed value needs to be greater than or less than the critical value for significance to be shown. You will find this information stated underneath each table of critical values.

Choosing which statistical test to use

Different inferential tests are used depending on (1) the research design and (2) the level of measurement. When deciding which test is appropriate in any situation you can ask yourself the questions in the diagram below:

Justifying your choice of test

On each spread that follows we have provided information that will help you justify your choice of tests, but be warned that such justifications need to be adapted to suit particular circumstances. Essentially you should:

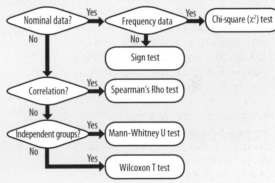

- Identify the **level of measurement** with reference to the actual data.
- State whether a test of correlation or difference is required and justify this.
- If a test of difference is required, state whether it is **independent groups** or **repeated measures**, and justify this statement.

EXAM CORNER

Practice for novel scenarios

1. Explain what is meant by the phrase 'significant at $p \leq 0.05$'. [2]
2. Suggest why a researcher may choose to use $p \leq 0.01$ in preference to $p \leq 0.05$. (Try to give two reasons.) [4]
3. What other term is used for the observed value? [1]
4. Identify the **four** pieces of information used to find the critical value. [4]
5. Identify the level of measurement that would be used in the examples below:
   a. Rating how stressful certain experiences are. [1]
   b. Counting the days a person has had off school. [1]
   c. Asking people to indicate the reasons for days off school. [1]

A2 Level only: Inferential tests: Spearman's Rank Order Correlation Coefficient

The first **inferential test** we will look at is a test of **correlation** – *Spearman's Rank Order Correlation Coefficient*. It is used to determine whether the correlation between two **co-variables** is significant or not.

For example on page 96 we described a study on happiness by Diener *et al.* (1993). They found that the correlation between income and happiness was +.12.

A figure of zero would be no correlation whereas a figure of +1.0 would be a perfect **positive correlation**. A correlation of +.12 may sound like a rather insignificant correlation but in fact it is **significant**.

The **observed value** of +.12 was calculated using a statistical test such as Spearman's Rank Order Correlation Coefficient. This observed value is then compared with the **critical value** found in a table of critical values (such as the table on the facing page) to see whether the observed value is significant. If the number of participants in this study was quite large (over 100) then .12 would be significant (as the number of participants increases the value needed for significance decreases). Incidentally if the observed value had been –.12 this would still be significant; it would be a significant **negative correlation**.

HEALTH WARNING – ETHICS

If you do conduct your own research studies, make sure no participants are younger than 16 and that you seek **valid consent**. If you are using sensitive information, such as tests of maths ability, then you must protect participants' **confidentiality**.

EXAM CORNER

1. Identify **two** ethical problems that might arise when conducting a study on finger length and numeracy, and state how these could be dealt with. [2 + 2]
2. Suggest problems that might occur when dealing with the ethical problems in the manner you suggested. [4]
3. Identify the co-variables in the study by Brosnan (above right). [2]
4. Identify an **intervening variable** in this study (the variable that links finger length to numeracy, for example). [1]
5. If you were going to study the relationship between digit ratio and literacy, state a possible alternative and null hypothesis for this study. [2]
6. Sketch a **scatter diagram** of the results on the facing page to check the outcome of the statistical test – does your graph show the same relationship as reported for the statistical test? [3]

FINGER LENGTH AND EXAM PERFORMANCE

Ring finger   Index finger

▲ Literacy hand
People with short ring fingers and long index fingers are better at literacy.

▲ Numeracy hand
People with long ring fingers and short index fingers are more likely to excel in numeracy.

A number of studies have looked at the relationship between finger length and various abilities such as numeracy or literacy. For example a study by Brosnan (2008) examined finger length in 75 British children aged between six and seven (boys and girls), and found that children with a higher digit ratio between their index and ring fingers were more likely to have a talent in maths, while those with a shorter digit ratio were more likely to have a talent in literacy.

This relationship is thought to be due to biological factors, specifically the production of **testosterone** and **oestrogen** in the brain. Male babies are exposed to more testosterone (a male **hormone**) during prenatal development and this affects their finger length. At the same time testosterone promotes the development of the areas of the brain which are often associated with spatial and mathematical skills, whereas oestrogen (a female hormone) is thought to do the same in the areas of the brain which are often associated with verbal ability.

In order to study the correlation between finger length and numeracy/literacy the researchers took photocopies of both the right and left hands of the children and measured the length of the index and ring fingers. They divided the length of the index finger by the length of the ring finger to calculate each child's 'digit ratio'.

The digit ratios were then correlated with the results from their *National Standard Assessment Tests* (SATs) for numeracy and literacy.

TRY THIS

You can repeat (**replicate**) the study above using GCSE scores instead of SATs results, or you could use online tests of literacy and/or numeracy. In order to determine if your results are significant follow the worked example on the facing page.

TRY THIS

Ideas for studies using a correlational analysis
* **Reaction time and number of hours of sleep** Does lack of sleep have any effects? For example it might be related to poor reaction time. You can measure reaction time using an online test.
* **Reaction time and time spent playing computer games** Perhaps playing computer games is related to reaction time.
* **Working memory and IQ** are predicted to be positively correlated. You can find tests for both at *www.bbc.co.uk*

WHEN TO USE SPEARMAN'S TEST

- The hypothesis predicts a *correlation* between two co-variables.
- The two sets of data are pairs of scores from one person or thing, i.e. they are *related*.
- The data are at least **ordinal** (i.e. not **nominal**). See page 144 for an explanation.

◀ Charles Edward Spearman (1863–1945)

You will never be required to do any calculations in an exam. Nevertheless, it is a good idea to calculate a statistic because it gives you a better 'feel' for the test and also helps you understand how to deal with observed and critical values, and draw a conclusion.

ALTERNATIVE AND NULL HYPOTHESIS

The term **alternative hypothesis** (H_1) is used because it is the alternative to the **null hypothesis** (H_0). The null hypothesis is required because statistical tests are looking at whether our samples come from a population where there is no effect or no relationship (in which case the null hypothesis is true, i.e. any relationship is due to chance) or whether our samples come from a population where there is a relationship (in which case we can reject the null hypothesis and accept the alternative).

The null hypothesis is a statement of no relationship (in a correlational analysis) or no difference. So it should always begin 'There is no correlation between...' or 'There is no difference between...'.

SPEARMAN'S RANK ORDER CORRELATION COEFFICIENT – A WORKED EXAMPLE

STEP 1. State the alternative and null hypothesis
Alternative hypothesis: The digit ratio between index finger and ring finger is positively correlated to numeracy skills. (This is a **directional hypothesis**, therefore requiring a **one-tailed test**.)
Null hypothesis: There is no correlation between digit ratio and numeracy skills.

STEP 2. Record the data and rank each co-variable and calculate the difference
Rank A and B separately, from low to high (i.e. the lowest number receives the rank of 1). If there are two or more of the same number (tied ranks), calculate the rank by working out the mean of the ranks that would have been given.

Participant number	Digit ratio	Numeracy score	Rank A	Rank B	Difference between rank A and rank B (d)	d^2
1	1.026	8	10	2.5	7.5	56.25
2	1.000	16	5.5	9	−3.5	12.25
3	1.021	10	9	5	4.0	16.0
4	0.991	9	4	4	0	0
5	0.984	15	3	8	−5.0	25.0
6	0.975	14	1	7	−6.0	36.0
7	1.013	12	7	6	1	1.0
8	1.018	8	8	2.5	5.5	30.25
9	0.982	17	2	10	−8.0	64.0
10	1.000	5	5.5	1	4.5	20.25
N = 10		Σd^2 (sum of differences squared) = 261.0				

STEP 3. Find observed value of rho (the correlation coefficient)

$$rho = 1 - \frac{6\Sigma d^2}{N(N^2 - 1)} = 1 - \frac{6 \times 261.0}{10 \times (100 - 1)} = 1 - \frac{1566}{990} = 1 - 1.58 = -0.58$$

STEP 4. Find the critical value of rho
$N = 10$; the hypothesis is directional so therefore a one-tailed test is used. Look up the critical value in the table of critical values (on right).
For a one-tailed test where $N = 10$, the critical value of *rho* ($p \leq 0.05$) = 0.564
Note that the observed value is negative – when comparing this figure with the critical value, only the value, not the sign, is important. The sign does, however, tell you whether the correlation is positive or negative. If the prediction was one-tailed and the sign (and therefore the correlation) is not as predicted, then the null hypothesis must be retained.

STEP 5. State the conclusion
As the observed value (0.58) is greater than the critical value (0.564) it might appear that we should reject the null hypothesis (at $p \leq 0.05$); **however, in this case the sign is in the wrong direction – a positive correlation was predicted but a negative correlation was found**. This means that we have to accept the null hypothesis and conclude that there is no correlation between digit ratio and numeracy skills.
If we had predicted a negative correlation then we could have rejected the null hypothesis.

Table of critical values of *rho* at 5% level ($p \leq 0.05$)

N =	One-tailed test	Two-tailed test
4	1.000	
5	0.900	1.000
6	0.829	0.886
7	0.714	0.786
8	0.643	0.738
9	0.600	0.700
10	0.564	0.648
11	0.536	0.618
12	0.503	0.587
13	0.484	0.560
14	0.464	0.538
15	0.443	0.521
16	0.429	0.503
17	0.414	0.485
18	0.401	0.472
19	0.391	0.460
20	0.380	0.447
21	0.370	0.435
22	0.361	0.425
23	0.353	0.415
24	0.344	0.406
25	0.337	0.398
26	0.331	0.390
27	0.324	0.382
28	0.317	0.375
29	0.312	0.368
30	0.306	0.362

Observed value of *rho* must be EQUAL TO or GREATER THAN the critical value in this table for significance to be shown.

Source: J.H. Zhar (1972) Significance testing of the Spearman's Rank Correlation Coefficient. *Journal of the American Statistical Association*, 67, 578–580. With kind permission of the publisher.

Exam advice...
Calculations of inferential tests will not be required in the exam but students will be expected to deal with observed and critical values - finding out whether a particular observed value is significant by using a critical values table. Make sure you know how to do this.

A2 Level only: Inferential tests: Chi-squared (χ^2) Test

The second **inferential test** we will look at deals with **nominal data**, i.e. data that are in categories. We use this test when we have counted how many occurrences there are in each category – called 'frequency data'. For example, we might be interested to find out whether men and women do actually differ in terms of their finger length ratio (as discussed on the previous spread). Research has found that adult women usually have ratios of one, i.e. their index and ring fingers are of equal length. The average for men is lower at 0.98, since they tend to have longer ring fingers than index fingers, suggesting greater exposure to testosterone in the womb. Of course, the Chi-squared Test (see below) does not prove this but can support this gender difference.

'Chi' is one of the letters of the Greek alphabet (pronounced as 'kie' to rhyme with 'pie'). The Greek symbol for chi is χ, which is why this symbol is used as the statistic for the Chi-squared Test.

CHI-SQUARED TEST – A WORKED EXAMPLE FOR A 2 × 2 TABLE

STEP 1. State the **alternative** and **null hypothesis**
Alternative hypothesis: There is a difference between men and women in terms of digit ratio (the ratio between the index and ring fingers). (This is a **non-directional hypothesis** that therefore requires a **two-tailed test**.)
Null hypothesis: There is no difference between men and women in terms of digit ratio.

STEP 2. Draw up a contingency table

	Male	Female	Totals
Digit ratio ≥ 1.00	5 (cell **A**)	12 (cell **B**)	17
Digit ratio < 1.00	10 (cell **C**)	9 (cell **D**)	19
Totals	15	21	36

This is a 2×2 *contingency table* as there are two rows and two tables. On the facing page there is a 3×2 contingency table as there are three rows and two columns. The first number is always rows and the second number is columns (to remember rows then columns, think of RC as in Roman Catholic).

* Many students get confused about the expected frequencies. These are not what the researcher expects – they are the frequencies that would occur if the data were distributed evenly across the table in proportion to the row and column totals.

The Chi-squared Test can be used to investigate a difference (as in the worked example on this page) or an association (as on the facing page).

There are online programs that will calculate Chi-squared for you – see for example http://math.hws.edu/javamath/ryan/ChiSquare.html (scroll about half way down the page). You could also use the statistics functions in Excel to calculate the statistic from your data table.

STEP 3. Compare observed and expected* frequencies for each cell
The expected frequencies are calculated by working out how the data would be distributed across all cells in the table if there were no differences, i.e. it was **random**.

	row × column / total = expected frequency (E)	Subtract expected value from observed value, ignoring signs (O − E)	Square previous value (O − E)²	Divide previous value by expected value (O − E)² / E
Cell **A**	17×15 / 36 = 7.08	5 − 7.08 = 2.08	4.3264	0.6110
Cell **B**	17×21 / 36 = 9.92	12 − 9.92 = 2.08	4.3264	0.4361
Cell **C**	19×15 / 36 = 7.92	10 − 7.92 = 2.08	4.3264	0.5463
Cell **D**	19×21 / 36 = 11.08	9 − 11.08 = 2.08	4.3264	0.3905

In some books Yates's correction is recommended, but Coolican (1996) says this is no longer modern practice.

STEP 4. Find the **observed value** of Chi-squared (χ^2)
Add all the values in the final column in the table above.
This gives you the observed value of Chi-squared as 1.984

STEP 5. Find the **critical value** of Chi-squared (χ^2)
Calculate degrees of freedom (df) by multiplying
(rows − 1) × (columns − 1) = 1
Look up the value in the table of the critical values (right).
For a two-tailed test, $df = 1$, the critical value of χ^2 $(p \leq 0.5) = 3.84$

STEP 6. State the conclusion
As the observed value (2.984) is less than the critical value (3.84) we must accept the null hypothesis (at $p \leq 0.05$) and therefore we conclude that there is no difference between men and women in terms of digit ratio.

Table of critical values of Chi-squared (χ^2) $(p \leq 0.05)$

df	One-tailed test	Two-tailed test
1	2.71	3.84
2	4.60	5.99
3	6.25	7.82
4	7.78	9.49
5	9.24	11.07

Observed value of χ^2 must be EQUAL TO or GREATER THAN the critical value in this table for significance to be shown.

Source: abridged from R.A. Fisher and F. Yates (1974) *Statistical Tables for Biological, Agricultural and Medical Research* (6th edition). London: Longman.

PARENTAL STYLE AND SELF-ESTEEM

Psychological research has identified three different parenting styles: *authoritarian* (parents dictate how children should behave), *democratic* (parents discuss standards with their children) and *laissez-faire* (parents encourage children to set their own rules). Buri (1991) found that children who experienced authoritarian parenting were more likely to develop high **self-esteem**.

TRY THIS

To conduct a study such as the one above you can access the *Parental Authority Questionnaire* (PAQ) at *https://dtreboux.files.wordpress.com/2013/06/parental-authority-questionnaire-2.docx*

There are various self-esteem questionnaires on the internet.

TRY THIS

Ideas for studies using a Chi-squared Test

- **Gender and conformity** Are women more conformist than men? Some studies have found this to be true, though Eagly and Carli (1981) suggest this is only true on male-oriented tasks. Try different types of conformity tasks and see whether some have higher or lower levels of female conformity, for example ask questions on a general knowledge test which are related to male or female interests. The answers from previous 'participants' should be shown so you can see if your real participant conforms to the majority answer.

- **Sleep and age** Research suggests that people sleep less as they get older. Compare older and younger participants in terms of average number of hours' sleep.

WHEN TO USE THE CHI-SQUARED (χ^2) TEST

- The hypothesis predicts a *difference* between two conditions or an *association* between variables.
- The sets of data must be *independent* (no individual should have a score in more than one 'cell').
- The data are in *frequencies* (i.e. **nominal**). See page 144 for an explanation. Frequencies must not be percentages.

Note This test is unreliable when the *expected* (i.e. the ones you calculate) frequencies fall below 5 in any cell, i.e. you need at least 20 participants for a 2×2 contingency table.

CHI-SQUARED TEST – A WORKED EXAMPLE FOR A 3 × 2 TABLE

STEP 1. State the **alternative** and **null hypothesis**

Alternative hypothesis: Certain parental styles are associated with higher self-esteem in adolescence. (This is a **non-directional hypothesis** and therefore requires a **two-tailed test**.)

Null hypothesis: There is no association between parental style and self-esteem in adolescence.

STEP 2. Draw up a contingency table

In this case it will be 3 by 2 (rows first then columns).

Parental style	Self-esteem		Totals
	High	Low	
Authoritarian	10 (cell **A**)	4 (cell **B**)	14
Democratic	5 (cell **C**)	7 (cell **D**)	12
Laissez-faire	8 (cell **E**)	2 (cell **F**)	10
Totals	23	13	36

STEP 3. Compare observed and expected frequencies

	row × column / total = expected frequency (E)	Subtract expected value from observed value, ignoring signs (O – E)	Square previous value (O – E)²	Divide previous value by expected value (O – E)² / E
Cell A	14 × 23 / 36 = 8.94	10 – 8.94 = 1.06	1.1236	0.1257
Cell B	14 × 13 / 36 = 5.06	4 – 5.06 = 1.06	1.1236	0.2221
Cell C	12 × 23 / 36 = 7.67	5 – 7.67 = 2.67	7.1289	0.9294
Cell D	12 × 13 / 36 = 4.33	7 – 4.33 = 2.67	7.1289	1.6464
Cell E	10 × 23 / 36 = 6.39	8 – 6.39 = 1.61	2.5921	0.4056
Cell F	10 × 13 / 36 = 3.61	2 – 3.61 = 1.61	2.5921	0.7180

STEP 4. Find the **observed value** of Chi-squared (χ^2)

Add all the values in the final column in the table above.
This gives you the observed value of Chi-squared (χ^2) = 4.0472

STEP 5. Find the **critical value** of Chi-squared (χ^2)

Calculate degrees of freedom (*df*): by multiplying (rows − 1) × (columns − 1) = 2
Look up the critical value in the table of critical values (on facing page).
For a two-tailed test, $df = 2$, the critical value of χ^2 ($p \leq 0.05$) = 5.99

STEP 6. State the conclusion

EXAM CORNER

Practice for novel scenarios

1. State the conclusion for the test above. [2]
2. Draw a contingency table to show the following data – old and young participants are asked whether they sleep more or less than eight hours per night on average. Of the old people 11 said they sleep more and 25 said they sleep less. Of the younger participants 31 said they sleep more than eight hours and 33 said they sleep less. [4]
3. State an appropriate alternative hypothesis (directional) and null hypothesis for this investigation. [2 + 2]
4. The observed (calculated) value of Chi-squared for the data from question 1 is 3.02 (one-tailed test). Is this value significant? Explain your decision and state whether this means you can reject the null hypothesis. [2 + 2]

A2 Level only: Inferential tests: Sign Test

The final three **inferential tests** are 'tests of difference' (on this spread and the next two spreads). What does this mean? A test of difference enables us to consider whether or not two samples of data are different from each other. For example, we might want to know whether people produce more accurate work in a noisy or quiet environment – we would be looking at a difference in participants' performance in the two conditions. The Chi-squared Test (on the previous spread) is both a test of difference and a **test of association**. Tests of association look at whether two variables both increase at the same time (positive association/correlation) or as one increases the other decreases (negative association/correlation).

Tests of difference are generally used for experiments. For example we might conduct an experiment to see if noisy conditions reduce the effectiveness of revision.

Case A – we could have two groups of participants:
- Group 1: participants revise in a silent room and are tested.
- Group 2: a different group of participants who revise in a noisy room and are tested.

Case B – we might have two conditions:
- Condition 1: participants revise in a silent room and are tested.
- Condition 2: the same participants revise in a noisy room and are tested.

Case A is an **independent groups design** (we have two separate groups of participants). Case B (we have two conditions but just one group of participants) is a **repeated measures design** as the same participants are tested twice.

The Sign Test (on this spread) and the Wilcoxon *T* Test (on the next spread) are used for repeated measures designs. The Mann–Whitney *U* Test (on pages 160–161) is used for independent groups designs.

In some experiments there are more than two conditions or groups – for example the classic research by Loftus and Palmer (1974) on leading questions had five different groups according to which verb was in the sentence (smashed, hit, etc.). There are specific statistical tests that are used for designs with more than two conditions/groups – but you don't need to worry about those.

Note There are **three** kinds of experimental design – repeated measures, independent groups and, finally, **matched pairs**. In a matched pairs study there are two groups of participants (as in independent groups design) but the groups are not independent – they are matched (e.g. on characteristics such as IQ, age, etc.). Therefore matched pairs experiments use repeated measures tests.

In statistical terms a test of difference is looking at whether two sets of scores are drawn from the same population (this is the null hypothesis) or from two different populations (this is the alternative hypothesis). For example, if we are looking at whether noise or no noise is better we either:
- Believe that there is no difference (the null hypothesis) – the scores from the two conditions inevitably will differ slightly but this difference is due to chance factors.
- Believe that there is a difference (the alternative hypothesis) – the fact that the scores from the two conditions differ is because each sample is drawn from a different population.

THE MATCHING HYPOTHESIS

Who do you find attractive? If everyone selected the most attractive people as potential partners we all might be fighting over a small group of beautiful men and women, but the **matching hypothesis** (Walster *et al.*, 1966) suggests that people are actually attracted to those individuals who most closely match their perceptions of their own level of attractiveness. Thus, although we may be attracted to physically attractive individuals as potential partners, a compromise is necessary to avoid rejection by our more attractive choices.

A number of studies have tested this hypothesis. For example, Murstein (1972) arranged for photos of dating and engaged couples to be rated in terms of attractiveness. The ratings showed a definite tendency for dating or engaged couples to have similar levels of attractiveness.

TRY THIS

You can replicate the study on the left using photographs of couples from magazines or the internet. Separate the photos so you can put all the males together and all the females together. Place all photos in a random order. Ask 'judges' to rate each individual for attractiveness. If you use a rating scale from 1 to 10 you might decide that similarity counts as having scores that are within 2 points of each other.

TRY THIS

Ideas for studies using a Sign Test
- **Evidence for extra sensory perception (ESP)** In the early days of ESP testing Zener cards (also called ESP cards) were used (above). Each pack consisted of 25 cards, five of each design. The cards were intended to be emotionally neutral to remove any response bias. A 'sender' (or agent) views each of the cards in the pack in turn and a 'receiver' guesses the symbol on that card. Before a trial begins the cards are placed in a random order. In order to demonstrate ESP a person must get more than five cards right – five is the level that would be expected by chance. If more than five cards are right you score a plus, otherwise you score a minus.
- **Inattentional blindness** refers to being unable to see things that are in plain sight. Show people the following video and ask if they did see a gorilla: *www.youtube.com/watch?v=vJG698U2Mvo*

You could also look at Richard Wiseman's replication of this at *www.youtube.com/watch?v=y6qgoM89ekM*

▶ Can we explain interpersonal attraction in terms of matching? That is, people seek partners who are similar to themselves in terms of attractiveness rather than seeking the most attractive individuals.

THE SIGN TEST – A WORKED EXAMPLE

STEP 1. State the **alternative** and **null hypotheses**
Alternative hypothesis: Partners who are dating or engaged have a similar level of attractiveness (i.e. match in terms of attractiveness). (This is a **non-directional hypothesis** and therefore requires a **two-tailed test**.)

Null hypothesis: There is no relationship between the level of attractiveness of dating or engaged couples.

STEP 2. Record the data and work out the sign
For each couple record the average rating score given to the male and female partners.

Then score a plus (+) if their average rating scores were the same and a minus (–) if their average rating scores were different. In the example below a rating scale of 1 to 5 was used and scores were expected to be identical to count as similar.

Couple	Average rating for male partner	Average rating for female partner	Similar or different?
1	3	4	–
2	4	3	–
3	5	5	+
4	1	2	–
5	1	1	+
6	3	3	+
7	5	5	+
8	4	4	+
9	3	1	–
10	4	4	+
11	5	2	–
12	4	4	+

STEP 3. Find the **observed value** of S
S = the number of times the less frequent value occurs.
In this case the less frequent sign is minus, so $S = 5$

STEP 4. Find the **critical value** of S
N = The total number of scores (less any zero values).
In this case $N = 12$ (no scores omitted). The hypothesis is non-directional – therefore a one-tailed test is used.

Look up the critical value in the table of critical values (see above right).

For a two-tailed test, $N = 12$, the critical value of S ($p \leq 0.05$) = 2

STEP 5. State the conclusion
As the observed value (5) is greater than the critical value (2) we must accept the null hypothesis (at $p \leq 0.05$) and conclude that there is no relationship between the level of attractiveness of dating or engaged couples (i.e. they do not match).

Table of critical values of S ($p \leq 0.05$)

N =	One-tailed test	Two-tailed test
5	0	
6	0	0
7	0	0
8	1	0
9	1	1
10	1	1
11	2	1
12	2	2
13	3	2
14	3	2
15	3	3
16	4	3
17	4	4
18	5	4
19	5	4
20	5	5
25	7	7
30	10	9
35	12	11

Observed value of S must be EQUAL TO or LESS THAN the critical value in this table for significance to be shown.

Source: abridged from R.F. Clegg (1982) *Simple Statistics*. Cambridge: Cambridge University Press.

WHEN TO USE THE SIGN TEST

- The hypothesis predicts a *difference* between two sets of data.
- The two sets of data are pairs of scores from one person (or a matched pair) = *related*.
- The data are **nominal** (i.e. not **ordinal** or **interval**). See page 144 for an explanation.

EXAM CORNER
Practice for novel scenarios
1. Identify **one or more** ethical problems that might arise when conducting a study on the matching hypothesis. [1 mark each]
2. Suggest how you might deal with the ethical problem(s). [2 marks each]
3. If you were going to study ESP using the Zener cards, state possible alternative and null hypotheses for this study. [2 + 2]
4. Is your alternative hypothesis directional or non-directional? [1]
5. Describe how you could obtain a volunteer sample for this study. [2]
6. Suggest an alternative sampling method and explain in what way this would be a better method than using a volunteer sample. [3]
7. Using made-up data or data you have collected, calculate the S value for your data set. Decide whether to accept or reject the null hypothesis. [2 + 2]
8. Explain why the Sign Test would be the appropriate test to use with this data. [2]

A2 Level only: Inferential tests: Wilcoxon Matched Pairs Signed Ranks Test

Like the Sign Test, the Wilcoxon Matched Pairs Signed Ranks Test is a **test of difference** for **repeated measures** or **matched pairs**. Whereas the Sign Test is only suitable for **nominal data**, the Wilcoxon *T* Test is suitable for **ordinal** or **interval data**. There are more 'powerful' tests that can be used with interval data – such as *t*-tests – but these are beyond the specification so you don't need to worry about them. The concept of 'power' refers to the fact that *t*-tests are better able to detect **significance** – this means that if you use the Wilcoxon *T* Test you might not find that your results are significant but if you used a *t*-test you might detect a significant difference – a bit like using a higher magnification microscope.

Wilcoxon Matched Pairs Signed Ranks Test – what a mouthful! The reason for this name is that Frank Wilcoxon produced another well-known statistical test called the *Wilcoxon Rank Sums Test* – therefore neither test can simply be called the Wicoxon Test. For ease of reference we have called it the Wilcoxon *T* Test because the statistic that is calculated for the Wilcoxon Matched Pairs Signed Ranks Test is called *T*.

Note **Matched pairs** is also a related design – there are two groups of participants but each participant in one group is matched with a participant in the other group on key variables, so in a sense it is like testing the same person twice.

THE MERE EXPOSURE EFFECT

There is a saying that 'familiarity breeds contempt', but psychological research has found that the opposite is generally true – we come to like things because of their familiarity. For example, people generally like a song more after they have heard it a few times, and advertisements often aim to increase our liking for a product through repeated exposure. Things that are familiar are less threatening and thus more likeable.

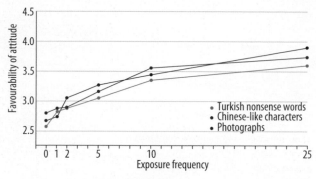

Robert Zajonc (pronounced 'zie-unts') conducted various experiments to demonstrate the *mere exposure effect*. For example, in one study Zajonc (1968) told participants that he was conducting a study on visual memory and showed them a set of photographs of 12 different men (face only). Each photograph was shown for two seconds. At the end participants were asked to rate how much they liked the 12 different men on a scale from 0 to 6. The key element of the study is that some photos were shown more often than others. For example, one photo appeared 25 times whereas another only appeared once.

Overall the frequencies were 0, 1, 2, 5, 10 and 25. The same experiment was repeated with invented Chinese symbols and also with Turkish words. All the results are shown in the graph on the left.

▲ Whose face is nicest? According to the *mere exposure effect* you should like the one you see most often.

TRY THIS

You can replicate the study above but don't need to have all six conditions. The final analysis can involve just comparing two of the stimuli – one frequent and one infrequent, as shown in the worked example on the facing page.

TRY THIS

Ideas for studies using a Wilcoxon *T* Test

- **Mere exposure again** The *mere exposure effect* can also be used to explain the fact that people prefer pictures of themselves that are reversed as in a mirror – because that is the way you usually see yourself and so it is more familiar (Mita *et al.*, 1977). You could take a few pictures of each participant with a digital camera and create a mirror image of each. Show them the photographs and record their ratings (on a scale of 1 to 5) for each photograph. Compare the ratings.
- **Right brain left brain** If you perform two tasks that involve the same brain hemisphere you should be slower on both tasks than if performing two tasks that involve the right and left hemispheres separately. For example, tap your right finger while reading a page from a book (both involve the left hemisphere). Then

repeat the finger tapping without doing any reading. On each occasion count how many finger taps you manage in 30 seconds and compare these scores.
- **Smiling makes you happy** You might think that you smile because you are feeling happy but psychological research shows it works the other way round too, i.e. you become happy because you are smiling. Laird (1974) told participants to contract certain facial muscles so he could measure facial muscular activity using electrodes. The instructions either resulted in something like a smile or like a frown. Participants who were made to 'smile' while rating cartoons for funniness rated the cartoons as funnier than those who were made to produce a frown. You could replicate this by asking people to smile for some cartoons and frown for others, and rate each cartoon for humour.

THE WILCOXON *T* TEST – A WORKED EXAMPLE

STEP 1. State the **alternative** *and* **null hypotheses**
Alternative hypothesis: Participants rate the more frequently seen face as more likeable than the less frequently seen face. (This is a **directional hypothesis** and therefore requires a **one-tailed test**.)
Null hypothesis: There is no difference in the likeability score for faces seen more or less often.

STEP 2. Record the data, calculate the difference between scores and rank
Once you have worked out the difference, rank from low to high, ignoring the signs (i.e. the lowest number receives the rank of 1).
If there are two or more of the same number (tied ranks) calculate the rank by working out the mean of the ranks that would have been given.
If the difference is zero, omit this from the ranking and reduce *N* accordingly.

Participant	Likeability for more frequently seen face	Likeability for less frequently seen face	Difference	Rank
1	5	2	3	9.5
2	4	3	1	3
3	3	3	omit	
4	6	4	2	6.5
5	2	3	−1	3
6	4	5	−1	3
7	5	2	3	9.5
8	3	4	−1	3
9	6	3	3	9.5
10	4	6	−2	6.5
11	5	2	3	9.5
12	3	4	−1	3

STEP 3. Find the **observed value** *of T*
T = the sum of the ranks of the less frequent sign.
In this case the less frequent sign is minus, so $T = 3 + 3 + 3 + 6.5 + 3 = 18.5$

STEP 4. Find the **critical value** *of T*
N = 11 (one score omitted). The hypothesis is directional – therefore a one-tailed test is used. Look up the critical value in the table of critical values (see right).
For a one-tailed test, *N* = 11, the critical value of $T (p < 0.05) = 13$

STEP 5. State the conclusion
As the observed value (18.5) is greater than the critical value (13) we must accept the null hypothesis (at $p \leq 0.05$) and conclude that there is no difference in the likeability score for faces seen more or less often.

WHEN TO USE THE WILCOXON *T* TEST

- The hypothesis predicts a *difference* between two sets of data.
- The two sets of data are pairs of scores from one person (or a matched pair) = related.
- The data are at least **ordinal** (i.e. not **nominal**). See page 144 for an explanation.

◀ Frank Wilcoxon (1892–1965), an American chemist and statistician.

Table of critical values of $T (p \leq 0.05)$

N =	One-tailed test	Two-tailed test
5	0	
6	2	0
7	3	2
8	5	3
9	8	5
10	11	8
11	13	10
12	17	13
13	21	17
14	25	21
15	30	25
16	35	29
17	41	34
18	47	40
19	53	46
20	60	52
21	67	58
22	75	65
23	83	73
24	91	81
25	100	89
26	110	98
27	119	107
28	130	116
29	141	125
30	151	137
31	163	147
32	175	159
33	187	170

Observed value of *T* must be EQUAL TO or LESS THAN the critical value in this table for significance to be shown.

Source: R. Meddis (1975) *Statistical Handbook for Non-statisticians*. London: McGraw-Hill.

EXAM CORNER

Practice for novel scenarios

1. Identify the maximum observed (calculated) value of *T* that would be required for significance with a two-tailed test with 25 participants. [1]

2. In a psychology experiment, 15 students were given a test in the morning and a similar test in the afternoon to see whether they did better when tested in the morning or afternoon. The researcher expected them to do better in the morning.
   a. Write appropriate alternative and null hypotheses for this study. [2 + 2]
   b. Invent data for the study – you need 15 pairs of scores. Explain why the Wilcoxon *T* Test would be the appropriate test to use with this data. [3]
   c. Follow the steps outlined above to calculate *T* for your data and then state the conclusion you would draw about the significance of the results. [2 + 2]
   d. One problem with this study is that the students might do better in the afternoon because they had done a similar test in the morning. Therefore the study was conducted again using a matched pairs design. Explain how this might be done (including the variables you would use for matching). [4]
   e. Explain how **counterbalancing** could be used to deal with the **order effects** if a repeated measures design was used. [3]

A2 Level only: Inferential tests: Mann–Whitney *U* Test

The final **inferential test** you need to study is one that is appropriate for **tests of difference** where there are **independent groups**, i.e. where the study involved two groups of participants each given a different level of the **independent variable**. One group might work in a noisy condition whereas the other group works in silence, or one group might be tested in the morning and the other group tested in the afternoon to see if time of day affects performance.

▲ The Capilano Suspension Bridge was used in the study by Dutton and Aron (see right). The bridge is narrow and long and has many arousal-inducing features: a tendency to tilt, sway and wobble, creating the impression that one is about to fall over the side; very low handrails of wire cable; and a 230-foot drop to rocks and shallow rapids below.

EXAM CORNER

Practice for novel scenarios

1. In a study to compare the effects of noise on performance a **matched pairs design** was used. Explain how this would be done, including a description of at least **two** variables that would be used for matching. Explain why you chose these variables for matching. [4]

2. What would be a suitable statistical test to use with this study? Justify your choice. [3]

3. Use **descriptive statistics** to summarise the results given in the worked example on the facing page, i.e. calculate measures of central tendency and dispersion, and also sketch an appropriate graph. [2 + 2 + 3]

4. A psychology class decides to replicate the study by White *et al.* on the right. Write appropriate alternative and null hypotheses for this study. [2 + 2]

5. Is your alternative hypothesis directional or non-directional? [1]

6. The students check the significance of their results using the Mann–Whitney test and find that $U = 40$ (there were 9 participants in one group and 13 in the other group). State what conclusion they could draw from their results. [2]

7. Repeat questions 2–5 with any of the other studies on this page. [marks as above]

FALLING IN LOVE

Psychologists have sought to explain the process of falling in love. One suggestion is that love is basically physiological arousal – arousal of your **sympathetic nervous system** which occurs when you are feeling scared or stressed or find someone physically attractive. Hatfield and Walster (1981) suggested that love is simply a label that we place on physiological arousal when it occurs in the presence of an appropriate object. A man or woman who meets a potential partner after an exciting football game is more likely to fall in love than he or she would be on a routine day. Likewise, a man or woman is more likely to fall in love when having experienced some bitter disappointment. The reason, in both cases, is to do with the two components of love: arousal and label.

This has been supported by various experiments, such as a memorable study by Dutton and Aron (1974). A female research assistant (unaware of the study's aims) interviewed males, explaining that she was doing a project for her psychology class on the effects of attractive scenery on creative expression. The interviews took place on a high suspension bridge (high arousal group; see left) or a narrow bridge over a small stream (low arousal).

When the interview was over, the research assistant gave the men her phone number and asked them to call her if they had any questions about the survey. Over 60% of the men in the high arousal condition did phone her compared with 30% from the low arousal group, suggesting that the men had mislabelled their fear-related arousal as sexual arousal.

TRY THIS

Another study which investigated the two-factor theory of love was conducted by White *et al.* (1981). In this experiment high and low arousal was created by asking men to run on the spot for two minutes or 15 seconds respectively, and then showing them a short video of a young woman. The more highly aroused men rated the woman as more attractive.

TRY THIS

Ideas for studies using a Mann–Whitney *U* Test

- **Digit ratio and gender** (see page 152). You can collect data on the digit ratios of men and women and analyse them using the Mann–Whitney test by comparing the scores for men and women.

- **Time of day** A number of studies have looked at how time of day affects our performance. For example, Gupta (1991) found that performance on **IQ tests** was best at 7pm as compared with 9am or 2pm, a factor which might be an important consideration when taking examinations.

- **Eyewitness testimony** You could repeat the classic evidence by Loftus and Palmer (1974) (see page 76) using just two conditions (e.g. leading question contains the word 'hot' or 'smashed') and compare the speed estimates given by the two groups of participants.

WHEN TO USE THE MANN–WHITNEY *U* TEST

- The hypothesis predicts a *difference* between two sets of data.
- The two sets of data are from separate groups of participants = *independent groups*.
- The data are at least **ordinal** (i.e. not **nominal**). See page 144 for an explanation.

The Mann–Whitney *U* Test is named after the Austrian-born US mathematician Henry Berthold Mann and the US statistician Donald Ransom Whitney who published the test in 1947. They adapted a test designed by Frank Wilcoxon that was for equal sample sizes (called the Wilcoxon Rank Sums Test – not the same as the one on page 158).

THE MANN–WHITNEY *U* TEST – A WORKED EXAMPLE

STEP 1. State the **alternative** and **null hypotheses**
Alternative hypothesis: Male participants interviewed on a high bridge give higher ratings of the attractiveness of a female interviewer than those interviewed on a low bridge. (This is a **directional hypothesis** and therefore requires a **one-tailed test**.)
Null hypothesis: There is no difference in the ratings of attractiveness given by those interviewed on a high or low bridge.

STEP 2. Record the data in a table and allocate points (see right)
To allocate points consider each score one at a time.
Compare this score (the target) with all the scores in the other group.
Give 1 point for every score that is higher than the target score and ½ point for every equal score. Add these up to calculate the score for the target score.
    Repeat for all scores.

STEP 3. Find the **observed value** of *U*
U is the lower total number of points. In this case it is 16.5

STEP 4. Find the **critical value** of *U*
N_1 = number of participants in group 1
N_2 = number of participants in group 2
Look up the critical value in the table of critical values (below).
For a one-tailed test, $N_1 = 10$ and $N_2 = 14$, the critical value of U ($p < 0.05$) = 41
Note   When you have a directional hypothesis, remember to check whether the difference is in the direction that you predicted. If it is not, you cannot reject the null hypothesis.

STEP 5. State the conclusion
As the observed value (16.5) is less than the critical value (41) and the results are in the predicted direction we can reject the null hypothesis (at $p \leq 0.05$) and therefore conclude that participants interviewed on a high bridge give higher ratings of attractiveness to a female interviewer than those interviewed on a low bridge, i.e. that physiological arousal leads to greater perceptions of attractiveness.

Attractiveness ratings given by high bridge group	Points	Attractiveness ratings given by low bridge group	Points
7	1.5	4	10.0
10	0	6	8.5
8	1.0	2	10.0
6	3.5	5	9.5
5	7.0	3	10.0
8	1.0	5	9.5
9	0.5	6	8.5
7	1.5	4	10.0
10	0	5	9.5
9	0.5	7	7.0
		9	3.0
		3	10.0
		5	9.5
		6	8.5
$N1 = 10$	16.5	$N2 = 14$	123.5

The two samples in the table above are unequal, which may happen when using an independent groups design.

Tables of critical values of U ($p \leq 0.05$)

CRITICAL VALUES FOR A ONE-TAILED TEST

N_2 \ N_1	2	3	4	5	6	7	8	9	10	11	12	13	14	15
2				0	0	0	1	1	1	1	2	2	2	3
3		0	0	1	2	2	3	3	4	5	5	6	7	7
4		0	1	2	3	4	5	6	7	8	9	10	11	12
5	0	1	2	4	5	6	8	9	11	12	13	15	16	18
6	0	2	3	5	7	8	10	12	14	16	17	19	21	23
7	0	2	4	6	8	11	13	15	17	19	21	24	26	28
8	1	3	5	8	10	13	15	18	20	23	26	28	31	33
9	1	3	6	9	12	15	18	21	24	27	30	33	36	39
10	1	4	7	11	14	17	20	24	27	31	34	37	41	44
11	1	5	8	12	16	19	23	27	31	34	38	42	46	50
12	2	5	9	13	17	21	26	30	34	38	42	47	51	55
13	2	6	10	15	19	24	28	33	37	42	47	51	56	61
14	2	7	11	16	21	26	31	36	41	46	51	56	61	66
15	3	7	12	18	23	28	33	39	44	50	55	61	66	72

CRITICAL VALUES FOR A TWO-TAILED TEST

N_2 \ N_1	2	3	4	5	6	7	8	9	10	11	12	13	14	15
2					0	0	0	0	1	1	1	1		
3			0	1	1	2	2	3	3	4	4	5	5	
4			0	1	2	3	4	4	5	6	7	8	9	10
5		0	1	2	3	5	6	7	8	9	11	12	13	14
6		1	2	3	5	6	8	10	11	13	14	16	17	19
7		1	3	5	6	8	10	12	14	16	18	20	22	24
8	0	2	4	6	8	10	13	15	17	19	22	24	26	29
9	0	2	4	7	10	12	15	17	20	23	26	28	31	34
10	0	3	5	8	11	14	17	20	23	26	29	33	36	39
11	0	3	6	9	13	16	19	23	26	30	33	37	40	44
12	1	4	7	11	14	18	22	26	29	33	37	41	45	49
13	1	4	8	12	16	20	24	28	33	37	41	45	50	54
14	1	5	9	13	17	22	26	31	36	40	45	50	55	59
15	1	5	10	14	19	24	29	34	39	44	49	54	59	64

For any N_1 and N_2 observed value of U must be EQUAL TO or LESS THAN the critical value in these tables for significance to be shown.

Source: R. Runyon and A. Haber (1976) *Fundamentals of Behavioural Statistics* (3rd edition). Reading, MA: McGraw-Hill.

Social psychology: Milgram (1963) Behavioural study of obedience

We end this chapter with two classic studies in psychology. The first is an example of social psychology – research into how the behaviour of other people affects us.

Stanley Milgram's study looked specifically at obedience to unjust authority. Milgram was seeking an answer to the question of why Nazis appeared so willing to obey orders and murder millions of Jews and other groups of people in the Second World War. Was such brutality simply a matter of obeying orders, as Adolf Eichmann – who had been in charge of the concentration camps – had claimed?

Milgram recognised that obedience is an indispensable part of social life. In order to live in communities, some system of authority is required. However, in the hands of unjust authorities do people obey? Milgram aimed to create a situation that allowed him to measure the process of obedience, even when the command requires destructive behaviour.

▲ Eichmann on trial in Jerusalem, Israel, in 1961. He was found guilty and hanged for his crimes. The presiding judge commented: *'Even if we had found that the Accused acted out of blind obedience, as he argued, we would still have said that a man who took part in crimes of such magnitude as these over years must pay the maximum penalty known to the law, and he cannot rely on any order even in mitigation of his punishment.'*

MEET THE RESEARCHER

Stanley Milgram
(1933–1984) grew up in a working-class Jewish family in New York. He investigated many social phenomena, though his name is forever associated with the obedience study. For example, he studied the 'small word problem' by sending letters to people in remote areas of the US and asking them to get a message to a target person. He showed that the average number of 'hops' was 5 or 6 people. He also studied familiar strangers – those people you see on your way to work or in local shops; you don't know them but they are familiar.

METHODOLOGY

The study was conducted in a **laboratory** environment so that conditions could be well controlled. It was not an **experiment** (see box at top right of facing page).

Participants

Milgram placed an advertisement in a New Haven newspaper. From the people who responded, he selected 40 males aged between 20 and 50 years. The advertisement led the participants to believe that they would be taking part in research about memory and learning. The men in the **sample** had a range of jobs, from postal clerks to engineers, and they varied in educational level from one who hadn't finished primary school to one with a doctorate. Each man was paid $4.50 for his participation in the study. He was told he would receive this simply for coming to the lab – payment did not depend on remaining in the study.

PROCEDURE

The study took place in a lab at Yale University. When participants arrived they were greeted by the 'experimenter', a 31-year-old man dressed in a grey technician's coat. Another 'participant' was at the lab, a mild-mannered and likeable 47-year-old accountant, Mr Wallace. In fact both of these men were accomplices of Milgram (called **confederates**).

The participants drew slips of paper to decide which of them would play the role of teacher or learner. The selection was rigged – the naïve participant was always assigned to the teacher role and the accomplice was always assigned the learner role.

Both learner and teacher were then taken to the experimental room where the learner was strapped into an 'electric chair' apparatus to prevent excessive movement. An electrode was placed on the learner's wrist, linked to a shock generator in the adjoining room.

▲ The 'learner' is strapped into a chair in a separate room. The 'teacher' sits next door to deliver shocks whenever the learner makes a mistake. The experimenter delivers 'prods' to encourage the 'teacher' to continue.

The shock machine

The teacher was taken to the adjoining room and seated in front of the shock generator. This large machine had 30 switches on it, each showing an incremental rise in voltage starting at 15 volts and going up to 450 volts. For every four switches, there were 'shock' labels, starting at 'slight shock' at 15 volts to 'intense shock' at 255 volts and finally 'XXX' at 450 volts, a potentially fatal shock. The experimenter gave the teacher a 'sample' shock to demonstrate that the machine was real.

The learning task

Once the study began, the teacher was told to administer a shock when the learner gave a wrong answer, and to escalate to a higher level of shock each time, announcing the shock level each time. The learner was told to make no comment or protest until the shock level of 300 volts was reached. At this point he should pound on the wall but thereafter make no further comment.

Feedback from experimenter

The experimenter was trained to give a sequence of four standard 'prods' if the teacher hesitated about delivering the shock or asked for guidance: 'Please continue'; 'The experiment requires that you continue'; 'It is absolutely essential that you continue'; 'You have no other choice, you must go on.' There were also special prods such as: 'Although the shocks may be painful, there is no permanent tissue damage, so go on.'

Dehoax

After the research was completed, the teacher was thoroughly 'dehoaxed' (**debriefed**) and the experimenter reunited the teacher and learner. They were then interviewed about their experience in this study.

FINDINGS

Quantitative data

Prior to the study Milgram surveyed 14 Yale psychology students. They estimated that 0–3% of the participants would administer 450 volts.

The findings from the actual study showed this was a wild underestimate. A large majority continued to the highest level. At 300 volts, five (12.5%) of the participants refused to continue. This was the point at which the learner made the only protest. All the participants had continued to this point.

A total of 26 of the 40 participants (65%) administered the full 450 volts. This does also mean that 35% of the participants defied the experimenter's authority.

Qualitative data

Many subjects showed nervousness, and a large number showed extreme tension: *'subjects were observed to sweat, tremble, stutter, bite their lips, groan and dig their finger-nails into their flesh'*.

Fourteen participants displayed *'nervous laughter and smiling'*. Their remarks and outward behaviour indicated that they were acting against their own values in punishing the learner. In the post-experimental interview (the 'dehoax'), these participants explained that they were not sadistic and that their laughter had not meant that they were enjoying shocking the learner.

Three participants had *'full-blown uncontrollable seizures'*. One participant had such a violent convulsion that the research session had to be stopped.

CONCLUSIONS

Milgram concluded that it is the circumstances in which the participants found themselves that amalgamated to create a situation in which it proved difficult to disobey. He suggested 13 elements in this situation that had contributed to these levels of obedience; for example:

- The location of the study at a prestigious university provided authority.
- Participants assumed that the experimenter knew what he was doing and had a worthy purpose, so should be followed.
- The participant didn't wish to disrupt the study because he felt under obligation to the experimenter due to his voluntary consent to take part.
- It was a novel situation for the participant, who therefore didn't know how to behave. If it had been possible to discuss the situation with others the participant might have behaved differently.
- The participant had very little time to resolve the conflict at 300 volts, and he didn't know that the victim would remain silent for the rest of the experiment.
- The participant assumed that the discomfort caused was minimal and temporary, and that the scientific gains were important.
- The conflict was between two deeply ingrained tendencies – not to harm someone, and to obey those whom we perceive to be legitimate authorities.

RESEARCH METHODS USED BY SOCIAL PSYCHOLOGISTS

All psychologists use the full range of methods: **experiments**, **observations** and so on. Within social psychology experimental research has been quite popular – though in fact many studies are well-controlled investigations rather than experiments. An experiment requires an **independent** and **dependent variable**. In Milgram's study the level of shocks varied but they weren't independent variables – they were a means of assessing how obedient each participant was. So his study was not an experiment but a controlled observation conducted in a **laboratory**.

One of the other well-known studies in social psychology was conducted by Solomon Asch (1956). He showed that people were willing to conform to the opinions of others even when the answer was clearly wrong. A group of people were shown three lines and asked to identify which of them was the same length as a standard line. A group of **confederates** sometimes gave the wrong answer but one-third of the time the true participant went along with them. This too was not an experiment but a well-controlled observation in a laboratory.

EVALUATION

Internal validity

Orne and Holland (1968) claim that this research lacks **internal validity** as the participants did not believe the electric shocks were real. It simply wouldn't have made sense that someone in a learning experiment would receive fatal shocks. Therefore participants behaved as they were expected to behave due to the **demand characteristics** of the study.

This has been further supported in a recent investigation by Gina Perry (2012). She read through Milgram's detailed archive of what actually happened in the study and found that the participants knew they weren't hurting anyone. In the follow-up questionnaire many participants said they were suspicious because, for example, the experimenter remained so calm.

On the other hand, Milgram (1974) reported that 75% of the participants strongly believed they were giving electric shocks.

Ethical issues

Baumrind (1964) claimed that Milgram caused psychological damage to his participants that could not be justified. Milgram defended himself in several ways. First, he did not know, prior to the study, that such high levels of distress would be caused. Second, he did consider ending the study when he observed the participants' behaviour, but decided that there was no indication of injurious effects (Milgram, 1974). Third, 84% of the participants did say afterwards that they were glad to have participated. Finally, the potential damage to participants should be weighed against the importance of the findings.

On the other hand, Perry (2012) has recently argued that Milgram failed in his duty of care for participants because some were waiting for up to a year before they were debriefed despite the fact that they had left the lab believing they had killed someone.

EXAM CORNER

1. Outline the procedures of Milgram's (1963) research 'Behavioural study of obedience'. [8]
2. *'Milgram's research is an example of research which is very unethical, but also very insightful'.* Discuss the extent to which you agree with this statement. [12]

Developmental psychology: Kohlberg (1968)
The child as moral philosopher

Our second classic study is an example of developmental psychology. This area of psychology focuses on how people change as they get older. Researchers consider such topics as how our sense of self changes and how our thinking and memories change from birth to death. The classic study we are going to examine researches how children's sense of right and wrong changes as they get older.

Lawrence Kohlberg could also be considered to be a **cognitive** psychologist because his view of moral behaviour was that it is governed by the way we think about situations of right and wrong and that our thinking matures as a part of ageing – it becomes more abstract. By contrast, **behaviourists** would suggest that moral behaviour is *learned* through reward and punishment, and not governed in any way by thinking – we behave 'morally' in order to avoid punishment. Freud proposed that our sense of right and wrong is learned through identification with our parents.

MEET THE RESEARCHER

Lawrence Kohlberg (1927–1987) found, as part of this research, that moral conversations encouraged people to move up to high levels of thinking. Together with Carol Gilligan, he set up a number of Cluster Schools (also called 'just' communities) in a number of schools, and even one in a prison. Members had the power to define and resolve disputes within the group, encouraging moral development.

▼ A moral dilemma

In Europe, a woman was near death from a rare type of cancer. There was one drug that the doctors thought might save her. It was a form of radium that a pharmacist in the same town had recently discovered. The drug was expensive to make but the pharmacist was charging 10 times what the drug cost him to make. He paid €400 for the radium and charged €4,000 for a small dose of it. The sick woman's husband, Heinz, went to everyone he knew to borrow the money, but he could only get together about €2,000, which is half of what it cost. He told the pharmacist that his wife was dying and asked him to sell it or let him pay later. But the pharmacist said, 'No. I discovered the drug and I'm going to make money from it'. Heinz got desperate and broke into the man's store to steal the drug for his wife.

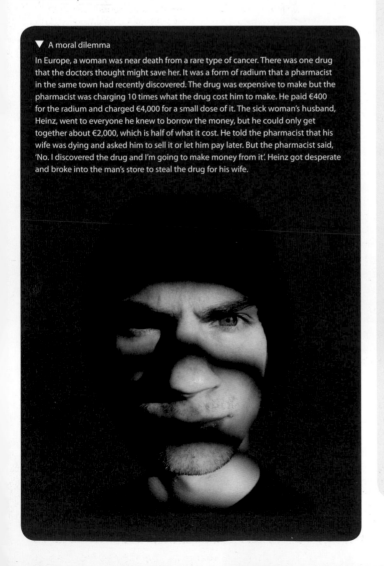

METHODOLOGY

Kohlberg undertook various studies related to moral development, using **interviews** to collect **qualitative data**. The study included cross-cultural comparisons and a **longitudinal** element.

Participants

Kohlberg and colleagues studied a group of 75 American boys from the age of 10–16 and again between age 22 and 28.

He also studied people in Great Britain, Canada, Taiwan, Mexico and Turkey.

PROCEDURE

To assess moral thinking Kohlberg created nine hypothetical moral dilemmas (such as the one on the left about the pharmacist). Each dilemma presented a conflict between two moral issues. Each participant was asked to discuss three of these dilemmas, prompted by a set of ten or more open-ended questions, such as:

- Should Heinz steal the drug? Why or why not?
- If the respondent favours stealing, ask: 'If Heinz doesn't love his wife, should he steal the drug for her?' Why or why not?
- If the respondent favours not stealing, ask: 'Does it make a difference whether or not he loves his wife?' Why or why not?
- Suppose the person dying is not his wife but a stranger. Should Heinz steal the drug for the stranger? Why or why not?

The boys' answers were analysed and common themes were identified so that the stage theory could be constructed. Each boy was re-interviewed every three years.

The same kind of interview was used with children and adults in other countries.

FINDINGS

The boys' answers were analysed and common themes were identified so that the stage theory could be constructed (see facing page). A stage theory is an account of how behaviour changes at different ages (stages). Kohlberg found that the younger children thought at the pre-conventional level and as they got older their reasons for moral decisions became less focused on themselves and more focused on doing good because relationships with others are important. The final level of development is related to moral principles.

The results in Mexico and Taiwan were the same except that development was a little slower.

CONCLUSIONS

Kohlberg concluded that the key features of moral development are:

- Stages are *invariant* and *universal* – people everywhere go through the same stages in the same order.
- Each new stage represents a more *equilibriated* form of moral understanding, resulting in a more logically consistent and morally mature form of understanding.

Moral discussion classes can be used to help children develop their moral thinking. Discussions between children at stages 3 and 4 result in the stage 3 child moving forwards.

RESEARCH METHODS USED BY DEVELOPMENTAL PSYCHOLOGISTS

Developmental psychologists focus on how children and adults change as they get older. Therefore they often conduct longitudinal research, i.e. a study that takes place over a period of years. Kohlberg began his research by studying 75 boys but he continued to interview the same boys once every three or four years over a period of 20 years (Colby *et al.*, 1983). Over that time stage 1 and 2 thinking dropped to nearly zero whereas stage 4 thinking had grown from almost zero at age 10 to 70% at age 36, with only 10% of the sample showing stage 5 thinking at age 36.

An alternative to longitudinal research is a **cross-sectional** study. Walker *et al.* (1987) also researched moral development but did it using a cross-sectional design – interviewing 80 people of various ages and comparing the moral development of people belonging to different age groups.

It takes a long time to complete a longitudinal study whereas cross-sectional research can be done fairly quickly. However, longitudinal study has the advantage of controlling individual differences.

▼ Kohlberg's stages of moral development.

THE PRECONVENTIONAL LEVEL Children accept the rules of authority figures and judge actions by their consequences. Actions that result in punishments are bad, those that bring rewards are good.	**Stage 1** The punishment and obedience orientation	This style of morality ignores the intentions behind a behaviour and focuses on obeying rules that are enforced by punishment (e.g. when one boy, Tommy, age 10, is asked 'Is it better to save the life of one important person or a lot of unimportant people?', he thinks of the value of life in terms of the furniture they possess).
	Stage 2 The instrumental purpose orientation	Children view actions as 'right' if they satisfy their own needs (e.g. Tommy, age 13, argues that someone in pain would be better off dead but her husband wouldn't like it – the wife's value is in terms of her instrumental value to her husband).
THE CONVENTIONAL LEVEL Individuals continue to believe that conformity to social rules is desirable, but this is not out of self-interest. Maintaining the current social system ensures positive human relationships and social order.	**Stage 3** Interpersonal cooperation	This is a 'good boy–good girl' orientation. What is right is defined by what is expected by others (e.g. Tommy, age 16, frames his answer more in terms of the wife's importance to the family relationships).
	Stage 4 The social-order-maintaining orientation	This marks the shift from defining what is right in terms of role expectations to defining what is right in terms of norms established by the larger social system (e.g. a different boy, Richard, age 13, expresses his views about mercy killing in terms of the right to destroy something God created).
THE POST-CONVENTIONAL (PRINCIPLED) LEVEL The post-conventional individual moves beyond unquestioning compliance with the norms of their own social system. The individual now defines morality in terms of abstract moral principles that apply to all societies and situations.	**Stage 5** The social contract orientation	Laws are seen as relative and flexible. Where they are consistent with individual rights and the interests of the majority, they are upheld (to preserve social order), otherwise they can be changed (e.g. Richard, age 20, considers the right that we all have to make the choice about our own life).
	Stage 6 The universal ethical principles orientation	Morality is defined in terms of self-chosen abstract moral principles. Laws usually conform to these principles, but where this is not the case, the individual acts in accordance with their moral principles.

EVALUATION

Sampling

One issue with this study is that Kohlberg's theory is based on interviews with boys. Carol Gilligan (1982) suggested that male morality might be quite different to female morality – it is based on justice rather than caringness. Indeed Kohlberg's moral dilemmas are more concerned with wrongdoing and are therefore more to do with justice.

Gilligan found evidence that showed that women tend to be more focused on relationships ('caring') than justice when making moral decisions. This suggests that Kohlberg's theory was gender-biased and restricted to only one type of morality.

However, many psychologists have come to recognise that Gilligan's critique was more of an expansion of Kohlberg's theory than an alternative to it (Jorgensen, 2006). The core concepts put forward by Kohlberg remain unchallenged, such as the invariant sequence of development and the importance of social interactions.

External validity

Gilligan (1982) also criticised Kohlberg's research because the evidence was not based on real-life decisions. The moral dilemmas were hypothetical scenarios which may have made little sense, especially to young children. Gilligan's own research involved interviewing people about their own moral dilemmas, such as the decision about whether to have an abortion.

Social desirability bias

One of the problems with **self-report** methods is that participants prefer to present themselves in a good light. Therefore they may describe their moral behaviour somewhat idealistically rather than what they would actually *do*. In addition Kohlberg was actually asking how people *think* rather than what they would do. Therefore this theory is about idealistic moral thinking than about behaviour.

To be fair, though, Kohlberg claimed it was a theory of reasoning. He did predict that those who reason in a more mature fashion should be inclined to more morally mature behaviour and he found some support for this (Kohlberg, 1975). When students were given the opportunity to cheat on a test, he found that only 15% of college students at the post-conventional stage cheated, whereas 70% of those at the pre-conventional stage did. However, Burton (1976) found that people only behave consistently with their moral principles on some *kinds* of moral behaviour, such as cheating or sharing toys, and concluded that generally it is likely that factors other than moral principles affect moral behaviour, such as the likelihood of punishment.

EXAM CORNER

1. Describe the findings and conclusions of Kohlberg's (1968) research 'The child as moral philosopher'. [10]
2. *'The usefulness of Kohlberg's research is limited by his inadequate sample.'* Evaluate the method and procedures used in Kohlberg's (1968) research 'The child as moral philosopher'. [10]

Some activities for you

Flashcards

Create a set of research methods flashcards. You can create them using 'old school' index cards or use a website such as *www.cram. com* to create a set of cards that you can share with your friends. You can either use this web-based program to create flashcards and then print them out, or you can use it to test yourself using the website or connect using a smart device.

Afterwards you can use flashcards in a variety of ways...

1. To test yourself.
2. To test your friends.
3. To play a research methods 'chain gang' with small groups of students – one student picks a card and then they have to explain the definition of that research methods term (without using any phrases that appear in the term being defined) to the next person in the chain. When that person has guessed the term they have to then define another randomly selected term to the next person and so on... The team that explains and identifies all of its research methods terms correctly wins!

Self-report

Pick an issue that is currently being debated in society, such as: 'Should we be giving money to overseas charities when we have people in need in the UK?'

Design a brief questionnaire, which includes open and closed questions and will collect quantitative and qualitative data about your chosen issue. Distribute the questionnaire to about 10 people.

Using the same questions, interview 10 people. Transcribe the interviews.

Compare the results you collected from the interview and from the questionnaire. Present the data in appropriate descriptive statistics or pick out key phrases or statements from the qualitative data.

Compare the two methodologies you used. Did you identify the advantages/disadvantages that were noted previously in this chapter?

Experimental designs

Copy and complete the table below, noting firstly which experimental design the statement relates to and then identifying whether you think the statement is offering an advantage or disadvantage of that experimental design. Please note that there are two advantages and two disadvantages for each of the three experimental designs.

	Statement	Design	Advantage or disadvantage?
1	Needs fewer participants than independent groups or matched participants design.		
2	Needs twice as many participants as a repeated measures design.		
3	No order effects as participants only take part in one condition.		
4	No order effects as participants only take part in one condition.		
5	There is no chance of intergroup differences as all participants take part in all conditions.		
6	There may be an uncontrolled intergroup difference that is responsible for any difference found in the DV.		
7	Takes time and resources to match participants.		
8	Order effects may occur and demand characteristics more likely.		
9	Less chance of demand characteristics as participants only take part in one condition.		
10	Less chance of demand characteristics as participants only take part in one condition.		
11	Even with really good matching there could still be an uncontrolled intergroup difference that is responsible for any difference in the DV.		
12	Participants may guess the aim of the study.		

ANSWERS ON PAGE 172

Kohlberg – can you think of a modern dilemma?

A criticism frequently levelled at Kohlberg's dilemmas is that they are hypothetical and not relevant to younger children (see the example about Heinz's ill wife).

So design a dilemma that an average 10-year-old child would be able to understand. Make sure that you use a situation with which they would be able to readily identify.

Milgram – can you really do better?

Many people criticise Milgram's research because of its ethical issues, such as deception or the risk of harm (stress, anxiety, humiliation or pain). But is it really fair to do this?

After reading up about ethical guidelines that psychologists have to comply with today, try to think of a way in which you could investigate Milgram's aim (see below) in an ethical way.

Milgram aimed to contrive a situation which allowed him to quantify exactly how obedient individuals would be in a controlled situation.

Decision saplings!

Diagnostic trees are tree-like diagrams that doctors and psychiatrists use when diagnosing disorders. They start off with one question and then using Yes/No answers they come to a conclusion about which disorder a person may have. Decision trees are similar tree-like models, that can include consequences and event outcomes.

When dealing with issues like methods, reliability, validity, etc., psychologists are often making many decisions and their choices depend on the potential consequences they might offer. One way to start thinking like a 'proper' psychologist could be to create 'decision saplings' (when they are really detailed enough they can become a fully grown tree). Take an issue like 'internal validity'; below you can see the sort of issues and methods of management a researcher would have to think about.

INTERNAL VALIDITY
Does the research measure what it claims to measure?

Does the x test really measure x? → Ask an expert in the field of x to check the x test to confirm if it does indeed test x

Is there any chance of socially desirable responses? → Ensure the Ps are told that the results will be confidential

Ethics committee

Collect the methodology and/or procedural sections of about 10 journal articles. You could also use the research summarised in the BPS's fortnightly Research Digest (a great subscription email that is free to receive – sign up now!).

One person in the group pretends to be the researcher and they have to defend their chosen methodology/procedure in terms of the ethics. They can describe methods that they used and explain why they think the safeguards they put in place were adequate for the safety of their participants.

Committee members (works best with about five other students) ask questions and may challenge the appropriateness of a researcher's ethical safeguards.

At the end the committee votes to indicate whether they think the research is ethical or not.

Location of research

Identify a construct that a psychologist may be interested in measuring, for example happiness.

Think of three behaviours you might look for if you were planning to 'observe' this construct; for example:
1. Smiling
2. Laughing
3. Saying positive statements

Ask five friends to spend five minutes chatting to each other in a classroom and observe how frequently they demonstrate each of these behaviours. Next, observe the same five friends for another five minutes chatting to each other in a less formal situation, like the student common room or a canteen.

Is there any difference in the frequency of observed behaviours when in the formal or less formal situations?

Which inferential test should you use?

Using the information in the following scenarios, identify which inferential test is appropriate to use.
1. A psychologist is conducting research into the film choice of different personality types. She talks to her participants and she decides whether they are extrovert or introvert and then asks them about the type of film they last saw at the cinema – horror, comedy, adventure.
2. A psychologist is comparing the time taken (seconds) by men and women to complete a lap of a race track.
3. A psychologist is conducting a Stroop test and is comparing the number of errors made when people complete the congruent condition and when the same people complete the incongruent condition.
4. A psychologist wants to investigate if there is a relationship between how well someone does in their exam (UMS marks) and how happy they are as measured by a happiness test.

ANSWERS ON PAGE 172

Make it better…

One way to test your understanding of concepts like reliability and validity is to look at research and spot any issues that research may have. Read through the following scenarios; what issues can you spot and what advice would you offer to improve the research?

ANSWERS ON PAGE 172

1. A psychologist is interested in finding out whether people's happiness levels are affected by the weather. A psychologist selects a local street and then asks every resident on that street to rate their happiness on a scale of 0 (no happiness) to 10 (the happiest they could ever be). He does this on two occasions, once on a Saturday in April on a day which is warm and sunny and once on a Monday in November, when the weather is cold and cloudy.
2. A headteacher notices the naughtiness of her students increases when they have charity days at the end of term. She believes this increase in naughtiness is due to the students wearing their own clothes rather than wearing their usual school uniform. In order to assess this she counts how many behavioural complaints are recorded by teachers on the school's administration software. She compares the number of behavioural complaints recorded on one day in the middle of term (when the students are all wearing uniform) and compares this to the number of behavioural complaints recorded on the last day of term (when the students are all wearing their own clothes).
3. A second-hand car salesman thinks red cars are easier to sell than any other car. On one Saturday when he opens his lot he has 15 red cars and 70 cars of other colours. By the end of the day he has sold 20% of the red cars, but only 10% of the cars of other colours. He decides after finding this he will only stock red cars on his lot.

Exam questions and answers

Questions on investigating behaviour may require descriptions (AO1), application to novel situation (AO2) or evaluation (AO3).

SHORT ANSWER QUESTIONS

1. Explain what is meant by null hypothesis. [2]
2. Explain the difference between an extraneous and confounding variable. [2]
3. Explain what is meant by random sampling. [2]
4. Identify what is being described in the following statements:
   a. A variable that is not the independent variable (IV) under study but which varies systematically with the IV. [1]
   b. An experimental design whereby each participant takes part in every condition under test. [1]
   c. Information collected directly from first-hand experience instead of using data collected by someone else. [1]
5. Explain what is meant by 0.05 level of significance. [2]

TRY THIS

Have a go at being the examiner
Bob's answer has been marked and the examiner comments are given.

Have a go at marking Megan's answers and write examiner's comments using the knowledge you have gained from Bob.

Bob's answer with examiner comments

1. Null means nothing, so a null hypothesis means that you predict that the IV will have no effect on the DV.
   Correct and clear explanation, sufficient detail for the full 2 out of 2 marks; both null and hypothesis are explained.

2. A confounding variable is anything in a study that might affect the results and the researcher has to try and control it, whereas an extraneous variable is more or less the same thing but the researcher doesn't bother to try and control these.
   This answer is muddled and inaccurate, so 0 marks, but it is a error lots of students make. A confounding variable is not the IV under study and varies systematically with the IV, which makes it unclear whether changes in the DV are due to the IV or the confounding variable, i.e. an alternative cause. In contrast extraneous variables do not vary systematically with the IV but could have an effect on the DV and thus make it more difficult to detect a significant effect.

3. Random sampling is when the researcher just picks who they want randomly, for example they could just stop anyone in the street.
   Inaccurate – Bob has described opportunity sampling, so 0 marks. Bob would need to explain that random means everyone in the target population has an equal chance of being selected using a random technique just as the lottery method.

4. a = confounding variable, b = repeated measures design, c = primary data
   All correct, for the full 3 marks.

5. 0.05 is the probability level that your results have occurred by chance, 0.05 means that there is a 95% probability that your results represent what is true and only a 5% probability they have occurred by chance.
   Correct and clear explanation, full 2 out of 2 marks.

Megan's answer

1. A null hypothesis is something that predicts nothing.
2. A key difference between the two is that confounding variables vary systematically with the IV, therefore any changes in the DV might be due to the IV or the confounding variable, whereas extraneous variables do not vary systematically and are more nuisance variables that can cloud a genuine significant effect.
3. Random sampling is when names are put in a hat and pulled out; everyone in the hat has an equal chance of getting picked. The researcher is not able to pick who they particularly want, it is all down to chance.
4. (a) extraneous variable, (b) repeated measures design, (c) primary data
5. 0.05 means your results are significant.

See page 175 for comments on Megan's answers.

Mark schemes for the investigating behaviour questions

Questions on investigating behaviour tend to be worth 1, 2, 3 or 4 marks. These questions require you to be very specific in what skills you demonstrate. Some example mark schemes are shown below.

A question that asks you to *identify* or *name* an element of the study, e.g. 'Identify the experimental design used in this study'. [1]

Mark	Description
1	Name the element/issue, e.g. matched pairs.
0	Inappropriate answer / no response.

A question that asks you to *explain* or *define* what is meant by a key term, e.g. 'Explain what is meant by matched pairs design'. [2]

Mark	Description
2	Explanation/definition is thorough and well detailed.
1	Explanation/definition is basic and less detailed.
0	Inappropriate answer / no response.

A question that asks you to *apply your knowledge* to the novel situation, e.g. 'Give **one** advantage of the experimental design used *in this study*'. [3]

When a question explicitly asks for an answer to 'in this study' you will be penalised if you do not contextualise your response.

Mark	Description
3	Appropriate advantage explained and applied well to the study.
2	Appropriate advantage explained. Some link to the study.
1	Appropriate advantage explained. No link to the study.
0	Inappropriate answer / no response.

QUESTION WITH A NOVEL SITUATION

Research such as that conducted by the National Institute of Child Health and Human Development (NICHD) has suggested that the more time a child spends in day care, the more aggressive and disobedient they are likely to be.

A team of researchers want to investigate the relationship between time spent in day care and levels of aggression. They propose an alternative directional hypothesis: 'There is a positive correlation between number of hours spent in day care and number of aggressive acts observed'.

The researchers study 12 children in a nursery school. They collect data concerning the number of hours each child spends per week in day care and then they observe the children in day care for one day and rate how aggressive they are by counting up how many 'aggressive acts' the child commits. The results from the study are below.

Participant number	Number of aggressive acts recorded during the day	Number of hours spent in day care per week
Child 1	3	12
Child 2	6	37
Child 3	2	40
Child 4	4	20
Child 5	1	10
Child 6	3	18
Child 7	2	40
Child 8	9	40
Child 9	0	37
Child 10	5	25
Child 11	2	37
Child 12	1	12

A correlation coefficient of +.26 was found.

a. Explain **one** issue of reliability in this study and explain how it could be dealt with in this study. [4]

b. Explain what is meant by a correlation coefficient. [2]

c. The psychologist proposed a directional alternative hypothesis in this study; explain why this was appropriate in this study. [2]

d. Identify the level of measurement of the 'number of hours spent per week in day care' and explain your answer. [3]

e. The researcher has used event sampling in this study. Explain what is meant by event sampling in this study. [3]

f. **A2 Level only:** Identify an appropriate inferential statistical test that could be used to analyse the data in this research and justify your choice. [3]

Bob's answer

a. One issue of reliability is that there is a team of researchers that are rating how aggressive each child is and may have different ideas about what aggression actually means. One researcher may record screaming as an act of aggression whilst another would only record physical acts like hitting and ignore things like screaming. This would mean that the observers were not being consistent in their approach and the study would lack reliability.

b. A correlation coefficient is a number between −1 and +1 that shows the direction and strength of a relationship between two co-variables.

c. They used a directional hypothesis because there has been lots of research done previously on the topic, e.g. the NICHD had already found a positive correlation between time in day care and aggression, etc., therefore these researchers could frame their research and were quite confident in what they expected to find.

d. Number of hours is interval data because number of hours has equal intervals, e.g. a child who spends 24 hours in day care spends twice as long as a child who spends 12 hours in day care.

e. Event sampling is used when observing behaviour. The researcher records every time they see the event happening. In this study the event is an aggressive act, so the observer records every time they see a child do it.

f. Spearman's Rho statistical test is the only appropriate one as it is the only one used for a correlation.

> Bob has provided an accurate, detailed and contextualised issue of reliability but has failed to consider how the issue could be dealt with. It is important to carefully read all questions as many require you to cover two elements. 2 out of 4 marks.

> Accurate and detailed as Bob has covered the meaning of the number as well as the direction of the relationship. 2 out of 2 marks.

> Accurate and well explained with clear reference to the novel situation. 2 out of 2 marks.

> Accurate level of measurement identified and clear explanation which is contextualised. 3 out of 3 marks.

> Accurate definition that is fully contextualised. 3 out of 3 marks.

> Bob has accurately identified an appropriate statistical test but has failed to fully justify why it is appropriate. In order to get full marks Bob would need to explain two reasons why the test is appropriate. 2 out of 3 marks.

TRY THIS

Have a go at being the examiner
Bob's answer has been marked and the examiner comments are given.
Have a go at marking Megan's answers and write examiner comments using the knowledge you have gained from Bob.

Megan's answer

a. Reliability means consistency in research and in this study one issue of reliability could be that 'aggressive act' has not been clearly operationalised, therefore different observers would have different interpretations of each child's behaviour. To solve this the team would have to fully operationalise aggressive acts prior to the study and then once the data is collected they could test how effective this was using inter-rater reliability, e.g. compare data collected and if there is 80% or more agreement you have solved the issue of reliability.

b. This is the number from a correlation.

c. This is a hypothesis that predicts exactly what will happen, e.g. there will be a positive correlation.

d. Ordinal.

e. Event sampling is taking the people available.

f. I would use the Spearman Rank Order Correlation Coefficient because this inferential test is appropriate for correlations and data needs to be at least of ordinal level. This study is correlational, e.g. day care and aggressive acts, and data is at least ordinal as time and number of acts are being measured.

See page 176 for comments on Megan's answers.

Exam questions and answers (continued)

Questions on investigating behaviour may require descriptions (AO1), application to novel situation (AO2) or evaluation (AO3).

QUESTION WITH A NOVEL SITUATION

The headteacher of a local comprehensive school has employed a psychologist to introduce a new positive psychology curriculum (PPC). This involves lessons for one hour per week that have been designed to promote learners' skills, strengths and goal achievement. The headteacher is hoping that this programme will increase the happiness and self-esteem of students.

To test whether this new curriculum does achieve its aim 10 students were selected from the group receiving the new programme using random sampling and were asked to complete a questionnaire prior to the implementation of the PPC. The questionnaire was repeated one year later, after students had completed PPC lessons.

One of the questions included in both questionnaires was 'How happy are you at present?' The learners responded using the scale below:

0	1	2	3	4
Very unhappy	Unhappy	Neither happy nor unhappy	Happy	Very happy

Responses are shown below:

Learner's ID number	Happiness score prior to PPC	Happiness score after 1 year of following PPC
1	1	3
2	4	4
3	3	4
4	3	3
5	2	3
6	2	2
7	3	4
8	4	4
9	1	3
10	2	2

a. Identify the independent variable in this research. [1]
b. Explain how the dependent variable has been operationalised in this research. [2]
c. Outline **one** disadvantage of random sampling in this study and explain an alternative method of sampling the psychologist could have used. [4]
d. Identify **one** issue of validity in this research and explain **one** way of dealing with this issue of validity. [4]
e. Calculate the mean happiness score of participants prior to PPC. [2]
f. Explain **one** advantage and **one** disadvantage of using the mean score as a measure of central tendency. [4]
g. Suggest a suitable directional hypothesis for this research. [2]
h. Identify **one** ethical issue in this research and explain how you would deal with this issue in this research. [4]
i. Identify and explain the level of measurement used in this study. [2]
j. The psychologist found that the quantitative data collected to represent happiness scores was not very detailed and so she decided to repeat her research, but this time collecting qualitative data. Explain how the psychologist could do this. You should identify and justify an appropriate methodology in your answer. [4]
k. **A2 Level only:** The psychologist used a Wilcoxon matched pairs signed ranks test to analyse the data. Justify why this test is appropriate for analysing the data collected in this research. [2]

Bob's answer with examiner comments

a. The IV is what is manipulated by the researcher and in this study it is whether the students have had the positive psychology curriculum or not.
There is no need to define what an IV is at the beginning – indeed the question only requires him to name the IV (PPC). Bob has accurately identified the IV contextualised in the study. 1 out of 1 mark.

b. The DV is defined numerically using the scale 0–4. This shows how happy each person is.
Correct and clear explanation. 2 out of 2 marks.

c. One disadvantage is that random sampling can be time consuming because you need to have everyone's name in the target population. One alternative could be systematic sampling.
A correct answer to this question must be contextualised as the question clearly states 'in this study'. Bob has failed to do this and has provided a generic disadvantage of random sampling (in fact it also isn't quite correct as researchers tend to use a smaller sampling frame). He has also simply named rather than actually explained an alternative sampling method. There are several possible creditworthy alternative sampling methods that could have been explained, e.g. stratified, volunteer, etc. 2 out of 4 marks (1 mark for the generic answer and 1 mark for naming an alternative method)

d. One issue of validity could be if the students have lied about how happy they are in the questionnaire. They may feel embarrassed to admit they are very unhappy and choose happy to avoid this. This would affect the accuracy of the data collected. One way to deal with this is if the psychologist explained to the students that their answers would be anonymous and kept confidential. This may make the students more truthful.
Bob has contextualised his answer and covered both elements, e.g. described an issue and explained how to deal with this specific issue. 4 out of 4 marks. There are several other possible creditworthy issues including students not understanding the scale, sampling issues, etc.

e. The mean is 2.5.
Bob has calculated the mean correctly but has failed to show his calculations. 1 out of 2 marks.

f. One advantage of the mean is that it is the most scientific of all measures of central tendency because it uses all scores in its calculations, e.g. everyone's happiness scores were taken into account when calculating the mean. A disadvantage would be that the mean is easily distorted by extreme scores, e.g. if one student had given a 0 score and then a 4, this would have brought the mean down in condition 1 and falsely inflated it in condition 2.
Both the advantage and disadvantage are well explained and have been contextualised, though this is not required in this question. This is nevertheless a good way to gain detail and therefore marks. 4 out of 4 marks.

Bob's answer continued

g. PPC does not make students happier.

Bob has produced a directional alternative hypothesis – he has stated the direction. However, he has not identified both conditions of the IV – before PPC and after PPC. He should have said 'Participants are happier after one year of having the PPC *than they were beforehand'*. The hypothesis also lacks operationalisation (mentioning one year), so 0 marks.

h. One ethical issue is valid consent. The sample of students used are below the age of 16 and therefore may not understand the implications of participating in this type of study and therefore cannot make the decision to consent to do so.

Bob has not addressed both elements of the question. He has identified and explained an ethical issue in a contextualised way but has failed to explain how he would deal with it. There are several possible creditworthy issues including a lack of confidentiality and a lack of protection from risk of harm. 2 out of 4 marks.

i. The data is quantitative because he has collected numerical data in the form of a happiness rating scale.

This answer is inaccurate so 0 out of 2 marks. Bob needs to describe the type of quantitative data collected, e.g. ordinal, and then explain in the context of the study why it is ordinal.

j. The psychologist could have used a semi-structured interview. She could have set up an interview time for each of the 10 students and asked them all the same basic questions such as: How happy do you feel generally? What sorts of things make you feel happy? and so on. She could then also ask further more individualised questions based on what the students say. I think this is a better method as you would get a greater understanding of how happy they are normally rather than on just the day they answered the questionnaire – for all we know the person who gave the rating of 1 might have had a massive argument with their friend that day and if they had been asked on a different day may have said 4! Using the interview would mean you get a proper understanding and not just a snap shot as in an interview you can really question people's experiences and ask them to elaborate and expand.

Bob has clearly identified an appropriate method and contextualised his response. His justification is good and linked to the research, though he has focused more on an issue with the original question (asking how you feel *at present*) instead of the real advantage of an interview, which is being able to discuss other issues related to the central question. 3 out of 4 marks.

k. This test was used because the researchers were looking for a difference and because data was ordinal.

This answer is not clear, nor is it contextualised. Bob needs to explain why it is a test of difference and why data is ordinal in this study by making reference to the happiness scale. Alternatively Bob could have made reference to the fact that it is a repeated measures design. 1 out of 2 marks.

TRY THIS

Have a go at being the examiner

Bob's answer has been marked and the examiner comments are given.

Have a go at marking Megan's answers and write examiner comments using the knowledge you have gained from Bob.

Megan's answer

a. The IV is the happiness score.

b. The DV is operationalised as them having PPC 1 hour a week or not.

c. Random sampling often results in you getting an unrepresentative sample if the sample size is quite small relative to the target population; in this study only 10 students were chosen from the whole year group and could be all girls and the same ability in school. They could use quota sampling where they take the first willing boy and a girl from each ability level.

d. One issue of validity could be researcher bias because the psychologist may hint to the students to give a low score before the PPC and a higher score after because she wanted the headteacher to think her PPC was brilliant. One way to solve this would be to get someone neutral who doesn't know the aim of the study to conduct both questionnaires.

e. $1 + 4 + 3 + 3 + 2 + 2 + 3 + 4 + 1 + 2 = 25$ $25 \div 10 = 2.5$
The mean is 2.5.

f. The mean is good because it is most commonly used, but a disadvantage of the mean is that it is easily influenced by extreme scores. If there are any really high or really low scores this can give you an unrepresentative mean.

g. Happiness scores are higher when students have completed PPC for one year compared to their score one year previously.

h. An ethical issue in this study is a lack of confidentiality. Students are telling the psychologist secret information about their feelings and may be really worried and upset if other people in the school found out. To deal with this the psychologist must not use the students' names and give them all a number. She should also keep their data locked in a secure place away from the school. This will ensure the happiness scores remain confidential.

i. The level of measurement used is ordinal because the data collected is from a happiness rating scale where participants had to select a number from 0–4 to indicate how happy they are.

j. I would have used an observation so I could see first hand how happy the students are. If you did this without them knowing you would get more realistic data than the rating scale because you wouldn't worry about social desirability bias.

k. This test was used because the data collected is ordinal, e.g. the students used a rating scale to assess their happiness. The study is also using a repeated measures design because the same students completed the questionnaire before the PPC and after it.

See page 176 for comments on Megan's answers.

Activity answers

Chapter 1 (page 24)

Assumptions, true or false?: F, T, T, F, F, T, T, T, T

Classic evidence, true or false?: F, T, F, F, T, T, F

What's active? 1. occipital and parietal lobes, 2. temporal lobes, 3. frontal lobes, 4. occipital lobes, 5. temporal lobes

Chapter 2 (page 44)

Fill in the blanks: psychosexual stages, order, oral, anal, phallic, latency, genital, libido, fixations, over-indulgence, under-indulgence, personality, orally fixated, pessimistic, sarcastic, envious, anally fixated, stubborn, possessive, tidy

The id, ego, superego: id, superego, ego, id, superego, ego, ego

Ego defences: displacement, regression, projection, repression

Crossword, across: 4. control, 8. prolonged separation, 9. six, 10. Rutter; down: 1. confidentiality, 2. affectionless, 3. Binet Scale, 5. fourteen, 6. qualitative (although the numbers of children in each group were counted which is quantitative) is correct, 9. forty-four

Chapter 3 (pages 64 and 65)

Sally: Classical conditioning – Sally associates her dogs with positive feelings such as companionship. Sally associates dogs as being better company than people. Operant conditioning – Sally is rewarded with feelings of happiness and being needed (positive reinforcement). Sally may walk her dogs to avoid a miserable home life (negative reinforcement). Sally avoids feeling lonely by spending time with dogs (negative reinforcement).

Relationship formation: classical, operant, repeat, reinforcement, rewarding, positive, reinforced, conditioning, associate, positive mood, association, loving

Methodology and findings: 1D, 2F, 3B, 4A, 5K, 6I, 7C, 8E, 9G, 10H, 11J

Match up: 1C, 2F, 3A, 4B, 5D, 6E

Chapter 4 (page 84)

Classic evidence, true or false?: T, F, T, F, T, T, T, T, F, T, T

Chapter 5 (page 104)

Assumptions, true or false?: F, T, T, F, T, F, F

Chapter 6 (pages 166 and 167)

Experimental designs: 1. repeated measures, advantage; 2. independent groups, disadvantage; 3. independent groups, advantage; 4. matched pairs, advantage; 5. repeated measures, advantage; 6. independent groups, disadvantage; 7. matched pairs, disadvantage; 8. repeated measures, disadvantage; 9. independent groups, advantage; 10. matched pairs, advantage; 11. matched pairs, disadvantage; 12. repeated measures, disadvantage

Make it better… 1. The psychologist should not have selected a 'local' street; he could have picked a random street in the UK to avoid biases. The Happiness scale may not really be measuring happiness – it might just be measuring their mood on that day, which may be affected by factors other than the weather. Perhaps ask residents to keep a mood diary over a month and then relate their scores to the weather reports for that month. People may be happier in April, not because of the weather but because they are being tested on a Saturday. The researcher should try to use the same day of the week in both April and November.

2. Behavioural complaints recorded by teachers may not be a good indicator of 'naughtiness'. The teachers may only record the most serious infractions rather than ALL naughtiness. Some teachers may not like recording behavioural complaints using the school's administration software. The headteacher would need to ensure that all staff are standardised in how to record behavioural complaints. There may be more 'naughtiness' at the end of term not because of the students wearing their own clothes, but because it is the end of term. The headteacher should hold an 'own-clothes' day during the middle of the term as well to check the findings are similar to the own-clothes day held at the end of term.

3. The car salesman is only considering the colour of the car; it may be that he sold more red cars because of the brand of car they were or that the red cars were priced more competitively. He should really try to match (on price, spec and mileage) the red cars with a car of 'other colour' and then see whether he sells more cars. Before the salesman started selling cars on that Saturday, he already thought that red cars sell more easily. This means his expectations may have affected his selling performance; he may have directed clients to the red cars more or offered better discounts if the clients showed an interest in a red car. He should really have another salesman, who is unaware of the 'red car' hypothesis, to sell cars on another Saturday and compare the sales results.

Which inferential test should you use? 1. Chi-squared test, 2. Mann–Whitney U test, 3. Wilcoxon Matched Pairs Signed Ranks Test, 4. Spearman's Rank Order Correlation Test

Examiner comments

Chapter 1

Question on explaining behaviours (page 26)
Bob's answer is well detailed in that he has considered several biological assumptions thoroughly and has applied them accurately to romantic relationships. Bob has focused on one relationship type in depth. **5 out of 5 marks**.

Megan's answer demonstrates a classic mistake that is commonly made – she has spent her time simply describing the assumptions of the biological approach with very little application to relationships. As a result her explanations are limited and superficial with unclear links to relationships. **2 out of 5 marks**.

Question on assumptions and therapies (page 26)
Bob has approached this question well. He has given a clear and well-detailed explanation of why the biological approach uses drug therapy. Bob has clearly linked one assumption to the underlying principles of drug therapy accurately. For full marks he should have discussed a second assumption and/or increased the use of biological terminology when describing the aim of drug therapy. **4 out of 6 marks**.

Megan has made a common mistake and focused more on describing the assumptions of the biological approach rather than focusing on how the assumptions link to the therapy. As a result Megan is unable to access the top mark band. However, she has covered two assumptions and therefore doesn't come far behind Bob. **3 out of 6 marks**.

Question on classic evidence (page 27)
Bob's answer is appropriate; however, his evaluative commentary is quite generic as he has discussed research methodology generally rather than applying it effectively to the key study. In some cases whole paragraphs could be used for another piece of classic evidence without changing anything and this is what makes it generic. Bob has considered a range of issues, e.g. causality, ethical issues, sampling, etc., and some is contextualised and not generic; it is therefore thorough, but he does not have the depth or application to the classic study to access the top mark bands. **10 out of 16 marks**.

Megan's answer is sophisticated and highly effective in that she has developed most of her evaluation points well, providing balanced arguments and at times taking it further by considering the implications, e.g. social sensitivity – these are all features of a sophisticated argument. Terminology is used to good effect and she has covered a range of issues and in most cases in appropriate depth. In order to achieve full marks Megan could further develop some evaluation points, e.g. sampling issues or alternative evidence. **15 out of 16 marks**.

Chapter 2

Question on classic evidence (page 46)
Bob's answer is both basic and limited. He has provided only superficial details regarding the psychological assessments used. Bob has wasted valuable time discussing the methodology and sample, as well as the impact the study has had – none of which is creditworthy. In order to move up the mark bands Bob would need to provide more precise details. **2 out of 6 marks**.

Megan's answer is more focused on procedures than Bob's. She has given some information about the sample but most of her second paragraph is about what Bowlby did. The answer is reasonably detailed, so **5 out of 6 marks**.

Question on evaluating approaches (page 47)
Bob has really embraced this question and considered the similarities and differences between the psychodynamic and behaviourist approach and contextualised them in therapy. His use of comparative terms, e.g. in contrast, similarly, both, whereas, etc., has meant he is able to demonstrate thorough analysis and has applied his knowledge of each approach and its therapies to this question (AO2 skill). Bob has covered a range of issues, e.g. effectiveness, appropriateness, ethics, research methodology, determinism and long-term effects, and has done so in depth. Bob has drawn a meaningful although basic conclusion. It is really more of a summary than a conclusion. A focused conclusion is important so **14 out of 16 marks**.

Megan has started this answer generally stating AO3 points, e.g. scientific/unscientific for the behaviourist and psychodynamic approaches respectively, with very little attempt to actually compare and contrast the two approaches. Megan must remember that this is an AO2 question and requires her to apply her knowledge by comparing and contrasting rather than simply making evaluative (AO3) comments. Furthermore, initially Megan has failed to contextualise the answer in therapy, preferring to consider the approaches generally until paragraph three. Megan has considered a range of issues but her analysis is quite basic. She has attempted to draw a conclusion at the end but this is not really based on any of the arguments presented. In order to build on this mark Megan would really need to focus on her AO2 skill and demonstrate that she is explicitly comparing and contrasting the similarities and differences rather than simply 'listing' them. In addition to this an informed and meaningful conclusion is required. **8 out of 16 marks**.

Chapter 3

Question on assumptions (page 66)
Bob's response certainly belongs in the top band with both assumptions being well detailed and clearly linked to human behaviour. Bob's use of terminology is good and research has been used to good effect. In order to further build on this Bob could attempt to write the three steps of classical conditioning more concisely and perhaps add some additional detail to the punishment element of operant conditioning. **4 + 3 out of 8 marks**.

Megan's answer is fairly typical of a mid band answer. Both assumptions are accurate but lack the necessary detail and the appropriate terminology illustrated by Megan. Martha could certainly enhance this by adding more detail to the nurture (empiricist) element of assumption 1 as well as adding in the terminology associated with the stages of classical conditioning / operant conditioning. **2 + 2 out of 8 marks**.

Question on a therapy (page 67)
Megan's answer is, on the whole, an effective and reasonably detailed answer; however, Megan has wasted significant time describing SD in paragraph one which receives no credit. Paragraph two is very well structured and coherent, and uses research to good effect in order to evaluate the effectiveness of SD. There are clear conclusions drawn throughout the answer and this is excellent practice. There is also clear evidence of range, e.g. treatment success, use and symptom substitution, but lacks some depth in parts. In order to build on this Megan needs to utilise the time she spent on paragraph one and use it to add additional detail to paragraphs three and four. **9 out of 12 marks**.

Bob's answer is effective and reasonably detailed, but Bob has wasted significant time describing AT in paragraph one which receives no credit. Paragraph two is well structured, coherent and uses research to good effect in order to evaluate the effectiveness of AT. There are clear conclusions drawn throughout the answer and this is excellent practice. Although there is evidence of a range of issues covered, e.g. success rates, drop out and symptom substitution, the latter points do lack some depth and detail. In order to build on this Bob needs to utilise the time he spent on paragraph one and use it to add additional detail to paragraphs three and four. Candidates are not penalised for uncreditworthy material but Bob could have used his time more valuably. **8 out of 12 marks**.

Chapter 4

Question on classic evidence (page 86)

Bob's answer is really well structured; it is in line with the mark scheme and provides appropriate coverage of the findings of both experiments. The use of a summary table is appropriate for the facts of this study and for this style of question. Unfortunately, there is one major inaccuracy – the verb 'bashed' was not in the study, as well as some minor inaccuracies such as some speed estimates being the wrong way round. As a result Bob cannot access the top mark band. To build on this and achieve full marks, Bob needs to make sure that all verbs/estimates are accurate. He did not need to include a conclusion at the end. **4 out of 6 marks**.

Megan has approached this question using a traditional essay format; although this is obviously acceptable; she might have used her time more effectively if she had drawn a table of results. There is some irrelevant information that receives no credit, e.g. the details of procedural elements. There are a few major inaccuracies, e.g. the findings of experiment two, as well as some minor inaccuracies in the speed estimates stated. Although findings have been covered, this has been done in a less detailed way than Bob, and indeed many of the speed estimates are quite vague. No credit is awarded for experiment two because the data are wrong – therefore Megan is only able to access a maximum mark of 3. In order to build on this Megan needs to include the exact speed estimate rather than rounding it off and make sure that there are some accurate findings stated for experiment two. **2 out of 6 marks**.

Question on the debate (page 87)

Bob's answer for you to mark

Eyewitness testimony has been found to be one of the strongest and most convincing types of evidence in a court of law. In this essay I plan to examine whether EWT can be trusted or whether it can be proven to be unreliable.

Leading questions or post event information can affect our recall. Backing this, Loftus and Zanni (1975) showed participants a car accident film. One group was asked 'Did you see a broken headlight?' and 7% reported seeing one. Another group was asked 'Did you see the broken headlight?' and 17% recalled it. This suggests that leading questions cause a person to remember something that wasn't there, which has major implications in how eyewitnesses are questioned by police, friends and in court. However, we must remember that 83% of participants did accurately recall the event, which shows that 'most' EWT is in fact accurate and that only some people are susceptible to post event information. Loftus (1979a) reinforces this viewpoint; where participants were shown a chain of pictures of a man pilfering a red wallet from a woman's bag, 98% remembered that it was red. Then leading questions were used to alter their recall but they continued to say it was red. Therefore, this disproves that leading questions affect memory and suggests we should trust EWT.

As a result of this type of research cognitive interviews have been developed which are based on research like this and have been adopted by the police. This interviewing technique has been scientifically proven to reduce the impact leading questions can have and results in higher levels of accuracy in EWT; this would suggest that if used we should trust the reliability of EWT.

Schemas can affect memory, as information that is already stored may distort our memory of an event. Schemas 'fill in the gaps' in our memories when they're incomplete, thus memories become distorted and eyewitness recall may be inaccurate, e.g. if you think of a bank robber you may automatically assume they are male, have a weapon and be wearing a mask but this may not be the case in reality. Yarmey (1993) asked 240 students to look at videos of 30 unknown males and classify them as 'good guys' or 'bad guys'. There was high agreement amongst the participants, suggesting that there is similarity in the information stored in the 'bad guy' and 'good guy' schemas. This suggests eyewitnesses may not select the actual criminal, but the individual who looks most like the schema of the criminal. This study lacks ecological validity, being done in an artificial environment, so it lacks the emotion people would feel while in a real crime, which questions its generalisability. This research also has important implications for the criminal, as it clearly shows that they may be incorrectly identified due to schemas. This sort of error was seen in the case of Ronald Cotton and Jennifer Thompson.

Eyewitnesses may not be reliable because the crimes they witness are unexpected and emotionally traumatising. Freud argued that extremely painful or threatening memories are forced into the unconscious mind. This process,

repression, is an ego-defence mechanism. Nowadays, psychologists might call this 'motivated forgetting', but in either form perhaps eyewitnesses are not reliable because the memory of the crime is too traumatising. However, the concept of repression is difficult to falsify, thus making scientific research nearly impossible. Indeed, other researchers suggest emotion will enhance memory and make it more reliable, e.g. flashbulb memories. This clearly shows how complicated the role of emotion is.

Research conducted by psychologists although valuable is often done in the lab where the participants act in such a way to please the researcher, and there's no consequence so the participants may not put much effort into remembering details compared with victims of a real crime. By contrast, researching the accuracy of EWT in real cases there's no way of knowing if the recollection was true or not as the researchers weren't actually there at the time. Also, as every crime is different, it's hard to draw valid conclusions as there isn't really much to compare with.

It is clear to see that reconstructive memory certainly poses a threat to the accuracy of EWT; however, the impact that emotion has, as well as leading questions, is less certain with some research suggesting these factors reduce accuracy, whilst other research suggests not. There is one message that is clear; the majority of eyewitnesses are able to recall details of real crimes quite accurately and other than the perpetrator are often the only people present to tell us what really happens. To this end they should be allowed to give their evidence to a jury but this must be considered with caution. *785 words*

Examiner's comments

Megan's essay begins with an interesting use of a case study, which doesn't add much to AO1 or AO3 but it does set the scene. Megan can be commended on her excellent descriptions of research in paragraph two (AO1) but she has failed to consider any evaluation (AO3) in terms of the research or that perhaps there may be contradictory evidence. The third paragraph is quite vague and less detailed, adding very little to either her AO1 or AO3 mark. The fourth and fifth paragraphs are purely AO1 and her description of repression/reconstructive memory is appropriate and detailed. Megan has drawn a meaningful, if unbalanced, conclusion. There is range and depth in this answer in terms of AO1 and the consideration of a number of well-chosen issues, e.g. leading questions, reconstructive memory, emotion, etc., and each is supported by appropriate research. However, the paragraph on children is less detailed and could certainly be improved; as a result Megan is unable to access the top band. Terminology is used to good effect (AO1). However, for AO3 Megan has failed to engage with the debate, considering only one side of it and presented a very unbalanced argument. Furthermore, she has not really considered the value of the research presented in terms of strengths and weaknesses either. Megan has however drawn a conclusion based on the evidence presented. **AO1 mark: 9 out of 10, AO3 mark: 4 out of 10, total: 13 marks out of 20**.

Bob's answer is well structured with evidence used effectively to discuss whether or not EWT is reliable. In the first paragraph Bob offers a brief introduction which sets out his clear intention to examine both sides of the debate – although it doesn't add much to either AO1 or AO3, it certainly sets the scene. In the second and third paragraphs Bob has provided a detailed analysis of the role of leading questions and used research which is described accurately (AO1) to show that leading questions may/may not affect EWT (AO3). Bob has drawn meaningful conclusions after each study – this is good practice. Furthermore, Bob has taken it a step further by discussing the consequences and positive implications of the research, e.g. the cognitive interview, which further adds to his AO3 mark. Bob has evaluated research throughout and this is a feature of top band answers. In paragraphs four and five Bob has used both research and theory effectively to convey both sides of the debate. Bob's overall conclusions are both evaluative and informed. There is range and depth in this answer and the consideration of a number of well-chosen issues, e.g. leading questions, reconstructive memory, emotion, etc., and each is supported by appropriate research. Terminology is used to good effect (AO1). Bob has demonstrated a sophisticated analysis with balanced arguments and evaluative commentary throughout (AO3), given the time available. **AO1 mark: 10 out of 10, AO3 mark: 10 out of 10, total: 20 marks out of 20**.

Chapter 5

Question on therapies (page 106)

Bob's answer reflects a good understanding of mindfulness but he has made an important mistake by not naming the principle discussed. As a result Bob is unable to access the top mark band and his answer falls in the 'principle is not named' but the description is 'accurate and detailed'. Naming the principle, e.g. gaining control of thoughts, would mean Bob would get full marks, but as it is he gets **3 out of 4 marks**.

Megan's answer begins promisingly, in that she has named the principle she is going to describe – this is good practice. However, her description of the CASIO factors is superficial because it lacks use of terminology. To access the top mark band she would need to explain what CASIO stands for. Furthermore, Megan's powers of expression and grammar could be improved. **1 out of 4 marks**.

Question on evaluating the approach (page 107)

Bob has provided an answer that engages with the quote and has some range and some depth. He has stated two key strengths and used the quote to help highlight the strengths of the positive approach relative to the other approaches studied. Both strengths are reasonably well detailed with a clear focus as to why they are strengths. In order to achieve full marks Bob could have brought in some research to illustrate the strengths stated as well as providing greater detail in the two evaluation points he has made. To increase range and depth, Bob could include an additional evaluation point. This answer lacked some of the key criteria for the top band. **7 out of 8 marks**.

Megan has covered three strengths in detail so has depth and range; however, she has not really engaged with the question as there is very little explicit reference to the quote provided. In order to build on her current mark Megan would need to make reference to the quote in a more explicit way. **4 out of 8 marks**.

Question on the debate (page 107)
Megan's answer for you to mark

The positive approach has proven to be very popular and as it is the most modern of all approaches it is commonly thought that it is the most relevant and applicable to society today. However, others argue that it has its roots firmly based in humanistic psychology and therefore is not a new approach at all.

The principles developed by the positive approach have been applied in education. Seligman says that putting positive psychology into the curriculum can increase students' happiness, self-worth and results in better behaviour. Gilman did a similar study and showed the benefits of having a positive curriculum are still there two years later. However, this research is correlational so we cannot say the positive psychology caused the positive outcomes.

Positive psychology has also been adopted in the workplace. A researcher has found that work can be one of our biggest sources of happiness. In order to further enhance and promote happiness employers now try to increase the fun factor in work and provide challenges and goals which increase self-esteem. From an economic point of view this can only be beneficial; a happy workforce is a productive workforce. The Gallup and Healthways Well Being Index shows that those countries in the top positions, e.g. Denmark, have high rates of literacy, growing economies, close family links and low migration rates. This therefore proves that any initiatives that develop and encourage well-being and happiness in work can have a cascading effect for all aspects of life.

It is clear to see that positive psychology can enhance the lives of everyone; however, we need to remain cautious because research is not exactly conclusive. Spence and Shortt (2007) questions the long-term effects of using a positive curriculum in education and suggests that all schools should not automatically put it into their curriculum until further, more long-term research has been carried out. Indeed, educationalists would have to decide what subjects they would have to remove from the curriculum if positive psychology was introduced and decisions would have to be made, e.g. is it better to remove geography and keep positive psychology? This is an extremely difficult decision.

In terms of work, even this is questionable as Diener found only a weak correlation of 0.12 between income and happiness, which plays down the importance that positive principles in the workplace can have.

All in all it is fair to say that positive psychology can be used to enhance the lives of everyone but we must be cautious in this assumption. After all, many of the concepts promoted by the positive approach, e.g. happiness, esteem and well-being, are subjective concepts that are really difficult to measure. We must remember that the positive approach is relatively new and further research is needed to uncover any long-term benefits it may have, and only then will we have an accurate picture of the positive impact this approach can have in today's society.

486 words

Examiner's comments

This question assesses AO1 skill (the ability to describe how positive psychology has been applied to benefit society) and AO3 (the ability to evaluate the applications and make judgements regarding how beneficial they are or not).

Bob has provided very detailed descriptions of how the positive approach has been applied to society, e.g. through education, the military and leisure time, and as a result he has depth and range and achieves an impressive **AO1 mark of 10 out of 10 marks**. However, Bob has very basic evaluative commentary as he has not really weighed up the strengths and weaknesses of the research, nor has he questioned whether the positive approach has been useful or not. Indeed, the only material that could be considered AO3 is his use of research, e.g. Seligman and Csikszentmihalyi, which shows that positive psychology could be effective – however, this is not stated explicitly. His conclusion is simply a summary of what he has written and is limited. As a result Bob achieves an **AO3 mark of 1 out of 10 marks, total 11 marks out of 20**. In order to achieve top mark bands candidates need to spend equal time on both AO1 and AO3 skills; this has clearly been an issue for Bob.

Megan's response begins philosophically where she makes the suggestion that to some people positive psychology is 'the' approach to understand today's society in line with the exam question. She also considers that the approach has not got the same appeal for everyone. Although a nice and interesting introductory statement, it does not really contribute to the AO1/AO3 mark given. Megan has considered a range of applications (e.g. education and employment), but not all applications are in the depth required for full marks, e.g. she has discussed positive psychology in education, but has not explained exactly how the principles have been used in PPC. She has really engaged with the question and presented a sophisticated and articulate analysis regarding the benefits the positive approach has in society. Her arguments are more balanced than Bob's as she has considered the idea that it may not have benefited society as well. This further contributes to the development of a sophisticated and articulate analysis of the debate. She has considered the value of supporting/contradictory evidence and been evaluative in her approach. She has reached an appropriate conclusion that is well informed but could be more detailed. **AO1 mark: 8 out of 10 marks, AO3 mark: 8 out of 10 marks, total: 16 out of 20 marks**.

Chapter 6

Short answer questions (page 168)
Megan's answers:
1. Lacks the required detail for full marks. **1 out of 2 marks**. A useful rule of thumb is if the question is allocated 2 marks you will need to write 2 points.
2. Accurate and very detailed. **2 out of 2 marks**.
3. Accurate and just enough detail. **2 out of 2 marks**.
4. **a.** incorrect; **b and c.** correct. **2 out of 3 marks**.
5. Nothing has been explained. **0 out of 2 marks**.

Question with a novel situation (page 169)
Megan's answers:
a. Megan has addressed both elements – the issue and how to solve it. It is in sufficient detail and contextualised, so therefore Megan receives **4 out of 4 marks**.
b. Megan's answer is very vague with no actual explanation of what a correlation co-efficient means. In order to achieve credit, Megan would need to make reference to the number range (−1 to +1), the sign (− or +) or that it is the value calculated from an inferential test. **0 out of 2 marks**.

c. Megan has clearly misunderstood what the question required, defining a directional alternative hypothesis rather than explaining why it is appropriate in this study. **0 out of 2 marks**.

d. Megan has incorrectly identified the level of measurement. **0 out of 3 marks**.

e. Inappropriate. **0 out of 3 marks**.

f. Correct identification of inferential test and fully justified. **3 out of 3 marks**.

Question with a novel situation (page 171)
Megan's answers:

a. Inaccurate; Megan has mixed up the IV and DV. **0 out of 2 marks**.

b. Inaccurate and muddled. **0 out of 2 marks**.

c. The disadvantage is accurate and sufficiently detailed. The alternative sampling method is appropriate and explained. Both elements of the question are contextualised. **4 out of 4 marks**.

d. The issue of validity is thoroughly explained and contextualised extremely well. The way of dealing with this issue is less detailed and there is not sufficient contextualisation. **3 out of 4 marks**.

e. Correct mean and calculations. **2 out of 2 marks**.

f. The advantage stated for the mean is not accurate; the disadvantage is thorough. There is no need to contextualise in this question. **2 out of 4 marks**.

g. Megan has identified the IV and DV as well as stating that the IV will have no effect on the DV, so has done enough for **2 out of 2 marks**.

h. Explanation of the issue is detailed and thorough and the way of dealing with this issue is appropriate. Both elements of the question are contextualised. **4 out of 4 marks**.

i. Megan has correctly identified the level of measurement as ordinal and has explained why within the context of the study. **2 out of 2 marks**.

j. Megan has identified an appropriate method, e.g. observation, but her explanation of how this could be carried out is limited and lacking in detail. There is no information about how she would actually observe happiness. She has justified her use of the alternative and this is contextualised. **3 out of 4 marks**.

k. Megan has made clear reference to ordinal data and the repeated measures design and has explained why they occur in this study. **2 out of 2 marks**.

References

Aghayousefi, A. and Yasin Seifi, M. (2013) Group quality of life therapy in patients with multiple sclerosis. *Practice in Clinical Psychology, 1(2)*, 10–14.

Alloy, L.B. and Abrahamson, L.Y. (1979) Judgment of contingency in depressed and non-depressed students: Sadder but wiser? *Journal of Experimental Psychology, 108*, 441–485.

Anastasi, J.S. and Rhodes, M.G. (2006) An own-age bias in face recognition for children and older adults. *Psychonomic Bulletin and Review, 12*, 1043–2047.

Anderson, S., Avery, D., DiPietro, E., Edwards, G. and Christian, W. (1987) Intensive home-based early intervention with autistic children. *Educational Treatment of Children, 10*, 352–366.

Argyle, M. (1986) *The psychology of happiness*. London: Methuen.

Asch, S.E. (1956) Studies of independence and conformity: I. A minority of one against a unanimous majority. *Psychological Monographs: General and Applied, 70(9)*, 1–70.

Astin, A.W., Green, K.C. and Korn, W.S. (1987) *The American freshman: Twenty year trends*. Los Angeles: University of California at Los Angeles Graduate School of Education, Higher Education Research Institute.

Atkinson, R.C. and Shiffrin, R.M. (1968) Human memory: A proposed system and its control processes. In K.W. Spence and J.T. Spence (eds) *The Psychology of Learning and Motivation*, vol. 2. London: Academic Press.

Azar, B. (2011) Positive psychology advances, with growing pains, American Psychology Association website, *www.apa.org/monitor/2011/04/positive-psychology.aspx*.

Badawy, A.A. (1999) Tryptophan metabolism in alcoholism. *Advances in Experimental Medicine and Biology, 467*, 265–274.

Baddeley, A.D. and Longman, D.J.A. (1978) The influence of length and frequency on training sessions on the rate of learning type. *Ergonomics, 21*, 627–635.

Bancroft, J. (1992) *Deviant Sexual Behavior*. Oxford: Oxford University Press.

Baumrind, D. (1964) Some thoughts on ethics of research: After reading Milgram's 'Behavioral study of obedience'. *American Psychologist, 19*, 421–423.

BBC (2009) Gay injustice 'was widespread'. Available online at *http://news.bbc.co.uk/1/hi/uk/8251033.stm* (accessed January 2015).

Berkowitz, L. (1970) The contagion of violence: An S-R mediational analysis of some effects of observed aggression. *Nebraska Symposium on Motivation, 18*, 95–135.

Blackmore, C., Beercroft, C., Parry, G., Booth, A., Chambers, E., Saxon, D. and Tantam, D. (2009) *A Systematic Review of the Efficacy and Clinical Effectiveness of Group Analysis and Analytic/Dynamic Group Psychotherapy*. Centre for Psychological Services Research, School of Health and Related Research, University of Sheffield, UK.

Boorman, S. (2009) NHS Health and Well-being Review: Final Report, November 2009. London: Department of Health, Central Office of Information (COI).

Bowlby, J. (1944) Forty-four juvenile thieves: Their characters and home-life. *International Journal of Psychoanalysis, 25(19–52)*, 107–127.

Bowlby, J. (1953) *Child Care and the Growth of Love*. Harmondsworth: Penguin.

Bowlby, J. (1969) *Attachment and Love. Vol. 1: Attachment*. London: Hogarth.

Bowlby, J., Ainsworth, M., Boston, M. and Rosenbluth, D. (1956) The effects of mother–child separation: A follow-up study. *British Journal of Medical Psychology, 29*, 211.

BPS (2009) *Code of Ethics and Conduct*. Available online at *www.bps.org.uk/system/files/documents/code_of_ethics_and_conduct.pdf* (accessed January 2015).

Braun, K.A., Ellis, R. and Loftus, E.F. (2002) Make my memory: How advertising can change our memories of the past. *Psychology and Marketing, 19(1)*, 1–23.

Bregman, E.O. (1934) An attempt to modify the emotional attitudes of infants by the conditioned response technique. *Journal of Genetic Psychology, 45*, 169–198.

Bricker, J.B., Peterson, A.V. Jr., Sarason, I.G., Andersen, M.R. and Rajan, K.B. (2006) Changes in the influence of parents' and close friends' smoking on adolescent smoking transitions. *Addiction, 101(1)*, 128–136.

Bridges, P.K., Bartlett, J.R., Hale, A.S., Poynton, A.M., Malizia, A.L. and Hodgkiss, A.D. (1994) Psychosurgery: Stereotactic subcaudate tractomy. An indispensable treatment. *British Journal of Psychiatry, 165(5)*, 612–613.

Brosnan, M. (2008) Digit ratio as an indicator of numeracy relative to literacy in 7-year- old British school children. *British Journal of Psychology, 99*, 75–85.

Buckout, R. (1980) Nearly 2,000 witnesses can be wrong. *Bulletin of the Psychonomic Society, 16*, 307–310.

Buri, J.R. (1991) Parental authority questionnaire. *Journal of Personality Assessment, 57(1)*, 110–119.

Burlingame, G.M., Fuhriman, A., Mosier, J. (2003) The differential effectiveness of group psychoanalysis: A meta-analytic perspective. *Group Dynamics: Theory Research and Practice, 17(1)*, 3–12.

Burt, R.S. (1986) *Strangers, Friends and Happiness* (GSS Technical Report No. 72). Chicago: University of Chicago, National Opinion Research Center.

Burton, R.V. (1976) Honesty and dishonesty. In T. Lickona (ed.) *Moral Development and Behaviour*. New York: Holt, Rinehart and Winston.

Buzan, T. (1993) *The Mind Map Book*. London: BBC.

Cahill, L. and McGaugh, J.L. (1995) A novel demonstration of enhanced memory associated with emotional arousal. *Consciousness and Cognition, 4*, 410–421.

Capafóns, J.I., Sosa, C.D. and Avero, P. (1998) Systematic desensitisation in the treatment of fear of flying. *Psychology in Spain, 2(1)*, 11–16.

Carmichael, L.C., Hogan, H.P. and Walters, A.A. (1932) An experimental study of the effect of language on the reproduction of visually perceived form. *Journal of Experimental Psychology, 15*, 73–86.

Chaney, G., Clements, B., Landau, L., Bulsara, M. and Watt, P. (2004) A new asthma spacer device to improve compliance in children: A pilot study. *Respirology, 9(4)*, 499–506.

Charlton, T., Gunter, B. and Hannan, A. (eds) (2000) *Broadcast Television Effects in a Remote Community*. Hillsdale, NJ: Lawrence Erlbaum.

Cherek, D.R., Lane, S.D., Pietras, C.J. and Steinberg, J.L. (2002) Effects of chronic paroxetine administration on measures of aggressive and impulsive responses of adult males with a history of conduct disorder. *Psychopharmacology, 159(3)*, 266–274.

Christopher, J.C. and Hickinbottom, S. (2008) Positive psychology, ethnocentrism and the ideology of individualism. *Theory and Psychology, 18(5)*, 563–589.

Cohen Kadosh, R., Levy, N., O'Shea, N. and Salvulescu, J. (2012) The neuroethics of non-invasive brain stimulation. *Current Biology, 22*, 108–111.

Colby, A., Kohlberg, L., Gibbs, J. and Lieberman, M. (1983) A longitudinal study of moral judgement. *Monographs of the Society for Research in Child Development, 48(1–2)*, Serial No. 200.

Comer, R.J. (2002) *Fundamentals of Abnormal Psychology*, 3rd edn. New York: Worth.

Coolican, H. (1996) *Introduction to Research Methods and Statistics in Psychology*. London: Hodder and Stoughton.

Coolican, H. (2004) Personal communication.

Cosgrove, G.R. and Rauch, S.L. (2001) Psychosurgery. Available online at *http://neurosurgery.mgh.harvard.edu/functional/Psychosurgery2001.htm* (accessed May 2015).

Costa, P.T., Jr., McCrae, R.R. and Zonderman, A.B. (1987) Environmental and dispositional influences on well-being: Longitudinal follow-up of an American national sample. *British Journal of Psychology, 78*, 299–306.

Crick, F. and Koch, C. (1998) Consciousness and neuroscience. *Cerebral Cortex, 8*, 97–107.

Csikszentmihalyi, M. and LeFevre, J. (1989) Optimal experience in work and leisure. *Journal of Personality and Social Psychology, 56*, 815–822.

Cumberbatch, G. and Gauntlett, S. (2005) Smoking, alcohol and drugs on television. A content analysis. Ofcom. Available online at *http://stakeholders.ofcom.org.uk/binaries/research/radio-research/smoking.pdf* (accessed June 2015).

Darley, J.M. and Latané, B. (1968) Bystander intervention in emergencies: Diffusion of responsibility. *Journal of Personality and Social Psychology, 8*, 377–383.

Davies, G., Tarrant, A. and Flin, R. (1989) Close encounters of the witness kind: Children's memory for a simulated health inspection. *British Journal of Psychology, 80(4)*, 415–429.

Dement, W.C. and Kleitman, N. (1957) The relation of eye movements during sleep to dream activity: An objective method for the study of dreaming. *Journal of Experimental Psychology, 53*, 339–346.

Devlin, Lord P. (1976) *Report to the Secretary of State for the Home Department on the Departmental Committee on Evidence of Identification in Criminal Cases*. London: HMSO.

Di Nardo, P.A., Guzy, L.T. and Bak, R.M. (1988) Anxiety response patterns and etiological factors in dog-fearful and non-fearful subjects. *Behaviour Research and Therapy, 26(3)*, 245–251.

Diener, E. and Seligman, M.E. (2002) Very happy people. *Psychology of Science, 13(1)*, 81–84.

Diener, E., Horwitz, J. and Emmons, R.A. (1985) Happiness of the very wealthy. *Social Indicators, 16*, 263–274.

Diener, E., Sandvik, E., Seidlitz, L. and Diener, M. (1993) The relationship between income and subjective well-being: Relative or absolute? *Social Indicators Research, 28,* 195–223.

Dion, K., Berscheid, E. and Walster, E. (1972) What is beautiful is good. *Journal of Personality and Social Psychology, 24,* 285–290.

Dutton, D.G. and Aron, A.P. (1974) Some evidence for heightened sexual attraction under conditions of high anxiety. *Journal of Personality and Social Psychology, 30,* 510–517.

Dweck, C.S. (1975) The role of expectations and attributions in the alleviation of learned helplessness. *Journal of Personality and Social Psychology, 31,* 674–685.

Eagly, A.H. (1978) Sex differences in influenceability. *Psychological Bulletin, 85,* 86–116.

Eagly, A.H. and Carli, L.L. (1981) Sex of researchers and sex-typed communications as determinants of sex differences in influenceability: A meta-analysis of social influence studies. *Psychological Bulletin, 90,* 1–20.

Ellis, A. (1994) *Reason and Emotion in Psychotherapy, Revised and Updated.* Secaucus, NJ: Carol Publishing Group.

Ellis, A. (1957) *How to Live with a 'Neurotic'.* Hollywood, CA: Wilshire Books.

Ellis, A. (2001) *Overcoming Destructive Beliefs, Feelings, and Behaviours: New Directions for Rational Emotive Behaviour Therapy.* New York: Prometheus Books.

Emmons, R.A. and McCullogh, M.E. (2003) Counting blessings versus burdens: An experimental investigation of gratitude and subjective well-being in daily life. *Journal of Personality and Social Psychology, 84(2),* 377–389.

Engels, G.I., Garnefski, N. and Diekstra, R.F.W. (1993) Efficacy of rational emotive therapy: A quantitative analysis. *Journal of Consulting and Clinical Psychology, 61(6),* 1083–1090.

Epstein, L.C. and Lasagna, L. (1969) Obtaining informed consent: Form or substance. *Archives of Internal Medicine, 123,* 682–688.

Farah, M.J. (2004) Emerging ethical issues in neuroscience. *Nature Neuroscience, 5(11),* 1123–1130.

Festinger, L., Riecken, H.W. and Schachter, S. (1956) *When Prophecy Fails.* Minneapolis: University of Minnesota Press.

Financial Times (2007) Happiness lessons: This is not a subject to add to the national curriculum [Editorial], 14 June. Available online at *www.ft.com/cms/s/0/dede57d0-1a13-11dc-99c5-000b5df10621.html?nclick_check=1* (accessed January 2009).

Foresight – UK Government Foresight Mental Capital and Wellbeing Project (2008) Final Project report. London: The Government Office for Science.

Foster, R.A., Libkuman, T.M., Schooler, J.W. and Loftus, E.F. (1994) Consequentiality and eyewitness person identification. *Applied Cognitive Psychology, 8,* 107–121.

Freud, S. (1900) *The Interpretation of Dreams.* New York: Macmillan.

Freud, S. (1909) Analysis of phobia in a five-year- old boy. In J. Strachey (ed. and trans.) (1976) *The Complete Psychological Works of Sigmund Freud: The Standard Edition, Volume 10.* New York: W.W. Norton and Co.

Freud, S. (1930) cited in Strachey, J. (1961) *The Standard Edition of the Complete Works of Sigmund Freud* (Vol. 21, pp. 57–145). London: Hogarth Press.

Freud, S. (1938) *An Outline of Psychoanalysis.* London: Hogarth Press.

Frisch, M.B. (2006) *Quality of Life Therapy: Applying a Life Satisfaction Approach to Positive Psychology and Cognitive Therapy.* Hoboken, NJ: Wiley and Sons.

Frodi, A.M., Lamb, M., Leavitt, L. and Donovan, W. (1978) Fathers' and mothers' responses to infant smiles and cries. *Infant Behavior and Development, 1,* 187–198.

Gallup and Healthways (2014) State of global well-being: Results of the Gallup-Healthways global well-being index. Available online at *http://info.healthways.com/wellbeingindex* (accessed May 2015).

Gallup, G., Jr. (1984, March) *Religion in America.* Gallup Report. Report No. 222. Princeton, NJ: Princeton Religion Research Center.

Geiger, B. (1996) *Fathers as Primary Caregivers.* Westport, CT: Greenwood.

Gettler, L.T., McDade, T.W., Feranil, A.B. and Kuzawa, C.W. (2011) Longitudinal evidence that fatherhood decreases testosterone in human males. *Proceedings of the National Academy of Sciences in the United States of America, 108(39),* 16135–16482.

Gill, G.K. (1998) The strategic involvement of children in housework: An Australian case of two-income families. *International Journal of Comparative Sociology, 39(3),* 301–314.

Gillham, J.E., Reivich, K.J., Jaycox, L.H. and Seligman, M.E.P. (1995) Prevention of depressive symptoms in schoolchildren: Two-year follow-up. *Psychological Science, 6,* 343–351.

Gilligan, C. (1982) *In a Different Voice: Psychological Theory and Women's Development.* Cambridge, MA: Harvard University Press.

Gneezy, U., Meier, S. and Rey-Biel, P. (2011) When and why incentives (don't) work to modify behaviour. *Journal of Economic Perspectives, 25(4),* 191–210.

Grant, G.M., Salcedo, V., Hynan, L.S., Frisch, M.B. and Puster, K. (1995) Effectiveness of quality of life therapy for depression. *Psychological Reports, 76,* 1203–1208.

Griffiths, M.D. (1994) The role of cognitive bias and skill in fruit machine gambling. *British Journal of Psychology, 85,* 351–369.

Greene, E. (1990) Media effects on jurors. *Law and Human Behavior, 14,* 439–450.

Guidelines for Psychologists Working with Animals (2012) Available online at *www.bps.org.uk/system/files/images/guideline_for_psychologists_working_with_animals_2012_rep55_2012_web.pdf* (accessed April 2015).

Gupta, S. (1991) Effects of time of day and personality on intelligence test scores. *Personality and Individual Differences, 12(11),* 1227–1231.

Haring, M.I., Stock, W.A. and Okun, M.A. (1984) A research synthesis of gender and social class as correlates of subjective well-being. *Human Relations, 37,* 645–657.

Harlow, H.F. (1959) Love in infant monkeys. *Scientific American, 200(6),* 68–74.

Hatfield, E. and Walster, G.W. (1981) *A New Look at Love.* Reading, MA: Addison-Wesley.

Heermann, J.A., Jones, L.C. and Wikoff, R.L. (1994) Measurement of parent behavior during interactions with their infants. *Infant Behavior and Development, 17,* 311–321.

Herzog, A.R., Rogers, W.L. and Woodworth, J. (1982) *Subjective Well-being among Different Age Groups.* Ann Arbor: University of Michigan, Survey Research Center.

Hollon, S.D., DeRubeis, R.J., Evans, M.D., Wiemer, M.J. and Garvey, M.J. (1992) Cognitive therapy and pharmacotherapy for depression. *Archive of General Psychiatry, 49(10),* 774–781.

Hopfield, J.J., Feinstein, D.I. and Palmer, R.G. (1983) 'Unlearning' has a stabilising effect in collective memories. *Nature, 304,* 158–159.

Howell, R.T., Chenot, D., Hill, G. and Howell, C. (2009) Momentary happiness: The role of need satisfaction. *Journal of Happiness Studies, 1,* 1–15.

Huff, C.R., Ratner, A. and Sagarin, E. (1986) Guilty until proven innocent: Wrongful conviction and public policy. *Crime and Delinquency, 32,* 518–544.

Humphrey, J.H. (1973) *Stress Education for College Students.* Hauppauge, NY: Nova.

Inglehart, R. (1990) *Culture Shift in Advanced Industrial Society.* Princeton, NJ: Princeton University Press.

Institute for Economics and Peace (2013) UK Peace Index: Exploring the fabric of peace in the UK from 2003 to 2012. Published April 2103, available online at *www.visionofhumanity.org/sites/default/files/UK_Peace_Index_report_2013.pdf* (accessed June 2015).

Jarrett, R.B., Basco, M.R., Risser, R., Ramanan, J., Marwill, M., Kraft, D. and Rush, A.J. (1998) Is there a role for continuation phase cognitive therapy for depressed outpatients? *Journal of Consulting and Clinical Psychology, 66,* 1036–1040.

Jarrett, R.B., Schaffer, M., McIntire, D., Witt-Browder, A. *et al.* (1999) Treatment of atypical depression with cognitive therapy or phenelzine: A double blind placebo controlled trial. *Archives of General Psychiatry, 56,* 431–437.

Johnstone, E.C., Crow, T.J., Frith, C.D., Husband, J. and Kreel, L. (1976) Cerebral ventricular size and cognitive impairment in chronic schizophrenia. *Lancet, 2,* 924–926.

Jorgensen, G. (2006) Kohlberg and Gilligan: Duet or duel? *Journal of Moral Education, 35(2),* 179–196.

Jost, A. (1897) Die Assoziationsfestigkeit in iher Abhängigkeit von der Verteilung der Wiederholungen. *Zeitschrift für Psychologie, 14,* 436–472.

Kabat-Zinn, J. (1990) *Full Catastrophe Living: Using the Wisdom of your Body and Mind to Face Stress, Pain and Illness.* New York: Delacarte.

Kahn, R.J., McNair, D.M., Lipman, R.S., Covi, L., Rickels, K., Downing, R., Fisher, S. and Frankenthaler, L.M. (1986) Imipramine and chlordiazepoxide in depressive and anxiety disorders. II. Efficacy in anxious outpatients. *Archives of General Psychiatry, 43,* 79–85.

Kohlberg, L. (1968) The child as a moral philosopher. *Psychology Today, 2,* 25–30.

Kohlberg, L. (1975) The cognitive developmental approach to moral education. *Phi Delta Kappan,* 670–677.

Koran, L.M., Hanna, G.L., Hollander, E., Nestadt, G. and Simpson, H.B. (2007) Practice guideline for the treatment of patients with obsessive compulsive disorder. *American Journal of Psychiatry, 164(7),* 5–53.

Koubeissi, M.Z., Bartolomei, F. and Picard, F. (2014) Electrical stimulation of a small brain area reversibly disrupts consciousness. *Epilepsy and Behavior, 37,* 32–35.

Kubzansky, L.D. and Thurston, R.C. (2007) Emotional vitality and incident coronary heart disease: Benefits of healthy psychological functioning. *Archives of General Psychiatry, 64(12),* 1393–1401.

Kuyken, W. and Tsivrikos, D. (2009) Therapist competence, co-morbidity and cognitive-behavioral therapy for depression. *Psychotherapy and Psychosomatics, 78,* 42–48.

Laing, R.D. (1965) *The Divided Self.* Harmondsworth: Penguin.

Laird, J.D. (1974) Self-attribution of emotion: The effects of facial expression on the quality of emotional experience. *Journal of Personality and Social Psychology, 29,* 475–486.

Lee, G.R., Seccombe, K. and Shehan, C.L. (1991) Marital status and personal happiness: An analysis of trend data. *Journal of Marriage and the Family, 53,* 839–844.

LeFrançois, G.R. (2000) *Psychology for Teaching*, 10th edn. Belmont, CA: Wadsworth Publishing Co.

Lepper, M.R., Greene, D. and Nisbett, R.E. (1973) Undermining children's intrinsic interest with extrinsic reward: A test of the overjustification hypothesis. *Journal of Personality and Social Psychology*, 28, 129–137.

Levitt, S.D., List, J.A. and Sadoff, S. (2010) The effect of performance-based incentives on educational achievement: Evidence from a randomised experiment. *Working Paper*. Cited in Levitt, S.D., List, J.A., Neckermann, S. and Sadoff, S. (2012) The behavioralist goes to school: Leveraging behavioral economics to improve educational performance. Zentrum für Europäische Wirtschaftsforschung GmbH: Centre for European Economic Research. Discussion Paper No. 12–038. Available online at *http://ftp.zew.de/pub/zew-docs/dp/dp12038.pdf* (accessed June 2015).

Lewis, C.C. (1995) *Educating Hearts and Minds: Reflections on Japanese Preschool and Elementary Education*. Cambridge: Cambridge University Press.

Linley, P.A., Joseph, S., Harrington, S. and Wood, A.M. (2006) Positive psychology: Past, present, and (possible) future. *The Journal of Positive Psychology*, 1(1), 3–16.

Loftus, E. (1975) Leading questions and eyewitness report. *Cognitive Psychology*, 7, 560–572.

Loftus, E. (1979a) *Eyewitness Testimony*. Cambridge, MA: Harvard University Press.

Loftus, E. (1979b) Reactions to blatantly contradictory information. *Memory and Cognition*, 7, 368–374.

Loftus, E. and Ketcham, K. (1992) *Witness for the Defense: The Accused, the Eyewitness and the Expert Who Puts Memory on Trial*, 2nd edn. New York: St Martin's Press.

Loftus, E. and Ketcham, K. (1996) *The Myth of Repressed Memory: False Memories and Allegations of Sexual Abuse*, 2nd edn. New York: St Martin's Press.

Loftus, E.F. and Palmer, J.C. (1974) Reconstruction of automobile destruction: An example of the interaction between language and memory. *Journal of Verbal Learning and Verbal Behaviour*, 13, 585–589.

Loftus, E.F. and Zanni, G. (1975) Eyewitness testimony: The influence of the wording of a question. *Bulletin of the Psychonomic Society*, 5(1), 86–88.

Lombroso, C. (1876) *L'Uomo Delinquente*. Milan: Hoepli.

Lovaas, O.I. (1987) Behavioural treatment and abnormal education and educational functioning in young autistic children. *Journal of Consulting and Clinical Psychology*, 55, 3–9.

Lyubomirsky, S. (2013) *What Should Make you Happy, but Doesn't, What Shouldn't Make you Happy, but Does*. London: Penguin.

MacKinnon, D. (1938) Violations of prohibitions. In H.A. Murray (ed.) *Explorations in Personality*. New York: Oxford University Press.

Maguire, E.A., Gadian, N.G., Johnsrude, I.S., Good, C.D., Ashburner, J., Frackowiak, R.S.J. and Frith, C.D. (2000) Navigation-related structural changes in the hippocampi of taxi drivers. *Proceedings of the National Academy of Science*, 97(8), 4398–4403.

Manstead, A.R. and McCulloch, C. (1981) Sex-role stereotyping in British television advertisements. *British Journal of Social Psychology*, 20, 171–180.

Mantzios, M. and Giannou, K. (2014) Group vs. single mindfulness meditation: Exploring avoidance, impulsivity, and weight management in two separate mindfulness meditation settings. *APHW*, 6(2), 174–191.

Mastekaasa, A. (1992) Marriage and psychological well-being: Some evidence on selection into marriage. *Journal of Marriage and the Family*, 54, 901–911.

Mayberg, H.S., Lozano, A.M., Voon, V., McNeely, H.E., Seminowicz, D., Hamani, C., Schwalb, J.M. and Kennedy, S.H. (2005) Deep brain stimulation for treatment-resistant depression. *Neuron*, 45(5), 651–660.

McAllister, L.W., Stachowiak, J.G., Baer, D.M. and Conderman, L. (1969) The application of operant conditioning techniques in a secondary school classroom. *Journal of Applied Behavior Analysis*, 2(4), 277–285.

McCrae, R.R. and Costa, P.T., Jr. (1990) *Personality in Adulthood*. New York: Guilford Press.

McDermut, W., Miller, I.W. and Brown, R.A. (2001) The efficacy of group psychotherapy for depression: An meta-analysis and review of empirical research. *Evidence-based Mental Health*, 4(3), 82.

Menzies, R.G. and Clarke, J.C. (1993) A comparison of in vivo and vicarious exposure in the treatment of childhood water phobia. *Behaviour Research and Therapy*, 31(1), 9–15.

Middlemist, D.R., Knowles, E.S. and Matter, C.F. (1976) Personal space invasions in the lavatory: Suggestive evidence for arousal. *Journal of Personality and Social Psychology*, 33, 541–546.

Milgram, S. (1963) Behavioral study of obedience. *Journal of Abnormal and Social Psychology*, 67, 371–378.

Milgram, S. (1974) *Obedience to Authority: An Experimental View*. New York: Harper and Row.

Miller, N.E. (1978) Biofeedback and visceral learning. *Annual Review of Psychology*, 29, 421–452.

Mita, T.H., Dermer, M. and Knight, J. (1977) Reversed facial images and the mere-exposure hypothesis. *Journal of Personality and Social Psychology*, 35, 597–601.

Moore, H.T. (1922) Further data concerning sex differences. *Journal of Abnormal and Social Psychology*, 17, 210–214.

Morris, K. (2014) Love step not naughty step: A New Year's resolution for parents? PurpleHouse Psychology Services. Available online at *www.mypurplehouse.co.uk/parenting-techniques/love-step-naughty-step-new-years-resolution-parents* (accessed February 2015).

Mowrer, O.H. (1947) On the dual nature of learning: A re-interpretation of 'conditioning' and 'problem-solving'. *Harvard Educational Review*, 17, 102–148.

Murstein, B.I. (1972) Physical attractiveness and marital choice. *Journal of Personality and Social Psychology*, 22, 8–12.

Myers, D.G. and Diener, E. (1995) Who is happy? *Psychological Science*, 6(1), 10–17.

Nelson, C.A. (2008) Incidental findings in magnetic resonance imaging (MRI) brain research. *Journal of Law, Medicine and Ethics (Summer)*, 36(2), 315–319.

Norem, J. (2001) *The Positive Power of Negative Thinking*. Cambridge, MA: Basic Books.

Nosek, B.A., Banaji, M.R. and Greenwald, A.G. (2002) Harvesting implicit group attitudes and beliefs from a demonstration website. *Group Dynamics*, 6, 101–115.

Nuffield Trust (2014) prepared by Spence, R., Roberts, A., Ariti, C. and Bardsley, M. (2014) *Focus on: Antidepressant prescribing. Trends in the prescribing of antidepressants in primary care*. London: The Health Foundation and the Nuffield Trust.

Orne, M.T. (1962) On the social psychology of the psychological experiment: With particular reference to demand characteristics and their implications. *American Psychologist*, 17, 776–783.

Orne, M.T. and Holland, C.H. (1968) On the ecological validity of laboratory deceptions. *International Journal of Psychiatry*, 6, 282–293.

Orne, M.T. and Scheibe, K.E. (1964) The contribution of nondeprivation factors in the production of sensory deprivation effects: The psychology of the 'panic button'. *Journal of Abnormal and Social Psychology*, 68, 3–12.

Öst, L.G. (1987) Age of onset in different phobias. *Journal of Abnormal Psychology*, 96, 223–229.

Oswald, A.J., Proto, E. and Sgroi, D. (2009) Happiness and productivity. IZA Discussion Paper No. 4645. Available online at *http://ftp.iza.org/dp4645.pdf* (accessed May 2015).

Pavlov, I.P. (1902) *The Work of the Digestive Glands*. London: Charles Griffin.

Perry, G. (2012) *Behind the Shock Machine: The Untold Story of the Notorious Milgram Psychology Experiments*. Brunswick, VT: Scribe Publications.

Piaget, J. (1970) Piaget's theory. In P.H. Mussen (ed.) *Carmichael's Manual of Child Psychology, vol. 1*. New York: Wiley.

Pines, M. (1998) *Group-Analytic Psychotherapy and the Borderline Patient: Circular Reflections*. London: Jessica Kingsley Publications.

Piliavin, I.M., Rodin, J. and Piliavin, J.A. (1969) Good Samaritanism: An underground phenomenon. *Journal of Personality and Social Psychology*, 13, 1200–1213.

Poloma, M.M. and Pendleton, B.F. (1990) Religious domains and general well-being. *Social Indicators Research*, 22, 255–276.

Popper, K.R. (1934) *The Logic of Scientific Discovery*. English translation, 1959, London: Hutchinson.

Pozzulo, J.D. and Lindsay, R.C.L. (1998) Identification accuracy of children versus adults: A meta-analysis. *Law and Human Behavior*, 22(5), 549–570.

Raine, A., Buchsbaum, M. and LaCasse, L. (1997) Brain abnormalities in murderers indicated by positron emission tomography. *Biological Psychiatry*, 42(6), 495–508.

Raine, A., Mellingen, K., Liu, J., Venables, P. and Mednick, S.A. (2003) Effects of environmental enrichment at ages 3–5 years on schizotypal personality and anti-social behavior at ages 17 and 23 years. *American Journal of Psychiatry*, 160, 1627–1635.

Reibel, D.K., Gresson, J.M., Brainard, G.C. and Rosenzweig, S. (2001) Mindfulness based stress reduction and health related quality of life in a heterogeneous patient population. *General Hospital Psychiatry*, 23(4), 183–192.

Robins, L. and Regier, D. (eds) (1991) *Psychiatric Disorders in America*. New York: Free Press.

Robinson, P.W., Newby, T.J. and Ganzell, S.L. (1981) A token system for a class of underachieving hyperactive children. *Journal of Applied Behaviour Analysis*, 14(3), 307–315.

Rosenbluth, R., Grossman, E.S. and Kaitz, M. (2000) Performance of early-blind and sighted children on olfactory tasks. *Perception*, 29(1), 101–110.

Rosenthal, R. (1966) *Experimenter Effects in Behaviour Research*. New York: Appleton.

Rosenthal, R. and Fode, K.L. (1963) The effect of experimenter bias on the performance of the albino rat. *Behavioural Science*, 8(3), 183–189.

Ruedy, N.E. and Schweitzer, M.E. (2010) In the moment: The effect of mindfulness on ethical decision making. Available online at *http://opim.wharton.upenn.edu/risk/library/WPAF2010-07-02_NR,MS.pdf* (accessed April 2015).

Rutter, M. and Sonuga-Barke, E.J. (2010) X. Conclusions: Overview of findings from the era study, inferences, and research implications. *Monographs of the Society for Research in Child Development*, 75(1), 212–229.

Sartre, J.-P. (1973) *No Exit*. New York: Vintage Books. (Original work published 1944.)

Schacter, D.L., Kaszniak, A.W., Kihlstrom, J.F. and Valdiserri, M. (1991) The relation between source memory and aging. *Psychology and Aging, 6(4)*, 559–568.

Schaffer, H.R. and Emerson, P.E. (1964) The development of social attachments in infancy. *Monographs of the Society for Research in Child Development, 29(3, Serial No. 94)*, 1–77.

Schinka, J.A., Musch, R.M. and Robichaux-Keene, N. (2004) A meta-analysis of the association between the serotonin transporter gene poly-morphism (5-HTTLPR) and trait anxiety. *Molecular Psychiatry, 9*, 197–202.

Seligman, M.E.P. (1970) On the generality of the laws of learning. *Psychological Review, 77*, 406–418.

Seligman, M.E.P. (2002) *Authentic Happiness: Using the New Positive Psychology to Realise your Potential for Lasting Fulfillment*. New York: Free Press.

Seligman, M.E.P. (2003) Foreword: The past and future of positive psychology. In C.L.M. Keyes and J. Haidt (eds) *Flourishing Positive Psychology and the Life Well Lived*. Washington DC: American Psychology Association.

Seligman, M.E.P. and Csikszentmihalyi, M. (2000) Positive psychology: An introduction. *American Psychologist, 55(1)*, 5–14.

Seligman, M.E.P., Ernst, R.M., Gillham, J., Reivich, K. and Linkins, M. (2009) Positive education: Positive psychology and classroom interventions. *Oxford Review of Education, 35(3)*, 293–311.

Sheldon, K.M. and King, L.K. (2001) Why positive psychology is necessary. *American Psychologist, 56*, 216–217.

Sheridan, C.L. and King, K.G. (1972) Obedience to authority with an authentic victim. *Proceedings of the 80th Annual Convention of the American Psychological Association, 7*, 165–166.

Silverman, M.S., McCarthy, M. and McGoren, T.E. (1992) A review of outcome studies of rational emotive therapy from 1982–1989. *Journal of Rational Emotive and Cognitive Behaviour Therapy, 10*, 111–186.

Simons, A.D., Gordon, J.S., Monroe, S.M. and Thase, M.E. (1995) Toward an integration of psychologic, social, and biologic factors in depression: Effects on outcome and course of cognitive therapy. *Journal of Consulting and Clinical Psychology, 63*, 369–377.

Skeels, H. and Dye, H.B. (1939) A study of the effects of differential stimulation on mentally retarded children. *Proceedings and Addresses of the American Association on Mental Deficiency, 44*, 114–136.

Skinner, B.F. (1938) *Science and Human Behavior*. New York: Macmillan.

Skinner, B.F. (1954) The science of learning and the art of teaching. *Harvard Educational Review, 24(2)*, 86–97.

Skodak, M. and Skeels, H. (1949) A final follow-up study of 100 adopted children. *Journal of Genetic Psychology, 75*, 85–125.

Slater, L. (2004) *Opening Skinner's Box: Great Psychological Experiments of the Twentieth Century*. New York: Norton.

Smirle, C. (2013) Profile of Rosalie Rayner. In A. Rutherford (ed.) *Psychology's Feminist Voices Multimedia Internet Archive*. Available online at *www.feministvoices.com/bonnie-strickland* (accessed February 2015).

Smith, J.W. (1988) Long term outcome of clients treated in a commercial stop smoking program. *Journal of Substance Abuse Treatment, 5*, 33–36.

Smith, J.W., Frawley, P.J. and Polissar, L. (1997) Six- and twelve-month abstinence rates in inpatient alcoholics treated with either faradic aversion or chemical aversion compared with matched inpatients from a treatment registry. *Journal of Addictive Diseases, 16(1)*, 5–24.

Solms, M. (2000) Dreaming and REM sleep are controlled by different brain mechanisms. *Behavioral and Brain Sciences, 23*, 843–850.

Soomro, G.M., Altman, D.G., Rajagopal, S. and Oakley-Browne, M. (2008) Selective serotonin re-uptake inhibitors (SSRIs) versus placebo for obsessive compulsive disorder (OCD). *Cochrane Database of Systematic Reviews, 1*. Available online at *http://summaries.cochrane.org/CD001765/selective-serotonin-re-uptake-inhibitors-ssris-versus-placebo-for-obsessive-compulsive-disorder-ocd* (accessed June 2012).

Spence, S. and Shortt, A.L. (2007) Research review: Can we justify the widespread dissemination of universal, school-based interventions for the prevention of depression among children and adolescents? *Journal of Child Psychology and Psychiatry, 48*, 526–542.

Spitz, R.A. and Wolf, K.M. (1946) Anaclitic depression. *Psychoanalytic Study of the Child, 2*, 313–342.

Sroufe, L.A., Egeland, B., Carlson, E. and Collins, W.A. (2005) *The Development of the Person: The Minnesota Study of Risk and Adaptation from Birth to Adulthood*. New York: Guilford.

Szasz, T. (1978) *The Myth of Psychotherapy*. Oxford: Oxford University Press.

Taylor, S.E., Klein, L.C., Lewis, B.P., Grunewald, T.L., Gurung, R.A.R. and Updegraff, J.A. (2000) Biobehavioral responses to stress in females: Tend-and-befriend, not fight-or-flight. *Psychological Review, 107(3)*, 411–429.

Teasdale, J.D., Williams, J.M.G., Soulsby, J.M., Segal, Z.V., Ridgeway, V.A. and Lau, M.A. (2000) Prevention of relapse/recurrence in major depression by mindfulness based cognitive therapy. *Journal of Consulting and Clinical Psychology, 68(4)*, 615–623.

Thomas, C.M. and Morris, S. (2003) Cost of depression among adults in England in 2000. *British Journal of Psychiatry, 183*, 514–519.

Tiihonen, J., Kuikka, J., Bergstrom, K., Lepola, U., Koponen, H. and Leinonen, E. (1997) Dopamine re-uptake site densities in patients with social phobia. *American Journal of Psychiatry, 154*, 239–242.

Tiihonen, J., Rautiainen, M.R., Ollila, H.M., Repo-Tiihonen, E., Virkkunen, M., Palotie, A., Pietiläinen, O., Kristiansson, K., Joukamaa, M., Lauerma, H., Saarela, J., Tyni, S., Vartiainen, H., Paananen, J., Goldman, D. and Paunio, T. (2015) Genetic background of extreme violent behaviour. *Molecular Psychiatry, 20(6)*, 786–792.

Toghyani, M., Kalantari, M., Amiri, S. and Molavi, H. (2011) The effectiveness of quality of life therapy on subjective well-being of male adolescents. *Social and Behavioural Sciences, 30*, 1752–1757.

Toon, K., Fraise, J., McFetridge, M. and Alwin, N. (1996) Memory or mirage? The False Memory Syndrome debate. *The Psychologist, 9(2)*, 73–77.

Trivers, R.L. (1972) Parental investment and sexual selection. In B. Campbell (ed.) *Sexual Selection and the Descent of Man*. Chicago: Aldine.

Tulving, E. and Psotka, J. (1971) Retroactive inhibition in free recall: Inaccessibility of information available in the memory store. *Journal of Experimental Psychology, 87*, 1–8.

Viguera, A.C., Nonacs, R., Cohen, L.S., Tondo, L. and Murray, A. (2000) Risk of recurrence of bipolar disorder in pregnant and non-pregnant women after discontinuing lithium maintenance. *American Journal of Psychiatry, 157(2)*, 179–184.

Wager, T.D., Phan, K.L., Liberzon, I. and Taylor, S.F. (2003) Valence, gender, and lateralisation of functional brain anatomy in emotion: A meta-analysis of findings from neuroimaging. *NeuroImage, 19(3)*, 513–531.

Walker, L.J., deVries, B. and Trevethan, S.D. (1987) Moral stages and moral orientations in real-life and hypothetical dilemmas. *Child Development, 58*, 842–858.

Walster, E., Aronson, V., Abrahams, D. and Rottman, L. (1966) The importance of physical attractiveness in dating behaviour. *Journal of Personality and Social Psychology, 4*, 508–516.

Watson, J.B. (1930) *Behaviorism*, revised edition. Chicago: University of Chicago Press.

Watson, J.B. and Rayner, R. (1920) Conditioned emotional reactions. *Journal of Experimental Psychology, 3*, 1–14.

White, G.L., Fishbein, S. and Rutstein, J. (1981) Passionate love and the misattribution of arousal. *Journal of Personality and Social Psychology, 41*, 56–62.

Wilson, R.M., Gaines, J. and Hill, R.P. (2008) Neuromarketing and consumer free will. *The Journal of Consumer Affairs, 42(3)*, 389–410.

Witter, R.A., Stock, W.A., Okun, M.A. and Haring, M.J. (1985) Religion and subjective well-being in adulthood: A quantitative synthesis. *Review of Religious Research, 26*, 332–342.

Wolpe, J. (1958) *Psychotherapy by Reciprocal Inhibition*. Stanford, CA: Stanford University Press.

Wolpe, J. (1973) *The Practice of Behavior Therapy*. New York: Pergamon Press.

Wood, W., Rhodes, N. and Whelan, M. (1989) Sex differences in positive well-being: A consideration of emotional style and marital status. *Psychological Bulletin, 106*, 249–264.

Yang, Y. and Raine, A. (2009) Prefrontal structural and functional brain imaging findings in antisocial, violent, and psychopathic individuals: A meta-analysis. *Psychiatry Research, 174(2)*, 81–88.

Yarmey, A.D. (1993) Stereotypes and recognition memory for faces and voices of good guys and bad guys. *Applied Cognitive Psychology, 7(5)*, 419–431.

Yuille, J.C. and Cutshall, J.L. (1986) A case study of eyewitness memory or crime. *Journal of Applied Psychology, 71(2)*, 291–301.

Zajonc, R.B. (1968) Attitudinal effects of mere exposure. *Journal of Personality and Social Psychology (Monograph), 9*, 1–29.

Glossary/Index

Glossary/Index

Multi-method approach 138

Multistore model Explains memory in terms of three stores (sensory (SM), short term (STM) and long term (LTM)). The transfer of data can be explained in terms of attention (SM to STM) and rehearsal (STM to LTM). 70

Mundane realism Refers to how a study mirrors the real world. The research environment is realistic to the degree to which experiences encountered in the research environment will occur in the real world. 112

Murders, brain abnormalities 16–17

Mustabatory thinking 74

Myers, D. and Diener, E. 96–99

Nativist approach The view that development is determined by innate factors, that most abilities simply need fine tuning but do not depend on experience for their development. 10, 12, 14

Natural experiments A research method in which the experimenter cannot manipulate the independent variable directly, but where it varies naturally, and the effect on a dependent variable can be observed. 120–121

Natural selection The major process that explains evolution whereby inherited traits that enhance an animal's survival and reproductive success are passed on to the next generation and are thus 'selected', whereas animals without such traits are less successful at survival and reproducing and their traits are not selected. 10–11

Nature Those aspects of behaviour that are innate and inherited. Nature does not simply refer to abilities present at birth but to any ability determined by genes, including those that appear through maturation. 7, 23, 42, 50, 63, 83

Nature–nurture debate The discussion about whether behaviour is due to innate or environmental factors. Such a debate is no longer appropriate as it is now accepted that both contribute and interact in such a way that it is not simply a matter of saying that one or the other determines behaviour. 7, 23, 42, 50, 63, 83

Naughty step 60–61

Negative correlation Describes a correlation where, as one co-variable increases, the other decreases. 90, 136–137, 152, 156

Negative reinforcement In operant conditioning, escape from an unpleasant situation increases the probability that a behaviour will be repeated, i.e. reinforces the behaviour. 50–51, 52, 58

Negative skewed distribution Most of the scores are bunched towards the right. The mode is to the right of the mean because the mean is affected by the extreme scores tailing off to the left. 146–147

Neisser, Ulric 4

Neural networks A system of highly interconnected neurons which means that the whole network behaves in a way that would not be predicted from the behaviour of individual neurons. 33

Neuroenhancement 20

Neuromarketing 20–21

Neuron A specialised cell in the nervous system for transmission of information. 11–12, 20

Neuroscience The study of how the brain and nervous system affect behaviour. 20–21, 82, 103

Neurosurgeons 14

Neurotransmitters Chemical substances, such as serotonin or dopamine, which play an important part in the workings of the nervous system by transmitting nerve impulses across a synapse. 11–14, 20, 22

Neutral stimulus In classical conditioning, the stimulus that initially does not produce the target response, i.e. it is neutral. Through association with the unconditioned stimulus (UCS), the NS acquires the properties of the UCS and becomes a conditioned stimulus producing a conditioned response. 50–51

New York Subway, study 119

NOIR 144

Nominal data A level of measurement where data are in separate categories. 144–145, 146, 150, 153, 154–155, 157, 158–159, 161

Nomothetic An approach to research that focuses more on general laws of behaviour than on the individual, possibly unique, case (the idiographic approach). 7, 23

Non-clinical Not medical; a non-clinical sample that has not got a diagnosed condition. 35, 75

Non-directional hypothesis predicts simply that there is a difference between two conditions or two groups of participants, without stating the direction of the difference. 114–115, 136, 151, 154–155, 157, 159

Non-participant observation The observer is separate from the people being observed. 130–131

Non-directional hypothesis A form of hypothesis that states a difference, correlation or association between two variables but does not specify the direction (e.g. more or less, positive or negative) of such a relationship. 114, 136, 151, 154, 155, 157

Noradrenaline A hormone associated with arousal of the autonomic nervous system (e.g. raised heart rate), and also a neurotransmitter. 12

Norem, J. 103

Normal distribution A symmetrical bell-shaped frequency distribution. This distribution occurs when certain variables are measured, such as IQ or the life of a light bulb. Such 'events' are distributed in such a way that most of the scores are clustered close to the mid-point; the mean, median and mode are at the mid-point. 147

Nosek, B.A *et al.* 119

Not guilty by reason of insanity (NGRI) 16, 19

NS *See* neutral stimulus.

Null hypothesis The assumption of no relationship (difference, association, etc.) between variables being studied. 114, 136, 150, 153, 154, 155, 157, 159, 161

Nurture Those aspects of behaviour that are acquired through experience, i.e. learned from interactions with the physical and social environment. 7, 18, 23, 42, 50, 63, 83

Obedience 162–163

Obedience orientation 165

Observation Can be structured or unstructured (no system). Can be used as a means of assessing the dependent variable in an experiment. 96, 118, 130–131, 133, 134, 148, 163

Observed value The number (value) produced after applying an inferential test formula. Sometimes also called 'calculated value' because it is calculated using an inferential test. 150–151, 152, 154, 155, 157, 161

Observer bias Observers' expectations affect what they see or hear. This reduces the validity of the observations. 130–131, 138

Obsessive-compulsive disorder (OCD) An anxiety disorder where anxiety arises from both obsessions (persistent thoughts) and compulsions (means of controlling the obsessional thoughts). 14

Occipital lobes One of four major sections of the brain. The occipital lobe is located at the back of the brain (furthest from the eyes) and contains the visual cortex. 10

Oedipus complex Freud's explanation of how a boy resolves his love for his mother and feelings of rivalry towards his father by identifying with his father. Occurs during the phallic stage of psychosexual development. In Greek mythology Oedipus unknowingly killed his father and married his mother. 30, 31, 41

Oestrogen A female sex hormone produced by the ovaries and by the adrenal gland. 40, 152

One-tailed test Form of test used with a directional hypothesis. 151, 153, 154, 157, 159

Online Refers to being connected via the internet to another source. You may be connected to a website or could be using an app on a mobile phone. Data can be collected from individuals. 119

Open questions Questions that invite respondents to provide their own answers rather than select one of those provided. Tend to produce qualitative data. 132, 148

Operant conditioning Learning that occurs when we are reinforced (negative or positive) for doing something, which increases the probability that the behaviour in question will be repeated in the future. Conversely, if we are punished for behaving in a certain way, there is a decrease in the probability that the behaviour will recur. 50–51, 52, 54, 56, 58, 60, 62

Operationalise Ensuring that variables are in a form that can be easily tested. A concept such as 'educational attainment' needs to be specified more clearly if we are going to investigate it. For example it might be operationalised as 'GCSE grade in Maths'. 62, 110–111, 114, 122

Opportunity sampling A sample of participants produced by selecting people who are most easily available at the time of the study. 16, 124–125

Psychic determinism Personality and behaviour are determined more by psychological factors than by biological conditions. 30

Psychoactive drugs 12, 16, 22

Psychoanalysis A form of psychotherapy, originally developed by Sigmund Freud, that is intended to help patients become aware of long-repressed feelings and issues by using techniques such as free association and dream analysis. 4, 30, 32, 34, 42, 73, 93, 103

Psychodrama 34–35

Psychodynamic/Psychodynamic approach Literally an approach that explains the dynamics of behaviour – what motivates a person. The approach has become synonymous with Freud's theory of personality. Freud suggested that unconscious forces and early experiences are the prime motivators. 6, 29–47, 55, 58, 72, 90, 95, 98, 102, 118

Psychological harm For example, lowered self-esteem, embarrassment or changing a person's behaviour or attitudes. 19, 59, 73, 79, 99, 128

Psychological tests 135

Psychology, history of 4

Psychosexual development/Psychosexual stages In psychoanalytic theory, the developmental stages that are related to the id's changing focus on different parts of the body. 30–31, 40, 42

Psychosurgery Medical operations that involve severing fibres or removing brain tissue with the intention of treating disturbed behaviour for which no physical cause can be demonstrated. Modern psychosurgery techniques, such as deep brain stimulation, do not involve permanent damage. 14–15, 22

Psychotherapy Any psychological form of treatment for a mental disorder, as distinct from physical forms of treatment. 14, 32, 35

Psychotic A loss of contact with reality, consistent with serious mental illness, which typically includes delusions, hallucinations and disordered thinking. 12

Publication bias 165

Publication, research 164

Punishment In operant conditioning, the application of an unpleasant stimulus such that the likelihood of the behaviour that led to it reoccurring is decreased. 50–51, 60–61, 128

Qualitative data Information in words that cannot be counted or quantified. Qualitative data can be turned into quantitative data by placing them in categories and counting frequency. 38, 132, 138, 148, 149, 163

Quality of Life Therapy (QoLT) 94–95

Quantitative data Information that represents how much or how long, or how many, etc., there are of something, i.e. a behaviour is measured in numbers or quantities. 132, 138, 144–145, 146, 148, 149, 163

Quasi-experiment Studies that are 'almost' experiments. A research method in which the experimenter has not manipulated the independent variable (IV) directly. The IV would vary whether or not the researcher was interested. The researcher records the effect of the IV on a dependent variable (DV) – this DV may be measured in a lab. Strictly speaking, an experiment involves the deliberate manipulation of an IV and random allocation to conditions by the experimenter – neither of which apply to a quasi-experiment and therefore causal conclusions can only tentatively be drawn. 16, 18, 120–121

Questionnaire Data are collected through the use of written questions. 76, 95, 96. 100, 118, 132–133, 134, 139, 148

Quota sampling Similar to a stratified sample except participants are not selected from strata using a random sampling technique. 124–125

Race, and happiness 96, 97

Raine, A., Buchsbaum, M. and LaCasse, L. 16–19, 22, 24, 27, 118, 141

Random allocation Allocating participants to experimental groups or conditions using random techniques. 116–117, 121

Random number generators 125

Random sampling A sample of participants produced by using a random technique such that every member of the target population being tested has an equal chance of being selected. 124–125

Randomised control trials An independent groups design where participants are allocated randomly to conditions. Often used to test medical treatments. 13

Randomly allocated/Randomly assigned Distributing participants to experimental groups or conditions using random techniques. 93, 95, 116, 121

Range The difference between the highest and lowest item in a data set. Usually 1 is added as a correction. 144–145

Rapid eye movement (REM) A kind of sleep when the body is paralysed except for the eyes. REM sleep is often equated with dreaming, though dreams also occur during other sleep periods. 33, 141

Ratio *See* fractions

Rational emotive behaviour therapy (REBT) A development of RET to emphasise the behavioural component of the therapy, i.e. that the aim of the therapy is to change a client's behaviour as well as their thinking. 74–75

Reality principle In psychoanalytic theory, the drive by the ego to accommodate to the demands of the environment in a realistic way. 31

Reciprocal inhibition Pairing two things together which are incompatible (such as anxiety and relaxation) so that one inhibits or eliminates the other. 54, 63

Reductionism An approach that breaks complex phenomenon into more simple components, implying that this is desirable because complex phenomena are best understood in terms of a simpler level of explanation. 7, 23

Refereeing 164

Regress In psychoanalytic theory, a form of ego defence whereby the individuals returns psychologically to an earlier stage of development rather than handling unacceptable impulses in a more adult way. Anxiety-provoking thoughts can thus be temporarily pushed into the unconscious. Often confused with repression. 30

Reinforcement If a behaviour results in a pleasant state of affairs, the behaviour is 'stamped in' or reinforced. It then becomes more probable that the behaviour will be repeated in the future. Can be positive or negative reinforcement – both lead to an increased likelihood that the behaviour will be repeated. 50–52

Relationship formation 11, 30, 31, 51, 71, 91

Reliability Consistency. 133, 134–135

REM sleep *See* rapid eye movement.

Repeated measures design Each participant takes part in every condition under test, i.e. each level of the IV. 116–117, 122, 151, 156, 158

Replicate/Replicated If a finding from a research study is true (valid) it should be possible to obtain the same finding if the study is repeated. This confirms the reliability and the validity of the finding. 16, 138, 152

Reporting investigations 162–163

Representation In psychoanalysis, an element of dreamwork which enables the latent content of a dream to be transformed into manifest content by translating thoughts and emotions into images. 32

Repression In psychoanalytic theory, a form of ego defence whereby anxiety-provoking thoughts and feelings are excluded from the conscious mind. Often confused with regression. 30, 80

Research Excellence Framework (REF) 164

Research funding 164

Research, location of 118–119

Researcher bias Anything that an investigator does that has an effect on a participant's performance in a study other than what was intended. This includes direct effects (as a consequence of the investigator interacting with the participant) and indirect effects (as a consequence of the investigator designing the study). Investigator effects may act as a confounding or extraneous variable. 122–123

Response-bias factors 77

Retrieval cues 76, 82

Review A consideration of a number of studies that have investigated the same topic in order to reach a general conclusion about a particular hypothesis. 96, 149

Rewards 6, 51, 60, 61, 91, 165

Right to withdraw Participants can stop participating in a study if they are uncomfortable in any way. This is especially important in cases where it was not possible to give valid consent. Participants should also have the right to refuse permission for the researcher to use any data they produced. 5, 19, 110, 126, 128, 129

Risk of harm During a research study, participants should not experience negative physical or psychological effects, such as physical injury, lowered self-esteem or embarrassment – beyond what would be normal for them to experience. 5, 59, 99, 119, 126–127, 128–129

Glossary/Index

Stress The subjective experience of a lack of fit between a person and their environment (i.e. where the perceived demands of a situation are greater than a person's perceived ability to cope). 12, 22–23, 72, 73, 93, 126, 135
Stress reduction 93

Structured interview Any interview in which the questions are decided in advance. 132–133

Structured observations An observer uses various 'systems' to organise observations, such as behavioural categories and sampling procedures. 130
Subjective interpretation 33

Subjective well-being (SWB) An individual's cognitive and affective evaluations of their own life. 96, 97, 98

Superego Part of Freud's conception of the structure of the personality. It embodies our conscience and sense of right and wrong as well as notions of the ideal self. It develops between the ages of 3 and 6. 30, 31, 37, 43, 44
Supernanny 51, 60

Symbolism In psychoanalysis, an element of dreamwork which enables the latent content of a dream to be transformed into manifest content by replacing elements of the dream with symbols. 32

Sympathetic nervous system The part of the autonomic nervous system (ANS) that is associated with physiological arousal and 'fight or flight' responses. 12, 160

Symptom substitution In therapy, the reappearance of symptoms in a different form possibly as a result of treating only the symptoms of a disorder rather than the underlying cause. 42, 53, 55, 67

Synapse A small gap separating neurons. It consists of the presynaptic membrane (which discharges neurotransmitters), the postsynaptic membrane (containing receptor sites for neurotransmitters) and a synaptic gap between the two. 11, 12

Synaptic cleft The gap between a transmitting and receiving neuron, about 10 nm wide. 11
Syndrome 12, 14

Systematic desensitisation A process by which a patient is gradually exposed to (or imagines) a threatening situation under relaxed conditions until the anxiety reaction is extinguished. 51–52, 54–55, 62, 63, 75

Systematic sampling A sample obtained by selecting every nth person (where n is any number). This can be a random sample if the first person is selected using a random method; you then select every nth person after that. 124–125
Szasz T.S. 15

Table of critical values A table that contains the numbers used to judge significance (whether the *null hypothesis* can be rejected). The *observed (calculated)* value of the *test statistic* is compared to the number in the table (called the *critical value*) to see if the observed value is significant. 151, 153, 154, 157, 159, 161
Tabula rasa 50, 52, 54

Target population The group of people that the researcher is interested in. The group of people from whom a sample is drawn. The group of people about whom generalisations can be made. 124–125
Taylor, S.E. *et al.* 23
Teasdale, J.D. *et al.* 93

Temporal lobes One of four major sections of the brain. The temporal lobes are located on either side of the brain below the parietal lobe and are involved, for example, in sensory processing and memory. 10
Tend and befriend response 23

Test of association A form of inferential test that analyses the association between two variables. 156

Test of difference A form of inferential test that analyses the difference between two sets of data – from an independent groups or repeated measures design. 156, 158, 160

Test statistic A form of inferential test that analyses the correlation between two variables, i.e. how much they increase or decrease jointly. 151

Test–retest method A method used to check external reliability. The same test or interview is given to the same participants on two occasions to see if the same results are obtained. 6, 134
Testosterone 41, 152, 154

Thalamus A structure lying under the cortex (subcortical) that has been described as the great relay station of the brain because most sensory information first goes to the thalamus, where it is processed and sent on to the cerebral cortex. 14, 16, 17

The field This is not the same as 'a field'. Conducting research in 'the field' usually means working with participants in an environment that is more familiar to them. 118–119, 121, 126
The Kiss (Klimt) 148
Therapist competence 73
Therapist-client relationship 33
Three Pillars, of QoLT 94

Time sampling An observational technique in which the observer records behaviours in a given time frame, e.g. noting what a target individual is doing every 15 seconds or 20 seconds or 1 minute. The observer may select one or more behavioural categories to tick at this time interval. 130–131
Toghyani, M. *et al.* 95

Token economy systems A form of behaviour modification which uses operant conditioning to positively reinforce appropriate behaviours using tokens (secondary reinforcers) that are exchanged for primary reinforcers (food or privileges). 51, 60
Toon, K. *et al.* 33, 45
Traffic accident study 76–79
Transcranial Direct Current Simulation (TDCS) 20
Traumatic memories 32, 33, 81

Tricyclic antidepressants A class of drugs used primarily to treat depression; may take several weeks before any effects are apparent. 13

Tripartite personality Freud's division of the personality into three contrasting components – id, ego and superego. 31, 32, 34
Trivers, R.L. 11
Tulving E. and Psotka J. 82
TV, effects of 120

Twin studies Research conducted using twins. If nature is the major influence on behaviour (rather than nurture) then we would expect monozygotic (MZ) twins to be more similar than dizygotic (DZ) twins in terms of a target behaviour such as intelligence or personality. Such studies may look at twins reared apart to reduce the confounding variable of shared environment. 83, 164
Twin study, fraudulent 164
Two-process model 58

Two-tailed test Form of test used with a non-directional hypothesis. 151, 153, 154, 155, 157, 159

UCR *See* unconditioned response.

UCS *See* unconditioned stimulus.

Unconditional positive regard Providing affection and respect without any conditions attached. 74

Unconditioned response In classical conditioning, the innate reflex response to a stimulus, such as salivating when presented with food. 41, 50

Unconditioned stimulus In classical conditioning, the stimulus that inevitably produces an innate reflex response, such as food producing a salivation response. 41, 50

Unconscious Lacking consciousness or awareness. In psychoanalytic theory, the unconscious part of your mind contains information that is either very hard or almost impossible to bring into conscious awareness. It holds your repressed thoughts which are too anxiety-provoking to allow into one's conscious. However, such material exerts a powerful influence over behaviour. 6, 30, 32, 34, 57, 58
Universal ethical principles orientation 165
Unstructured interview 132–133
Urinal, study 127
US Army, positive approach 102

Valid consent Participants must be given comprehensive information concerning the nature and purpose of the research and their role in it, in order that they can make an informed decision about whether to participate. 5, 13, 15, 19, 39, 55, 79, 110, 126, 128, 129, 152

Validity Refers to whether an observed effect is a genuine one. 70, 98, 102, 112–113, 122–123, 131, 133, 134–135, 165
Valium 12

Variable Anything of relevance in a study that can vary or change. See *confounding variable, continuous variable, dependent variable, extraneous variable and independent variable.*

Variance A measure of dispersion of a set of scores. It is the square of the standard deviation. 73
Viguera, A. *et al.* 22

YEOVIL COLLEGE
LIBRARY